Third-Party Peacemakers in Judaism

Third-Party Peacemakers in Judaism

Text, Theory, and Practice

DANIEL ROTH

UNIVERSITY PRESS

OXFORD
UNIVERSITY PRESS

Oxford University Press is a department of the University of Oxford. It furthers the University's objective of excellence in research, scholarship, and education by publishing worldwide. Oxford is a registered trade mark of Oxford University Press in the UK and certain other countries.

Published in the United States of America by Oxford University Press
198 Madison Avenue, New York, NY 10016, United States of America.

© Oxford University Press 2021

All rights reserved. No part of this publication may be reproduced, stored in a retrieval system, or transmitted, in any form or by any means, without the prior permission in writing of Oxford University Press, or as expressly permitted by law, by license, or under terms agreed with the appropriate reproduction rights organization. Inquiries concerning reproduction outside the scope of the above should be sent to the Rights Department, Oxford University Press, at the address above.

You must not circulate this work in any other form
and you must impose this same condition on any acquirer.

Library of Congress Cataloging-in-Publication Data
Names: Roth, Daniel, Rabbi, Dr., 1975- author.
Title: Third-party peacemakers in Judaism : text, theory, and practice / Daniel Roth.
Description: New York : Oxford University Press, 2021. |
Includes bibliographical references and index.
Identifiers: LCCN 2020052882 (print) | LCCN 2020052883 (ebook) |
ISBN 9780197566770 (hardback) | ISBN 9780197566794 (epub)
Subjects: LCSH: Conflict management—Religious aspects—Judaism. |
Mediation—Religious aspects—Judaism. | Peace in rabbinical literature. | Jewish ethics.
Classification: LCC BJ1286.C65 .R68 2021 (print) | LCC BJ1286.C65 (ebook) |
DDC 296.3/6—dc23
LC record available at https://lccn.loc.gov/2020052882
LC ebook record available at https://lccn.loc.gov/2020052883

DOI: 10.1093/oso/9780197566770.001.0001

1 3 5 7 9 8 6 4 2

Printed by Sheridan Books, Inc., United States of America

*In loving memory of my beloved father, Larry Roth z"l,
a genuine lover of peace and pursuer of peace*

Contents

Preface ix
Acknowledgments xvii

Introduction: Terms and Methodology 1

1. From Muhammad to *Sulha*: Religious and Traditional Cultural Models of Third-Party Peacemaking 9

2. Judaism's Paradigmatic Third-Party Peacemaker: Legends of Aaron, the Pursuer of Peace, in Classical Rabbinic Literature 37

3. From Rabbi Meir to Beruria: Legends of Third-Party Peacemakers in Classical Rabbinic Literature 91

4. From Rabbi Yosef Syracusty to Rabbi Nissi al-Nahrawani: Historical Accounts and Stories of Third-Party Rabbinic Peacemakers in Medieval and Early-Modern Rabbinic Literature 141

5. *Rodfei Shalom*, *Metavkhei Shalom*, *Pashranim*, and *Nikhbadim*: Historical Accounts and Stories of Third-Party Lay Peacemakers in Medieval and Early-Modern Rabbinic Literature 207

Conclusion: The Text, Theory, Practice, and Scope of Third-Party Peacemakers in Judaism 253

Notes 267
Bibliography 333
Index 349

Preface

In the winter of 2003, in the middle of the Second Intifada during which extreme violence was taking place between Israelis and Palestinians, I was busy studying Greek as part of the requirements for my MA in Talmud at the Hebrew University of Jerusalem. I was struggling to see how all of the philological-historical skills I was working so hard to acquire in order to analyze ancient rabbinic texts were benefiting the world I was living in.

I decided to take a course in mediation, as this had been a longtime passion of mine and it felt incredibly practical. At the end of the course I asked the instructor, Michael Tsur, if he was aware of any books that connect religion, and in particular Judaism, with conflict resolution. While he hadn't heard of any book on the subject, he did refer me to two books on the relationship between culture and conflict resolution: Kevin Avruch's *Culture and Conflict Resolution* and David Augsburger's *Conflict Mediation across Cultures*.[1]

I knew then that I wanted to write my PhD dissertation on Judaism and conflict resolution; I just didn't know where and on what specifically. I began searching the web for PhD programs in conflict resolution all over the world, but none of them seemed to indicate any interest in religion. Then I came across a web page of an academic conference that had taken place the previous year right outside of Tel Aviv, at Bar-Ilan University's Program on Conflict Management and Negotiation (currently known as the Conflict Resolution, Management and Negotiation Graduate Program). The conference was called "Religion and Conflict Resolution." It featured Prof. Gerald Steinberg, founder and director of the program at Bar-Ilan, together with others, including Rabbi Dr. Marc Gopin and Dr. R. Scott Appleby.[2] The program website also advertised itself as wanting to advance the field of mediation and conflict resolution within the context of Jewish tradition and culture.[3] This convinced me that the right place to conduct my research was at Bar-Ilan, which as a religious university had an appreciation for the integration of religion and science.

I enthusiastically met with Prof. Steinberg and pitched to him my original thesis topic—the study of contradictory interpretations of biblical conflict narratives through the lens of a mediator. He wasn't convinced. He chastised me for not presenting an academic research question appropriate for conflict resolution studies, and proceeded to show me the door to the hermeneutics department down the hall. However, he also gave me the phone number of someone who was working for an NGO called Common Denominator, whose goal was to bridge the religious-secular divide in Israel, and encouraged me to write my dissertation about their work.

The wind was completely knocked out of me.

For a year or so after this encounter, I was incredibly frustrated and discouraged. I so desperately wanted to connect my two passions, Judaism and conflict resolution, but couldn't seem to figure out how. I eventually contacted the person Prof. Steinberg recommended. After pitching my idea of conflict resolution workshops using the interpretation of biblical conflicts stories, he handed me a book that would change my life: Rabbi Dr. Marc Gopin's *Between Eden and Armageddon: The Future of World Religions, Violence, and Peacemaking*.

In this now foundational book in the field of religion and peacebuilding, Dr. Gopin describes Aaron, the biblical high priest and older brother of Moses, as "the ideal Jewish peacemaker," contrasting his mediation methods to contemporary models. He also writes about the legend of Rabbi Meir (3rd cent. CE) serving as a third-party peacemaker between a husband and wife. He concludes:

> The ideal Jewish peacemaker's path, as seen from the Aaron and Rabbi Meir stories, involves the development of pious or moral character worthy of respect, the conscious creation of role models of peacemaking, purposeful acts of humility that sometimes involve personal sacrifices or loss of face, active or empathetic listening, a method of helping people work through destructive emotions, and finally, the gift of abundant if not unlimited time.[4]

Regarding a story from the later rabbinic literature describing Aaron as a peacemaker in the context of healing religious-secular conflicts in Israel, Gopin writes that "working with these traditions interpretatively . . . could both stimulate the creation of indigenous conflict resolution methods and simultaneously offer a healing connection between Jews."[5] Gopin also advocates for establishing conflict resolution training that would be grounded in the *mitzva* (commandment) to "seek peace, and pursue it" (Ps. 34:15).[6]

I vividly recall reading these sections of his book and being simultaneously inspired and bewildered. Inspired because I felt these lines were speaking to me and I wanted to do my part as a scholar-practitioner of Jewish conflict resolution; bewildered because I recall thinking, "That's it? In all of rabbinic literature there are only two stories of rabbinic peacemaking?" I knew then that this was what I wanted to write my PhD dissertation on.

It turns out, though, that this would not be a simple task. I recall writing to one of my Talmud professors at Hebrew University, Prof. Menachem Kahana, about the idea of writing my dissertation on this topic. He responded by remarking that Prof. Saul Lieberman, the famous twentieth-century Talmud scholar, was known to say that the well-known rabbinic dictum "Torah scholars increase peace in the world" (Berakhot 19a) is proof that the rabbis had a sense of humor.[7]

I was determined to prove that rabbis don't have a sense of humor!

Over the next several years, I went through an incalculable amount of rabbinic literature representing many generations of scholarship, as well as conducted countless word searches in various databases (such as the Bar-Ilan Responsa Project) looking for phrases that might lead me to cases of people involved in conflict resolution either as third parties or as a side in the conflict—but with little success. (Only one story from that period of research eventually found its way into this book, along with the Aaron and the Rabbi Meir stories mentioned by Gopin.) I had even considered interviewing contemporary rabbis to see how they serve as third parties in conflicts.

A major breakthrough finally came when I came across the term *pius*, "reconciliation." This inspired me to search for examples in rabbinic literature where rabbis or laypeople would either reconcile between conflicting sides or reconcile with others with whom they were in conflict. Later, I came across other terms and concepts I had never heard of, such as *pashranim* (compromisers), *metavehkei shalom* (mediators of peace), and finally, *rodfei shalom* (pursuers of peace). I had heard of a *rodef shalom* (pursuer of peace) in the singular, in the rabbinic description of Aaron, but never in the plural, *rodfei shalom*.

I eventually returned to Prof. Steinberg and proceeded to write my PhD dissertation at Bar-Ilan University, under the incredible supervision of Prof. Moshe Rossman, who had been teaching courses on conflict resolution and early modern Jewish history at the Bar-Ilan Conflict Resolution, Management and Negotiation Graduate Program since its inception. The title of my dissertation was "The Tradition of Aaron the Pursuer of Peace between People as a Rabbinic Model of Reconciliation," and my academic research question was, To what extent does the legend describing Aaron as a pursuer of peace between individuals indeed represent *the* rabbinic model of reconciliation?[8] To answer this question I compared the rabbinic legend of Aaron as a pursuer of peace to other cultural models of third-party reconciliation, such as the Arab-Islamic *sulha* process. I also compared it to other rabbinic legends I had found telling of rabbis serving as third-party peacemakers or as reconciling with others they were in conflict with. Finally, I examined the legend of Aaron in light of Jewish laws pertaining to third-party peacemaking and reconciliation or forgiveness between individuals.

Toward the end of 2011, as I was submitting the final draft of my dissertation, two things happened. First, I came across a doctoral dissertation called "Traditional Jewish Perspectives on Peace and Interpersonal Conflict Resolution," by Rabbi Dr. Howard Kaminsky.[9] My heart stopped. However, as I eagerly worked my way through this incredibly thorough work, and later when I spoke with its author on the phone, I understood that Kaminsky limited the scope of his research to models of conflict resolution that did *not* involve a third party. In fact, at the end of his dissertation he writes, "The next stage of research, which would logically flow as a corollary to this study, would be an analysis of Jewish perspectives on interpersonal conflict resolution that does involve a third party."[10] Phew! I then proceeded to rework about a dozen footnotes pertaining to areas where our research overlapped, but the main body of my research, which pertained to third parties, was not made superfluous.

Second, Prof. Robert Eisen of George Washington University, who was one of my dissertation readers, gave me the following advice, after sharing his comments for changes on my dissertation: "Make your *book* about the 'mediator' in Jewish tradition. What role does the mediator play in dispute resolution in Judaism? This way you can basically keep everything you have, but take some of the weight off the Aaron tradition." Book?! I could still barely get my head around finishing my dissertation!

A few years later, though, I decided to take Prof. Eisen's advice, but it did not include "keeping everything" I had. Refocusing my book to be about only third-party peacemakers required me to drop about 50% of my dissertation and to research about 50% new material. I began reading up on religious and traditional cultural models of conflict resolution in general, and those regarding third parties (thanks in part to my international graduate students) in particular. In light of a complaint I justifiably received from several of my female graduate students, I searched through early rabbinic literature for potential examples of women serving as third parties. I also looked for more examples of laypeople serving as peacemakers. A graduate student of mine, Rabbi Dr. Offer Ashual, referred me to a letter he had come across of a seventeenth-century traveler to Safed, Palestine, describing third-party lay peacemaking, while a former professor of mine from Hebrew University, Prof. Robert Brody, referred me to a tenth-century story of a well-respected layperson named Bishr b. (son of) Aaron making peace between two powerful rabbis in Babylonia.

Yet the biggest breakthrough came one late night while sitting with my friend Ḥanan Benayahu. I shared with him how incredibly difficult it was to find stories of rabbis serving as mediators or peacemakers. He stood up walked over to the floor-to-ceiling bookcases in his study and handed me a stack of books that his late father, the famous professor of early-modern Jewish history, Meir Benayahu, had written. He assured me that I was bound to find examples there, especially in the travel diary of Rabbi Ḥayim Yosef David Azulai, about whom his father wrote a seminal, two-volume book. As I stayed up that night reading through the fascinating travel diary of this eighteenth-century rabbi, I knew that Ḥanan had just handed me the missing pieces needed for writing my book.

However, as opposed to my doctoral dissertation, I did not want to write a book strictly about text and theory. I wanted to include implications for the practice of third-party peacemaking today as well—in particular, reflections on my own experiences using many of the cases of third-party peacemakers featured in this book in various conflict resolution trainings, educational programs, academic courses, and actual conflict situations.

At more or less the same time I had formally started my doctoral research, I began teaching what I had learned at the Pardes Institute of Jewish Studies, where I had already been teaching Bible and Talmud for several years. In 2009 I created the Peace and Conflict Track at Pardes,[11] which integrated Jewish text with conflict resolution theory and hosted lectures by conflict resolution practitioners. Two years later, through the encouragement of a few idealistic students of mine, and as part of being a senior research fellow at Marc Gopin's Center for World Religions, Diplomacy, and Conflict Resolution (CRDC) at George Mason University, the Peace and Conflict Track morphed into the Pardes Center for Judaism and Conflict Resolution (PCJCR).[12]

The original mission statement of the new center was "to create a global network of *rodfei shalom*, uniting individuals and communities across personal, political, and religious divides around the shared values of Judaism and conflict resolution." This began with a mini-course called "The *Rodef*

Shalom in Judaism" taught by Pardes alumni in synagogues and on campuses in various cities around the United States; an online version of the course co-taught by Marc Gopin and me; and a culminating national retreat.[13]

Between 2012 and 2019, the center offered three main programs: (1) The Pardes Rodef Shalom Schools Program, which engaged roughly thirty Jewish middle schools in the United States, and included teacher training and coaching as well as a seven-unit curriculum for students; (2) The Pardes Rodef Shalom Communities Program, which focused on American community rabbis and top Jewish lay leaders from different denominations, offering retreats, resources, and cohort programs; and (3) The 9AdarProject: Jewish Week of Constructive Conflict, which the center created as an awareness week around the Jewish value of "Disagreements for the Sake of Heaven," commemorating the tragic events some 2,000 years ago when the two dominant rabbinic schools of thought ceased to disagree constructively and instead engaged in a violent clash over how open or closed to be toward non-Jews in general, and making war or peace with Rome in particular.[14]

The following statement was the foundation of two Rodef Shalom programs:

> The *rodef shalom* is a rabbinic model of a Jewish peacemaker who pursues peace between individuals, families, and communities. Throughout Jewish history, there were people known in their communities as *rodfei shalom*. Today, to be a *rodef shalom* means to be mindful in seeking to understand, respect, and assist in constructively balancing conflicting needs and perspectives, between individuals and communities, in the spirit of *maḥloket leshem Shamayim* (disagreements for the sake of Heaven).

In the beginning of 2019, I transitioned from my position at Pardes to become the director of Mosaica's Religious Peace Initiative, under the guidance of its founder and president, Rabbi Michael Melchior.[15] Mosaica is an Israeli NGO that seeks to cultivate a culture of conflict resolution, dialogue, and consensus building among individuals, families, communities, cultures, and religions through developing, implementing, and disseminating models of third-party intervention. Mosaica is devised of two branches: The Religious Peace Initiative and The Center for Conflict Resolution by Agreement. The Religious Peace Initiative is a strategic network of religious leaders who serve together behind the scenes as "insider mediators" advancing religious peace in the context of the Israeli-Palestinian Conflict and mitigating life-threatening crisis situations as they arise using their existing, extensive network of relationships. The Center for Conflict Resolution by Agreement supports several professional programs of conflict resolution, dialogue, and consensus building, often through Israeli government tenders. One of these programs, "Tochnit Gishurim" (Network of Community Mediation Centers Project), is an Israeli government tender of The Ministry of Labor, Social Affairs, and Social Services and has been operated by Mosaica for nearly 15 years. The program currently helps support a national network of 47 Community Mediation and Dialogue Centers and 20 initiatives (that are in the process of becoming centers), which includes over 1000 active volunteer community mediators throughout all of Israeli society. My experience at Mosaica working closely with senior Jewish and Islamic leaders who serve as "insider religious mediators", as well as with the community mediation centers, has been an extremely formative experience. The more I personally have had the opportunity to engage in the practice of mediation and third-party peacemaking the more I understand and appreciate the many texts and theories I write about in this book.

In addition to my work at Pardes, and Mosaica, I have also had the opportunity to teach many of the cases in this book in academic graduate courses. Since completing my PhD, I have taught several hundred Israeli graduate students from all sectors of society (secular Jews, religious Zionists, Arabs, and even some ultra-Orthodox Jews). Moreover, I have taught many of these cases to several hundred non-Jewish international students from literally all over the world as part of courses I have taught at Tel Aviv University's International Program in Conflict Resolution and Mediation;[16] at Bar-Ilan University's International Summer Program, Identity Based Conflict Resolution;[17] and at Hebrew University's summer program, Religion in the Holy Land: Faith's Role in Peace and Conflict.[18] Teaching these stories to graduate students from all over Israel and from China, India, Africa, North America, Europe, South America, and elsewhere has taught me a tremendous amount about their own religious and cultural models of peacemaking—which in turn has better informed me with regard to how I relate to the various cases presented on these pages.

This book, therefore, is the sum total of both my textual and my theoretical research, as well as that of my experiences in practically applying much of this research over the past nearly twenty years.

Daniel Roth
Jerusalem, February 2021

Acknowledgments

As I noted in the Preface, I am deeply indebted and grateful to numerous teachers, colleagues, and friends who played a central role in the story behind this book.

First and foremost, my thanks go to Rabbi Dr. Marc Gopin, whose writing not only was the inspiration for my research, but who also played a critical role in encouraging and advising me over the years of writing this book. Dr. Gopin also mentored me regarding how to bridge theory with practice and bring the book alive through actually engaging in the practice of religious peacebuilding. Dr. Rob Eisen, who in addition to strongly encouraging me to write this book, invested endless amounts of time and energy reading over the complete manuscript and offering invaluable comments and guidance during our ḥavruta (study partner) sessions.

I want to thank my professors at Bar-Ilan University's Conflict Resolution, Management and Negotiation Graduate Program, and in particular, my PhD advisor, Prof. Moshe Rosman, who challenged me to think deeper about how to integrate text with conflict resolution theory. Especial thanks are due as well to Professors Gerald Steinberg, Michal Alberstein, and Ephraim Tabory, who served as the directors of the program over the years and supported me in completing this book.

My deepest thanks also go to the leadership of the Pardes Institute of Jewish Studies, Rabbi Leon Morris, Dr. David Bernstein and Joel Weiss, who not only supported my work in the Pardes Center for Judaism and Conflict Resolution (PCJCR) over the years, but also encouraged and enabled me to take the necessary time to sit and write this book. I also want to thank Elisheva Blum, who was the Assistant Director of the PCJCR, without whose professionalism and friendship I never would have been able to reach the finish line.

I want to express my deepest gratitude and admiration to the senior leadership of Mosaica for giving me the opportunity to apply the texts and theories of this book into practice. Rabbi Michael Melchior, the President of Mosaica, through his daily instruction and modeling to me of what it actually means to be a rabbinic peacemaker in practice, in particular in advancing religious peace and mitigating crisis situations in the context of the Israeli-Palestinian Conflict. And Nurit Bachrach, the CEO of Mosaica, who has introduced and connected me to the ever growing movement of community mediation and dialogue centers in Israel, which are the contemporary equivalent of the lay third-party peacemaking traditions discussed in this book.

Several friends and colleagues played a role in offering advice, encouragement, and comments. They include Hanan Benayahu, Dr. Pinchas Roth, Dr. Offer Ashual, Dr. Yehudah Galinsky, Dovid Jacob, Emanuel Cohn, and of course Rabbi Dr. Howard Kaminsky, whose own book on Judaism and conflict resolution served as the standard-bearer I wished to come close to.

A special thanks to my friend Micah Selya, a Torah scribe, for the beautiful cover art of Rabbi Ḥayim Palagi's call to establish community volunteer *rodfei shalom* (pursuers of peace).

I want to acknowledge and thank Dr. Jenny Labendz and Deena Nataf, each of whom played a critical role in helping review and edit various drafts of this book over the years.

Thank you to the many students I have had the privilege of teaching over the years, from the Pardes Institute and from the graduate programs at Bar-Ilan University, Tel Aviv University, and the Hebrew University. My students both studied and argued with me over many of the texts discussed in this book, and read various early sections, offering important insights and comments from which I learned so much.

Many thanks to Cynthia Read and the entire Oxford University Press editing staff, who have done more to advance academic literature on religious peacebuilding than any other academic press. It is a great honor to have my book join this important list of publications.

Finally, I want to express my deepest gratitude for the strong, loving support of my family: my mother, Marsha Roth, for her years of support, love, encouragement, and devotion; my children, Uriel, Rachel, Hadas, and Eden, who were very patient over the many years I spent researching and writing this book, celebrating each milestone with me along the way; and most of all, my closest advisor, friend, lawyer, and wife, Leora. There are simply no words to express my gratitude for all that she has done to support me throughout every point in this long journey.

I dedicated this book in memory of my late father, Larry Roth, who was a real *mensch* and natural *rodef shalom* (pursuer of peace), and whose image was truly the guiding inspiration for all the research behind this book.

Introduction

Terms and Methodology

The goal of this book is to present an array of case studies featuring third-party peacemakers, sometimes referred to as *rodfei shalom* (literally, pursuers of peace), found within Jewish rabbinic literature that can serve as important textual inspirations and historical precedents necessary for fostering indigenous Jewish practices of third-party peacemaking and mediation today. This is not a history book of third-party peacemakers tracing historical developments from one time period to the next, but rather a study organized around typologies of third-party peacemakers found within rabbinic literature.

The book seeks to build upon and expand the academic study of both religious and traditional cultural models of conflict resolution, and as such is primarily geared toward scholars interested in the interplay between religion, culture, and conflict resolution/peacebuilding. However, as I have attempted to bridge theory and practice, it is also my intention that rabbis, educators, and laypeople as well as conflict resolution practitioners will find within these pages critical sources of inspiration and wisdom for working in the practical field of third-party peacemaking and mediation today. Furthermore, since many of the cases of third-party peacemakers presented in this book have not previously been explored by Judaic studies scholars, or at least not from within the context of conflict resolution studies, it is also my intention that this book contribute to the vast area of Judaic studies as well.

I chose the term "third-party peacemaker" for this book in order to allow for a broad and fluid understanding of the roles a third party can play in intervening in a conflict situation. This includes the role of mediator, in which the third party works together with both sides in conflict for the purpose of bringing them to a mutually agreed-upon, noncoercive compromise agreement; the role of reconciler, where regardless of whether or not there is a formal agreement solving the problem between the sides, the third party reconciles between them and helps them reestablish and heal their relationship; the role of equalizer, in which the third party uses its status to bring the sides in conflict to the table to ultimately make peace; the role of coach, advising one of the sides how best to engage in the conflict; the role of anger-absorber; and the role of guarantor to keep the peace and make sure it holds up. I am defining all these third-party roles and processes as "peacemaking."[1] I am not including in this definition examples in which rabbis served as arbitrators to ultimately enforce a ruling upon two conflicting sides. However, as we shall see, the lines between mediation and arbitration are not always as clear as they are perceived to be in modern-Western contexts.[2]

All the case studies of third-party peacemakers explored in this book are found, as noted earlier, in rabbinic literature. By this I am referring to the broadest definition of the term, which includes both classical rabbinic literature, such as Mishna, Talmud, and Midrash (200–1000 CE), and medieval and early-modern rabbinic literature (1000–1850 CE). For the vast majority of Jews today, rabbinic Judaism, which aligns itself with both the Written Law (i.e., the Bible) and the Oral Law (i.e., rabbinic tradition and interpretation), even if radically reinterpreted or rejected, still represents the normative corpus of religious Jewish literature over the ages (as opposed to, e.g., Karaite Judaism, which rejected the Oral Law). Within this large body of literature there are many laws and interpretations of laws and customs that prescribe how one should behave. There are also many legends that describe how famous people supposedly behaved, which also serve as important sources of inspiration for how people should behave. And finally, there are accounts of historical events that tell of how people actually behaved.

The majority of the book will focus on thirty-six case studies of third-party peacemakers found in rabbinic literature from the third to the nineteenth centuries. At the ends of Chapters 2, 3, 4, and 5, there are summary tables, which present the cases examined in that chapter according to the case number (1–36). Throughout the book, I will frequently be referring back to these tables and case numbers. Each case study represents one example from rabbinic literature of a third party attempting to make peace between two conflicting parties. Some of the third parties, such as Aaron, will be the subject of more than one case (see Table 2.1, cases 1–4). Some case studies explore only the peacemaker and not the particular case (Table 4.1, case 15), and some describe a custom of third-party peacemaking germane to a particular community (Table 5.1, case 32; Table 5.2, case 33).

I have divided the book into five chapters. Chapter 1 is entitled "From Muhammad to *Sulha*: Religious and Traditional Cultural Models of

Third-Party Peacemaking," and its goal is to establish the theoretical lens through which the case studies of third-party peacemakers in Judaism can be analyzed. I begin this chapter by reviewing the study of religion and peacebuilding in general, and Judaism and conflict resolution in particular. I then bring, as examples of research conducted in religious peacebuilding, paradigmatic peacemakers in other religious traditions, such as the prophet Muhammad in Islam. In the second part of the chapter, I survey the literature relating to traditional cultural models of conflict resolution and peacemaking, focusing on the traditional Arab-Islamic process of *sulha* and how it compares to modern-Western models of conflict resolution and reconciliation. This chapter concludes with Table 1, which compares the *sulha* process to the Interactive Problem-Solving Workshops based on the ten theoretical questions for comparison outlined later in this section. These questions will serve as a point of comparison for all the subsequent case studies found in rabbinic literature presented in this book.

The four chapters within which the case studies are presented can be divided between Chapters 2 and 3, which present legends of third-party peacemakers found in the more authoritative, classical rabbinic literature; and Chapters 4 and 5, which feature historical accounts and stories of third-party peacemakers in medieval and early-modern rabbinic literature. This division does not come to suggest historical progress from the earlier rabbinic stratum to the later, but rather is a means to distinguish between the different types of case studies, namely, legends on the one hand, and historical case studies and stories (which I will define as hybrids between historical accounts and legends) on the other. Thus, the chapters move from most paradigmatic and legendary to least paradigmatic but most historical (often also comprising far more detail).

In light of this, Chapter 2 is entitled "Judaism's Paradigmatic Third-Party Peacemaker: Legends of Aaron, the Pursuer of Peace, in Classical Rabbinic Literature." There I explore the various legends of Aaron as the pursuer of peace in classical rabbinic literature. The first part of the chapter focuses on Aaron's identity as the ideal peacemaker in Judaism, and the second part examines legends that tell of his peacemaking methods. But Aaron is not the only example of third-party peacemakers found in classical rabbinic literature, and in Chapter 3, "From Rabbi Meir to Beruria: Legends of Third-Party Peacemakers in Classical Rabbinic Literature," I present eight legends of third-party peacemakers, beginning with the case perhaps most similar to Aaron, that of Rabbi Meir, and ending with the case most different from

Aaron, that of the simple jesters. I also discuss two cases of women serving as third parties, which differ from all other examples of third-party peacemakers presented in this book, one of them being Beruria, the famous learned wife of Rabbi Meir.

In Chapters 4 and 5, I investigate historical accounts and stories of third-party peacemakers in medieval and early-modern rabbinic literature. Chapter 4, "From Rabbi Yosef Syracusty to Rabbi Nissi al-Nahrawani: Historical Accounts and Stories of Third-Party Rabbinic Peacemakers in Medieval and Early-Modern Rabbinic Literature," focuses on cases of rabbis who served as third-party peacemakers. I distinguish between those of high social status who succeeded in their peacemaking efforts and those of lower social status who were less successful peacemakers. Afterward, I discuss exceptions to this distinction, and the correlation between status and success. In Chapter 5, "*Rodfei Shalom, Metavkhei Shalom, Pashranim*, and *Nikhbadim*: Historical Accounts and Stories of Third-Party Lay Peacemakers in Medieval and Early-Modern Rabbinic Literature," I focus primarily on historical accounts of lay leaders serving as third-party peacemakers in historical Jewish communities.

In the Conclusion, entitled "The Text, Theory, Practice, and Scope of Third-Party Peacemakers in Judaism," I outline certain conceptual and theoretical common trends and variations of third-party peacemakers in Judaism and their relationship to other religious and traditional models. I also reflect on further implications and directions for future studies and practical applications.

The cases described in this book consist of legends (Chaps. 2 and 3) and historical accounts and stories (Chaps. 4 and 5). The Cambridge Dictionary defines the word *legend* as "a very old story or set of stories from ancient times, or the stories, not always true, that people tell about a famous event or person." Legends, while they may not always be completely true, play an important role in the cultural and ethical teachings of a particular group. Within the parameters of rabbinic literature, I am identifying as "legends" all cases found in classical rabbinic literature. This includes the cases found in *Aggada* (Table 3.1, cases 5–10; Table 3.2, cases 11–14), often translated as rabbinic legend literature, as well as all early rabbinic portrayals of Aaron as the paradigmatic peacemaker (Tables 2.1, 2.2).

The second category of case studies can be identified as historical accounts. According to the Cambridge Dictionary, the word *account* means "a written or spoken description of an event." Therefore, by historical accounts, I am referring to all cases that are found in firsthand reports of particular historical events. These historical accounts of third-party peacemaking were preserved mostly in legal queries, known as rabbinic responsa literature, sent to rabbis describing local communal conflicts (Table 4.3, cases 24–26; Table 5.1, cases 28–32; Table 5.2, cases 34–35). There are also cases found in rabbinic travel diaries or letters written by travelers (Table 4.2, cases 18–23; Table 5.2, case 33). While these accounts clearly also contain within them storytelling by the author, since they are nevertheless firsthand accounts of particular events, I am identifying them as historical.

There are several cases that do not fit neatly into either of these categories, which I will refer to simply as "stories." This is because they were written about events or people that the rabbinic authors did not witness firsthand but which had taken place either in the author's lifetime or a generation or two before. These stories may be historical, but they also contain elements within them that may not be completely factual, such as glamorizing the hero of the story or ascribing miraculous powers to him; in this case they are closer to being legends. In this hybrid category I am including cases found in medieval and early-modern rabbinic historiographical works (Table 4.1, case 17; Table 4.3, case 26; Table 5.2, case 36), as well as in early-modern rabbinic books that recorded the story in the context of teaching a spiritual or ethical lesson (Table 4.1, cases 15–16).

In addition to exploring the case studies of third-party peacemakers, I have made a point to discuss all areas of Jewish law as they pertain to third-party peacemaking, either as part of my analysis of the various case studies or as separate, introductory chapter sections in Chapters 4 and 5 that explore the Jewish imperative for rabbis and laypeople to be third-party peacemakers.

The three primary questions to be explored in Chapters 2–5 are: (1) Who are the various third-party peacemakers found in rabbinic text, and what are their methods of peacemaking? (2) How do they compare to each other and to other religious and traditional cultural models of third-party peacemaking, which can shed light on the theoretical model of the case study? (3) What are the practical implications of these cases for peacemaking today? Consequently, my methodology for analyzing each of the thirty-six case studies is based on three layers of analysis: text, theory, and practice.

The first layer, text—the raw material to be analyzed in this book—consists of rabbinic legends and historical accounts. One must do a close textual, historical, and literary analysis of these difficult ancient texts and the stories preserved within them. This includes studying the various manuscripts and parallel versions of each textual case study. It also includes taking into account previous academic scholarship that may have analyzed these texts from a historical or literary perspective. However, as already noted, many of the cases presented in the book are being critically analyzed for the first time as part of this study. Since this can at times be tedious and exhausting for the reader, even one who is not a neophyte with regard to rabbinic literature, I have done my best to present only the necessary textual and historical information needed to appreciate and understand the case at hand.[3]

With regard to the case studies found in classical rabbinic literature (Chaps. 2 and 3) that I have identified as legends, it is also critical to include in this layer of textual analysis how these primary textual legends were interpreted by later rabbinic commentaries over the generations. (This differs from the historical case studies [Chaps. 4 and 5], which did not merit rabbinic commentaries.) Since the goal of analyzing these legends is so that they can serve as inspirations for third-party peacemaking today, it is essential to explore how they were understood by later rabbis in subsequent generations; this creates an important body of wisdom in its own right with significance for practical application today.

The second layer of analysis is to delineate the theoretical model of third-party peacemaking embedded within the thirty-six cases of legends and historical accounts by comparing them to other models of third-party peacemaking found in both Jewish literature and other religious and traditional models of conflict resolution. In order to do this, I have outlined ten questions that will serve as categories for theoretical comparison throughout the book: (1) What is the conflict, including its roots, and what is the identity of the conflicting sides, as well as the relationship and power dynamics between, the sides in conflict? (2) What is the identity of the third-party peacemakers, how many are intervening, and what can be learned from this number regarding the cultural model of peacemaking? (3) What is the social status of the third-party peacemakers, and how respected are they by the sides and by the community at large? (4) How strongly is the third party connected to and familiar with the sides in conflict? (5) Who takes the initiative to intervene: the third party, the community at large, or one or both of the sides in conflict? (6) Does the third party meet with each side separately, going back and forth between them, or does everyone meet together? (7) Does the third party attempt to bring the sides in conflict to a formal compromise agreement that in essence resolves the material aspects of the dispute? (8) Does the third party attempt to transform the perceptions of each side, restore damaged honor, and, ultimately, reconcile their relationship, and if so, how? (9) Does the third party undergo any personal self-sacrifice for the purpose of making peace? And finally, (10) what is the result of the third party's intervention? Has the peacemaker succeeded in making peace and reconciling the sides, or did he or they fail? What factors may have contributed to the success or failure of the intervention? Only in the minority of the cases will all ten questions be answered, yet having all of them as a basis for comparison is essential for the theoretical comparisons (see Tables 1–5).

The final layer of analysis relates to the potential practical implications of these case studies to serve as indigenous Jewish models of peacemaking today, and in particular for conflict resolution training and educational programs.[4] Consequently, at the end of several of the sections throughout this book, I will add a short addendum called "Practical implications for third-party peacemaking today." In these short excursions, I will share reflections based on my personal experiences using these cases in various settings for over fifteen years in educational programs, conflict resolution trainings, academic courses, and practical fieldwork.

1
From Muhammad to *Sulha*
Religious and Traditional Cultural Models of Third-Party Peacemaking

The ever-evolving nature of conflict in today's world poses a constant challenge to the interdisciplinary study of conflict resolution, the elements and boundaries of which its practitioners must adapt and update in order to respond appropriately.[1] In this book I will argue that in the race to discover the newest and most scientific solutions to today's conflicts, we must not forget to also look back and consider ancient religious and traditional cultural remedies, which contain within them incredible wisdom for contemporary conflict engagement. This is especially true in light of how many of today's conflicts contain strong elements of ethno-religious tension that too often the new wisdoms are ill equipped to resolve. The old ones may just contain within them the missing antidote needed for reconciliation.

This book seeks to contribute to two parallel subfields of conflict resolution studies, both of which strongly promote the dusting off of ancient wisdom models as a requisite for humanity's moving forward. The first is the study of religion and peacebuilding, in particular religious' models of conflict resolution, which prescribes how people *ought* to act; the second is the study of indigenous or traditional cultural models of conflict resolution and peacemaking, which describes how people *actually* act. In this chapter, the dual theoretical introduction to these two areas will serve as an important analytical framework within which the many cases of peacemakers presented in this book will be analyzed.

The Study of Religion and Peacebuilding

Since the late 1990s, as religion has played an increasing role in the world's conflicts, there has been a greater interest in the role of religion in conflict resolution and peacebuilding.[2] In academic programs of conflict resolution and peace and conflict studies, as well as in divinity schools, courses, specialty tracks, and centers have been opened that focus on the theory and practice of religion and peacebuilding.[3] An important common paradigm that often unites these diverse programs and centers is the assumption that in spite of its being the catalyst for so much war and violence from time immemorial, religion can, and indeed must, serve as an essential source of conflict resolution and peacebuilding.[4] This assumption is commonly known as the "ambivalence of the sacred," a term first coined by Dr. R. Scott Appleby some twenty years ago in his book *The Ambivalence of the Sacred: Religion, Violence, and Reconciliation*.[5]

The study of religion and peacebuilding can be divided into two broad, primary disciplines and subsequent areas of research. The first is the study of religious people today from within the various disciplines of the social sciences.[6] This includes both religious organizations and religious individuals who are involved in studying violence, conflict, conflict resolution, and peacebuilding today.[7] From within a Jewish context, when conducting research into contemporary Jewish interreligious peacebuilders involved in the Jewish/Israeli–Muslim/Palestinian conflict, three Jewish religious peacebuilding leaders to study, among others, would be the late Rabbi Menachem Froman, Rabbi Michael Melchior, and *rodef shalom* Eliyahu McLean.[8]

The second primary discipline employed in studying religion and peacebuilding is that of religious studies and in particular the study of religious texts and hermeneutics as they pertain to violence, peace, and conflict resolution.[9] This too can be divided into two broad areas. The first focuses on the "ambivalence of the sacred." This hermeneutical paradox claims that religious texts can be interpreted to promote either interreligious conflict and violence or interreligious peacebuilding and coexistence. A key aspect of this textual ambiguity often revolves around the tension between particularism and universalism, with the assumption that the former promotes further violence and the latter the potential for peace. This is often referred to as *scope*. As Marc Gopin wrote regarding the Scope of Monotheistic Ethical Concern in Relation to War and Peace: "A key challenge to peacemaking in all of the monotheistic traditions is their tendency to limit prosocial ethical values to members of the religion, or in group."[10] Within a Jewish context, an excellent example of this is Prof. Robert Eisen's *The Peace and Violence of Judaism: From the Bible to Modern Zionism*, which traces throughout their historical evolution the many examples of Jewish texts that have been interpreted to promote particularism and violence or universalism and coexistence.[11]

The second area of interest into religious texts within the field of religion and peacebuilding can be referred to as "religious models of conflict resolution." These models have already been identified within the broader field of conflict resolution studies, yet have a comparable model within religious traditions, including texts, legends, rituals, symbols, and laws. These models prescribe how religious adherents should behave. Gopin, one of the founders of the field of religion and peacebuilding in general, and as we shall see, Judaism and conflict resolution in particular, refers to this as "paradigms" or "methods" of religious conflict resolution, claiming that "there is a vast reservoir of information in sacred texts on peacemaking."[12] Katrien Hertog, in her book *The Complex Reality of Religion and Peacebuilding: Conceptual Contributions and Critical Analysis*, refers to this area of study as "Religion as Living Tradition," noting that "sacred scriptures offer wisdom and insights about the nature of peace and the task of peacemaking as well as ethical precepts and inspirational texts . . . references are made to the need and duty of peacemaking."[13]

One of the foremost examples of a study on religious models of conflict resolution, which also had a major impact on my own thinking and research, is the work of Mohammed Abu-Nimer. In his study of Islam and peacebuilding, Abu-Nimer refers to this area as "Islamic models of conflict resolution" or "Islamic principles and values of peacebuilding."[14] Abu-Nimer was motivated to investigate this area in light of the apparent clash between Western models of conflict resolution and Arab-Islamic models, which will be discussed in this chapter's section entitled "Comparing Traditional Models of Third-Party Peacemaking to Modern-Western Models." The principles and values that Abu-Nimer touches upon include social justice, universality and human dignity, the quest for peace, third-party peacemaking, forgiveness, and patience. For each of these, Abu-Nimer cites several traditional Islamic sources from the Quran, the *hadith*,[15] and more that promote that value or principle. These values, Abu-Nimer notes, are relevant for a variety of conflict contexts, "from interpersonal and family tensions to disputes among countries and nations."[16] While Abu-Nimer does not delve deeply into any of these topics with an exhaustive survey of everything written on the topic from within Islam or with a comparison between the Islamic and contemporary conflict resolution models, his study represents a very important step forward in tapping into the vast body of Islamic resources as they pertain to the broader study of conflict resolution.

Jewish Models of Conflict Resolution

Within a Jewish context, three scholars have contributed in the most significant way to defining and advancing the field: Prof. Marc Gopin, Prof. Gerald Steinberg, and Dr. Howard Kaminsky.[17] As noted in the Preface, Gopin, in addition to being one of the overall founders of the field of religion and peacebuilding, is also one of the primary founders of the field of Judaism and conflict resolution. He wrote his groundbreaking study on Jewish models of conflict resolution in his book *Between Eden and Armageddon: The Future of World Religions, Violence, and Peacemaking*, in the chapter entitled "New Paradigms of Religion and Conflict Resolution: A Case Study of Judaism."[18] This chapter is studied in every course on Judaism and peacebuilding, and is without a doubt one of the foundational studies of the field. Its goal was to develop an authentic Jewish model of conflict resolution that would be able to speak simultaneously to both the religious and ultra-Orthodox Jewish community, which in general is suspicious of modern models of conflict resolution and peacebuilding, and the secular and non-Orthodox community, which is often very suspicious of or at least does not connect to traditional Jewish models of how to run society.

The purpose of such a Jewish model of conflict resolution would be to serve not only as a bridge between religious Jews and secular Jews, but also as a model for conflict resolution and healing wounds of the past—in particular, Jewish trauma from the Holocaust—as well as for conflict resolution and peacemaking in the context of the Israeli/Jewish–Arab/Muslim conflict.[19] Gopin does not argue that his study is *the* model; rather, he is interested in developing a dialogue on such models of conflict resolution and inspiring additional, more in-depth studies on these subjects.[20]

Gopin notes that there have been many studies written on peace and war from within Jewish tradition, but there has been no research into models of conflict resolution within classical Jewish rabbinic literature that relate to such topics as conflict prevention, de-escalation, and post-conflict healing.[21] Throughout the entire chapter referred to earlier, Gopin compares these Jewish models with the accepted rational models of conflict resolution studies, and claims that any process of conflict resolution demands an integration of the two.[22]

Gopin divides his study into five sections, each of which enumerates a specific Jewish model of conflict resolution:

1. *Mourning, post-trauma, healing, and deep conflict resolution.* Here Gopin claims that in every serious and prolonged conflict there is loss of life, land, property, and time. These losses often fuel the continuation of violent conflict. Consequently, one cannot deny the past; it is important to engage with it and find models of healing instead. The Jewish model, which can serve as such a model for healing and bring about transformation toward the other side, is *aveilut* (mourning), the laws and customs of which can be employed in a reciprocal manner by both sides of the conflict.[23]

2. *Conflict prevention as the first stage of conflict resolution: theory and practice.* Within the area of conflict prevention, Gopin distinguishes between the models or rabbinic values that deal with how one relates to one's own "self" and those that relate to how one relates to the "other." Among the examples of rabbinic values that are geared toward how one relates to oneself, he lists "benevolent care of the self" and "becoming like God in the acts of benevolence and peacemaking." Two notable examples of values that promote "conflict prevention and the interpersonal relationship" that he mentions are constructive conflict (disagreements for the sake of Heaven) and seeking peace.

3. *Unilateral gestures of aid as conflict resolution.* In this section Gopin cites the verse in Exodus 23:5: "If you see your enemy's donkey buckling under its burden, even if you do not want to ease it, you must nevertheless unload it with him." He identifies this verse, along with its accompanying rabbinic explanations, as a Jewish model of unilateral gestures of aid toward an enemy with the purpose of shifting the enemy's perceptions, which ultimately brings about a transformation of the relationship and renewed mutual trust between the sides. Gopin claims this verse in Exodus is "the *mitzva* of conflict resolution."[24]

4. *Reconciliation and transformation: the process of teshuva.* Gopin finds within the many laws of *teshuva* (repentance) the primary Jewish model for transformation, which can turn enemies into friends. The process of *teshuva* includes restitution, remorse, confession, and a commitment not to repeat the hurtful acts in the future. In this context Gopin also relates to apologies and forgiveness as the culmination of the *teshuva* process.[25]

5. *Conflict management, resolution, and reconciliation: the ideal Jewish peacemaker.* In this section Gopin introduces the ideal third-party peacemaker in Judaism, specifically Aaron, the high priest and brother of Moses in the Bible. In rabbinic literature, Aaron is identified as a "lover of peace

and pursuer of peace" (Table 2.1). Gopin brings another example of an ideal third-party peacemaker, Rabbi Meir, a well-known second-century rabbi, about whom a legend is told in classical rabbinic literature of how he pursued peace between a husband and wife (Table 3.1, case 6).

This last section, which focuses on third-party peacemakers, will be the focus of this book, and thus I will return to discuss these peacemakers in great depth, as well as Gopin's comments on them.

The second scholar who can be identified as one of the first to research Jewish models of conflict resolution is Prof. Gerald Steinberg. Steinberg, who founded Bar-Ilan University's Conflict Resolution, Management and Negotiation Graduate Program, wrote two articles on this topic. The first, "Conflict Prevention and Mediation in the Jewish Tradition,"[26] was published in *Jewish Political Studies Review*. There Steinberg claims that culture influences the different approaches to conflict resolution, and consequently each culture employs a different approach.[27] In the Jewish tradition there are examples and principles of conflict resolution found in the Bible, Talmud, commentaries, and legal works (*halakha*).[28] Steinberg explores Jewish approaches to conflict resolution and mediation in light of known models in conflict resolution literature. He brings several examples of such models, including the notion of *peshara* (compromise) as an example of mediation and alternative dispute resolution.[29] However, the bulk of the article serves as an introduction to others in that volume, which do not deal with Jewish models of conflict resolution but rather with Jews, either today or throughout history, and conflict resolution.

Steinberg's second article, "Jewish Sources on Conflict Management: Realism and Human Nature," lays out several Jewish models of conflict resolution in a much more fundamental way. The article was published as the introduction to an important source book put out by Michal Roness of the Bar-Ilan program, *Conflict and Conflict Management in Jewish Sources*,[30] which briefly discusses numerous models of conflict resolution through a clear presentation of the Jewish sources on the topic. Steinberg's primary goal for this article is to present the argument that the Jewish tradition of conflict resolution is closer to the philosophical-political approach of rationalist realism, which he ascribes to Thomas Hobbes, and not to the more dominant approach within religion and peacebuilding studies today, such as that of Gopin, which he describes as the "idealistic" approach, and which advocates transforming relationships between conflicting sides.[31] This distinction reflects a difference between two general approaches to conflict resolution studies today, which may be referred to as the difference between Conflict Management, which defines conflict as opposing material interests between sides, and Peace and Conflict Studies, which understands conflict as perceived opposing needs and differences in interpreting realities, but which can be transformed.[32]

It is therefore apparent that models of conflict management do not aspire to change worldviews of the sides or even the relationship between them, but rather seek to deal with the reality as it is and to manage the conflict through models such as separating between the sides, avoiding conflict, and rational problem-solving. Steinberg also emphasizes that any discussion on Jewish models of conflict resolution should be limited to intra-Jewish conflicts, as external conflicts between Jews and non-Jews need to be managed differently.[33] In this regard, Steinberg does not see himself as part of the larger field of religion and peacebuilding; indeed in many ways he stands in opposition to it.[34] Yet through his articles on Judaism and conflict management, his founding of an academic program, and the conferences it has sponsored on religion and conflict resolution, he has done a significant amount toward advancing it.

Steinberg divides this second article into five sections, each one serving to prove his realist claim regarding the nature of the Jewish approach toward conflict management:

1. *Makhloket—constructive conflict—for the sake of Heaven*. In this section Steinberg discusses the well-known concept of *makhloket*, or "disagreement for the sake of Heaven" (Mishna Avot 5:17), wherein there are continued positive relationships and mutual respect despite disagreement. He identifies this Jewish concept with the model in conflict resolution literature known as "constructive conflict."[35] He argues that separating sides into different groups, such as splitting a community into two communities, is sometimes preferred over perceived communal *shalom bayit* (peace within the home), if the latter will not alleviate tension and conflict. This is addressed in the next section.

2. *Conflict management: the examples of Abraham and Jacob*. Here Steinberg describes the concept in conflict resolution studies referred to as "cutting the cake," which Abraham employed with his nephew Lot when they decided to separate from one another instead of continuing to fight. Other groups and families in the Bible, such as Jacob and his father-in-law Laban,

did likewise. Similarly, Steinberg mentions that the biblical-rabbinic model of cities of refuge, to where an accidental murderer can escape, also operates in accordance with this same principle, as it effects separation between the sides and mitigates a continued blood feud.[36]

3. *Win-win models in the Jewish tradition.* In this section, Steinberg connects the win-win model in conflict resolution studies with the Talmudic concept of "This one benefits and this one doesn't lose" (Bava Kamma 20b).[37]

4. *Forgiveness and its limitations.* Steinberg claims that the topics of forgiveness and reconciliation have received a lot of attention in conflict resolution studies, in large part due to their centrality in Christianity. In his opinion, however, the Jewish approach is different. It reflects the realist approach, which limits the potential of forgiveness and reconciliation. Steinberg identifies the many pitfalls within the forgiveness-reconciliation models, which make it more difficult for the one apologizing, and presents cases in which the victim is not obligated to forgive.[38]

5. *Truth, justice, compromise, and shalom bayit.* Here Steinberg explores the various sources in rabbinic literature that say one is allowed to change the truth (i.e., lie) for the sake of peace. Such peace, Steinberg claims, is a pragmatic peace, designed to avoid conflict, and is preferable to telling the truth.[39] In this context he mentions the legend of Aaron as a third-party peacemaker, pursuing peace and keeping the peace by changing the truth. This will be discussed in depth in Chapter 2.

The fact that despite coming from very different theoretical and ideological orientations Gopin and Steinberg both cite Aaron as a prime example of a third-party peacemaker in Judaism testifies to the relevance of this example to diverse Jewish communities and identities.

At the end of his article, Steinberg, like Gopin, reemphasizes that his primary goal is "to start and to stimulate a wider discussion of Jewish approaches to intercommunal and interpersonal conflict."[40] Although both influencers represent opposing ideologies and approaches to the field of conflict resolution studies, they can both be considered the "forefathers" of this new field of Jewish models of conflict resolution. Both of them touch upon several subject areas within Jewish texts, including third-party peacemaking and in particular with regard to Aaron, with the hope of encouraging other scholars to investigate these areas in greater depth. I shall return to the difference in approaches between these two founding scholars throughout this book as I explore to what extent did the third-party peacemakers attempt to resolve disputes over material resources through *peshara*—in accordance with Steinberg's realist approach; and to what extent did they focus more on transforming the perceptions of and relationship between the sides in conflict—more in accordance with Gopin's "idealistic," transformative approach.[41]

A third scholar, who has conducted by far the most rigorous research in the field of Judaism and conflict resolution, is Dr. Howard Kaminsky. Kaminsky's original motivation for researching this field, and writing his doctoral dissertation on it at Columbia University's Teachers College, was to establish the textual and theoretical basis of Judaism and conflict resolution with the ultimate goal of creating a Jewish conflict resolution educational curriculum for Jewish schools. As he reworked his dissertation into a book, *Fundamentals of Jewish Conflict Resolution: Traditional Jewish Perspectives on Resolving Interpersonal Conflicts*,[42] he expanded his motivation to include serving as a guide for people's everyday interpersonal relationships.

Kaminsky is extremely thorough. First, he carefully examines the *halakha* (Jewish law) that pertains to a particular model; next, he presents all the parallel literature in contemporary conflict resolution; and finally, he compares and contrasts the two. He defines the scope of his research as interpersonal conflict resolution, and provides lengthy discussions on core topics such as constructive conflict and the Jewish concept of "disputes for the sake of Heaven," *tokhaha* (rebuke) and interpersonal dialogue, asking and granting forgiveness, anger management, and more. However, he explicitly excludes models that relate to intergroup conflicts and third-party peacemaking and conflict resolution, and therefore his research has little to contribute to the topic of this book.[43]

Nevertheless, Kaminsky's approach to research makes a tremendous contribution to the larger field of conflict resolution and sets a whole new standard for exploring religious models—both in terms of the depth of his textual analysis and comparisons to contemporary conflict resolution theories, as well as their implications toward practice. This book seeks to be the first attempt at examining in depth, according to the standards Kaminsky has set, the identity and methods of third-party peacemakers in Judaism.

Before introducing the subject of traditional cultural models of third-party peacemaking—the second area of research this book seeks to contribute to—I will cite a few examples of how religious texts and legends have been used by conflict resolution scholars in presenting paradigmatic third-party peacemakers.

Paradigmatic Peacemakers in Religious Traditions: Muhammad, Krishna, Deganawida, and Jesus

The phenomenon of focusing on ideal, paradigmatic third-party peacemakers drawn from sacred texts, such as Aaron the high priest, is of course not unique to Judaism. It is found in Christianity, Islam, and Hinduism, and doubtless in other faith communities as well.

The Prophet Muhammad

As already mentioned, one of the Islamic values of peacebuilding noted by Mohammed Abu-Nimer is third-party peacemaking. Abu-Nimer cites traditional Islamic sources that encourage peacemaking and finds important inspiration for serving as a peacemaker in the texts that describe the life and teachings of the prophet Muhammad. As Abu-Nimer states, "Peacemaking and reconciliation of differences and conflict are preferred and highlighted by the Prophet's tradition."[44] He refers to the following famous legend as an example of how the prophet engaged in third-party problem-solving and peacemaking:

> The groups of Quraysh now collected stones for the rebuilding, each group gathering separately, and they built until they reached the spot of the *ruku* [the sacred black stone]. Then all the people quarreled, because each group wished the honor of lifting the stone into place; so bitter were the quarrels that the groups made alliances and prepared to fight.... The situation remained thus for four or five nights; the Quraysh assembled in the mosque to consult and reach a decision; and the oldest man among them said at last, "Why not let he who next enters through the door of this mosque be the arbiter in this quarrel, and let him decide it?" They agreed, and the first man who entered was the apostle of Allah [i.e., Muhammad]. And they said, "This is the faithful one! We agree that he shall judge." When he came near they told him of the problem and he said, "Bring me a cloak." When they had brought one, he placed the *ruku* in it with his own hands, saying, "Let every group take hold of a part of the cloak." Then all of them lifted it together, and when they reached the spot, the apostle placed it in position with his own hands, and the building was continued over it.[45]

Abu-Nimer describes this story as "a classic example of peacebuilding. It illustrates the creativity of a peaceful problem-solving approach conducted by a third party."[46] In this narrative, Muhammad serves as a problem-solver who is respected and accepted by all sides. Instead of ruling in a win-lose manner, he "expands the pie," finding a creative, win-win solution to the scarcity of the small, black stone, so that all can feel connected. He places the stone in a larger cloak so all can hold on to it, and then he himself does the final placing of the stone.

Abu-Nimer points to Muhammad as a role model of other values that promote conflict resolution as well, such as forgiveness. When the prophet first returns to Mecca, he forgives those who fought with him.[47] This precedent served as an important inspiration for Nigerian peacemaker Imam Ashafa to forgive his enemies and work to build peace.[48] Abu-Nimer concludes:

> Peacemaking was one of the Prophet's central qualities while living in Mecca. . . . His creative methods of peacemaking and advocating justice were highly praised by believers and nonbelievers. Islamic conflict resolution methods can easily rely on these classic cases of intervention.[49]

Lord Krishna
In Hinduism, Lord Krishna, the reincarnation of Lord Vishnu, is often cited as the ideal third-party peacemaker. His most famous attempt at making peace was between the Pandavas and Kauravas in the Mahabharata epic, where he went back and forth as a mediator and peacemaker between the sides trying, unsuccessfully, to avoid the bloody civil war that ensued. Aalok Sikand, in his article on Hindu perspectives on dispute resolution, discusses at length the model Lord Krishna lays out in mediating a famous conflict. He concludes: "Krishna's mediation attempts . . . give advice on how one should communicate to a party. Like Krishna, a mediator should state the purpose for his or her communication: peace."[50] Similarly, Anthony Wanis-St. John, in his article, "Ancient Peacemakers: Examples of Humanity," writes regarding Krishna's conflict intervention: "Krishna's peace bid, though not successful, remains an important ancient example of preventative mediation and diplomacy. Krishna is a proactive seeker of peaceful outcomes who nevertheless leaves the human parties to make their final choices with autonomy."[51]

Deganawida
Among the Iroquois people, Deganawida (16th cent.), which is a sacred name not to be uttered out loud, is commonly referred to as "the Great Peacemaker." He is credited with making peace between five warring nations (and later six) and transforming them into the "League of the Iroquois," considered one of the first democratic confederacies. "The Peacemaker is a

legendary yet historical figure, memorialized in traditions held to be sacred by indigenous peoples among the Iroquois Nations—and, generally, among Native Americans and Native Canadians today."[52] The numerous legends told about his interpersonal and intergroup peacemaking efforts continue to serve as important sources of inspiration even beyond the Iroquois people.[53] I shall return to discuss a couple of examples of his peacemaking methods in comparison with third-party peacemakers in Judaism in Chapters 3 and 4.

Jesus

In Christianity, Jesus is frequently cited as the ideal peacebuilder (even though there are no legends of him serving directly as a third-party peacemaker). John Paul Lederach, one of the foremost scholars of conflict transformation in general and within a Christian context in particular, writes about the imperative to "embody the reconciling love of God found in the Word-became-flesh, the person of Jesus in his day-to-day world."[54] Similarly, Ken Sande[55] writes in his book *The Peacemaker: A Biblical Guide to Resolving Personal Conflicts*, "Imitating Jesus in the midst of conflict is the surest path to restoring peace and unity with those who oppose us."[56] Religious Christian peacemakers at the Tanenbaum Center for Interreligious Dialogue cite biblical quotations of Jesus as inspiration for their worldwide conflict resolution work. Abuna Chacour, for example, who worked for many years in peacemaking between Israelis and Palestinians, describes how Jesus's Beatitudes, in particular, "Blessed are the peacemakers for they will be called the children of God" (Matthew 5:12), played a pivotal role in shaping his life's mission to be a servant of God as a peacemaker.[57]

Similar to Aaron and other legendary Jewish peacemakers, Muhammad, Krishna, Deganawida, and Jesus serve, each in their own way, as important role models of peacebuilders for religious practitioners of conflict resolution. The use of role modeling shifts a practitioner's focus, at least in some measure, from the particular skills and actions he or she engages in as a peacemaker to the personal characteristics necessary to be like the role model. In this way, religious traditions of peacemaking can provide a healthy challenge to the secular pursuit of conflict resolution, as these traditions encourage the practitioner to look inward at his or her own character as part of the process of helping resolve other people's conflicts. The legends found inside religious traditions serve as important sources of inspiration for how people *ought* to strive to behave. One of the key questions, therefore, that

I will explore throughout this book is, Who are the role models of peacemaking in Judaism, and how do they compare with each other and—to a certain extent—with role models found in other religions?

Traditional Cultural Models of Conflict Resolution and Peacemaking

The second area of research this book seeks to build on and advance is that of traditional cultural models of conflict resolution, and in particular third-party peacemaking. This refers to descriptions of how traditional or indigenous communities behave in peacemaking. Research of traditional cultural models of peacemaking, sometimes also referred to as indigenous processes of peacemaking, began in the 1990s and came as a critique of the "first generation" of conflict resolution studies, which dates back to the 1970s. This generation ignored the cultural aspects of conflict and conflict resolution, and assumed that the various newly developed problem-solving models were culturally neutral.[58]

This second generation of research has been based primarily on studies in social anthropology and ethnography, and has also developed alongside the study of religion and peacebuilding over the last twenty-five years. To a certain degree, the study of traditional cultural models of conflict resolution served as one of the important inspirations for the study of religious models of peacebuilding.[59] John Paul Lederach, one of the founders of both areas of study, coined this as the "elicitive approach," which calls for learning from local cultural traditions of conflict transformation. This would include religious traditions as well.[60]

The descriptions of peacemakers in traditional cultural models found in this research do not serve as paradigmatic, ideal peacemaking models like those found in the religious traditions discussed in the previous section, but they do serve as important examples of how everyday people actually act as third parties in conflict situations, with, inevitably, varying degrees of successes. It is worth noting that the descriptions of these traditional processes can occasionally be "idealized" or "romanticized" in the culture and conflict resolution literature, describing only how they are *supposed* to work while ignoring, or playing down, the many case studies where the peacemaker did not succeed—and indeed may have caused additional harm. Uncritical portrayal of conflict resolution models can be likened to advertising a prescription drug without listing its potential damaging side effects. I will therefore do my best to portray the strengths and limitations through examining both the successful and the failed case studies presented in this book.

One of the scholars who helped establish this area of research is Kevin Avruch. Avruch, in his seminal book *Culture and Conflict Resolution*, notes in his section entitled "Third-Party Processes and Roles," that certain ethnographic research suggests that where there is no strong third-party "go-between," conflicts tend to escalate and become violent very quickly.[61] Similarly, David Augsburger, in his groundbreaking book *Conflict Mediation across Cultures*, writes that "throughout virtually all traditional societies, mediation of conflicts by trusted persons or groups is the most frequently used process of dispute settlement."[62]

The most encompassing and scholarly research in this field to date, however, is Hamdesa Tuso and Maureen P. Flaherty's edited compendium *Creating the Third Force: Indigenous Processes of Peacemaking*.[63] In this impressive collection of scholarly essays, the identity and methods of indigenous models of third-party peacemakers are examined from over twenty cultural contexts around the world. In the final chapter, Tuso concludes:

> The most significant mission found in indigenous processes of peacemaking is the ability to manage conflict so that it does not escalate. The leadership in indigenous communities mobilize the *Third Side* for the purpose of creating the *Third Force*.[64]

Tuso identifies twelve interrelated cultural norms these third-party peacemakers use: (1) conflict resolution is mandatory; (2) truth and justice are sought; (3) individual and family take responsibility; (4) elders are the key players in conflict resolution; (5) storytelling is used; (6) spirituality is considered; (7) the individual community, nature, and the supernatural are considered; (8) unity is a goal; (9) justice is sought; (10); apology and forgiveness are required; (11) damaged relationships are repaired; and (12) rituals are present.[65] These general observations are very helpful in that they point to the fact that in traditional third-party peacemaking models there is a consistent phenomenon of well-respected local mediators involved in the process who strive not only to resolve the conflict but to reconcile the sides as well. In order to illustrate this in greater detail, I will present here several examples of third-party peacemakers researched initially by anthropologists that have drawn the attention of conflict resolution scholars.

Examples of Traditional Cultural Third-Party Peacemakers: From the Leopard-Skin Chief to the *Sulha* Process

The Leopard-Skin Chief

The earliest case of a traditional third-party peacemaker to be discussed in conflict resolution literature is the "leopard-skin chief" of the Nuer people in South Sudan. Both Augsburger and Avruch[66] cite the anthropological research conducted by E. E. Evans-Pritchard as part of their discussions on cultural models of third parties in conflict resolution.[67]

The leopard-skin chief, according to Evans-Prichard, is not actually a chief, as he has no political or legal authority. Rather, he is a spiritual figure who possesses the ability to curse or bless. He serves as the primary mediator (often joined by the elders of the community) in various forms of intra- and intertribal disputes, such as after a homicide. In such a case, he offers the murderer his home as asylum, and conducts animal sacrifices as part of atonement for the murderer. He then proceeds to go back and forth between the two groups, ultimately bringing about a settlement of reparations that the sides agree to out of respect for him.

The *Monkalun*, the *Taojie*, and the *Jurgamar*

Since the Evans-Prichard study, numerous traditional models of third-party peacemaking have been noted in conflict resolution studies. To name just a few, Augsburger, and more recently Barnes and Magdalena, cite anthropological studies on the *monkalun* (lit., advisor or mediator) found among one of the indigenous peoples of the Philippines known as the Infugao. The *monkalun* are neutral, third-party "go-betweens" with no official position or authority to rule on a particular dispute, who are selected by the parties or community due to their prestige and reputation for wisdom within the population. Bee Chen cites anthropological studies of traditional rural Chinese mediators, known as *taojie*, as part of his discussion comparing these traditional, "collectivist" models with modern-Western "individualistic" forms of mediation.[68]

Abu-Nimer and Kadayifci make use of research on the institution of *jirga* among the Pukhtoon in Afghanistan and Pakistan as example of traditional models of third-party peacemaking in an Islamic context.[69] Members of the *jirga*, known as *jirgamar*, can be described as "gray-bearded elders." They are well-respected members of the community, considered impartial and known as possessing significant communal and religious knowledge.[70] Approached individually by one side, they then conduct shuttle diplomacy between the two parties. When the time is right, the *jirgamar* invite both sides to join them in a large circle in a public space, with many members of the community watching from the side. This symbolic circle contributes to the creation of common identity and helps bring reconciliation between the conflicting sides. They also invite each side to present their case, and then for each member of the *jirga* to express their opinion until there is a unanimous consensus as to how to resolve the conflict.[71]

The *Schmagluch*

The *schmagluch* of Beta Israel, the community of Jews who came to Israel from Ethiopia, are another excellent example of a traditional third-party peacemaker.[72] Yitbarakh Nagat describes how the *schmagluch* serve as Beta Israel's "'gatekeepers' and leaders, responsible for peace and harmony in their community."[73] Community tradition has it that this practice dates back to the seventy wise men chosen by Moses to help lead the Jewish people. Today, the *schmagluch* continue to serve their community in the State of Israel and act not only as third-party peacemakers within their community but also between the community and the Israeli authorities. The state formally recognizes the *schmagluch*'s role in helping to bridge the vast cultural gap between their community traditions and customs from Ethiopia and their new lives in the modern State of Israel.

Sulha

The most researched model of traditional third-party peacemaking is the Arab *sulha* model, on which numerous anthropological studies have been conducted and to which conflict resolution scholars have frequently referred.[74] This traditional-Arab model, also known as *sulh* or *musalaha*,[75] has the specific goal of restoring the honor and social harmony among the parties and in the community as a whole, and bringing matters back to how they were before the outbreak of the conflict.[76] Its origins are estimated to reach as far back as pre-Islamic Arabia,[77] and it is practiced today in various regions of the Middle East, including Jordan, Lebanon, northern and southern Israel, and elsewhere.[78] Despite regional variation, there exists a common structure of the *sulha* process.

The *sulha* process addresses conflicts that focus heavily on issues such as dignity, honor, and humiliation.[79] The incident most commonly responded to through the *sulha* process is murder, especially if it is committed in the context of a blood feud, but it is sometimes used for physical injuries, theft, or other injuries to one party's dignity that transgress the social norms of the community.[80] The relationship between the parties is asymmetric: one side is considered the attacker and is in the wrong, while the other side is considered the victim and is in the right.[81] Sometimes, the asymmetric relationship between the sides parallels a power imbalance between them, and the *sulha* process favors the more powerful entity.[82] This imbalance is expressed throughout the entire process, as we will see. Employing *sulha* always involves conflicts between groups, such as families, extended families, or tribes; it is not used in conflicts between individuals.[83]

The third party, known as either the *jaha* (respected delegation),[84] the *muslihs* (facilitator of the *sulha*),[85] or the *wasit* (mediator),[86] stands at the center of the *sulha* model. It always comprises a few, generally three or four, highly respected and socially powerful individuals.[87] The respect they command and their social power may derive from their position as elders,[88] heads of their tribe or village,[89] members of a family of mediators,[90] politically powerful or well-connected individuals,[91] or individuals of significant economic means.[92] In certain cases, the third-party peacemaker is not only a respected communal lay leader but also a holy man, such as an imam or sheikh, who possesses important "moral and spiritual legitimacy"; this is very helpful for being seen as trustworthy by the conflicting sides.[93]

The peacemaker must also be learned in the customs and traditions of the *sulha* and its processes,[94] as well as knowledgeable in the history of the region and the conflict.[95] If the mediators are not respected and skilled enough, this can lead to the failure of the process and/or the lessening of the mediators' social status.[96] Conversely, if they succeed in bringing about peace between the two parties, their social status is significantly elevated.[97] The third-party mediators need to be neutral, in that they must have positive, long-standing relationships with each side.[98] This includes participating in "social events and celebrations, which involve many of the disputants that they have worked with."[99]

It is important that the third party have a great deal of patience, since the *sulha* process may take years to complete.[100] Often mediators must be willing to sacrifice their own honor and well-being as they serve as anger absorbers, being cursed and humiliated by the parties in conflict.[101] Initiating a *sulha* should come from the perpetrator in the conflict, not from the third party, though it may on occasion come from the latter,[102] and it is important that initiative be taken soon after the incident.[103]

The role of the third party in the *sulha* process is to mediate between the two sides indirectly, as the parties do not meet in person during the process.[104] The third party must first visit the home of the victim's family and afterward the perpetrator's family in order to get both parties on board to participate in the process.[105] They must listen to the stories of each side, and receive approval from both to serve as the *jaha* delegation.[106] Sometimes the initiative comes from the third side, and they need to establish who the guilty party is.[107] Next, the third party brings about a ceasefire,[108] after which they set or suggest an agreement that will be acceptable to each side, and which will include the payment of damages and the restoring of honor.[109] Sometimes the agreement includes the exile of the guilty party, especially in the case of murder.[110]

After the *sulha* agreement is reached and reparations made, there is a direct reconciliation encounter between the two parties, called the *musalaha* or simply the *sulha*.[111] Usually the ceremony begins in a neutral space, such as the town square, at a time when everyone is able to participate.[112] At the beginning of the encounter, the perpetrator or their representatives, along with the aggressor's family, ask for forgiveness and shake the hands of the victim's family, who are standing in a line opposite the family of the perpetrator. This handshake represents both the perpetrator's apology and the victim's forgiveness.[113]

This stage of physical contact between the sides is considered the tensest part of the *sulha* process, and there have been cases in which a member of the victim's family refuses to shake hands, specifically in order to signify that they do not forgive; there have even been outbursts of violence at this stage.[114] After this, there are speeches by notables, such as the main mediator, who will emphasize the importance of the reconciliation and of social harmony; and by a representative of the victim, who will express forgiveness for what was done.[115]

Next, the two parties, along with the third party and other notables, move to the home of the victim's family to drink bitter coffee together, and from there they move to the home of the perpetrator's family to share a meal.[116] Sometimes at this stage, the victim's side will announce the relinquishment of the reparations payment and other negotiated terms as a sign of good will.[117] Any deviation from these customs can hurt one of the parties, reopening the wounds between them and even undoing the *sulha* process.[118] The reconciliation encounter can include other ceremonies in accordance with different regional customs, and these also symbolize the restoring of honor and a return to harmonious and normalized relationships between the two parties.[119]

Comparing Traditional Models of Third-Party Peacemaking to Modern-Western Models

Several scholars have researched traditional cultural models of conflict resolution through comparing them to modern-Western models of mediation and dispute resolution, often critiquing the application of the modern-Western models in a traditional, non-modern cultural context.[120] Such comparisons are very important for establishing an analytical framework through which other cultural models of peacemaking, such as the case studies to be explored throughout this book, can be characterized and contextualized, allowing consideration for paths not taken as well. This is significant both for a theoretical understanding of these legendary peacemakers and for their potential practical application in the future in contemporary modern cultures.

Many of these comparisons were done between the *sulha* process and Western models of conflict resolution. One such pioneer in conducting cross-cultural comparisons was Paul Salem,[121] who critiqued the use of Western conflict resolution in non-Western contexts, in particular in Arab-Islamic culture. The basis for his critique was the conclusions he drew from researching the differences between these two peacemaking models with regard to the cultural assumptions that serve as the base of conflict resolution in general. The following are a few of the differences that he mentions:

1. *The influence of psychology.* One difference derives from the influence of psychology on contemporary Western culture, wherein those influenced by it see conflict as the result of different perspectives. Consequently, much of the actual conflict may be engendered by subjective rather than objective reality. By contrast, in a culture that has not been influenced by psychology, such as the Arab-Islamic culture, it is very difficult to look at conflicts in this way.

2. *The influence of postmodernism.* The modern-Western approach is highly influenced by postmodernism, which holds that more than one side can be correct; in the Arab-Islamic cultural context, which does not accept

the postmodernism approach, one side is right and the other side is wrong. One side is "good" and the other side is "bad," and it is not possible for both sides to be right and good.

3. *The influence of science.* The modern-Western world has also been influenced by science and therefore tends to look at conflict as the collision of different natural forces, which can be broken down into their different elements in order to solve the problem. In traditional, non-Western cultures, there is a tendency to understand all phenomena in the world, including conflicts, according to religious, magic, or ethical explanations, and not through "objective" or neutral explanations.

4. *The willingness to "open up."* Another difference relates to self-revelation in front of the other side. In the West, people are more used to engaging in conversations in which personal experiences, feelings, and interests are all directly revealed to the other party. In other cultures it is more comfortable for participants to remain within formal roles, and not to reveal personal information to the other side.

5. *The identity of the third side.* In the West, the ordinary person is accustomed to adhering to the rules of the state, and therefore when entering a process of conflict resolution is willing to accept the rules of a neutral mediator, regardless of the mediator's identity. In traditional Arab-Islamic culture, the concept of the "good citizen" who obeys the rules of the state is far less developed, and as a result, parties to a conflict need the third party to be a well-known, authoritative person, admired within the community, who acts according to known traditional customs.

As mentioned, Salem mentions only cultural assumptions that are liable to bring about differences between Western and traditional approaches to conflict resolution. However, he does not relate to actual differences between the Western and the traditional processes of conflict resolution. Such a comparison was first done by Mohammed Abu-Nimer.[122] Abu-Nimer found a number of such differences. The following is the essence of his findings:

1. *The root of the conflict.* In the Western approach there are conflicting interests and positions both between the individuals at the center of the conflict and in the process, and in general, the conflict is managed around material resources (e.g., money, land). In the Arab-Islamic approach, even if the conflict at first glance is about material assets of individuals, the values of honor, shame, and dignity stand at the center of the matter. Response to the

conflict is not only that of individuals directly involved; the entire community is also involved: on the level of family, *hamula* (clan), tribe, and even religion.

2. *The goal of the process.* In the West, conflict is considered to have the potential to bring about prosperity and progress within society. Consequently, the goal of the conflict resolution process is to solve the problem that caused the injustice and inequality between the sides, and thereby change the status quo—generally, in favor of the weaker side. In traditional Arab-Islamic culture, conflict is considered negative and dangerous; it should be avoided or resolved immediately, because it will bring about only disruption and destruction of the social order. Therefore, the goal of the conflict resolution process is to restore the previous social order as quickly as possible, and therefore protect the status quo—which in general favors the stronger party in the conflict.

3. *The components of the process.* The Western process of conflict resolution is built upon rationalism, which includes direct negotiation between the sides, concluding in an agreement created by the parties themselves and therefore accepted by them. The third party needs to be both a seasoned professional in conflict resolution and neutral—meaning not connected to either of the sides. The purpose of the third party is to assist the sides in working together to draw up the agreement. By contrast, in the Arab-Islamic conflict resolution process, the negotiation does not take place directly, which would be considered another expression of humiliation by the victim's side. All negotiation is done via the third party, which in this case is a group of highly respected elders, people of stature and influence in the society, who are connected to both sides to a similar extent. Their purpose is to be the intermediaries between the two sides and in the end to formulate the agreement which both parties will be obligated to accept, in accordance with the societal norms and traditions.

In his analysis, Abu-Nimer succeeds in highlighting important cultural differences with regard to conflict resolution processes, but his findings are limited to the stages of negotiation and the composing of a formal agreement. He does not address the possible next stage: the reconciliation encounter between the two sides.

A third study that compared the two cultural models was conducted by George Irani and Nathan Funk.[123] Irani and Funk raise many of the same points Abu-Nimer already articulated, among them the emphasis on satisfying the needs of all individuals involved as being characteristic of Western cultural approaches. By contrast, the emphasis in the Arab-Islamic approach is on honor, reputation, and dignity, not only of the individuals but of the entire group with whom the individual is identified. The goal of the Western process is to arrive at a "win-win" agreement that meets the interests of both sides equally—or at least fairly; in Arab-Islamic culture the goal is to return to a state of harmony and solidarity between the sides.

Irani and Funk mention the differences regarding the identity of the third party, as Salem and Abu-Nimer noted. They also point out the emphasis in the Arab-Islamic approach on specific acts of reconciliation such as acknowledging guilt, apology, reparations, and forgiveness. These elements, according to them, are absent in the Western approach, which focuses primarily on the process of negotiation and the agreement, and not on reconciliation.

Regarding the end of the process, Irani and Funk point out that the Arab-Islamic model concludes in an impressive ceremony between the sides, which includes handshakes and a joint meal, whereas the Western conflict resolution process concludes in a formal agreement signed by both sides. Irani and Funk's research expands the scope of comparison between the cultural models in that they include the concept of reconciliation. They claim, as do others who have made similar comparisons, that the acts of reconciliation that have been described here are to be found only in the traditional model of conflict resolution.[124]

Some scholars have noted that there are modern-Western third-party models that also seek to restore relationships and foster reconciliation. Jeanmarie Pinto, in her description of third-party peacemaking among the Navajo Nation, compares this indigenous model to both "transformative mediation" and "settlement mediation."[125] Transformative mediation is different from settlement mediation (sometimes also known as pragmatic mediation) in that it focuses on changing the nature of the relationship between the parties in conflict as opposed to focusing solely on reaching an agreement on the issue, and in that way is similar to traditional cultural models. Nevertheless, Pinto points out, the Navajo model is still different from such modern models in that it aims to both restore the relationship between the sides and bring them to an agreement. Moreover, the third party, who is a well-respected insider as opposed to a professional outsider, makes use of prayer in the process, is assertive in bringing the sides to agreement, and includes members of both sides' families and the larger community in the process, which again makes the Navajo model also very different from both modern-Western models of mediation.

Another approach for comparing traditional models to modern-Western models that promote the restoration of relationships and do not merely bring the sides to an agreement was developed by Doron Pely. In his in-depth study of the *sulha* process, Pely first offers several comparisons with contemporary conflict resolution theories. He then suggests that the closest Western model to the traditional *sulha* is "restorative justice."[126] According to Pely, the goal of this approach is to repair the harm caused to the victim by the perpetrator through a collaborative process that includes both sides as well as community members, in an effort to transform the relationship between both the sides and the community.[127] Indeed, many scholars have suggested that the roots of restorative justice are in indigenous models of peacemaking, the *sulha* process among them.[128] Pely notes that although restorative justice theory makes use of "reintegrative shaming" while *sulha* employs what he refers to as "reintegrative honoring," the two models are very similar.

Despite the many similarities between the traditional *sulha* model and contemporary restorative justice, there is at least one important difference between them. Restorative justice is a process that works within a conflict context where there is already an established victim-perpetrator dynamic and is therefore an inherently asymmetric restorative process from beginning to end. In the *sulha* process, while it is true that very often one side may unquestionably be considered the guilty party and the other the clear victim, at times it is up to the third party to either determine this sensitive question or relate to the sides as if both are equally responsible for the conflict. In many of the cases examined throughout this book, the relationship between victim and perpetrator is not at all clear-cut, requiring the third-party peacemakers to relate to each side as more or less equals in their contribution to the conflict.

There is still a need to conduct an additional cross-cultural comparison between the third-party, traditional peacemaking model of the *sulha* and a modern-Western third-party model. This model needs to be based on third-party intervention that aims to reconcile and heal the relationship between the sides and not make do with merely bringing them to an agreement, that takes place on the communal and not just the individual level, and that does not have a clear victim-perpetrator dynamic. Such a comparison will serve as an important theoretical lens through which the various case studies of third-party peacemakers found in Judaism will be analyzed.

Interactive Problem-Solving Workshops and *Sulha*

For the sake of comparison between modern-Western and non-Western traditional cultural models[129] of third-party peacemaking, I will briefly present here a modern-Western, third-party, intergroup model commonly known as Interactive Problem-Solving Workshops (IPSW; also referred to as "Problem-Solving Workshops" or "Interactive Conflict Resolution").

The IPSW model, which is rooted in social psychology, was first designed in the late 1960s by John Burton and later by others such as Leonard Doab and Herbert Kelman.[130] IPSW is designed to address international or intercommunal conflicts that are rooted in the basic psychological needs of each side, such as dignity, identity, and security.[131] It was initially used in the pre-negotiation stage of international or intercommunal conflicts as a type of Track II diplomacy, aimed to foster creative solutions that responded to each of the conflicting sides' needs and fears such that it could later serve as a foundation for a formal peace agreement between them.

Since the late 1990s and the early twenty-first century, the IPSW model has also been employed for the purpose of promoting reconciliation between conflicting groups in conflicts that are defined as intractable, violent, prolonged ethno-religious group conflicts.[132] Engaging in IPSW typically comes after a formal agreement resolving the dispute has already been achieved, but at times may be needed in the pre-negotiation stage.[133] In the context of reconciliation, the goal is to bring about a more harmonious relationship between the two sides through emotional and cognitive changes in the identities of the parties involved.[134] Scholars, however, have not distinguished between these different contexts by name, so for the purpose of this book I will refer to them as Interactive Problem-Solving Workshops for negotiated agreements and Interactive Problem-Solving Workshops for reconciliation.

The third-party in both models of IPSW plays a vital role, since it is they who invite the parties in conflict to participate in the process. The third-party is made up of professional scholar-practitioners who are skilled in various approaches to conflict resolution and interpersonal communication, and who also have basic historical knowledge about the conflict and the region.[135] They are intended to be entirely neutral, not connected to either side of the conflict. The third-party is generally composed of three or four people, but does not exceed eight.[136] Their role is to guide the parties through the different stages of the process and, to a certain extent—especially in the reconciliation workshops—to function as their psychologist.[137] Under no circumstances is the third-party to offer their own suggestions.[138]

The workshop itself consists of a small number of influential representatives (between three and eight from each side), who meet in total secrecy for a three- to five-day workshop in a private, neutral space, such as a seminar room in a university.[139] When the IPSW is performed in the pre-negotiation stage, the third-party facilitates collaborative dialogues between the sides, bringing them to a deeper understanding of each side's needs and then discussing creative potential solutions that are mutually satisfying and could later lead to a formal agreement between the leadership of the conflicting sides.

When the goal of the IPSW is reconciliation, the third-party facilitates a joint analysis of the history of the conflict, with the goal of each side's acknowledging each other's narrative—and perhaps even creating a new, mutual narrative that both sides accept and share. The hope is that through the process of these professionally facilitated dialogues there will be mutual self-recognition of each side's guilt for their part in hurting the other side, offers of both apologies and forgiveness, and mutual assurances not to return to prior behaviors.[140] These transformations should take place in both the individuals participating in the workshop and, later, with their assistance, within the conflicting populations they represent as a whole.[141]

Presenting Interactive Problem-Solving Workshops as an example of a modern-Western cultural model of third-party peacemaking is particularly appropriate, since as noted earlier in this chapter, many of the model's original pioneers, such as Burton, believed that the model was entirely culture-neutral and could be applied in any cultural context—a claim highly critiqued since the study of culture and conflict resolution began.[142]

Various elements of IPSW and the *sulha* process stem from specific cultural contexts, which can account for at least some of the differences between them. Nevertheless, both models can be defined as culturally specific, third-party peacemaking models that share a basic outline:

1. They respond to an intergroup conflict that consists of both material and relationship aspects, at the root of which is injury to at least one party's dignity, honor, identity, or rights.
2. The third-party intervenes in order to lead the two sides toward an agreement that resolves the material aspects of the conflict.

3. The third-party ultimately leads the sides to a direct reconciliation encounter which is intended to repair their relationship by means of, *inter alia*, recognition of guilt, apologies, forgiveness, and assurances about the future.

Both models operate on the belief that dignity and honor lie at the heart of the conflicts they seek to address. However, in the IPSW model they are considered basic psychological needs of human beings, while in the traditional-Arab *sulha* model they are seen as a social-religious right. In addition, whereas in IPSW the parties are considered equals—at least as a core component of the workshop process—with each side considered a contributor to their shared problem and bearing both guilt and hurt, in the *sulha* model there is a process through which victim and perpetrator dynamics are clearly established.

Each model is of course based on a third-party peacemaker, although there are significant differences between the two models when it comes to both the identity and the role of the third-party. In IPSW, the third-party is a professional or an academic skilled in interpersonal communication who is not connected to either side in the conflict. By contrast, the third-party in the *sulha* model is a well-respected community or religious leader within the society, connected to both sides in the conflict and deeply knowledgeable of the history of the conflict's region as well as the customs of the *sulha*.

IPSW dictates that the third-party facilitates a direct, interactive conversation between the two sides, allowing each to share their needs and fears and then ultimately bringing them to an agreed-upon, negotiated agreement that meets both sides' needs. The *sulha* process uses the third-party as a go-between, meeting separately with each side to hear their stories, setting the sum of the damages to be paid, and enacting other sanctions as necessary. They base their decisions on community precedent and serve much more as arbitrators in setting the agreement between the two sides.

Both cultural models conclude with a direct meeting between the two sides in a neutral space. In the IPSW model this would be a private space that is identified with the third-party; in the *sulha* process it would be a public space that both sides identify with, followed by further meetings in the private homes of each side. These meetings consist of acknowledgments of guilt, requests for forgiveness, and promises that matters will not return to their previous state, but whereas in IPSW these sentiments may be articulated through direct communication, the traditional-Arab model relies heavily on nonverbal, symbolic actions.

Both models strive to repair the relationship between the two sides and to reestablish harmony between them. The IPSW model seeks to do this by building a new relationship entirely, based on a newly created agreements and a shared narrative—or at least by deeply understanding the conflicting narratives. The goal of the traditional-Arab model is to restore the same harmonious relationship that existed before the conflict, returning both parties and the community as a whole to status quo.

This cross-cultural comparison of third-party peacemaking models as presented in Table 1.1 will serve as an important analytical framework of the ten categories I have chosen for the theoretical comparison between the various case studies of third-party peacemaking found within Judaism (see Tables 2.1, 3.1, 4.1, 5.1). In addition, many of the case studies will be compared back to the *sulha* process and the Interactive Problem-Solving Workshops. The comparison also has numerous implications with regard to the practice of establishing hybrid models that seek to integrate traditional cultural models of third-party peacemaking, such as *sulha*, with contemporary models, such as mediation.[143]

Table 1.1 Cultural Models of Third-Party Peacemaking

Parameters for Comparison	Interactive Problem-Solving Workshops (IPSW)	Traditional–Arab Islamic *Sulha* Process
The Conflict		
1. The case	• Intergroup conflict (nations, ethnic groups) at the root of which is an affront to basic psychological needs such as honor, identity, and security • Both parties considered equals	• Intergroup conflict (families, clans) at the root of which is an affront to fundamental community values such as honor and rights • One side considered victim, the other perpetrator
The Third-Party Peacemaker		
2. Number	3–4; maximum 8	3–4; can range from 1 to 20
3. Social status	Professional scholar-practitioners trained in dialogue facilitation who have a basic understanding of the history of the conflict	Highly respected community leaders or religious leaders, versed in the *sulha* process and very knowledgeable about the history of the region and the conflict

Continued

Table 1.1 *Continued*

Parameters for Comparison	Interactive Problem-Solving Workshops (IPSW)	Traditional–Arab Islamic *Sulha* Process
4. Connection to sides in conflict	Neutral outsiders with no connection to either side	Strongly connected to both sides

The Third-Party Peacemaker's Methods

5. Initiative to intervene taken by	Third-party	Generally perpetrator, sometimes third party
6. Meeting with sides in conflict	Third-party meets with unofficial, influential representatives of the two sides together in a neutral and private location identified with the third party.	Third-party meets with each side separately, and only at the end do the two sides meet in a neutral public location associated with both sides, then afterward in each side's home.
7. Bringing sides to a compromise agreement	Third-party facilitates interactive problem-solving workshops in the pre-negotiation stage to think collaboratively and creatively of potential solutions that meet both sides' needs and could later lead to a formal agreement between the leadership of the conflicting sides	Third-party serves as intermediary between the leaders of the two sides and in the end sets the amount for reparations through the *sulha* agreement, according to traditional precedents
8. Transforming perspectives, reconciling the relationship	Third-party facilitates interactive reconciliation dialogue workshops in post-negotiation stage (and sometimes in pre-negotiation stage)	Third-party oversees ritualistic reconciliation, which includes numerous symbols after the *sulha* agreement has been accepted
9. Personal self-sacrifice	n.a.	Third parties will often endure personal sacrifice and humiliation

Result of Third-Party Intervention

10. Success/failure of intervention	• Transforming previous perceptions of the other • Mutual understanding of the other's needs, which can lead to a formal peace agreement • Reconciliation of the conflicting narratives, thus creating a new reality	Restoration of social harmony to pre-conflict reality

2
Judaism's Paradigmatic Third-Party Peacemaker

Legends of Aaron, the Pursuer of Peace, in
Classical Rabbinic Literature

In the previous chapter, I claimed that numerous religious traditions preserve legends telling of their founding figures serving as paradigmatic peacemakers, such as Jesus, Muhammad, Krishna, and Deganawida. In Judaism, the undisputed "ideal peacemaker" is the biblical Aaron, the high priest and older brother of Moses, who will be the subject of this chapter.

The Bible itself does not identify Aaron specifically as a peacemaker; the numerous elaborate portrayals of him as such can be traced back to the beginning of post-biblical rabbinic literature.[1] Contemporary scholars have often understood that the true motivation for this portrayal was polemical, and not merely the result of rabbinic hermeneutics (as this chapter will demonstrate). In other words, the attempts of these early rabbis to "rebrand" Aaron's biblical image as that of a peacemaker should be seen in the context of their struggle for power with the *kohanim*, the ruling priestly class responsible for Temple worship, toward the end of the Second Temple period. The rabbis did not deny that the *kohanim* serving in the Temple in Jerusalem were indeed the biological descendants of the first high priest, Aaron, but rather they argued that they, the rabbis and not the *kohanim*, were Aaron's true disciples, emulating his righteous ways.[2]

At this end of this chapter I will raise the possibility of an additional factor of cultural influences that may have inspired the rabbis to identify Aaron the high priest as a peacemaker. However, my primary goal with this book is not to try to convince readers of the historical evolution of events, texts, or ideas, but rather to argue that there are rich textual and historical precedents of third-party peacemakers within Judaism that have important implications for establishing indigenous Jewish mediation and peacemaking today. Therefore, in this chapter I will trace and define Aaron's identity and methods as a third-party peacemaker through exploring the foundational early-rabbinic texts that describe him as such. These core rabbinic texts do not stand alone within rabbinic textual tradition, but rather are always accompanied by centuries of rabbinic commentaries (in particular, premodern rabbinic commentaries) that are often of equal significance in establishing normative precedent for Jews today. I will therefore present the earlier core rabbinic texts together with their various understandings and interpretations found in the commentaries.

I have divided the chapter into three parts. The first is structured around three tannaitic passages (the earliest layer of classical rabbinic literature, roughly 3rd cent. CE). This stratum of rabbinic literature firmly establishes Aaron as the paradigmatic third-party peacemaker in Judaism. The second part of the chapter describes Aaron's methods of peacemaking and explores three contexts in which he functioned as a peacemaker. These are found in four rabbinic books from the post-talmudic stratum known as the Minor Tractates. This delineation between the two layers of rabbinic literature, however, is not necessarily to suggest a process of historical evolution of these legends; rather, it stems from the fact that the earlier texts primarily discuss *who* Aaron was and the later ones focus more on *how* Aaron would pursue peace.

I will explore each of these foundational rabbinic texts, which describe Aaron's identity and methods as a peacemaker, through three analytical questions: (1) How was the text interpreted by later rabbinic commentaries and contemporary scholars? (2) How does the description of Aaron as a third-party peacemaker in the text compare to other models of third-party peacemakers found both in Jewish tradition, which will be discussed in greater detail later in this book, and in other traditional cultural models described in conflict resolution and anthropological research? (3) What are the practical implications of these core rabbinic texts, together with their commentaries, for practitioners and trainers of conflict resolution today?

At the end of the chapter I will compare Aaron to other traditional models of third-party peacemaking, in particular that of the "saint peacemaker."

Aaron's Identity as a Third-Party Peacemaker in Tannaitic Literature

The First Source

"Be of the disciples of Aaron: A lover of peace and a pursuer of peace." (Mishna Avot 1:12)

The most famous of the three earliest rabbinic sources, and indeed of all rabbinic sources that identify Aaron as a pursuer of peace, is the third-century text of the Mishna, which preserves within it a statement ascribed to the well-known first-century rabbinic sage, Hillel:

> Hillel says:
> Be a disciple[3] of Aaron:
> a lover of peace
> and a pursuer of peace,
> a lover of people,
> and one who draws them close to Torah.[4]

This mishna, like many ancient rabbinic texts, as we shall see, is full of ambiguities. As a result of its cryptic nature, questions asked by the commentaries over the centuries gave rise to a wealth of creative expressions of the ideal character of a peacemaker. I will focus our discussion on four central questions that arise regarding this mishna that relate to the central question of the identity and character of Aaron as a pursuer of peace: (1) Why was there a need to open with "a disciple/of the disciples of Aaron? (2) Why be both a lover and a pursuer of peace? (3) What does *shalom* (peace) mean? and (4) Was Aaron also a "lover of people" who drew them closer to Torah?

Why Was There a Need to Open with "A Disciple/of the Disciples of Aaron"?

One question asked by the commentaries on this mishna is why it opens with the words, "Be a disciple of Aaron" or in the standard printed additions, "be of the disciples of Aaron." Why didn't Hillel simply state, "Be a lover of peace and a pursuer of peace"?[5]

From a historical perspective, Stuart A. Cohen, a political scientist and historian, argued that Hillel's statement must be understood in the context of his attempts to shift political leadership from the *keter kehuna* (the priestly crown) to the *keter Torah* (the crown of the Torah, or the rabbis), and that "those who were 'disciples of [*talmidei*] Aaron' [Avot 1:12] were implicitly superior to the high priest's genetic offspring."[6] Meaning Hillel, as one of the founders of rabbinic Judaism, emphasized that the true heirs of Aaron were not his biological children, the *kohanim*, but rather his disciples, namely, the rabbis, who sought to emulate his superior character traits.

Traditional commentaries on the Mishna, however, searched for wisdom pertaining to peacemaking in Hillel's words. Rabbi Shmuel de Uçeda, a rabbinic scholar and mystic living in Safed, Palestine, in the early sixteenth century, explains in his commentary on this mishna:

> Perhaps he said, "Be of the disciples of Aaron," and did not [just] say, "Be a lover of peace," since every person in their own eyes is a lover of peace, and even if he is a person of strife and conflict he does not see any fault with himself. Therefore, [Hillel] had to give clear guidelines, saying, so long as you are not like Aaron, you are not a lover of peace. . . . And he did not say, "Be like Aaron" . . . for to be exactly like [Aaron] is impossible in this world, and therefore [Hillel] set a lower standard: "Be one of his disciples," even if you can't be exactly like him. And [Hillel] said, "of his disciples," and did not say, "and like his disciples," because it is enough that he does not need to be exactly like Aaron; [but] he should nevertheless really be one of his disciples and not just like one of [them].[7]

Uçeda makes an important observation: Many people see themselves as lovers and pursuers of peace when they are in reality full of conflict and strife, and that is why Hillel started with Aaron, whom he considered the standard-bearer of what it means to be a pursuer of peace. Having such a model thus allows one to determine if a person is truly behaving as a pursuer of peace. He also stresses the importance of setting realistic goals to strive for: while not expecting to be exactly like the paradigmatic Aaron, one should nevertheless not settle for being merely "like" one of his disciples.

Rabbi Yosef b. Ḥayim Yaavetz (Spain, 15th cent.) offers a complementary point regarding the interpretation of the mishna's opening line: "Do not say, 'I am a child of well-off people, a child of the wise people of old; how can I go to the house of such a lowly person to place peace between him and his wife?'

Are you greater than Aaron, who was the high priest, the older brother of Moses, king of Israel, who would do so?"[8] In other words, the mishna needed to preface its call to pursue peace with "be of the disciples of Aaron" in order to establish a critical precedent and standard: no one can hold themselves up to be more important and of higher social status than Aaron, and if he was willing to pursue peace wherever and however needed, so too should his subsequent "students."

Indeed, as we saw in the previous chapter with regard to Muhammad, Krishna, and Jesus, one of the ways in which religious conflict resolution models stand out from other forms of conflict resolution work is the central importance of role models. Religious communities view select figures from their sacred texts and histories as paradigmatic peacemakers, whose legacies resonate for centuries. Identifying Aaron as the ideal Jewish peacemaker does not seek simply to clarify the personality of an ancient biblical persona for historical or literary purposes, but rather is clearly intended to uphold Aaron as a role model whose behavior should be imitated. As Marc Gopin writes in his discussion on "the Ideal Jewish Peacemaker":

> It is . . . significant that the rabbis do not speak about conflict resolution abstractly but do so by installing those values in a particular personality. This raises some important issues, for further study elsewhere, about whether the field of conflict resolution has focused too much on skills and not enough on the formation of character, namely, the ideal personality of the peacemaker. Religion focuses heavily on role modeling and on the development of moral character. More reflection is required on whether this is simply a different way to attain the same goal as conflict resolution training that focuses on objective skills, or whether there is something that these paradigms can learn from each other.[9]

Practical Implications for Third-Party Peacemaking Today

Using these texts when training rabbis, Jewish educators, and lay leaders, or when lecturing to students, or Jewish and Muslim "activists for tolerance," I often like to ask participants to reflect on and share who their personal *rodef shalom* role model is. The very first unit, for example, of a middle school curriculum I was involved in creating was called "Be of the Students of Aaron," and asks students to discuss with their parents, and later research and present contemporary examples of, whom they consider a "student of Aaron" today. It can be someone the student or participant knows intimately such as a family member or former teacher, or someone like Aaron, whom they only know of. Israeli university students have cited Prime Minister Yitzhak Rabin, Prime Minister Menachem Begin, and the last Lubavitcher Rebbe as their role models of a *rodef shalom*, while Christian students of mine have chosen figures such as Jesus, Pope Francis, and Mother Teresa. Muslim students have often referred to family or community religious leaders in their community today, or those who were active during their childhood.

No matter who is chosen as a *rodef shalom* role model, it is essential in conflict resolution training for people not only to acquire rational problem-solving skills but to build a picture of themselves as pursuers of peace. Moreover, they need to build an awareness of how their own role models would engage in a particular conflict, and how they can serve as both an inspiration and a standard for the students' own engagement. This is clearly an important contribution that Jewish and religious models of conflict resolution have to offer, as it inspires and motivates students and practitioners to want to engage in the pursuit of peace.

But I would argue that this is still insufficient. Students of conflict resolution and peacemaking must also learn contemporary, rational conflict resolution, communication, and problem-solving skills that Western conflict resolution approaches have to offer. Therefore, to answer Gopin's question, these two approaches indeed have much to learn from one another and are not merely attaining the same goal through different means.

Why Be Both a Lover and a Pursuer of Peace?
Another question that commentaries on this mishna felt compelled to discuss was what it means to be a pursuer of peace. Moreover, why was there the need to state both "[Be] a lover of peace" and "[Be] a pursuer of peace"? Different answers are suggested among the classical commentaries.[10] One can be found in the earliest rabbinic comment on Mishna Avot, in the post-talmudic, Minor Tractate of *Avot d'Rabbi Natan*,[11] which states:

> "A lover of peace and a pursuer of peace": Even if you run after it from city to city, from district to district, from country to country, do not desist from making peace. For it is equal in weight to all the other *mitzvot* [commandments] in the Torah.... And Scripture says, "Depart from evil, and do good; seek peace, and pursue it [Ps. 34:15]." Rabbi Yosei says: If a person sits in his

house and does not go out to the marketplace, how will he make peace between people? Rather, by going to the marketplace he sees people fighting and he enters between them and [effects a] compromise between them.[12]

Though this text does not relate directly to the distinction between "pursuer of peace" and "lover of peace," it does emphasize that to be a "pursuer of peace" one must proactively go out to make peace wherever there is conflict. The implication may be that it is not enough to passively be a "lover of peace," waiting for conflicts to come to him instead of taking the initiative. This unique, proactive mitzva is considered to be equal to all other commandments in the Torah.[13]

The same idea is further expressed in a statement in the name of Rabbi Yosei, which is found in *Avot d'Rabbi Natan* a few lines after the excerpt just cited. It strengthens the notion that if one does not go out to the "marketplace" where conflicts are taking place and only stays within his home, he is not actively pursuing peace.[14]

Regarding the methods of Aaron in pursuing peace, we will see later on in this chapter, as well as throughout the book, that a key characteristic of pursuing peace in Judaism is to take the initiative and not wait to be invited to be a third-party peacemaker. This is in sharp contrast to typical modern mediation today, where it would be very unlikely that an individual mediator would take the initiative to intervene in the interpersonal conflicts of others.[15] The strong communal ethos these rabbinic texts and commentaries reflect is closely aligned with the traditional cultural models of third-party peacemakers I explored in Chapter 1 and will discuss throughout the book.

A second explanation for Hillel's charge to be both a lover and a pursuer of peace is found in the commentary of the Maharal of Prague (Rabbi Yehuda Loew, 1512–1609). It clearly builds off of the first explanation we explored, yet is slightly modified:

And [concerning] that which is said, "A lover of peace and a pursuer of peace": The explanation of "lover of peace" is that there should be no conflict between people; and "pursuer of peace" [means] that if there is conflict, one should pursue after it in order to make peace. And that is where "pursuing" is needed: until he is able to return them to peace. For it is the manner of people that once they have entered into a conflict, each one distances himself as far as possible from the other, and a matter that is far needs pursuing after it.[16]

The Maharal's distinction between the two characteristics is not hierarchal; there is no preference for actively pursuing peace over passively loving peace. Rather, the Maharal is distinguishing between "loving peace" as preventing conflict and "pursuing peace" as exhausting every effort to make peace and resolve issues once there is conflict. Conflict prevention includes a wide range of strategies and initiatives that help preempt potential violence and conflict.[17] Therefore, to be a lover of peace would mean continuously working to create a healthy community that would neutralize potential conflicts, while being a pursuer of peace requires an immediate increase in efforts to extinguish the fire that has already been kindled.

A third explanation regarding the seemingly superfluous words of the mishna can be found in the commentary of Rabbi Yitzḥak b. Shlomo of Toledo (Spain, 14th cent.):

> There are people who love peace in theory; however, they do not trouble themselves to pursue it and engage in it in practice. Not so Aaron, for he would pursue with all his strength to place peace between individuals and husband and wife.[18]

Rabbi Yitzḥak b. Shlomo understands that to love peace means to appreciate its value in theory, while to pursue it means to turn theory into practice, as Aaron was known to do.[19] It is similar to the explanation in *Avot d'Rabbi Natan*, as it too compares various degrees of engaging in the pursuit of peace, but here the distinction is not between passively or actively responding to conflict but rather between doing so in theory or in practice.

A fourth direction taken by the commentaries on this mishna is that the difference between a lover of peace and a pursuer of peace is that the first concerns one's own interpersonal conflicts while the latter pertains to the conflicts of others. Rabbi Shmuel de Uçeda writes:

> And he said, "lover of peace," [meaning peace] for himself and for his household [with regard to his relationships with others]; and "pursuer of peace," [meaning] to make peace, to bring peace between a person and his fellow and between husband and wife. And this is the meaning of the word "pursuer": that he pursues and actually goes to his fellow's home to make peace between him and his wife. And first he needs to love peace for himself. And since he considers peace a good thing and he loves it for himself, he will be drawn also to make peace between others.[20]

Here, "lover of peace" is defined as how one interacts in one's own interpersonal relationships, while "pursuer of peace" refers to how one serves as a third-party peacemaker.[21] As we shall see in Chapter 5, it was fairly widespread in Jewish communities during the Middle Ages and early-modern era to refer to laypeople who actively engaged in third-party peacemaking as "pursuers of peace."

Practical Implications for Third-Party Peacemaking Today

All four explanations of the difference between being a "lover of peace" and a "pursuer of peace" have important implications for peacemaking today. The first explanation distinguishes between being passive and being proactive in the pursuit of peace. For me, reflecting upon the text's words "even if you have to run after it . . . from country to country" has served as a motivating mantra every time I have found myself traveling for the purpose of trying to heal a fractured relationship, whether between my own family members or between Jewish and Muslim leaders in the Middle East. Such ancient religious wisdom statements can play a critical role for practitioners by helping them remain motivated and driven in their pursuit of peace, especially when the conflict seems so incredibly unsolvable.

The second explanation of "lover of peace" and "pursuer of peace," which differentiates between conflict prevention and conflict resolution, has extensive implications for today. In fact, the very term I have been using to describe third-party interveners in this book is "peacemaker," which implies someone responding to conflict that already exists, and, according to this definition, is serving as a "pursuer of peace." That being said, it is important to recognize the great significance of being a "lover of peace" in the sense of engaging in conflict prevention.

A good example of the call for conflict prevention can be found in the very first line of the 1945 United Nations charter, which explains that the purpose of the organization is "to save succeeding generations from the scourge of war" (United Nations, 1945). In recent years this call for "conflict prevention" has attracted much attention in both international diplomacy and conflict resolution education.[22] I will return to the concept of conflict prevention again in Chapter 3 in the context of the role of women in third-party peacemaking.

The third explanation, which understands "lover of peace" as embracing peace in theory and "pursuer of peace" as actively doing something about it, can be understood in a modern context as the distinction between the theory of conflict resolution and peacemaking and their actual practice, which are too often detached from one another. As noted in the preface of *The Handbook of Conflict Resolution: Theory and Practice*, "As an area of scholarship and professional practice, conflict resolution is relatively young.... Practice and theory have been only loosely linked."[23]

This comment may be offering a critique against those who separate between the two, such as mediators who have never studied the theory behind their practice and academics who conduct research on conflict analysis and resolution but have never assumed the role of a third-party peacemaker. Indeed, as I write these words, I am burdened with the dilemma of whether I am "allowed" to express these sentiments, as I may be crossing the line between the pure realm of theoretical and academic study and the messy realm of practical conflict resolution.

The fourth explanation, which defines a "lover of peace" in terms of one's own interpersonal relations and a "pursuer of peace" as acting as the third party, also raises an important question for conflict resolution work today: to what extent should peacemakers first work on their own inner peace and relationships with others before entering into other people's problems as third-party peacemakers?[24]

I recall several years ago attending a conference on religion and peacebuilding at Emory University where Bernard Lafayette, a well-known civil rights activist, was one of the keynote speakers. He spoke beautifully, but the part that impacted me most was his off-script comment that a high percentage of the time NGOs commit to "saving the world" is wasted in people fighting with their coworkers in the cubicle next to them. I have no idea how true this is, but Lafayette had unintentionally (and serendipitously) made a powerful point: at an international conference on religion and global peacebuilding, we must not forget to engage in interpersonal peacekeeping as well; in other words, to actively seek to be "lovers of peace" and not just run to be third-party "pursuers of peace."

Lafayette's comment also draws attention to the difference between modern mediators and traditional peacemakers such as Aaron and his disciples. If a modern mediator—or a therapist, for that matter—yelled at their children and fought with their neighbor before showing up at the mediation or therapy session, I doubt anyone would know or even care, so long as in the room they facilitated a professional process. However, if Aaron were to have done so, it is possible that his entire ability to serve as a communal role model and inspiration for making peace would have been irreparably damaged. Likewise, as we will see at the end of this chapter, the third-party saint peacemaker, who I claim is the traditional cultural model of third-party peacemaking most similar to Aaron, would have also been very careful to never engage in conflict with others, as this would have hindered their ability to serve as a third-party peacemaker.

What Does Shalom (Peace) Mean?
A question often overlooked, yet so essential to our analysis of the mishna and the field of conflict resolution in general, is, What does the word *shalom* mean?[25] One could argue that the vast majority of violent struggles take place over competing interpretations over the very definition of "peace." One medieval commentator who addressed this question was Rabbi Don Yitzhak Abarbanel (Portugal, Spain, Italy; 15th cent.) in his commentary *Nahalat Avot*:

> With regard to the words of *shalom* which Hillel mentions in our mishna, and in all places that *shalom* is mentioned in Scripture, the commentators always thought that it refers to an agreement between two parties in conflict.... Therefore they explained that "a lover of peace and a pursuer of peace" [means] that a person should make peace between people who are fighting... as if the matter of *shalom*, according to them, does not occur unless there is a fight and conflict beforehand.[26]

Here Abarbanel derides those who restrict Hillel's directive to mean that one should resolve conflicts and help others arrive at peace agreements. He continues:

> And [the other commentaries] did not know the great value of *shalom*, and they did not see its preciousness and the splendor of its greatness, since in addition to orchestrating agreements between conflicting parties—as they thought—*shalom* also relates, separate from the issue of fights and conflicts, to the common good, and to people's agreements and their mutual love, which is the [most] necessary element for the gathering together of a nation; and it is the string that ties together and binds everything.

Abarbanel understands *shalom* not as a problem-solving measure or a description of the solution to particular problems through peace agreements, but as a constant state that should be pursued and developed in and of itself, through pursuit of the "common good" and loving relationships between people. He concludes:

> In general, *shalom* relates to the health of a matter and its wholeness [*sheleimut*, from the same root as *shalom*], its goodness, and its beauty. Therefore, God is called *Shalom*, since He is the One who ties together the whole world and stands everything in order in accordance with its particular nature, because when a matter is in its appropriate order it will be peaceful and upright.[27]

In line with Abarbanel's distinction, Royce Anderson, in his article "A Definition of Peace," distinguishes between Western and Eastern definitions of peace. After exploring the word for peace in English, Hebrew, Arabic, and several other languages, he concludes:

> Western definitions of peace tend to emphasize the absence of violence; Eastern definitions tend to be positive in the sense that peace means the presence of certain characteristics rather than the absence of negative characteristics. A truly global understanding of peace should include both the absence of factors such as violence and the presence of factors such as balance, harmony, and unbrokenness.[28]

Anderson also associates his two definitions of peace with Johan Galtung's distinction between "negative peace," which concerns lowering levels of violence, and "positive peace,"[29] which pertains to cultivating social harmony and positive relationships.[30] It is interesting to note that this cultural distinction between East and West echoes what we saw in the Introduction, where several scholars suggested that Western conflict resolution processes conclude with a formal, signed peace agreement, while non-Western models such as *sulha* end in a reconciliation ceremony. It is therefore possible that Abarbanel is distinguishing here between bringing the sides in conflict to a formal compromise agreement and transforming the relationship between the sides in conflict and bringing about reconciliation. This distinction will accompany us throughout the many cases to be studied in this book.[31]

Practical Implications for Third-Party Peacemaking Today

The distinction Abarbanel makes raises an important question regarding who can be considered a "pursuer of peace" today. If *shalom* means only bringing sides to an agreement that ends a particular conflict, then Aaron's natural disciples today would be mediators and third-party peacemakers. However, if *shalom* means the well-being and harmony of the community, then the answer to the question is greatly expanded and is, simply put, everyone! During my years working with Jewish conflict resolution education in schools, this notion of a more holistic concept of peace held a very powerful message. Many conflict resolution education programs in schools focus on a select group of student mediators who respond to conflicts in the school; this would be consistent with Abarbanel's first explanation. In accordance with Abarbanel's second explanation, however, the entire school community must be engaged in being pursuers of peace and in cultivating a culture of peace in the school—and not simply "putting out fires."

In the context of my work at Mosaica, this distinction has come up in two instances. First, in the context of Mosaica's Religious Peace Initiative, I have used this quote of the Abarbanel to help explain the difference between elite religious peacebuilding and cultural religious peacebuilding.[32] Elite religious peacebuilding means engaging the most senior influential Islamic and Jewish religious leaders, either separately or, ideally, together, to discuss what a peace agreement between Israelis and Palestinians could look like from within their religious textual traditions. It also involves mediating life threatening crisis situations, which requires bringing the conflicting parties to concrete agreements. This is more in line with Abarbanel's first definition of peace, as agreement between conflicting sides. Cultural religious peacebuilding, on the other hand, is much more in line with Abarbanel's second definition of peace, as it means creating a culture of peace on a more holistic, grassroots level that is not in response to a particular crisis situation.

A good example of cultural religious peacebuilding from my work at Mosaica is the Iftar of Mediation. This event brought together Islamic sheikhs, Religious Zionist rabbis, Muslim and Jewish community mediators, and others to have a festive (kosher) *iftar* meal together in the Bedouin Muslim city of Rahat in the south of Israel.[33] There were no discussions of peace agreements in this gathering, but there was a lot of *shalom/salaam* developing between the participants.[34] Another good example of this was an event Mosaica, together with Interfaith Encounter Association, organized in honor of the Jewish fast day of Tisha Be'av and the Islamic fast day of Arafah coinciding. The online zoom event brought together a religious Zionist rabbi and Islamic Movement sheikh (both connected to Mosaica) to speak about the meaning of the day and its connection to "loving one's neighbor" each according to their respective religious traditions.[35] These cultural activists are not resolving active conflicts, but rather are building a culture of peace within and between their respective communities. For the purposes of this book, we will limit ourselves to the first definition, exploring third-party peacemakers who enter into an existing conflict in attempt to mediate and often also to reconcile between the sides.

Was Aaron Also a "Lover of People" Who Drew Them Closer to Torah?
Another important question asked concerning this mishna is, What is the connection between being a "lover of peace and a pursuer of peace" and that which is expressed in a later part of the mishna, that is, to be a "lover of people" and "one who draws them close to Torah?" Were Aaron's peacemaking efforts ultimately about bringing people closer to the Torah, to Judaism, to God?

From a historical perspective, historian Peter Schäfer, similar to other historians, understands Hillel's description of Aaron as part of the tension between rabbis and priests at the end of Second Temple period. He describes Hillel and the general historic background somewhat forcefully, as "disguising" Aaron's priestly identity in the Mishna, portraying him instead as "a pious peace-maker and, above all, someone who has made the Torah, of all things, the center of his and his fellows' life. A rabbinized Aaron, deprived of all his priestly authorities and glory, rabbinic Judaism incarnate! Quite a metamorphosis indeed."[36]

Some commentaries understood that being a disciple of Aaron pertains only to the latter's being a lover and a pursuer of peace, while loving people and drawing them closer to the Torah was a separate statement made by Hillel not connected to Aaron.[37] However, most commentaries believe that Aaron would also engage in bringing people closer to the Torah, primarily by preventing them from sinning against one another and committing other transgressions.[38] Their opinion is based on a later legend of Aaron greeting the wicked with *shalom*, which we shall discuss later in this chapter.

Resolving this issue is important to our pursuit of how to characterize Aaron's identity as a peacemaker in rabbinic literature, and subsequently what it means for others to follow in his ways. If someone is engaged only in the pursuit of peace but not at all in bringing people closer to the Torah, could they too be recognized as being of the disciples of Aaron?

This also raises an additional question, although not directly asked by the commentaries on the mishna: what was the scope of Aaron's peacemaking; between which two parties would Aaron pursue peace? Being a "lover of people" is a very universalistic and broad scope, but "drawing people close to Torah" seems to be bringing the parameters back to an internal, particularistic Jewish focus. Most commonly we find Aaron pursuing peace between two individuals or between husband and wife. However, one post-talmudic source, *Mishnat Rabbi Eliezer*, states: "Aaron would pursue peace between a person and his fellow, between a husband and his wife, between a family and another family, between a tribe and another tribe."[39] *Mishnat Rabbi Eliezer* addresses the scope of the directive in terms of the kinds of people and the size of the groups among whom one should pursue peace. It expands the scope of pursuing peace to include both interpersonal and intergroup situations.

Practical Implications for Third-Party Peacemaking Today

This later source, *Mishnat Rabbi Eliezer*, has important implications with regard to the field of conflict resolution. How many academic conflict resolution programs or NGOs focus on either international peacemaking or interpersonal mediation? Very few attempt to engage in both. However, what about non-Jews, beyond the tribes of Israel? It is indeed hard to believe that Aaron could have served, or even been perceived, as a peacemaker between, say, the Israelites and the Canaanites. This question is always raised, especially but not only, by my non-Jewish graduate students when studying this mishna. We will explore the critical question of scope again in Chapter 4 with regard to the case of a rabbi who was known to pursue peace among non-Jews (Table 4.1, case 15). I will also touch upon this question in the Conclusion.

The Second Source

> "Moses rebuked; Aaron pursued peace and was loved by all." (*Sifra, Mekhilta d'miluim*)

The mishna in Avot does not relate at all to two additional questions: From where do we know that the biblical character Aaron, the high priest and brother of Moses, was indeed a pursuer of peace?, and How would he pursue peace? The first question is addressed in the other tannaitic sources that identify Aaron as a pursuer of peace, and they do so by comparing him with Moses. We will come back to the second question, as it is the focus of the later, post-talmudic legends of Aaron as a pursuer of peace.

The second tannaitic source that establishes Aaron as the paradigmatic Jewish peacemaker appears in the *Sifra*, a third-century collection of Midrash, in the section known as *Mekhilta d'miluim*:[40]

> From where do we know that Aaron was a pursuer of peace among [the people of] Israel?
>
> It is written (Num. 20:29): "And when all the congregation saw that Aaron was dead, [they wept for Aaron for thirty days, all the house of Israel]." But regarding [the death of] Moses it is written (Deut. 34:8): "The children of Israel wept for Moses in the Plains of Moab thirty days." Why did "all the house of Israel" weep for Aaron, but only "the children of Israel" weep for Moses? Because [Aaron] never said to a man or a woman, "You have sinned."[41] But because Moses would rebuke them, [the Torah] said of him: "The children of Israel wept for Moses in the Plains of Moab for thirty days." And likewise it is explicitly stated in the tradition about Aaron (Mal. 2:5[42]): "My covenant was with him of life and peace"; he was a pursuer of peace among Israel.[43]

The Midrash asks for the biblical source for the notion[44] that Aaron was a pursuer of peace among the Jewish people, comparing him with Moses, who would rebuke the people and was therefore presumably not a pursuer of peace.[45] Two answers are given, one based on the Torah and one based on the later book of Malachi, referred to here as "the tradition" (*kabbala*)—meaning the prophetic tradition.[46] The proof in the Torah is based on a difference in wording in the description of Israelites' mourning after the deaths of Moses and Aaron.[47] "The children of Israel" is taken to refer to only a portion of the people, whereas "*all* the house of Israel" is taken to refer to all the people.[48] The implication is that since Aaron was popular as well as beloved by all the people, he must have been a pursuer of peace.

The Midrash's prophetic proof for Aaron's being a pursuer of peace appears in the context of the prophet Malachi rebuking the Levites and priests of his day for not acting like their forefather, of whom

> My covenant was with him of life and peace, and I gave them to him, and of fear, and he feared Me, and was afraid of My name. The law of truth was in his mouth, and unrighteousness was not found in his lips; he walked with Me in peace and uprightness, and did turn many (*rabim*) away from iniquity. (Mal. 2:5–6)

This midrash interprets the words of the prophet, "My covenant was with him of life and peace," as referring to Aaron, and "life and peace" means he was a pursuer of peace.[49]

Two important points can be raised on this text regarding Aaron's identity in contrast to that of his younger brother, Moses. The first is that as a result of his pursuit of peace he was popular and beloved by everyone. Linking popularity to the pursuit of peace can be problematic, for what if popularity and honor becomes his or her primary motive instead of a successful outcome of the mediation process?

Joseph Ginat documents several examples where the status and popularity of the third side in *sulha* decreased when the process was unsuccessful[50] and significantly increased when it was successful.[51] One extreme example of this is a case where a community leader actually arranged for a murder to take place in which it would appear as though one *hamula* (clan) had committed the crime against an opposing *hamula*—just in order for him to be invited to be the third-party peacemaker! The leader's motive behind this absurd situation was to gain in popularity, as he was running for mayor of the village.

This is of course an extreme example of how the third side can place their own interests in gaining popularity and influence before the interests of the actual sides in conflict.[52] However, the case highlights how peacemaking can corrupt the third side with the increased status and popularity it brings.

Is a popular and revered leader who unites the people preferred over a leader who says hard words and subscribes to unpopular policies? The midrash seems to be quite positive and complimentary toward Aaron, in that he was a uniting personality and *therefore* loved by all. Later we shall see later rabbinic texts that proclaim, "There is no one more humble of spirit than a pursuer of peace," and whose ego is not a factor in the peacemaking process.

The second point regarding the identity and character of Aaron that comes out of this text is that the reason everyone loved him is because he didn't act like Moses, who rebuked the people and told them they were wrong. Instead, he "pursued peace." The midrash stops short of saying what Aaron *did* do when people sinned, but it establishes that he did not rebuke them, and for this he was beloved by all the people.

For theoreticians and practitioners of conflict resolution this contrast can be very unhinging, as it appears to propose a binary of two extreme options: fight and flight. Moses would fight with the people even though it damaged his relationship with them, while Aaron seems to have been silent, in "flight mode"—in essence enabling the people to continue sinning. Yet a central argument in the field of conflict resolution is that there is a third option, often referred to as "constructive communication." Constructive communication involves discussing the difficult issue in a manner that not only does not damage the relationship between the sides, but perhaps even strengthens it.

The commentaries on this midrash indeed felt a certain unease with this contrast between Aaron and Moses, and therefore offered some additional details regarding Aaron's pursuit of peace. Rabbi Abraham ibn Ḥayim (Morocco, 17th cent.) wrote in *Korban Aharon*, his commentary on *Sifra*, that "Aaron would not return them [to the fold] by means of rebuke at all, but by means of love and peace."[53] Similarly, Rabbi Yaakov David Biderman of Wyszogród (Poland, 19th cent.) wrote in his commentary, "Aaron also prevented Israel from sinning, but he did so through placation and reconciliation, and that is the essence of the commandment to rebuke: to prevent people from sinning in the future and to get them to regret what they did in the past."[54]

According to these commentaries,[55] Aaron pursued peace not by being passive and running away from the difficult issue, but rather by engaging the people in a manner different from that of Moses. Aaron's goal was to get the sides to refrain from their inappropriate behavior *and* maintain their relationship with each other.[56] The commentaries do not explicitly disparage Moses for having rebuked; after all, the Torah unambiguously commands (Lev. 19:17): "You shall rebuke your neighbor." Rather, they attempt to explain Aaron's method of pursuing peace as an effective alternative to rebuke, altering people's behavior without having them become defensive and scornful.

In a later version of this same midrash,[57] we do find Moses described as not being mourned by all the people because he "rebuked them with *harsh words*." The addition of "harsh words" appears to be a subtle critique of his behavior, hinting that this midrash favors Aaron's methods over those of Moses.[58]

Practical Implications for Third-Party Peacemaking Today

I have used this early rabbinic source found in the *Sifra* in various trainings from rabbis and social justice activists to middle school students. For example, in the Pardes Rodef Shalom Schools Program curricular unit 1, "Be of the Students of Aaron," participants are asked to debate the question, Who is the greater hero: Moses or Aaron? Using the excerpt from the *Sifra* cited earlier, Moses is presented as a *rodef tzedek* (pursuer of justice) who is not afraid to speak up against something wrong even if that makes him unpopular, while Aaron is a *rodef shalom* who strives to maintain good relationships with the sides in the conflict. Teachers are encouraged to note at the end of the debate, "We need both types of heroes in the world—the *rodfei tzedek* (pursuers of justice) and the *rodfei shalom*. While Moses may not have been as popular as Aaron, he is not considered less of a hero than his brother."

I have also used this midrash from as an introductory source for educational units and practical trainings focused on the Jewish concept of *tokhaha* (rebuke) as a form of constructive communication.[59] After studying the midrash together with its commentaries cited earlier, and before practicing practical non-violent communication skills, participants are asked, "How would Aaron have communicated and offered feedback differently from Moses?" This is important for establishing that a third-party peacemaker is not simply a conflict avoider but has the tools for discussing difficult conversations constructively.

The Third Source

"Moses judged; Aaron pursued peace." (*Tosefta* Sanhedrin 1:2)

The third tannaitic source that establishes Aaron's identity as Judaism's paradigmatic peacemaker is *Tosefta* Sanhedrin. The *Tosefta* discusses a disagreement among the Sages regarding the merits and drawbacks of *bitzua* or *peshara*, both of which have been understood to mean a form of compromise, as opposed to a strict judicial ruling.[60] The portion of the text that pertains to Aaron discusses one rabbi's opinion that compromise is strictly forbidden:[61]

Rabbi Eliezer b. Rabbi Yosei the Galilean says:
Anyone who compromises (mivatze'a) is a blasphemer before God, as it is said (Ps. 10:3): "The compromiser (botze'a) curses and scorns the Lord."[62]

Rather, let the law pierce through mountains.
For so Moses said: "Let the law pierce through mountains."
But Aaron would make peace between a person and his fellow,
as it is said (Mal. 2:6): "He walked with Me in peace and uprightness."[63]

Like the midrash in the *Sifra* we saw earlier, the *Tosefta* distinguishes between Moses and Aaron and invokes the same passage from the book of Malachi. However, here Moses is described as advocating for strict law while Aaron would seek peace. The *Tosefta* is cited, with minor differences, in both the Jerusalem and the Babylonian Talmuds. The commentaries on the version in the Babylonian Talmud wrestle with what they perceive to be an inner contradiction within the opinion of Rabbi Eliezer b. Rabbi Yosei the Galilean: if compromise is forbidden and strict justice is preferred, and Moses is associated with strict justice, then Aaron, according to this opinion, must have been a sinful, blaspheming compromiser![64] This is an unlikely and unsettling characterization, from the commentaries' perspective, of a revered biblical character and progenitor of the priestly line. The commentaries offer four different approaches to resolve this textual tension.

One approach, adopted by the twelfth-century German commentator Rabbi Eliezer b. Natan (the "Ra'avan") and the late-nineteenth and twentieth-century Polish-German scholar Rabbi Yosef Tzvi Halevi Diner, is that the second part of the text, which introduces Moses and Aaron into the mix, is not actually a continuation of Rabbi Eliezer b. Yosei the Galilean's words or position. They both point out that, essentially, the characterization of Aaron is actually a counterargument to Rabbi Eliezer Rabbi Eliezer b. Yosei's position. They assert, as it were, that he cannot be correct, since none other than Aaron the high priest engaged in compromise.[65] Both commentators address the editorial complexity of rabbinic texts, where elements are sometimes inserted or rearranged in misleading ways, perhaps by the redactor of the source as an attempt to debunk Rabbi Eliezer b. Rabbi Yosei the Galilean's argument. Most traditional commentators, however, maintain the editorial unity of the text, attributing both parts to Rabbi Eliezer b. Rabbi Yosei the Galilean, but they differentiate between compromise (*bitzua*), which he forbade, and pursuing peace, for which Aaron is to be praised. A second interpretation therefore was to focus on timing. Rabbi Shlomo Yitzhaki, commonly known as Rashi, the famous eleventh-century French commentator, describes Aaron's activities thus: "When he would hear that there was a dispute between [people], he would pursue them and make peace between them before they could come to him for judgment."⁶⁶ Rashi apparently considered Aaron to have been a judge, like Moses, and he did engage in compromise, but only in the context of pursuing peace. But since he did so before the sides actually came for a judicial ruling, even Rabbi Eliezer would permit it.

Rabbi Meir Halevi Abulafia (known as the Yad Rama, after his commentary; Spain, 13th cent.) explains this perspective on Rabbi Eliezer's opinion in terms of instructions to judges:

> Once they have come before you for judicial ruling, even before you hear their arguments, you are forbidden from then on to compromise. . . . But Aaron was a lover and a pursuer of peace, and when he heard that people had a fight, he would initiate and make peace between them before they came for judgment.⁶⁷

The perspective of Rashi and Rabbi Abulafia is particularly significant because it portrays Aaron's peacemaking activities not in contrast to the role of a judge, but as one aspect of a judge's opportunities or perhaps even responsibilities. These two commentators thus move Moses and Aaron closer together in terms of their identities as judges; but Aaron would also take initiative to mediate conflicts through compromise before entering into a formal legal process.

A third interpretation that seeks to distinguish between Aaron's role as a third-party peacemaker and judicial compromise is taken by Rabbi Yeshayahu di Trani of thirteenth-century Italy, known as the Riaz:

> Even according to the opinion that holds it is forbidden to compromise at all [i.e., that of Rabbi Eliezer b. Rabbi Yosei the Galilean], it is because such a compromise comes from the judges. But if the compromise comes from the litigants themselves, who are aware of the issues in the compromise and are satisfied with it, even after the case has been closed it is also possible to reconcile litigants who forgive each other. And this is the meaning of "Aaron was a lover of peace and pursuer of peace, and a peacemaker between a person and his fellow." And one who holds that it is forbidden to compromise says . . . what is done with the knowledge of the litigants themselves is not compromise but peacemaking, when [peacemakers] go to the trouble to reconcile litigants until they are satisfied and there is peace between them. And there is no greater mitzva than this, and this is what Aaron would do. Indeed, one may not force them or do it for them, but

[may] appease and reconcile them. But the compromise that is forbidden is one that is imposed upon them.[68]

The Riaz differentiates between judges imposing compromise upon litigants, which is what Rabbi Eliezer b. Rabbi Yosei the Galilean forbade in the *Tosefta*, and a process through which a judge peacefully facilitates reconciliation and an agreed-upon compromise between the conflicting sides without coercion. According to all, such a process is considered a great mitzva and can be done even after there was a formal ruling on the case. This distinction has been referred to as the distinction between a "judicial *ruling* of compromise" and a "judicial *mediation* of compromise."[69] This distinction between the judge's peacemaking role and the judicial imposition or coercion of compromise is subtle but essential.

The fourth and final approach taken by the commentaries asserts that Aaron's *not* being a judge was precisely what made it permissible for him to initiate compromise; judges, however, may not do so under any circumstances. According to the *Tosafot*, a collection of early-medieval Franco-German commentaries—in this case identified as the fourteenth-century French students of Peretz b. Eliyahu of Corbeil:[70] "Since [Aaron] was not a judge and cases did not come to him but to Moses, certainly for him it was permissible [to compromise]."[71] Rabbi Alexander Zusslin Hakohen (Germany, 14th cent.) adds legal force to this interpretation: "From this we learn that a judge may not compromise, even after the case has concluded."[72] But the flip side of this ruling is that someone who is *not* a judge may mediate a compromise even after a case has been concluded and a judicial ruling issued.

This distinction between Moses as a judge and Aaron as a peacemaker can be found in *Avot d'Rabbi Natan*, which cites a similar midrashic reading of the Bible as the *Sifra* cited earlier:

> Regarding Moses, what does it say? "The children of Israel wept for Moses in the Plains of Moab thirty days" (Deut. 34:8). And regarding Aaron what does it say? "And when all the congregation saw that Aaron was dead, they wept for Aaron for thirty days, all the house of Israel." (Num. 20:29). And why, for Aaron, did all of Israel cry and for Moses only some cried? Because Moses was a judge, and it is impossible for a judge to rule favorably for both litigants to the same manner; rather, he must rule favorably for one [side] and convict

the other side. Aaron was not a judge, but rather a peacemaker between people; therefore all of Israel cried for Aaron and for Moses only some cried.[73]

We will see in Chapter 5 that in Jewish communities throughout history there were people referred to as *rodfei shalom* who, similar to how Aaron is described according to this last interpretation, were not judges but rather laypeople; had no authority to coerce the sides to accept a compromise agreement; and acted outside of the former courts, occasionally, such as in Morocco (case 32), intervening even after judicial rulings had already been issued.

Practical Implications for Third-Party Peacemaking Today

The discussion in this section presented four interpretations of the relationship between compromise, referred to as *bitzua*, over which there is a rabbinic disagreement in the *Tosefta* whether it is a prohibition or a *mitzva*, and *redifat shalom*, the "pursuit of peace," as exemplified by Aaron. Each of these interpretations has direct implications for understanding the contemporary relationship between judges and mediators today. A mediator (Heb.: *megasher*, from the word *gesher*, bridge), as defined by contemporary Israeli law, is "someone whose role it is to assist litigants (without formal authority to rule on the matter) to arrive at an agreement that resolves the conflict between them in a process of mediation (*gishur*), through engaging in noncoercive negotiation."[74]

According to the Ra'avan's understanding of Rabbi Eliezer b. Rabbi Yosei the Galilean, there is no place for any form of compromise, whether it be a judge's ruling in court or a layperson's initiative outside of court. This may serve as support for those who take issue with various forms of ADR (alternative dispute resolution, which includes court-ruled compromise, arbitration, and mediation).[75]

According to Rashi's understanding, a judge can and should serve as a form of mediator so long as he engages in negotiations between the sides before the case comes before him, but not once the formal case has begun. By contrast, the *Tosafot* hold that a judge can never serve as a mediator, but others can and should be encouraged to proactively mediate between the disputants. This disagreement between Rashi and the *Tosafot* is similar to the various legal debates taking place today over judges mediating between disputants prior to the formal opening of the trial.[76]

Finally, the position of the Riaz, that a judge may at any time facilitate peacemaking and reconciliation between the sides, bringing them to an agreed-upon compromise without any form of coercion, is strikingly similar to a very "new" form of conflict resolution known as "judicial conflict resolution" (JCR). In JCR, a judge in his or her courtroom is perceived as performing numerous functions, including at times that of mediator. In this role they strive to either bring the disputants to a noncoercive agreement or facilitate dialogue and transformation, with the goal of healing the relationship between the sides.[77]

The distinction made by the *Tosafot* and *Avot d'Rabbi Natan* between Aaron the pursuer of peace, or mediator, and Moses the ruler-judge has important implications for understanding the relationship between pursuers of peace and pursuers of justice. What is being presented here is a model of dual leadership. There is a need for rulers and judges who speak and rule based on what is just and true even when it may come at the expense of what is popular and appeasing, and there is a need for pursuers of peace and mediators who help bring parties to an agreement, heal relationships, and cultivate communal harmony. In Israel, this can best be described as the difference between the role of the prime minister and the role of the president. The prime minister is charged with making difficult and often unpopular decisions in the pursuit of justice as he or she perceives it; the president, on the other hand, is supposed to be a uniting figurehead, representing consensus and popular with everyone.

It is important to emphasize that the rabbis did not see these two models of leadership as being in opposition to one another but rather as complementing each other. A good example of this can be found in a later midrash discussing the verse "And he went, and met him in the mountain of God, and he kissed him" (Ex. 4:27), which tells of Aaron meeting Moses after many years of separation due to Moses's exile. The midrash describes this encounter and kiss as being metaphorically the same as the verse in the book of Psalms (85:11): "Loving-kindness and truth meet; justice and peace kiss." In this midrash Aaron is likened to loving-kindness and peace, while Moses is likened to truth and justice.[78] These potentially conflicting values are represented by two paradigmatic leadership models that complement one another.[79]

Aaron's Methods of Third-Party Peacemaking

We have seen that Aaron's identity as Judaism's ideal third-party peacemaker was firmly established in the earlier tannaitic stratum of rabbinic literature, which was redacted no later than the third century CE. The three main sources we have examined so far in this chapter reverberate throughout Jewish literature, garnering commentary and meriting citation across the centuries and around the world.

However, while those sources identified Aaron as the paradigmatic peacemaker, and contrasted him with Moses, they did not articulate much of his *methods* for third-party peacemaking. That changed in the post-talmudic era between the sixth and ninth centuries, where we find different legends describing Aaron's methods of pursuing peace. These are preserved in four separate rabbinic sources, all of which are part of what are known as the "Minor Tractates" of the Talmud:[80] the first two, *Avot d'Rabbi Natan*, version A,[81] and *Avot d'Rabbi Natan*, version B,[82] describe Aaron's peacemaking methods in the context of commenting on the mishna in tractate Avot that we have been exploring here. The third source appears in *Kalla rabbati* 3:1 as part of a discussion of the attributes of a Torah scholar.[83] Finally, the fourth reference, in *Derekh eretz zuta* 11:18—also known as *Perek hashalom* ("Chapter of Peace")—is part of a collection of rabbinic statements concerning the value of peace.[84]

These legends seem to be an elaboration on both the earlier rabbinic sources and the verse in Malachi 2:6.[85] All four sources expand on Aaron's methods, but additional related material varies between them. The sources describe Aaron pursuing peace in three different contexts, using slightly different methods for each: (1) with the "wicked," (2) between husband and wife, and (3) between individuals.

In this section I will first examine the legends cited in each of these contexts and delineate the characteristics of the peacemaking methods they present. Second, I will demonstrate how those characteristics resonate throughout the rest of rabbinic literature in earlier as well as later sources and commentaries. Third, I will compare Aaron's third-party peacemaking methods with those of other cultural traditional methods, and will attempt to identify the most similar to those in rabbinic literature that describe Aaron's modus operandi. Throughout the chapter, I will share reflections on possible implications for third-party peacemaking today.

Pursuing Peace with the Wicked by Greeting Them with *Shalom*

The first context in which Aaron is portrayed as a pursuer of peace is with regard to greeting the wicked with the word *shalom*:

> Rabbi Meir says:
> What is the meaning of "And did turn many away from iniquity" (Mal. 2:6)?
> When Aaron would walk along a road and meet a wicked person,
> [Aaron] would offer him [i.e., greet him with] shalom.
> The next day, that person would seek to commit a sin.
> He would say, "Woe is me! How will I look up and see Aaron afterward!
> I am embarrassed before him, since he offered me shalom."
> And lo and behold that person would restrain himself from the sin.[86]

According to *Avot d'Rabbi Natan*, Aaron's custom of greeting the wicked with *shalom* results in proactively preventing them from wrongdoing.[87] The midrash derives this from the same verse in Malachi that we have seen throughout this chapter.[88] Aaron's practice of greeting the wicked might not be connected to the field of peacemaking but rather used as a means of preventing people from committing transgressions. As noted, several medieval commentaries on Mishna Avot 1:12 cite this text as proof of the descriptions there of Aaron as "a lover of people and one who draws them close to Torah."[89] However, it could be argued that this is a narrow approach to understanding the nature of Aaron's pursuit of peace.

By greeting someone with *shalom*, Aaron is showing the person honor and including them in his community, making them feel connected and part of his identity group. This may be seen as a form of conflict prevention: staying connected to those who may currently be at the fringe of society and offering them respect prevents them from leaving the fold, as they don't want to damage that connection. Moreover, a gift of respect and restoration offered unilaterally by a possessor of great honor might change the way that person perceives himself and his actions, causing him to rethink whatever crime he was about to commit—whether against God or against another person.[90] We will see later on in *Kalla rabbati*, in the section entitled "Pursuing Peace between Two Individuals," that the first thing he would do when he met with each side in a conflict was to say "peace be upon you"—offering them honor and opening them up to rethinking their contribution to the conflict.

Aaron's practice of greeting even the wicked or those who may be excluded from the "in-group" is reminiscent of Jesus's teaching: "And if you greet only your brothers, what more are you doing than others? Do not even the gentiles do the same?"[91] Likewise, Muhammad emphasized the importance of greeting people, both "those whom you know and those whom you don't know."[92]

Kalla rabbati's narrative on Aaron also includes reference to his peaceful greetings to the wicked, but in an entirely different way:

> There is no one more humble of spirit than a pursuer of peace.
> Think to yourself: How could one pursue peace if he did not humble his spirit as he walked? How so? A person curses him – he says to him, "*Shalom*."
> A person fights with him—he remains quiet.[93]

This time, the sinner himself attempts to hurt the pursuer of peace: he curses him or fights with him. But the response is a respectful "*Shalom*," or simply silence. In contrast to the narrative in *Avot d'Rabbi Natan* cited earlier, here Aaron is not proactively greeting a wicked person with *shalom* in order to build connection so they won't commit inappropriate behavior; he is responding to violent behavior with a nonviolent, peaceful "*Shalom*." This character trait of Aaron's somewhat reminds us of Jesus's famous instruction to "turn the other cheek" (Matthew 5:39; Luke 6:29). It also points to one of the definitions we saw in Mishna Avot of a "lover of peace" as opposed to a "pursuer of peace," that is, that the former refers to interpersonal relations while the latter describes a third-party peacemaker.[94]

It is critical for religious peacemakers to understand Aaron's behavior here, because it demonstrates that the quintessential peacemaker insisted on being in peace even with those who fought with him *ad hominem*, not just as a third-party peacemaker. It also draws important similarities between Aaron and other cultural models of third-party peacemakers. We will see this quality in several of the peacemakers mentioned in the book, such as the saints of the Atlas Mountains, who also claim to not engage in conflict themselves, and Rabbi Yosef Syracusty, who was described in one of the eulogies for him as being "of the insulted but not of the insulting."[95]

Practical Implications for Third-Party Peacemaking Today

In various *rodef shalom* conflict resolution workshops I have run, I've often begun with a short icebreaker I refer to as "The *rodef shalom* who runs to say '*shalom*' first."[96] Participants have to stand up and run to greet another workshop attendee whom they did not previously know and say "*shalom*." They are then asked to study together a short Jewish (and depending on the context, Islamic) text that relates to how to greet another person, such as the text about Aaron greeting the wicked with *shalom*.[97] I will then open up a discussion with, "Why, in your opinion, would Aaron say *shalom* even to the wicked? Have you ever tried greeting someone who may be considered your enemy? What happened?" The idea is that the *shalom* we are studying and attempting to establish as part of the training is not simply about how to extinguish conflicts, as we saw in the words of Abarbanel,[98] but how to build community and create a culture of *shalom*.

Pursuing Peace between Husband and Wife

A second context in which Aaron's methods of pursuing peace are portrayed pertains to making peace between a husband and wife.[99] *Avot d'Rabbi Natan* (see Table 2.1, case 1) states:

> If a man was hostile to his wife and sent her away from his house, Aaron would go to him and say to him, "My son, why were you hostile to your wife?" He would answer, "She sinned[100] against me." [Aaron] would say to him, "I guarantee that she will no longer sin against you."
>
> He would go[101] to the wife and say to her, "My daughter, why were you hostile to your husband?" She would say to him, "He hit me and cursed me." He would say to her, "I guarantee that he will no longer hit you or curse you."
>
> And thus would Aaron act throughout his life, until he would bring her to [her husband's] house and she would become pregnant and give birth to a son, and she would say, "[God] gave me this son only in the merit of Aaron."
>
> And there are those who say that more than three thousand Israelites were named Aaron. And when he died, more than twenty-four thousand sons and grandsons removed their shoes before his coffin [in mourning].[102]

This legend, like the previous one, is also based on the verse from Malachi and the earlier tannaitic *Midrash Sifra*, though neither is cited explicitly. This is the first legend we have seen so far that portrays an actual third-party intervention in a conflict between two sides. Aaron's methods are laid out fairly clearly. The legend describes the conflict itself ("a man was hostile to his wife and sent her away from his house"); Aaron's intervention by approaching each party separately, inquiring about their complaint, and assuring each one as a guarantor of peace; and finally the results of his intervention: a reconciliation between the couple and ultimately a lot of children named Aaron as a result of his having saved their marriage.

Aaron's practice is described completely differently in *Kalla rabbati* (Table 2.1, case 2):

> He would hear about a husband and wife who were fighting.
>
> He would go to the husband and say to him, "Since I heard you were arguing with your wife, if you divorce her, you might find another like her or you might not. And if you do find another like her and you argue with her, the first thing she will say to you is, 'This is what you did to your first wife.'"[103]

While this legend does not state explicitly that the couple reconciled, it is implied, and later in the source it says that eighty thousand children were named Aaron as a result of his making peace between their parents. The description of the conflict is similar to that in *Avot d'Rabbi Natan* cited earlier, but with a salient difference: in *Kalla rabbati*, Aaron approaches only the husband, trying to convince him not to divorce his wife. His logical argument is that a new wife may not be any better than his present one. This distinction can be described as the difference between the third party's acting as a peacekeeping guarantor and his or her acting as a conflict coach. But despite this, both versions present Aaron as intervening on his own initiative in a conflict between spouses and trying to convince at least one of them to reconcile.

The definition of conflict coaching is "A process in which a coach and client communicate one-on-one for the purpose of developing the client's conflict-related understanding, interaction strategies, and interaction skills."[104] This is essentially what Aaron is doing in the piece from *Kalla rabbati*, where he sits with the husband and convinces him not to divorce his wife. As a conflict coach, Aaron meets with just the husband and discusses the strengths and weaknesses of each of the husband's options.

Aaron's third-party role in the *Avot d'Rabbi Natan* piece is that of guarantor; he assures each party that their spouse will no longer cause physical or emotional harm to them. Isak Svensson writes, "Third-party security guarantees are one of the most prominent techniques mediators and other third parties can utilize if they seek to enhance the prospect of peace."[105] Svensson continues, emphasizing that one of the most important ingredients for the success of such a peace guarantee is the reputation of the third side: "Third parties that, to a great extent, care about their reputation as peace guarantors will be prone to deliver on their promises."[106]

Medieval commentators record yet a third legend that describes how Aaron helped reconcile husbands and wives. Most likely it is based on an earlier one about Rabbi Meir, which we shall see in Chapter 3 (Table 3.1, case 6).[107] It is attributed to Rashi[108] on Mishna Avot 1:12 and reads as follows (Table 2.1, case 3):

> A man said to his wife, "I swear that you will not derive benefit from me until you spit in the eye of the high priest." Aaron heard, and he went to that woman and said to her, "So-and-so, my eye bothers me, and your saliva has medicinal properties. Spit in my eye." And she spit [in his eye]. Because of this it was said of Aaron (Num. 20:29), "they wept [for Aaron for thirty days], all the house of Israel"—meaning both men and women. And regarding Moses it says only the children of Israel [wept for him], as it is written (Deut. 34:8), "The children of Israel wept for Moses."

According to this version, the husband's intention is simply to humiliate his wife. Forswearing any benefit or pleasure from him toward her until she spits in Aaron's eye has nothing to do with Aaron specifically, or even with anything his wife has done to him. Nevertheless, Aaron is willing to fulfill the husband's absurd terms by creating a situation in which the wife will spit in his eye—all in order to reconcile the spouses. Here we have an example of the humility of spirit that *Kalla rabbati* referenced.

Another striking feature of this legend is that Aaron lies (about his eye trouble) in order to make peace, a practice we will see more of. Furthermore, unlike the versions in *Kalla rabbati* and *Avot d'Rabbi Natan*, here Aaron does not engage in direct, logical arguments with either party (i.e., as a conflict coach), nor does he serve as a peacekeeping guarantor. His approach here is shocking, as it appears to be simply placating a bully. We see the peacemaker demonstrating tremendous humility and self-sacrifice for the sake of making what he construes as peace. We will return to discuss this method later in Chapter 3 when we see the roots of this late medieval legend in the story about Rabbi Meir.

Practical Implications for Third-Party Peacemaking Today

I have never used these three legends in trainings and educational workshops. The cultural gaps between these ancient texts and my participants, who adhere to a very different definition of what can be considered a healthy relationship between spouses today, are too great to even attempt to bridge.

Pursuing Peace between Two Individuals
(Table 2.1, case 4)

The third context in which Aaron is described as pursuing peace, which has drawn the most attention from conflict resolution scholars, is between two individuals. With regard to this context, all four sources we have been exploring cite the same legend, with slight variants.[109] I will present here the version of the legend as found in *Kalla rabbati* and cite variants as needed from the other three versions.[110] (For a complete synopsis of all four sources see Table 2.2.)

Kalla rabbati introduces this section by emphasizing Aaron's practice of humbling himself: "If two were fighting, [Aaron] would humble himself and go to the one and appease him regarding the other, and vice versa. For that was the practice of Aaron the righteous." From this point in the legend, *Kalla rabbati* parallels the other three sources, as follows (Table 2.2):

> He would hear about two [individuals] who were fighting.
> He would go to the one and say to him, "Peace be upon you, my master."
> And he would say to him, "Peace be upon you, my teacher and master.
> What does my teacher seek here?
> And he would say to him, "Your friend so-and-so sent me to appease[111] you.
> For he was saying, 'Woe is me, for I have sinned against my friend.'"
> Immediately that person would think to himself, "Such a righteous person comes to appease me?" And he would say to [Aaron], "My master, I am the one who sinned against him."

> [Aaron] would go to the other and say the same.
> The two [individuals] would meet on the road.
> One would say to the other, "Forgive me, my teacher, for I have sinned,"
> and the other would say the same to the first.[112]

The common core components of the legend found in all four versions are that Aaron, who is clearly of higher social status than the sides engaged in conflict, goes first to one side with an invented story indicating the other side regrets the fight and wants to reconcile. He then goes to the other side and tells that party the same story, thus leading each side to think differently about the situation—which in turn leads the two sides to reconcile.

The legend can be divided into three parts: (1) the conflict, (2) Aaron's intervention, and (3) the encounter between the sides as a result of the intervention. The first part of the legend mentions the conflict but reveals almost no details. There is no mention, for example, of what each side did to the other that caused the conflict. We can deduce that there is a breakdown in the relationship between the two sides. This is perhaps even more apparent in the parallel line in the version found in *Derekh eretz zuta*, which reads, "When Aaron would see two people hating each other."

Likewise, it is clear from the continuation of the legend that damaged honor is at the heart of the conflict,[113] and it is the task of the pursuer of peace to help repair the resulting broken relationship. We shall see that this is a common thread in many conflicts described in rabbinic literature; even when there were actual details of who did what to whom, or how much each side may have owed the other financially, at the heart of the conflict is the deterioration of the relationship. Similarly, as we have seen in Chapter 1, damaged honor and broken relationships are classic reflections of traditional or non-Western attitudes toward the very nature of conflict.

In addition, we learn from this terse description in the *Kalla rabbati* piece that while there are no details as to the identities of the parties in conflict, the two sides are described symmetrically, as social equals, with each presented as both victim and aggressor. Two individuals fight with *each other*.[114] This symmetrical relationship is sustained (in all four sources) throughout the legend, from the opening description of the conflict, through Aaron's balanced intervention, and until the meeting at the end.

The setup of two power-equals, with a third-party peacemaker who is significantly more respectable and powerful than the sides, is an ideal description of conflict mediation, yet it is somewhat detached from reality.

More often than not there are power discrepancies between the sides, which challenge the ability of the third party to mediate between them. In conflict resolution contexts, such as in Interactive Problem-Solving Workshops (Table 1.1), this is called the "myth of equals."[115] We will see that the vast majority of the cases examined throughout this book are far from this pure and ideal conflict triangle of power dynamics.

Before addressing in detail the middle section of the legend, which describes Aaron's methods of pursuing peace, it is worth exploring first the end of the legend, in which the two sides meet and reconcile. *Kalla rabbati* portrays the two parties meeting on the road, perhaps each one on the way to the home of the other to apologize, and then simultaneously asking for forgiveness and acknowledging his own wrongdoing.

In contrast to the legend as presented in *Kalla rabbati*, both versions of *Avot d'Rabbi Natan* portray a physical show of renewed affection and resumption of the relationship between the two parties: "When they went to the marketplace and met each other, they hugged and kissed one another."[116] In this version the two parties meet in the public marketplace intentionally, to reconcile after Aaron told each side that the other had told him, "Woe is me, for I have sinned against my fellow, who is greater than I. Here I am standing in the marketplace; go and ask him for me."[117] Waiting in the marketplace to reconcile is reminiscent of the *sulha* practice, explained in Chapter 1, which encourages the reconciliation encounter not to take place in a private room as in modern-Western models, where no one else would see, but in the public space, so that the entire community would know and participate. Moreover, the description of the reconciliation in which the two sides hug and kiss each other is also characteristic of a successful traditional reconciliation process.[118]

The end of the legend therefore reflects the beginning of the legend, in that the conflict is about a damaged relationship and the resolution is about repairing that relationship; there is no signed compromise agreement here that "solves the problem." Rather, there is a repairing of damaged honor and a process in which the two sides restore the relationship and the friendship. Several medieval commentaries refer to this last stage as *piyus* (reconciliation).[119] Moreover, nearly all scholars who studied this legend appropriately identified it with the concept of "reconciliation" familiar within the academic field of conflict resolution studies discussed in Chapter 1.[120]

Now that I have presented the conflict and the reconciliation encounter, I will turn to Aaron's methods of intervention as a third-party peacemaker between individuals. Scholars of conflict resolution have identified several ways Aaron pursued peace. I will analyze six of them: (1) taking the initiative to intervene, (2) meeting with each side separately, (3) serving as an emissary of the offender, (4) being a calming influence, (5) bending the truth, and (6) modeling humility and self-sacrifice. These six core characteristics define Aaron's methods of third-party peacemaking as found in the different versions of the legend and in the later commentaries that explored them.

Aaron Would Initiate the Intervention

The first characteristic of Aaron's peacemaking efforts was noticing conflict in the community and initiating intervention without being invited in by one or both of the sides. Aaron, at least in the *Kalla rabbati* and *Derekh eretz zuta* versions, is described as observing what is going on between the parties by "hearing" or "seeing." This highlights his attentiveness as an involved and caring peacemaker in the community. Similarly, as the commentaries on Mishna Avot 1:12 explain with regard to a "pursuer of peace" as opposed to a "lover of peace," one has to go out to the marketplace and actively seek it. This characteristic is also common among later Jewish *rodfei shalom* discussed in Chapter 5, who almost always are described as "entering in [to the conflict]" on their own initiative and not waiting to be invited.

Rabbi Yitzchok Adlerstein, when distinguishing secular mediation processes from religious ones, emphasizes Aaron's taking the initiative and not waiting to be invited in to mediate:

> Aaron, it seems, did not content himself in mediating disputes, in acting as an impartial guide or arbitrator to move along the process of peace to those who sought it. He actively created it—by generating interest in it to those who did not otherwise show any interest in achieving it![121]

This is indeed one of the primary cultural differences between modern-Western, individualistic societies and traditional non-Western, collectivist societies, the latter of whom show willingness for third-party peacemakers to intervene on their own initiative in what may be perceived as "other people's conflicts." According to Mohammed Abu-Nimer, one of the lessons Western conflict resolution approaches can learn from non-Western, Middle Eastern approaches is to "adopt the involvement of the community and society," which intervenes and encourages the sides to reach agreement.[122]

Aaron Would Meet with Each Side Separately

Another salient feature of Aaron's methods noted by scholars is his use of meeting with each side separately.[123] Gopin writes that Aaron "did not sit people around a table and conduct a dialogue or negotiation," as many modern-Western models of conflict resolution would suggest, such as in the Interactive Problem-Solving Workshops model discussed in Chapter 1. He met with each side alone and engaged in shuttle diplomacy, "which honors both sides by entering into their own spaces and honoring the boundaries of their world."[124] Aaron used this same method in pursuing peace between husband and wife, as we saw in case 1.

Throughout this book we shall see examples of third-party peacemakers meeting with the two sides in conflict separately (see Table 2.1, criterion 6). As we saw in Chapter 1, contrary to modern models of conflict resolution, the use of private caucus by third-party peacemakers is a core ingredient of traditional, non-Western intervention, particularly in the Arab *sulha* process.[125] The Aaron legend is therefore an expression of such traditional third-party peacemaking models, such as the *sulha*, which were likely familiar to the authors of the Aaron legend (Table 2.1, case 4).

Aaron Would Serve as an Emissary of the Offender

In *Kalla rabbati* (and similarly in *Avot d'Rabbi Natan* B and *Derekh eretz zuta*), Aaron not only intervenes in the conflict and sits with each side separately, he also presents himself to both parties as a messenger of reconciliation sent to represent the offending side: "Your friend so-and-so sent me to appease you." This too is reminiscent of the role of the third side in the *sulha* process, in which the norm is for the offending side to approach respected peacemakers and beg them to serve as *jaha* (emissaries) for him.[126] Elias Jabbour, who serves as a third-party peacemaker in *sulha* processes in the Galilee, writes:

> The *jaha* should tell the offended side, "We are asked by the offender and his family to come and pay you a visit in order to have the honor of offering their repentance and to express their sorrow for what has happened and to ask you to be kind—to have a great deal of honor on your own part and to let us take the case into our hands and see how we can help to restore peace between you."[127]

In general, there is no direct contact between the two sides until the peacemakers broker a settlement;[128] an offender who approaches his victim directly is considered an exceptional and strange case. Ginat describes such a case among the Bedouin in Israel's Negev region, in which a relative of the murderer approached the tent of the victim directly:

> In this case the senior relative humiliated himself by crawling into the tent. Prostrating himself he refused to be served the traditional cup of coffee until the family of the murdered man agreed to a settlement of the dispute. In order to preserve his honor regarding the Bedouin tradition of offering hospitality even to enemies, the paterfamilias relented and agreed to an end of the blood dispute. This unprecedented behavior was frowned upon by mediators because it indicated that blood disputes could be settled without their services, albeit by strange behavior.[129]

The model of the third-party peacemaker serving as an emissary of the offending side may be the exception and not the rule in terms of how rabbinic law evolved. Rabbi Yaakov ibn Haviv (1445–1516), after leaving Catholic Catalonia for Ottoman Thessaloniki during the Spanish Inquisition, observed several differences between the local customs in his new home and what he held to be the law, which in turn caused tension between the Jewish community of Thessaloniki and the newcomers from Spain.[130] One such custom that he criticized and encouraged to have changed was that of an offender sending a third-party peacemaker to the victim on his behalf. Ibn Haviv claimed this practice was misguided and not a reflection of normative Jewish law:

> It seems to be a mistaken practice, which is the custom in our day, that if one man sins against another, insulting him with words, a middle man comes in between them and makes peace, speaking with the insulted one so that he should be appeased [enough] to receive the appeasements of the one who insulted. And after this introduction, [the offender] comes to ask forgiveness from him.
>
> [This is contrary to Jewish law.] Rather, [the offender] must go himself in front of the [one he] insulted and say to him, "I have wronged you." And if he does not accept, then he should bring people with him and return to entreat him in front of them to forgive him . . . for this shame and humiliation are to atone for him and for what wrong he has done to his fellow, even if he only insulted him with words.[131]

As a result of ibn Haviv's position, many subsequent codifiers of Jewish law ruled that ideally the individual himself must go and ask for forgiveness and reconciliation; only if the first attempt is unsuccessful, or if the individual knows for certain the offended side will not agree to reconciliation without an emissary first, is he permitted to send such a representative.[132]

Other authorities argued that it is permitted to send a third party *ab initio*, since what is important is the appeasement of the offended party not the atonement of the offender.[133] One of these rabbis was Rabbi Hayim Palagi (Turkey, 1788–1868), who argued with ibn Haviv's position based on the legend of Aaron pursuing peace between individuals:

> If you say that the offender must go first, how is it that [the rabbis] gave such praise to Aaron the priest? "He walked with Me in peace and uprightness" (Mal. 2:6). For "they wept [for Aaron for thirty days], all the house of Israel" (Num. 20:29). And according to [ibn Haviv's opinion], as a result of Aaron's actions the offender would not have fulfilled his obligation [to ask forgiveness].... The intervention of Aaron would spoil, according to the strict letter of the law, what is supposed to take place [i.e., the offender must go first without the intervention of a third party], and how could they praise [Aaron] for that?[134]

According to Rabbi Palagi, the Aaron legend, which describes Aaron intervening before the sides approach each other, stands in direct opposition to the ruling of Rabbi ibn Haviv, who claims the offender must go first to appease the offended without the intervention of a third party.[135]

Nevertheless, it appears that while direct peacemaking without the initial intervention of a third-party peacemaker is considered the norm in Jewish rabbinic tradition, it is very rare in Arab-Islamic practice. In other words, the appointment of an emissary is considered the rule in Arab-Islamic traditions and the exception in Jewish rabbinic law. In this regard, Jewish rabbinic tradition is more similar to the accepted practice in Western culture, where the offender is expected to approach the offended party and apologize without the introduction of a mediator.[136]

Aaron Would Be a Calming Influence

The portrayal of Aaron as an emissary of the perpetrator, however, is not found in one version of the legend, that of *Avot d'Rabbi Natan* A—which is perhaps the most well-known of them all. Here Aaron tells a slightly different story:

Two people were fighting with each other.

Aaron would go and sit with one of them and say to him,

"My child, see what your friend is saying. He is beating his chest [and tearing his clothes] and strangling his mind and pulling out his hair,[137] saying, 'How can I look up and see my friend? I am embarrassed before him, since I sinned against him.'"

And he would sit with him until he removed all the jealous rage from his heart.

And Aaron would go and sit with the other one, and say [the same] to him.

In this version Aaron presents himself as a concerned third-party observer who claims to have seen the other side beating themselves up in regret for how they acted toward the one to whom Aaron is speaking. It stresses the depth of each side's regret at far greater length than the other three versions of the legend do, which tell only of Aaron functioning as an emissary of reconciliation. Another important addition found solely in this version is that Aaron "would sit with him until he removed all the jealous rage from his heart." Gopin comments, "This combination of listening, staying with someone who is enraged, and having an open-ended time frame seems to be crucial to conflict resolution in traditional cultures in general."[138]

Indeed, the very first thing the *jaha*, the third-party peacemakers in the *sulha* process, are supposed to do is sit with the victim's side, and listen to their entire story and hear their pain.[139] By contrast, modern-Western models of reconciliation such as the Interactive Problem-Solving Workshops model discussed in Chapter 1 encourage the parties to meet and communicate their pain directly.

Pely notes that at the initial stages of the *sulha* process, when the delegation attempts to recruit the victim's family to take part in the reconciliation, "the dignitaries may also resort to the extraordinary measure of acting as venting buffers for the victimized family's sense of rage, helplessness and frustration." Pely explains that this unburdening process, which functions as a form of role reversal in the social hierarchy in that the most respected members of the community are showing respect to the victim's family, while the family is, as it were, showing them a lack of respect, is a necessary ingredient in facilitating the reconciliation process, without which it would be unlikely to succeed.[140]

Aaron Would Bend the Truth

Perhaps the most obvious method, and for many the most problematic one as well, is the fact that at the core of Aaron's efforts is a lie (or a "bending of the truth"), as he tells each side that the other regrets their behavior and wants to reconcile. Solomon Schimmel refers to this as Aaron "sometimes using white lies,"[141] while Gopin emphasizes the "moral problematics" of Aaron's method of lying.[142] Friedman and Weisel deduce from the tradition that "Aaron makes it quite apparent that Jewish law recognizes that lying to bring peace is a commandment."[143] Indeed, in Jewish rabbinic tradition, and perhaps in the Bible as well,[144] it is generally accepted that one is permitted to lie for the sake of peace.

In the Babylonian Talmud (Yevamot 65b) there is a disagreement among the rabbis whether "changing the truth for the purpose of peace" is permitted or perhaps a mitzva (a meritorious act). Maimonides (Rabbi Moses b. Maimon, also known as the Rambam; Spain, Egypt; 1138–1204) rules that it is permitted, and a person is not considered a liar if "he made peace between two people and added and subtracted from the statements each one of them made to heighten their feelings of closeness."[145] Rabbi Yitzhak b. Yaakov Alfasi (known as the Rif; Algeria, Spain; 1013–1103) seems to rule according to the opinion that it is a mitzva to lie for the sake of peace.[146]

This preference for "social harmony over truth," as Steinberg describes it,[147] is not unique to Judaism. In Hinduism, Krishna, who as we saw in Chapter 1 was identified as a peacemaker role model, was known for having bent the truth in order to pursue peace.[148] In Arab-Islamic tradition as well, a peacemaker is permitted to lie for the sake of peace. In the *hadith* of *Sahih al-Bukhari*, a tradition is brought in the name of Um Kulthum bint Uqba, who heard Muhammad say, "He who makes peace between the people by inventing good information or saying good things is not a liar."[149] Pely notes that this *hadith* establishes an important historical and legal precedent for the common practice of third-party peacemakers in the *sulha* process engaging in what he refers to as creative reframing, "a practice used extensively by *sulha* practitioners whereby the peacemakers take extensive liberty with impressions and information that they convey to the disputing sides in the service of helping them develop a more positive attitude toward each other, even if it includes substantially misquoting or even inventing texts and narratives."[150]

A good example of this can be found in Ginat's account of a conflict that took place between Druze and Christians in Israel's Galilee during which one of the peacemakers suggested lying to the two sides in order to help broker the peace:

> He suggested to the other mediators that they wait for an hour among the olive trees instead of entering the village, and then return to the Christian family and say that the Druze notables had agreed to 'atwa [initial payment in exchange for a ceasefire]. He reasoned that any condition imposed by the Christian family would be humiliating to the Druze notables. He felt that it would not be difficult to persuade the Druze villagers to agree to 'atwa and begin negotiations for *sulha*, but he did not want a surfeit of conditions imposed by the Christian family to be a stumbling block to the negotiations.[151]

It is evident that in Jewish and other traditional cultures and religions, a peacemaker is allowed to lie for the sake of making peace in order to restore social harmony. In Chapter 3 we shall see additional rabbinic legends (cases 6, 7, and 8) where the third-party peacemaker lies in order to reconcile between the sides. By contrast, modern-Western models of peacemaking and mediation generally assume the "transparent honesty" and trustworthiness of the mediator,[152] and any mediator who would lie, even with worthy intentions, would destroy his credibility in subsequent peacemaking efforts.[153]

There were dissenting opinions within rabbinic literature that sought to limit the practice of lying for the sake of peace.[154] One such example that relates directly to the legend of Aaron may be found in the nineteenth-century compilation of hasidic writings of Rabbi Yehoshua Heshel of Rimanov. Like other hasidic masters, as we shall see in the next section, Rabbi Yehoshua Heshel was troubled by the language describing Aaron as a *rodef* (pursuer), since it is said in the book of Ecclesiastes (3:15): "And God seeks that which is *nirdaf* (pursued)." Classical rabbinic literature understands this to mean that God will always be on the side of the pursued, "even when a righteous person is pursuing a wicked person."[155] If so, asks Rabbi Yehoshua Heschel, why did the rabbis praise Aaron for being a "lover of peace and a *pursuer* of peace"; why not "say lover of peace and maker of peace, for what does pursuing have to do with peace?" He answers:

> For certainly the main attribute of peace is founded upon the path of truth, because from the attribute of truth comes forth the attribute of peace. And therefore, the person making peace must also speak the truth and distance

himself from lies. However, since on occasion it is impossible to bring forth peace without lying, it is therefore permissible to change [the truth] for the sake of peace. For "great is transgressing for a holy purpose."[156]

But truthfully, that peace should be achieved through lying is considered a despicable thing and a pursuit [i.e., with negative connotations] for the attribute of peace. And even though in the end, when peace has been achieved and out of the great love and connection between [the sides in conflict] the lie becomes canceled and forgotten entirely, nevertheless at the outset, when the person emits a lie out of his mouth, it is considered pursuit [in a negative manner] for the attribute of holiness.

And this was the attribute of Aaron the priest, who loved peace and pursued peace, meaning that due to his great love . . . of peace [and because] he yearned to constantly increase peace in the world . . . he would also pursue peace through lies in order that there should always be peace upon Israel.[157]

Although Rabbi Yehoshua Heschel and other commentators hold that lying for the sake of peace is indeed very problematic and may be considered a type of "pursuing" in its most negative meaning, Aaron was unique in that he was able to pursue peace by changing the truth. This is an example of the ends—achieving peace, justifying the means—employing manipulation and deception. It also reflects the understanding of peace as primarily the restoration of social harmony and normative relations between conflicting sides, and not as solving the problems between the sides or healing the various offenses each party committed against the other in the past.

Aaron Would Model Humility and Self-Sacrifice

The final core characteristic of Aaron's methods of peacemaking was his willingness to lower himself in humility and shower the parties in conflict with honor. As noted earlier in the version of the legend in *Kalla rabbati*, the peacemaker is described as one who acts out of humility in the pursuit of peace: "There is no one more humble of spirit than a pursuer of peace." This source, after telling of how Aaron would respond with *shalom* or with silence to people cursing, states, "If two were fighting, [Aaron] would humble himself and go to the one and appease him regarding the other, and vice versa. For that was the practice of Aaron the righteous."[158]

Gopin understands humility as one of the key ingredients of Aaron's method in his efforts to transform the way the conflicting sides perceive themselves, the other, and the conflict:

The actions of the third party are a critical role-model for the conflicting parties. They demonstrate that the mediator must be prepared to lose a little face in order to do something sublime, something spiritual, a *mitzva*.... The more that this dignified individual is willing to humble himself, the more powerful the model of peacemaking. This means that the psychological strength and moral character of the peacemaker/mediator is an essential element in conflict resolution.[159]

Indeed, we shall see throughout the rest of the book that there are numerous cases of peacemakers who sacrificed their own honor and well-being as part of their efforts to make peace between conflicting sides (see category 9 "personal self-sacrifice" each Tables, 1.1, 2.1, 3.1, 3.2, 4.1, 4.2, 4.3, 5.1, 5.2).[160]

Humility is likewise seen as an important means of preventing conflict in Islam, as it is said in the *hadith of Sunan Abu-Dawud*, narrated by Iyad ibn Himar: "The Prophet [Muhammad] (peace be upon him) said: 'Allah has revealed to me that you must be humble, so that no one oppresses another and boasts over another.' "[161] The humility of the third party is also essential in the *sulha* process. Pely emphasizes throughout his book the importance of recognizing that the offense is very much about dishonor and that the reconciliation process is very much about restoring honor. The third-party delegation, as has been noted, must be prepared to humble themselves and honor the victim's family even, or especially, at the expense of their own honor. He mentions that he personally witnessed several instances where the dignitaries were "abused verbally, sometimes in quite an aggressive manner, by the victim's family members—particularly women and youngsters."[162]

Jabbour refers to the *jaha* as the "anger absorber," saying, "Everything in *sulha* depends on how wise the members of the *jaha* are." The peacemaker must know when and how to act humbly and absorb other people's anger in order to bring peace.[163] Jabbour recounts the story of a well-respected peacemaker who humbled himself to bring peace in a *sulha* process.[164] Upon his arrival as part of the *jaha* delegation at the house of a murder victim, the women of the house went up to the roof and poured ashes on their heads, to the extent that "this good man's black beard turned gray because of the ashes." The peacemaker, however, did not get angry and rebuke the women for this; rather, he said to them, "You have the right to do that. Go on, go on." According to the story, the women wondered to themselves: "What kind of 'angel' do we have here? Perhaps we should be ashamed." Jabbour explains:

They wanted to express their anger. In this respect the role of the delegation may often have to serve as an anger or shock absorber for the other side. "You are angry? Don't throw it on your enemy—throw it on us. We will take the anger on ourselves."[165]

This raises the question of boundaries: How far should third-party peacemakers humble themselves, and what should they do if this method does not prove successful in transforming the situation?

The hasidic master Rabbi Moshe Hayim Ephraim of Sudilkov (Poland, 1748–1800), like Rabbi Yehoshua Heschel cited in the previous section, was bothered by the description of Aaron as a pursuer of peace. He held that its negative connotations include that of destroying the other side, which seems contrary to peacemaking. He cites in the name of his grandfather, the Ba'al Shem Tov (founder of the Hasidic movement), that Aaron would degrade himself to pursue peace only when he knew that as a result, the two conflicting sides would "regret their actions of their own accord as soon as they realized that Aaron, the high priest, needed to trouble himself and go to each of them and speak with them with regard to the disputed matter in order to mediate peace . . . and for this they would become ashamed of their actions and repent for their bad deeds."[166]

But if one of the conflicting sides happened to be "foolish and of a crude nature" and did not appreciate the fact that Aaron, the high priest, was willing to lower himself, speak with this crude individual, and help him make peace with his fellow:

> [Aaron] would have to change his method and pursue that person, defeat them, humiliate them, show them their shortcomings and their lowly value in order that afterward he could make peace between him and his fellow and between him and his Father in heaven and bring him closer to Torah. And this is what is alluded to by "lover of peace and pursuer peace" (Mishna Avot 1:12), meaning sometimes [Aaron] had to act as a *rodef* [pursuer] in order to mediate the peace. . . . And he was allowed to do this, even though it is not an attribute of piety to pursue a Jew. . . . All of his actions were for the sake of Heaven, and he would not do anything out of his own desires . . . only for the sake of God . . . he was able to stand up to the challenge of the hour, and change matters from the paths of the world for the sake of the paths of peace.[167]

Rabbi Sudilkov understands that sometimes Aaron needed to change his methods and shift from humbling himself and serving as a role model for the sides in conflict to "defeating" the side that was not interested in making peace. This act of humiliating one of the parties in conflict is a form of *pursuing* that is indeed negative, but it is for the sake of a holy goal.

The rabbi of Sudilkov likens this delicate and questionable method of "pursuing peace" to a professional doctor who knows how to use potentially fatal medicines in order to save the patient; but someone less skilled, or an amateur, could just as easily kill the ailing individual:

> [When] a professional and wise doctor, brilliant in the mixed natures of human beings . . . comes to a very sick person and hears [of his ailment], he is able to process the matter and give him medicines, even though they are very sharp and bitter, and [the person is] almost at the danger of dying from them. However, he understands very well that this person needs the medicine. But a different doctor . . . is not allowed to do this, for he is not wise and an expert like [the first doctor], and he could easily make a mistake and lose a life.[168]

The dilemma of when a peacemaker should employ the use of force is of course very prevalent in the context of international third-party peacemaking.[169] Similarly, the peacemaker in Islamic societies is not always successful in bringing peace out of humility; sometimes he is forced to ensure peace through the use of force, as the Quran states:

> And if two parties among the Believers fall into a quarrel, make ye peace between them: but if one of them transgresses beyond bounds against the other, then fight ye (all) against the one that transgresses until it complies with the command of Allah; but if it complies, then make peace between them with justice, and be fair: for Allah loves those who are fair (and just).[170]

Nizar Hamzeh, describing Hezbollah peacemakers operating within Lebanon as a means of gaining popularity and influence, points out that avoiding vendetta "requires not only spiritual influence but also physical force." He quotes Sayyid Ibrahim Amin al Sayyid, a Hezbollah third-party peacemaker, who says:

> In preventing vendetta, we avoid using force. . . . In some conflicts . . . the vendetta was prevented and a truce established without using force. In

other conflicts, however . . . a truce was established first by force then followed by a mediator's visit to both parties.[171]

Fredrik Barth articulates this point very well when he quotes Nalkot Pacha, considered a saint and peacemaker among the Swat Pathans in Pakistan, as saying that in order to make peace, "both holy status and force" are required. He goes on to tell of a case in which one of the conflicting sides appeared at a peacemaking gathering armed with weapons in an attempt to impose its will. The peacemaker, however, outsmarted them, revealing his own hidden armed men who subsequently helped establish a balanced and peaceful settlement between the two sides.[172]

Practical Implications for Third-Party Peacemaking Today

Each of the methods employed by Aaron in serving as a peacemaker between individuals has practical implications for mediators today. Actions such as taking the initiative to intervene, meeting with each side separately, serving as an emissary of reconciliation, and serving as a calming influence for the sides in conflict are all critical for the practice of peacemaking today. I personally find myself reflecting on Aaron's methods as part of my work at Mosaica.

Once, after conducting a panel for rabbis and sheikhs about their role as mediators within their own communities, one of the rabbis came up to me and asked for help in establishing a local forum of rabbis and sheikhs within his city in Israel. Only a few days later, there was an actual violent incident between the communities, and Mosaica decided to take the initiative and attempt to intervene. We visited the city as a delegation of two rabbis and two sheikhs. First, we met with a local influential sheikh, to whom we had a prior connection. Then we met with the local influential rabbi who had participated in our panel, and with whom we also had a prior relationship.

There would be numerous setbacks and challenges throughout the process (which as of this writing is still taking place). For one, there already existed a forum of religious leaders from the area through which some of these leaders had already met. The problem was that each time they met as part of that forum, the distrust between them grew—while the professional facilitators and governmental organization gathering them together had little knowledge of this. After analyzing the situation, we concluded that the problem was that the forum was being run like an Interactive Problem-Solving Workshop, grounded in modern-Western psychological methods, and was not appropriate enough to the local cultural and religious dynamics actually taking place.

Our method was to be like Aaron. Over the next few months, we went back and forth, listening to each side separately. Then we attempted to build a deep relationship and friendship between the two religious leaders, who could then work together and add more relationships of deep trust and friendship to the budding circle—including those who were considered even more extremist in their religious and political ideologies. With no pressure of formal, set meeting times, we are slowly attempting to bring the leaders of the two communities together and slowly help them facilitate a reconciliation process between all sides.

This traditional cultural method, following in the model of Aaron, may not look nice on paper—so often required by Western donors, who want to see how many meetings took place, who was at the meetings, what the outcomes and outputs were, etc. However, the Aaron model is the correct way to cultivate a real and deep culture of peace in Jewish-Muslim relations in the Middle East.

Aaron's practice of "changing the truth" is often very difficult for modern-Western students and participants in training workshops to come to terms with, and is occasionally greeted with cynicism and dismissed as being problematic, impractical, and unethical. There is a direct cultural clash between this population and the ancient religious and cultural assumptions behind Aaron's method in the legend. I have therefore had to address Aaron's lying for the sake of peace in various ways depending on the training and educational context and goals of each encounter.

For example, in the context of the Pardes Rodef Shalom Schools Program, Unit 1: "Be of the Students of Aaron" after much internal debate, we decided not to include Aaron's lying for the sake of peace in the middle school curriculum, as the feeling was that it had the potential to do more harm than good—either by giving legitimacy to lying or by risking the students' dismissing these rabbinic peacemaking models as childish. However, in training adults and lecturing to graduate students, I use this difficult text as a window to comprehending different cultural understandings of the relationship between truth and peace.

I have often experienced sharp differences in reaction between North American, European, and secular Jewish Israeli graduate students of mine on the one hand, and African, Indian, Chinese, and Japanese graduate students on the other. The latter group expressed much less reservations about Aaron's method, often citing sources from their own cultural and religious traditions in support of it. I recall how once a Muslim graduate student of mine from the Galilee wrote a beautiful essay on how she had successfully used this exact tactic of bending the truth in pursuing peace between different members of her family and how meaningful it was for her to find support for her method in the Aaron legend.

In my current role as the director of Mosaica's Religious Peace Initiative, I have had the opportunity to serve as a third-party peacemaker, where this issue has come up. For example (without disclosing any sensitive details), once, in a sensitive crisis situation between Palestinians Israelis, one of the sides came up with a compromise that they could live with. However, telling the other side that it was their opponent's idea risked the chances of reaching an agreement. We deliberated over whether or not we should present the suggestion as our own. As we went back and forth over this delicate question, the textual discussion explored in this chapter was very much present in my mind.

The hasidic parable likening Aaron to a doctor who knows when to be humble and when to humiliate or humble others has within it profound wisdom regarding what it means to be a third-party peacemaker today. How often do well-intended mediators enter into a conflict without fully understanding the "medical history" of the different sides, with all their wounds and scars—whether they be from the conflict or from other traumatic experiences? What are the potential risks of applying the same medicine for different patients without taking that history into account?

In various *rodef shalom* conflict resolution trainings I have facilitated as well as graduate courses I have taught, I often remind participants of this parable in every single session, as I feel it emphasizes the complexity and nuance of what it means to be a professional third-party peacemaker. Sometimes it is appropriate for the mediator to be a humble listener and anger absorber, a facilitator—in other words, an *ohev shalom* (lover of peace)—while other times the mediator must take sides as a *rodef shalom* (pursuer of peace), serving more as an "equalizer" in an asymmetric conflict.[173] An amateur who attempts to intervene in other people's conflicts and employs only one method of intervention may end up causing more harm than good. This has often led to fascinating conversations and debates about hot topics such as the Boycott Divestment and Sanctions (BDS) movement against Israel, from more liberal-oriented students on the left; and the legitimacy of using military force in times of conflict, from more conservative-oriented students on the right.

Comparing Aaron to the Third-Party Saint Peacemaker

In this chapter I presented all of the early rabbinic sources describing Aaron's identity and methods as a third-party peacemaker, together with their later commentaries. While the various commentaries did not always agree, they all share the core assumption that Aaron, the high priest and older brother of Moses, is the paradigmatic third-party peacemaker in Judaism.

I have also compared and contrasted the various rabbinic descriptions of Aaron as a peacemaker with other cultural models of third-party peacemaking. I have noted numerous similarities to traditional, non-Western models, particularly to the Arab *sulha* process, discussed at length in Chapter 1. There too, the third-party peacemakers are "highly respected insiders" as opposed to "neutral, professional outsiders," as is often the case in modern-Western forms of mediation. Moreover, the methods of the peacemaker in the *sulha* process are similar to those of Aaron, as described in the various rabbinic sources: the peacemaker initiates contact with the conflicting sides (if the perpetrator does not do so first); meets with each side separately; represents himself as an emissary of the other side; sits with each side until their rage is quieted; employs manipulations such as lies to advance the process; and recognizes the significance of modeling humility and reestablishing honor, thereby reconciling and restoring friendship between the conflicting sides.

While I believe this cross-cultural comparison is accurate, I would argue that an even more precise comparison can be made between the various rabbinic descriptions of Aaron as a peacemaker and the Bedouin saint peacemaker found among the Berbers of the Atlas Mountains of Morocco.[174]

These "Saints of the Atlas Mountains," who live alongside Sufi Muslim Berber tribes, are known as *igurramen* (sing.: *agurram*). Anthropologist Ernest Gellner, who studied these saints, defines their characteristics:

> Ideally, an *agurram* is one who is descended from the Prophet ... is visibly a recipient of divine blessing, *baraka*, mediates between men and God and arbitrates between men and men, dispenses blessing, possesses magical powers, is a good and pious man, observes Koranic precepts ... is

uncalculatingly generous and hospitable and rich, does not fight or engage in feuds (nor, by extension, in litigation); hence turns the other cheek.[175]

Gellner points out that not all *igurramen* fit this definition exactly, but since our focus is the ideal, legendary character of Aaron as a pursuer of peace, the description is very helpful.

Just as the Jewish priestly status that began with Aaron, the first high priest and forefather of the *kohanim*, is passed on from father to son to this day, Berber *igurramen* claim to be direct descendants of the prophet Muhammad and therefore chosen by God because of their status. By contrast, the more common Islamic clerical leadership prominent to this day in urban communities (as opposed to nomadic), known as the *ulama*, draw their religious authority not from their lineage, but rather from their scriptural knowledge of Islamic law—much as rabbis do, in contrast to *kohanim*.

The saints live separately but alongside the Berber tribes and serve as spiritual leaders alongside the political lay leadership of the tribes, for whom they facilitate annual elections for the tribal chiefs.[176] This dual leadership of political ruler and *agurram* is reminiscent of how some rabbinic sources, discussed earlier, portray the dual leadership roles of Aaron, the high priest and peacemaker, and his brother, Moses, the ruler and judge. The saints' compound was considered a sanctuary city, to where a murderer could flee from his pursuers. Likewise, the altar in the Temple, where the *kohanim*—all of whom belong to the tribe of Levi—served, functioned as sanctuary for the accidental murderer (according to the rabbis of the Talmud, the Levite cities also served this purpose).[177]

The Berber saints, like the *kohanim*, were the mediators between God and the people, in charge of all the sacrificial worship (the *kohanim* served in the Tabernacle in the wilderness and later in the Temple). Some of the *igurramen* were known for possessing a type of *baraka* (divine blessing),[178] while the *kohanim* were charged with blessing the people with the blessing (*berakha*) of peace, as it is written in the book of Numbers (6:22–27):

And God spoke to Moses, saying: "Speak to Aaron and to his sons, saying: Thus you shall bless the children of Israel; you shall say to them:
May God bless you and keep you; May God make His face shine upon you, and be gracious to you; May God raise His countenance to you, and give you peace. So shall they put My name on the children of Israel, and I will bless them (*avarkhem*)."

Other characteristics attributed to Aaron in rabbinic literature that we have explored in this chapter also appear in Gelner's description of the *igguramen*. He writes that the saints "claimed not to feud or litigate at all. A mediator who was himself involved in a network of hostilities and alliances would not be much use for mediation and sanctuary."[179] This recalls what we saw in *Kalla rabbati*, as well as in some commentaries on Mishna Avot with regard to being a "lover of peace," that Aaron would not fight with others and would instead be quiet or even respond to verbal abuse with a *shalom*. But in terms of this book, the most significant similarity between the rabbinic vision of Aaron, agreed upon by all rabbis, and the Berber *igurramen*, is that Aaron became known as the ideal mediator not only between the people and God but between people as well.

Gellner writes that the *igurramen* "[need] not only to mediate with God, but also to help with inter- and intratribal political mediation."[180] Like other traditional, non-Western third-party mediators, they go back and forth between the two sides in conflict. For example, Gellner describes how in cases of homicide the *agurram* would negotiate between the two sides until peace was restored through an agreement, payment of blood money, and the exile of the murderer.[181] Like Aaron—according to some sources, "the saints are, ultimately, arbitrators rather than judges: they cannot enforce their verdicts, but depend on the acceptance of that verdict by the tribesmen."[182] Their attempts to persuade and pressure the sides play a central role in the process, similar perhaps to how Aaron was portrayed in some sources as approaching spousal conflict.[183] Gellner even mentions a case where the saints lie in order to ensure that the conflict will be resolved.[184]

Ginat writes that Gellner relayed to him in a personal communication one more interesting fact about these saint mediators that draws an even closer connection to Aaron: "Only one Saint at a time serves as the mediator. . . . In Bedouin and rural Arab societies there are cases where only one mediator is used but it is more usual, and always in blood disputes, for there to be more than one mediator."[185] In other words, the saints did not form a delegation of third-party peacemakers but rather operated alone. Likewise, Aaron is always described in rabbinic legend literature as intervening alone and not as part of a delegation. In Chapter 5 we shall see that unlike Aaron and these saints, Jewish lay mediators (sometimes referred to as *rodfei shalom*) were always described in the plural, as part of a delegation, and never operated alone.

The striking similarities between the portrayal of Aaron the high priest as the ideal peacemaker within rabbinic literature and the anthropological descriptions of the saints of the Atlas Mountains raises an interesting question regarding the motivation of the rabbis to portray Aaron as they did. Is it possible that in addition to the potential historical motivations of the rabbis of late Second Temple times to rebrand the first *kohen* as a peacemaker who brings people closer to Torah (as discussed in the beginning of this chapter), as well as the various hermeneutical motivations based upon rabbinic interpretation of certain Biblical verses (as also discussed), that there were also cultural influences informing the rabbis' description of Aaron?

It would be a far stretch, of course, to claim that Hillel, for example, knew of the saints of the Atlas Mountains and then shaped Aaron in the saints' image. However, is it not conceivable that the rabbinic author or authors of the later legends found in the Minor Tractates of the Talmud describing Aaron's methods of peacemaking may have been influenced by cultural models of third-party peacemaking, similar to those employed by the saints or the *sulha* model, with which they were familiar from within their own communities?

Putting aside these potential cultural influences, there are striking similarities between the portrayal of Aaron in rabbinic literature and the peacemaking activities of the saint—but with one important difference.

As noted in the beginning of this chapter, the era in which the rabbis were expounding on the character traits of Aaron as a pursuer of peace was one during which the power structure was beginning to shift from priestly based to rabbinically based.[186] The priestly class at top of the societal pyramid was being challenged by the rabbis. Indeed, Hillel, who was one of the founders of rabbinic Judaism, did not say, "Be of the *children* of Aaron," but rather "Be of the *disciples* of Aaron." The attributes and behaviors of Aaron the high priest were not to be inherited but taught, learned, and most important, emulated.[187] Anyone could be a disciple of Aaron, even those—or perhaps especially those—who were not his descendants. In essence, the early rabbis may have imagined the legendary character of Aaron the high priest as the ideal third-party peacemaker, similar to the traditional cultural model of the ideal saint-peacemaker which is based upon lineage; but simultaneously turned him into a rabbi with disciples—like Hillel himself![188]

In the next chapter I will explore legends of third-party peacemakers in classical rabbinic literature such as the Talmud and Midrash (5th–6th cent. CE). These peacemakers could very well be identified as the "disciples of Aaron," as they were not *kohanim* but rabbis and lay leaders.

Table 2.1 Legends of Aaron, the Pursuer of Peace

Parameters for Comparison	Highly Respected Peacemaker			Individuals
Case Number	1. Aaron (Avot d'Rabbi Natan B)	2. Aaron (Kalla rabbati)	3. Aaron (Pseudo Rashi)	4. Aaron (Avot d'Rabbi Natan A, B; Kalla rabbati; Derekh eretz zuta)
The Conflict				
1. The case	Husband and wife	Husband and wife	Husband and wife	Two individuals, breakdown in relationship
The Third-Party Peacemaker				
2. Number	1	1	1	1
3. Social status	High	High	High	High
4. Connection to sides in conflict	Strongly connected insider	Strongly connected insider	Strongly connected insider	Strongly connected insider
5. Initiative to intervene taken by	Third party	Third party	Third party	Third party
6. Meeting with sides in conflict	Separately	Separately	Separately	Separately
7. Bringing sides to a compromise agreement*	———	———	———	———
8. Transforming perspectives, reconciling the relationship	Peace guarantor: he won't hit her and she won't sin against him	"Conflict coach": advises husband not to divorce his wife	Bends the truth in order to allow wife to spit in his eye to placate husband	• Serves as a calming force • Removes rage • Bends the truth, telling each side the other wants to reconcile • Acts as emissary of forgiveness
9. Personal self-sacrifice	———	———	Offers to be humiliated	Models humility
Result of Third-Party Intervention				
10. Success/ failure of intervention	Success: reconciliation, name their son "Aaron"	———	———	Success: reconciliation, embracing, ask each other forgiveness

*In earlier sources (Tosefta), Aaron is described as bringing the sides to a compromise agreement.

Table 2.2 Synopsis of the Legend of Aaron Pursuing Peace between Individuals (case 4)

Avot d'Rabbi Natan A, chap. 12, 24b (MS New York 25)	Avot d'Rabbi Natan B, chap. 24, 25b (MS Parma 327)	Kalla rabbati 3:1, 216–17 (MS Parma 327)	Derekh eretz zuta 11:18 (MS Oxford 2339)
		If two were fighting, [Aaron] would humble himself and go to the one and appease him regarding the other, and vice versa. For that was the practice of Aaron the righteous.	
Two people were fighting with each other.	A person would be hostile with his fellow.	He would hear about two [individuals] who were fighting.	When Aaron would see two people hating each other,
Aaron would go and sit with one of them and say to him, "My child, see what your friend is saying. He is beating his chest [and tearing his clothes] and strangling his mind and pulling out his hair, saying, 'How can I look up and see my friend? I am embarrassed before him, since I sinned against him.'" And he would sit with him until he removed all the jealous rage from his heart.	Aaron would go to him and say to him, "My child, why were you hostile to your fellow? He has just come to me crying and pleading, saying, 'Woe is me for I have sinned against my fellow, who is greater than I. Here I am standing in the marketplace; go and ask him for me.'"	He would go to the one and say to him, "Peace be upon you, my master." And he would say to him, "Peace upon you, my teacher and master. What does my teacher seek here?" And he would say to him, "Your friend so-and-so sent me to appease you. For he was saying, 'Woe is me, for I have sinned against my friend.'" Immediately that person would think to himself, "Such a righteous person comes to appease me?" And he would say to [Aaron], "My master, I am the one who sinned against him."	he would go to one of them and say to him, "Why do you hate so-and-so? He already came to me at my house and splayed himself before me, and said to me, 'I sinned before so-and-so; reconcile for me.'"

Continued

Table 2.2 *Continued*

Avot d'Rabbi Natan A, chap. 12, 24b (MS New York 25)	*Avot d'Rabbi Natan* B, chap. 24, 25b (MS Parma 327)	*Kalla rabbati* 3:1, 216–17 (MS Parma 327)	*Derekh eretz zuta* 11:18 (MS Oxford 2339)
And Aaron would go and sit with the other one, and say to him, "My child, see what your friend is saying. He is beating his chest and tearing his clothes and saying, 'Woe is me! How can I look up and see my friend? I am embarrassed before him, since I sinned against him.'" And he would sit with him until he removed all the jealous rage from his heart.	He would go to the friend and say to him, "My child, why were you hostile to your fellow? He has just come to me crying and pleading, saying, 'Woe is me, for I have sinned against my fellow, who is greater than I. Here I am standing in the marketplace; go and ask him for me.'"	[Aaron] would go to the other and say the same.	And he would leave that one and go to the other and say what he said to the first.
And when they would meet each other they would hug and caress and kiss each other.	When they went to the marketplace and met each other, they hugged and kissed one another. And thus Aaron would do all of his days, until he made peace between a person and his fellow.	The two [friends] would meet on the road. One would say to the other, "Forgive me, my teacher, for I have sinned," and the other would say the same to the first.	And he would make peace and love and friendship between a person and his fellow.

3

From Rabbi Meir to Beruria

Legends of Third-Party Peacemakers in Classical Rabbinic Literature

In the previous chapter, I outlined the identity and methods of Aaron as the paradigmatic pursuer of peace in Judaism. Yet he is not the only example of third-party peacemaking found in classical rabbinic literature.[1] In this vast array of early rabbinic literature, one can find additional legends that describe a third party attempting to make peace between two conflicting groups. Many of these legends, like those of Aaron, have served as important sources of inspiration for subsequent generations to engage in peacemaking. In this chapter, I will both examine each of these legends by unpacking their textual, literary meaning and trace their resonance throughout the history of rabbinic commentary as a model for peacemaking.

I will also explore the identity and methods of third-party peacemakers against the backdrop of the legends of Aaron examined in Chapter 2, as well as compare them to other theories and cultural models of third-party peacemaking from around the world. Finally, I will share possible implications of these legends for the field of conflict resolution today, as well as reflections on how I have applied many of these legends in various *rodef shalom* training and educational programs. This includes critical reflections regarding the limitations and problematics of some of these legends for such training programs today.

The chapter is divided into four sections, starting with the third-party peacemaker most similar to Aaron and his methods and at the "top" of the rabbinic social hierarchy, and concluding with those farthest from it. We will begin with Rabbi Meir, the "highly respected third-party rabbinic peacemaker," continue with legends of less respected rabbinic peacemakers, and conclude with legends of lay peacemakers and women.

The Highly Respected Third-Party Rabbinic Peacemaker

Rabbi Meir: Peacemaking through Being a Calming Influence (Table 3.1, case 5)

The legend of a peacemaker most similar to the rabbinic legends about Aaron is that of Rabbi Meir, the highly respected rabbi of second-century Palestine. It is found in the Babylonian Talmud (6th cent. CE). As with each of the legends examined in this chapter, I will first present the legend in its original and discuss its literary meaning before analyzing its theoretical model of third-party peacemaking.

> There were two people who, being egged on by Satan, quarreled with one another every Friday afternoon. Rabbi Meir came to the place (i.e., the house where they were arguing) and stopped them [from quarreling] and settled them down on three Friday afternoons. When he had finally made peace between them, he heard Satan say, "Alas for this man [i.e., himself, Satan], whom Rabbi Meir has driven from this house!"[2]

There is much to be unpacked in this short and somewhat cryptic legend. The identity of the quarreling individuals is unknown, but they are presented as equal sides; neither takes precedence in social status or contribution to the conflict. In other words, the conflict, as in the legend of Aaron pursuing peace between two individuals, is symmetrical.[3] The cause of their quarrel is also not specified, but it is possible that the mention of Friday afternoon is significant: Sabbath preparations and end-of-the-week activities such as shopping and delivering food and money to the poor can lead to tension in a household.[4]

Rabbi Meir's peacemaking between the quarreling housemates is so powerful that it drives out Satan from the household. The beginning of the story singles out Satan as the cause or sustainer of the strife; the end indicates Satan can remain in the house only so long as the conflict continues. Satan enters when there is a quarrel and incites the parties to continue their struggle, but does not enter or remain in a peaceful home.

Rashi articulates this in his commentary on a statement elsewhere in the Talmud regarding a group of scholars studying together at the home of an ill person. Whereas the intention of the gathering is to bring about healing for the patient in the merit of Torah study, the Talmud notes that caution is warranted because an assembly of students, who characteristically quarrel as they study and analyze Jewish texts, would bring Satan into the mix—further endangering the one who is sick. Rashi explains: "Satan is the Angel of Death[5] who, when he sees them fighting with one another, eggs them on."[6] In other words, quarreling drives out the Divine Presence and is the cause, not the result, of Satan's entering a home.

But Rabbi Meir manages to make peace and drive out Satan, who represents the opposite of Rabbi Meir in this piece, from the home of the quarrelers. Rabbi Meir's method is described as "stopping them from quarreling" and "settling them down" from fighting on three consecutive Fridays, with no further explanation of how he does it. This might be intended not to obscure but to highlight his approach to peacemaking: his mere presence on three occasions was enough to prevent them from quarreling and to push Satan out of the house. William Ury describes Rabbi Meir's method:

> A simple experiment will reveal, in its most elementary form, the influence of the third side. Introduce a neutral third person into any argument between two people. Even if the third person does not talk, the parties' tone will usually begin to moderate and their behavior will become more controlled. If the third person commands special respect, the effect will become even more pronounced.[7]

Rabbi Meir's subtle methods can also be intimated in a later midrashic source, which says that when Rabbi Meir would see two people walking together on a path he would call to them, "Peace be upon you, masters of conflict!" But when he would see three people walking together on a path, he would call to them, "Peace be upon you, masters of peace!"[8] Meaning, the mere presence of a third party may help function as a calming influence (of course, so long as they act as the third party and do not take sides).

In the legend in tractate Gittin, Rabbi Meir may also be acting as a spiritual healer whose role is to banish Satan from the house, thereby transforming the dynamic of the dwelling's residents. In other religious and indigenous models of peacemaking, the peacemaker may be found playing a similar role in banishing the evil spirit and thereby restoring peace.[9] An example of this may be found in the Iroquois legend of the Great Peacemaker, Deganawida. According to the legend, he climbed onto the chimney of the house of a well-known cannibal and, as a result of the cannibal looking down and seeing the reflection of Deganawida in the boiling pot of human flesh and mistaking it for his own, Deganawida, who represented the Great Spirit of goodness, succeeded in ridding the Evil Spirit from the cannibal—thereby transforming him into a better person and even a friend. As Jean Houston writes:

> The roles of the Great Spirit and Evil Spirit are played here by Deganawida and the cannibal.... With the coming of Deganawida, a new dispensation was at hand, and the cannibal, instead of being banished, was shown his true being and spent the rest of his life as a healer who brought the Good News of life and peace to replace death and suffering. Having been healed of his cannibalism ... the man became Deganawida's primary ally and friend.[10]

The rabbinic portrayal of Rabbi Meir is very similar to the rabbinic portrayal of Aaron. He is a well-respected third side who takes the initiative to enter into the conflicts of others who are less respected than he and make peace. Rabbi Meir also exemplifies humility and self-sacrifice by staying with the quarreling parties in their home for three straight Friday afternoons. Similar to the Aaron legend, the root of the conflict is unclear; the Talmud appears to be emphasizing the relationship and unfriendly atmosphere rather than any particular issue.

Likewise, the result of Rabbi Meir's intervention, as with Aaron's, is not a signed compromise agreement between the two sides but rather the expulsion of the negative atmosphere that takes the literary form of "Satan." Rabbi Meir, like Aaron, is not engaged in classical problem-solving conflict resolution but rather conflict transformation, reestablishing healthy relations and reconciliation between the two sides. The primary difference between these two legends is that Rabbi Meir does not meet with each side separately, and more important, does not bend the truth or use manipulative tactics to make peace between the two sides.

Rabbi Meir is a model of third-party rabbinic peacemaking, albeit not nearly to the extent Aaron was within early rabbinic literature. Nevertheless, this legend about Rabbi Meir was cited in later rabbinic literature to encourage peacemaking. For example, in his collection of responsa, Rabbi Moshe Isserles, the famous codifier of Jewish Law commonly known as the Rema (Poland, 16th cent.), cites this story as part of his praise for and defense of his friend and relative, Rabbi Meir Katznellenbogen Padua (known as Maharam Padua; 1473–1565), who was known to be a rabbinic peacemaker (see Chap. 5 and Table 5.1, case 31).[11]

Rabbi Haim Yosef David Azulai (*Avodat hakodesh* 1:7), whom we shall discuss at length in Chapter 4, is another example of a model rabbinic peacemaker. He alludes to this legend in the context of encouraging people to seek peace within their own home. It is quite likely that legends such as those of Aaron and Rabbi Meir serve as important sources of inspiration for Rabbi Azulai's own peacemaking.[12]

Another, more recent place the Rabbi Meir legend is cited as a source for understanding peacemaking is found in the responsa of Rabbi Yekusiel Yehuda Halberstam (Galicia, Israel; 1905–1994). There he invokes this story to explain why the hymn "*Shalom Aleikhem*" ("Peace be upon you"), welcoming in the angels of peace (*malakhei hashalom*), is sung every Friday night as part of bringing in the Sabbath. After citing the Rabbi Meir story, Rabbi Halberstam comments, "[The angels of peace] help drive away contention that arises on the Sabbath eve."[13] Rabbi Halberstam implicitly likens Rabbi Meir to the angels of peace who visit people's homes Friday night, helping banish contention among family members.

The legend of Rabbi Meir as a highly respected third-party peacemaker pursuing peace between two equal sides in conflict is much more the exception than the rule in classical rabbinic literature. Indeed, in many of the legends we shall discuss in this chapter there are significant power discrepancies between the two sides in conflict, which forces the third-party peacemaker to employ strategies different from those of Rabbi Meir.

Rabbi Meir: Peacemaking through Humility and Appeasement
(Table 3.1, case 6)

Rabbi Meir is found pursuing peace in a second legend in classical rabbinic literature, this time between a husband and wife with significant power differences between them. His primary method of peacemaking is through enduring humiliation and appeasing the more powerful side. As noted in Chapter 1, Rabbi Meir is the only peacemaker in Jewish tradition other than Aaron who merited the attention of a contemporary conflict resolution scholar, Marc Gopin.[14] This story is found in several places in the corpus of rabbinic literature of Palestine. This is the version in the Jerusalem Talmud.

> Rabbi Zevadya, the son-in-law of Rabbi Levi, would tell the following story:
> Rabbi Meir would lecture in the synagogue of Hammata every [Friday] night.

There was a woman who would regularly listen to him there. Once, the lecture lasted longer than usual. She left, and as she came home she found that the lamp had gone out. Her husband said to her, "Where have you been?" She replied to him, "I was listening to the lecturer."[15] He said to her, "[I swear] that this woman will not enter this house until she goes and spits in the face of that lecturer."

R. Meir perceived [the situation] with divine inspiration, and he pretended to have a pain in his eye. He said, "Any woman who knows how to whisper [a healing incantation] for an eye, come and whisper it." Her neighbors said to her, "Here is your opportunity to go home! Pretend to whisper [an incantation] for him and spit in his eye!" She went to him. He said to her, "Do you know how to whisper [an incantation] for an eye?" In her awe of him, she said to him, "No." He said to her, "They spit into it seven times, and it is good for [healing it]." After she spit, he said to her, "Go tell your husband, 'You told me [to spit] one time, but [I] spit seven times.'"

R. Meir's disciples said to him, "People scorn the Torah like that? Had you told us, would we not have brought him and flogged him on his bench and appeased him to his wife?"

He said to them, "Should Rabbi Meir's honor be unlike (i.e., greater than) his Creator's honor? If regarding the Name of the Holy One written in holiness Scripture says that it should be erased with water (during the *sota* ritual) in order to bring peace between a man and his wife,[16] all the more so Rabbi Meir's honor!"(JT Sota 1:4 [16d]):[17]

This story is not an easy one for contemporary egalitarian readers, as it reflects clear power differences between the genders, yet it nevertheless serves as an important case study of a well-respected rabbinic peacemaker. I shall come back to address the challenges and problematics of using this story as a model for peacemaking today at the end of my analysis.

The story begins with describing the source of the marital conflict in this story, from the perspective of the husband at least: the woman's prioritizing attendance at Rabbi Meir's lecture over being home with her husband on the Sabbath eve.[18] Returning home to find the lamp extinguished is both literal and figurative, as Sabbath lights are known in classical rabbinic literature as a symbol of domestic peace and harmony,[19] and they are connected specifically with women.[20]

When the husband takes an oath not to allow his wife back in the house until she spits in Rabbi Meir's face, this too has both literal and symbolic meaning. In rabbinic literature, spitting in someone's face is considered a particularly severe form of disrespect, and possibly even a form or personal injury that requires payment of restitution.[21] Spitting in Rabbi Meir's face would reinforce the wife's renewed preference for—and duty to—her husband over Rabbi Meir.[22]

To the horror of his disciples, Rabbi Meir allows himself to suffer the humiliation of having the woman spit in his eye. He justifies the personal disgrace of a great Torah scholar, which disgraces the Torah itself, through an analogy with the biblical *sota* ritual, used in the case of a woman suspected of adultery. Part of that ritual includes the Ineffable Name of God being written on a scroll and subsequently washed away with water. If God is willing to suffer such humiliation for the sake of restoring marital harmony, reasons Rabbi Meir, so can he. One might go so far as to say that Rabbi Meir was likening his own eyes to God's very Name and the woman's saliva to the water that washes away God's Name in the *sota* ritual.

As in the legend about Rabbi Meir we explored at the beginning of this chapter, the goal here is not to address the underlying issues at play in this conflict, but to restore the status quo of marital harmony by fulfilling the terms of the husband's vow and allowing the woman to return home. Rabbi Meir is not a neutral third party in this story. He himself contributed to the dispute, and therefore he needs to be personally involved in its resolution, specifically by accepting upon himself a measure of humiliation.

This method of peacemaking between a husband and wife by means of the humiliation of the peacemaker appears in another talmudic legend, but here the third party is not the source of the conflict; the husband is simply dissatisfied with his wife's cooking.[23] This brief story involves two other rabbis of Rabbi Meir's generation, Rabbi Yehuda and Rabbi Shimon, each with his own perspective on the acceptability of disgracing a sage for the sake of peace:

> A man said to his wife, "I swear that you will not benefit from me until you feed my food to Rabbi Yehuda and Rabbi Shimon!" Rabbi Yehuda tasted and said, "This is an *a fortiori* inference: If to make peace between a man and his wife the Torah said, '[God's] Name, which is written in holiness, shall be erased [during the *sota* ritual] in the bitter water for a case of doubtful [adultery]'; all the more so should I [undergo this]!" Rabbi Shimon did not taste, and said, "Let all the widow's (i.e. that woman's) children die, but do not remove Shimon from his honor!" (Nedarim 66b)[24]

The husband apparently intends to humiliate his wife by forcing her to demonstrate her poor cooking to two major rabbis.[25] Intentionally or not, however, this involves a certain amount of humiliation, or at least self-abnegation, on the part of those rabbis. Like Rabbi Meir, Rabbi Yehuda reasons that this self-effacement is perfectly acceptable for the sake of restoring marital harmony. He cites the precedent of dishonoring God, as it were, during the *sota* ritual, whose purpose is also to restore marital harmony.

Rabbi Shimon is unwilling to accept the humiliation of a sage for any reason. On the surface, he seems to be self-interested and negative, but it is also possible to see Rabbi Shimon's response as an attempt to offer an alternative method for restoring marital harmony here. Indeed the Talmud itself, in its elaboration of this story, suggests that Rabbi Shimon turned down the food in order not to accustom the husband to making such vows with impunity.[26]

The tension between Rabbi Meir and Rabbi Yehuda on the one hand, who took the approach of enduring humiliation and appeasing the husband, and that of Rabbi Meir's disciples and Rabbi Shimon on the other hand, who rejected this approach, raises an important question as to which of these approaches should serve as the appropriate model for third-party peacemaking today. Rabbi Menashe Klein, a contemporary American-Israeli, ultra-Orthodox rabbi, writes in a responsum related to a marital conflict: "If I can be of help in any way, I am prepared. For the Holy One, blessed be He, commanded to have His name erased, Heaven forbid, for the sake of peace in the home, and Rabbi Meir had his eye spit in for the sake of peace in the home; so what can I say?"

Rabbi Klein finds in Rabbi Meir an important role model and inspiration for engaging in the pursuit of peace within the home. What is notable is that the context within which he cites this legend is in ruling that couples in dispute should turn only to rabbis for help. According to the opinion of Rabbi Klein, it is absolutely forbidden to involve a therapist in marital disputes.

By contrast, Shulamit Valler, a contemporary Israeli historian and feminist, asserts that Rabbi Meir's and Rabbi Yehuda's decisions to placate the husband are extremely problematic. She stresses the high price paid in giving in to the husband's whims, and the patriarchal viewpoint those decisions represent. In her view, Rabbi Meir and Rabbi Yehuda express through their actions that "the most effective way to grapple with the worsening of a man's attitude toward his wife is to appease him and restore his damaged pride. There is no doubt that this path is not egalitarian, and it often does the woman an injustice."[27] Valler therefore presents the position of Rabbi Shimon and Rabbi Meir's disciples as the desired, alternative model to that of Rabbi Meir and Rabbi Yehuda. This alternative expresses that "one should not give in to the husband's demands, but rather, on the contrary, one should point out his errors using verbal threats or even physical punishment."[28]

Marc Gopin, as a scholar-practitioner of religion and conflict resolution, understands the story as an important critique of "a certain elite, [contemporary] priests or rabbis who may think that peacemaking is beneath them," while at the same time clearly acknowledging the problems of applying "too literally these rabbinic methods, which after all come from a civilization of two thousand years ago."[29] He nevertheless identifies some important lessons to be learned for the contemporary peacemaker.

First, Gopin stresses the significance of Rabbi Meir's personal and professional stature. As a third-party peacemaker of "great power due to his spiritual position," Rabbi Meir swallows his own pride and enables the injured party, in this case the husband, to be released from his anger—a necessary step in the reconciliation process.[30] Second, Gopin argues that this form of peacemaking stands contrary to Western expectations of the mediator, whose personal, moral, and ethical qualities are irrelevant to the process, and who is also personally disconnected from the dispute. Drawing upon similarities between this legend of Rabbi Meir and the legend of Aaron pursuing peace between individuals, in particular according to the version in *Kalla rabbati*, which states that "there is no one more humble of spirit than the pursuer of peace," Gopin concludes:

> The ideal Jewish peacemaker's path, as seen from the Aaron and Rabbi Meir stories, involves the development of a pious or moral character worthy of respect, the conscious creation of role models of peacemaking, purposeful acts of humility that sometimes involve personal sacrifice or loss of face, active or empathic listening, a method of helping people work through destructive emotions, and, finally, the gift of abundant if not unlimited time."[31]

Gopin's observations are in line with the description of the *sulha* process in Chapter 2, where the third-party peacemaker has to be willing to serve as an anger absorber, if needed, as part of the process, allowing the victim's side to express their rage and then begin to shift toward forgiveness. Yet we also saw, in particular in the words of Rabbi Moshe Ḥayim Ephraim of Sudilkov in *Degel Maḥaneh Ephraim*, that sometimes peacemakers needed to set certain boundaries to this behavior when one side is asserting power over the other and becoming even more arrogant as a result of the humility expressed by the peacemaker. It is therefore important to emphasize the potential problems with Rabbi Meir's approach in this legend and the critique expressed through the voices of his students and Rabbi Shimon. These two legends involving a husband and wife, with the accompanying internal tension apparent in both of them, serve as valuable case studies of the importance of the peacemaker's willingness to endure self-sacrifice and humiliation for the sake of peace, and simultaneously the potential limits and dangers to this approach.

It is also important to highlight some of the differences between the legends of Rabbi Meir and the rabbinic legends of Aaron pursuing peace between individuals and between husband and wife. Unlike Rabbi Meir and Rabbi Yehuda, Aaron was not forced into an act of abasement and humiliation by either party in those disputes; rather, he chose to humble himself when intervening in disputes between common people. He experienced a far lower degree of humiliation than that which Rabbi Meir and Rabbi Yehuda endured. What is more, Aaron related to the two parties absolutely equally, without granting one side an advantage over the other—also unlike Rabbi Meir and Rabbi Yehuda.

There is, however, the legend we explored in Chapter 2, which describes Aaron pursuing peace between a husband and wife in a nearly identical situation to Rabbi Meir: he is also forced by a husband's vow to have a woman spit in his eye as a condition for reconciliation. Yet as noted, this was a later tradition undoubtedly based on the earlier legend of Rabbi Meir, and Aaron allowed himself to be disgraced most likely due to the fact that the sides in conflict were not considered equal in status.

Practical Implications for Third-Party Peacemaking Today

I have personally used the first legend of Rabbi Meir (Table 3.1, case 5) in many of the training and educational programs I have run. For example, it is included in the Pardes Rodef Shalom Schools Program curricular Unit 2, entitled "The Strategies of the Rodef Shalom," which is geared toward a Judaic studies course at the middle school level.[32]

In a previous class, students brainstormed the various roles third-party *rodfei shalom* can play in different conflict scenarios. Now they are asked to study the Rabbi Meir legend carefully, attempting to elicit Rabbi Meir's strategy from it. After discussing the narrative together and the theory of how a well-respected third party can de-escalate tension, students engage in role-playing.

Two students are asked to act out in front of the class a scenario of two eighth graders quarreling, one claiming, for example, that the other took their school uniform and the other denying it. A third student is then asked to enter into the conflict as the principal of the school, and then later another student enters as a popular and well-respected tenth grader. Finally, two peers who are close to both sides are asked to intervene. Afterward, students add to their initial list of a *rodef shalom*'s strategies what they learned from studying the Rabbi Meir legend and participating in or observing the role play. New strategies they might add include serving as a calming presence and transforming relationships.

In contrast to the first legend of Rabbi Meir, the second one in which he serves as a peacemaker between a husband and wife (Table 3.1, case 6), raises serious challenges in its applicability for *rodef shalom* training today because of its various complexities. Several years ago, at the very first Pardes Rodef Shalom Retreat, which I cofacilitated with Marc Gopin, I used this legend as a case study for third-party peacemaking. The participants, who ranged from young social justice activists and rabbinic students to conflict resolution professors and rabbis, were asked to first study the legend in small groups and then to do a role-playing exercise. The scenario was "one week later," and the couple (whom I referred to as Andy and Nate, based on the parallels between this story and the then-popular movie, *The Devil Wears Prada*) were once again fighting.

I had participants break into groups of four, with two people playing the roles of Andy and Nate and the other two playing the *rodfei shalom*, Aaron and Elisheva (the name of the biblical Aaron's wife). They were asked to enact a private conversation between Elisheva and Andy, and then one between Aaron and Nate, while the other two observed and offered feedback. My thinking was that they would take their contemporary conflict resolution skills and apply them to this scenario loosely based on the legend, thereby offering alternative approaches to the two found in the legend—that of Rabbi Meir and that of his students. I thought this was a very clever idea.

I was mistaken.

At some point in the middle of the activity, one of the participants, a rabbi, stood up and said how deeply offended she was by our even suggesting that such a misogynistic text be used. Moreover, it was very uncomfortable for her to enter into such a problematic scenario. Prof. Gopin, whom prior to the session I had (wrongly) not consulted about using this legend, quickly chimed in, explaining the peacemaking values that can be found in this legend while simultaneously acknowledging its clear problematics. It was a hard lesson for me to learn about the practical limitations of using these ancient legends, which originate in such a different cultural setting from that of modern participants in a training setting. I have not used this legend since.

In the following section I will explore four stories where not only are the sides in conflict considered of unequal status, but one of the sides is considered more respectable than even the third-party peacemaker.

The Less Respected Third-Party Rabbinic Peacemaker

The peacemakers we have seen up to this point such as Aaron and Rabbi Meir, as well as the many traditional third-party peacemakers discussed in Chapter 1, were well-respected religious leaders, indeed considered more distinguished than the two sides in conflict. However, the third party was not always in this position, and sometimes they found themselves in an asymmetric conflict, where one of the sides was considered more respected and more powerful not only than the other side, as is the norm,[33] but actually more distinguished than the third-party peacemaker as well. This scenario is too often ignored by conflict resolution scholars, many of whom prefer to discuss more idealized cases where the third party is worthy of the most respect. Consequently, these legends did not merit serving as sources of inspiration for similar third-party peacemakers in subsequent generations.

In anthropological studies such scenarios are in fact discussed. Joseph Ginat, for example, cites several examples of *sulha* mediators who were not respected and skilled enough, which led to the failure of the process and/or to the lowering of the mediator's social status.[34] Including Jewish legends of this nature in this book is meant to have an important sobering effect on our understanding of the complex nature of third-party peacemaking in Judaism.

In classical rabbinic literature I have found two primary ways for a less respected third-party peacemaker to deal with this power discrepancy. One is to change the truth to placate the more powerful, offended side (similar to what we saw in the second Rabbi Meir legend, Table 3.1, case 6), and the other is to clarify the truth of the situation in conversation with the weaker, offending side.

Rabbi Yaakov bar Iddi: Pursuing Peace through Bending the Truth
(Table 3.1, case 7)

The first story in which a less respected third-party peacemaker is portrayed can be found in the Jerusalem Talmud.[35] It tells of Rabbi Yohanan bar Nappaha, head of the rabbinical academy in Tiberias, who lived at the end of the third century CE. Rabbi Yohanan becomes angry at Rabbi Elazar b. Pedat, who was an immigrant from Babylonia, and Rabbi Yaakov bar Iddi, a student of Rabbi Yohanan, successfully calms his teacher down by offering him three interpretations of Rabbi Elazar's perceived offense. However, it is unclear whether these suggested interpretations are realistic or not:

> Rabbi Yohanan [bar Nappaha] was leaning on Rabbi Yaakov bar Iddi [for support while he walked],[36] and Rabbi Elazar [b. Pedat] saw him and hid from him. [Rabbi Yohanan] said, "That Babylonian did two things to me. First, he did not greet me,[37] and second, he did not transmit the law in my name."
>
> [Rabbi Yaakov bar Iddi] said to him, "That is the custom of [Babylonians]. A lesser person does not greet a greater person, for they fulfill the verse (Job 29:8): 'The young men saw me and hid themselves, and the aged rose up and stood.'"
>
> While they were walking, he saw a rabbinic study hall. [Rabbi Yaakov bar Iddi] said to [Rabbi Yohanan], "This was where Rabbi Meir would sit and expound, and he would transmit the law in the name of Rabbi Yishmael, but he would not transmit the law in the name of Rabbi Akiva."
>
> [Rabbi Yohanan] said to him, "But everyone knows that Rabbi Meir was the student of Rabbi Akiva!"
>
> [Rabbi Yaakov bar Iddi] said to him, "And everyone knows that Rabbi Elazar [b. Pedat] is the student of Rabbi Yohanan!"
>
> [Rabbi Yaakov bar Iddi] said, "Should one pass [directly] in front of the *Adori*[38] idol [or should one cross the street]?"
>
> [Rabbi Yohanan] said, "Why would you give it such an honor? Pass before it and blind its eye!"
>
> [Rabbi Yaakov bar Iddi] said, "Rabbi Elazar acted appropriately toward you by not passing [directly] in front of you."
>
> [Rabbi Yohanan] said to him, "Rabbi Yaakov bar Iddi, you know how to appease." (JT Mo'ed Katan 3:7 [83c]).

There are two things for which Rabbi Yoḥanan bar Nappaḥa is upset at Rabbi Elazar b. Pedat. First, Rabbi Elazar did not greet him, and second, at some point Rabbi Elazar had neglected to give Rabbi Yoḥanan credit for a certain teaching. Rabbi Yaakov bar Iddi, whom Rabbi Yoḥanan was physically and perhaps (symbolically) psychologically leaning upon, offers three different explanations that attempt to recast Rabbi Elazar's behavior in a positive light. But at no point in this story are we told that Rabbi Yaakov bar Iddi actually knew what motivated Rabbi Elazar's actions.

Rabbi Yaakov bar Iddi's first explanation is that the Babylonian custom is for students to refrain from greeting their teachers. We should begin, therefore, by asking: is it reasonable to assume that Rabbi Elazar did in fact refrain from greeting Rabbi Yoḥanan because he was observing the Babylonian custom of respect, and we have here an example of a cultural misunderstanding?[39]

Ofra Meir, a contemporary literary scholar of rabbinic legend literature, understands that Rabbi Yaakov bar Iddi was indeed telling the truth when he cleverly transformed Rabbi Yoḥanan's insult of Rabbi Elazar, "that Babylonian!," into an explanation that casts his behavior in a positive light specifically as a Babylonian. Furthermore, Meir argues, Rabbi Yaakov bar Iddi was not only honest and correct in his defense of Rabbi Elazar, he expressed multiple levels of truth and served as a skilled third-party peacemaker. She explains Rabbi Yaakov bar Iddi's point to be that a student's respect for a teacher cannot be ascertained simply by means of external expressions, but is determined by internal intentions. She writes, "Rabbi Yaakov bar Iddi not only understood [Rabbi Elazar b. Pedat's] actions correctly, he also understood the heart of his teacher, and knew how to get him to see that his emotional reaction with regard to his honor caused him to err in his interpretation of the reality."[40]

I am not convinced. Misinterpreting cultural norms is of course a genuine cause of strife between two people, but there is good reason to doubt the corroborating sources for this custom.[41] Indeed, the practice of greeting one's rabbi is well attested to in the Babylonian Talmud,[42] and in the version of this story found in the Babylonian Talmud, Rabbi Yaakov bar Iddi's explanation does not even appear. It is reasonable to conclude, therefore, that the story knowingly depicts Rabbi Yaakov bar Iddi using a falsehood as a means of placating Rabbi Yoḥanan, and in reality there is no such Babylonian custom.

There is also question whether Rabbi Yaakov bar Iddi's second interpretation of Rabbi Elazar b. Pedat's behavior is true. He tells Rabbi Yoḥanan that everyone already knows Rabbi Elazar is Rabbi Yoḥanan's principal disciple, and therefore there is no need for him to credit Rabbi Yoḥanan explicitly when he transmits the law. He draws an analogy between Rabbi Elazar and Rabbi Meir, the very same famous sage of several generations prior whom we met in the previous section. Rabbi Meir never cites his principal teacher, Rabbi Akiva, in classical rabbinic literature, and he also almost never[43] cites Rabbi Yishmael, another sage of his teacher's generation, who was not his principal teacher. In the Babylonian Talmud's version of this story,[44] Rabbi Yoḥanan and Rabbi Elazar are compared to the biblical figures of Moses and Joshua: an unequivocal teacher-student relationship. But was Rabbi Yoḥanan's relationship to Rabbi Elazar comparable to either of those two clear teacher-student relationships?

While some commentators and rabbinic legal authorities take for granted that Rabbi Yaakov bar Iddi was telling the truth,[45] there is, once again, good reason to doubt this. The relationship between Rabbi Yoḥanan bar Nappaḥa and Rabbi Elazar b. Pedat is not at all simple. Rabbi Elazar, according to another source in the Jerusalem Talmud, was not Rabbi Yoḥanan's principal disciple, but rather a student-colleague (*talmid ḥaver*).[46] On many occasions in the Jerusalem Talmud, Rabbi Elazar disagrees with Rabbi Yoḥanan, and in some places it is even stated, "When Rabbi Yoḥanan heard [the objection], he said, 'Rabbi Elazar has taught us wisely.'"[47] We know too that Rabbi Elazar studied under the tutelage of other important rabbis of that generation, both before and after he moved from Babylonia to Palestine.[48]

There are also clues regarding who actually taught Rabbi Elazar the allegedly unattributed law (which pertains to levirate marriage) that indicate Rabbi Elazar did not actually learn it from Rabbi Yoḥanan and therefore had no need to cite him. In the Babylonian Talmud's version of this story, the law is referred to right before the incident we have been exploring, but here the Babylonian sage Shmuel, a former teacher of Rabbi Elazar, had also taught the law in question, and it is likely Rabbi Elazar learned it from him before he moved to Palestine and became Rabbi Yoḥanan's student. Likewise, another passage in the Jerusalem Talmud records Rabbi Yoḥanan protesting that Rabbi Elazar had learned a certain law from him.[49] However, another rabbi steps in and says the law was already recorded in the Mishna, indicating that in all likelihood Rabbi Elazar had not learned it from Rabbi Yoḥanan—despite the latter's insistence that he had.[50]

It seems, therefore, that Rabbi Yoḥanan had an unrealistic view of himself as Rabbi Elazar's principal teacher. Rabbi Yaakov bar Iddi, one assumes, knew this, but he chose to accept Rabbi Yoḥanan's view of that teacher-student relationship and to use it as the basis, albeit false, of a positive light in which to cast Rabbi Elazar's behavior. Specifically, he argues that Rabbi Elazar's lack of attribution is actually a tribute to the immeasurable debt he owes Rabbi Yoḥanan.

Rabbi Yaakov bar Iddi then revisits the issue of Rabbi Elazar's ignoring Rabbi Yoḥanan bar Nappaḥa. This time, instead of arguing that it is the Babylonian way of showing respect for one's teacher, Rabbi Yaakov bar Iddi argues that distancing oneself from a person (or, in his analogy, an idol) is a universal sign of respect. He engages with Rabbi Yoḥanan socratically,[51] allowing the great rabbi to articulate the main point himself.[52] This apparently convinces Rabbi Yoḥanan, as it leads directly to the conclusion of the story, in which Rabbi Yoḥanan praises Rabbi Yaakov bar Iddi as one who truly knows how to appease.

There are multiple ways to view Rabbi Yaakov bar Iddi's relationship to the truth in his role as a third-party peacemaker in this story. A helpful contrast can be drawn between the method he employs with Rabbi Yoḥanan and that of two other rabbis who, in the Babylonian Talmud's version of the story, had previously attempted but failed to mollify Rabbi Yoḥanan. In that version of the story, Rabbi Ami and Rabbi Assi rebuke Rabbi Yoḥanan for his anger. They compare his anger toward Rabbi Elazar b. Pedat to a fight that broke out generations earlier between two sages, which was so bitter that it became violent, involved the tearing of a Torah scroll and eventually leading to the place in which it occurred turning into a place of idolatry. They essentially tell Rabbi Yoḥanan that his anger, and any such anger, is entirely unjustified because it can only lead to destruction.

Rabbi Yoḥanan bar Nappaḥa's anger does indeed seem unjustified. For one, why did he not greet his student first? A tradition about Rabban Yoḥanan b. Zakkai, one of the earliest and most venerated sages in rabbinic literature, states that he was so quick to greet others that not even a non-Jew in the marketplace was ever fast enough to greet him first.[53] Furthermore, the Mishna states that a pious person should be "slow to anger and quick to appease."[54] This hardly describes Rabbi Yoḥanan bar Nappaḥa's behavior, and one can understand why others would want to point this out to him.

In response to Rabbi Ami and Rabbi Assi's rebuke, however, Rabbi Yoḥanan bar Nappaḥa becomes even angrier. He retorts that Rabbi Elazar is not his peer; this is not a fight between equals in social status, as was the fight between the earlier sages.[55] Rabbi Yoḥanan not only rejects the analogy, but he sees in it an expression of the same disrespect for his elevated social and rabbinic status that had upset him in the first place. Of course, based on the evidence regarding the actual relationship between Rabbi Yoḥanan and Rabbi Elazar in other places in rabbinic literature, the two were in fact much closer to each other in social status than Rabbi Yoḥanan held.

Rabbi Ami and Rabbi Assi based their argument on truth, and tried to show Rabbi Yoḥanan the reality and the danger he was heading toward in his anger. But Rabbi Yoḥanan was not prepared to accept the truth. By contrast, Rabbi Yaakov bar Iddi accepted Rabbi Yoḥanan's mistaken view and used it as the basis for a new, albeit false, perspective. The last line in the Babylonian Talmud's version of the legend, similar to the one presented in the Jerusalem Talmud, portrays Rabbi Yoḥanan saying to Rav Ami and Rav Assi, "Why do you not know to appease the way Iddi our colleague knows?"

In some ways, Rabbi Yaakov bar Iddi is similar to the paradigmatic figure of Aaron. He functions as a third-party peacemaker who voluntarily enters into a conflict in order to help mollify an offended party, and he incorporates a measure of bending the truth into his method, typical of Aaron and many traditional, non-Western peacemaking norms. But he is also different from Aaron in other important ways, both in his identity and in his methods.

First, while Rabbi Yaakov bar Iddi is a rabbi, he is of lesser status than Rabbi Yoḥanan, who leans on him as they walk. Second, unlike Aaron, Rabbi Yaakov bar Iddi does not relate to both parties in the conflict equally. He doesn't shuttle back and forth between the two sides in order to get at the root of the problem between the two or to discover the truth behind Rabbi Elazar b. Pedat's behavior. Rather, as a less respected third-party peacemaker, he focuses exclusively on the more distinguished figure and the affront he suffered to his personal honor. This is similar to many non-Western models of third-party peacemaking, which focus on restoring the status quo and preserving the honor of high-status individuals and institutions in society. While there is no evidence that Rabbi Yaakov bar Iddi is held up as a role model for third-party peacemaking in later rabbinic literature, he was praised by Rabbi Yoḥanan bar Nappaḥa himself.

Reish Lakish: Pursuing Peace through Bending the Truth
(Table 3.1, case 8)

The next legend is the first of several examples of an unsuccessful third-party peacemaker that I will analyze in this book. In this legend, the third party is even farther from being seen as a role model of success since, as we shall see, he fails to make peace between the sides. The legend, which tells of a third-party peacemaker who is less respected than one of the sides in the conflict and lies for the sake of making peace, appears in Genesis Rabba (6th cent. CE) and the Jerusalem Talmud (5th cent. CE). Rabbi Yehuda Nesiya (the grandson of the famous Rabbi Yehuda the Prince, compiler of the Mishna) is the injured party and, as in the previous story, a highly distinguished rabbi. In fact, he is not only a rabbi but the "Patriarch," or political leader and representative of the Jews to the Roman government.

Rabbi Yehuda Nesiya's honor is insulted by a scholarly man named Yosei of Maon, who appears nowhere else in rabbinic literature. Yosei of Maon takes it upon himself to expound biblical verses in a way that criticizes the Jewish political and rabbinic leadership of the day—embodied at that time by Rabbi Yehuda Nesiya—placing upon him all the responsibility for the suffering or wrongdoing of the nation as a result of corruption.[56] Reish Lakish, a well-known rabbi, attempts to mollify Rabbi Yehuda Nesiya in the same way the previous story showed Rabbi Yaakov bar Iddi mollifying Rabbi Yoḥanan: he invents an interpretation of the other party's behavior that casts it in a positive light. The following is the version of the story that appears in Genesis Rabba:

> Yosei of Maon expounded in the synagogue of Maon:[57]
> "*Hear this, priests*
> *Attend, House of Israel*
> *And give ear, royal house,*
> *For right conduct is your responsibility!*" [Hos. 5:1]

[Meaning]:

"*Hear this, priests*"—In the future the Holy One, blessed be He, will take the priests and stand them up for judgment, saying to them, "Why did you not toil in Torah? Did you not receive the benefit of the twenty-four priestly gifts [i.e., the required tithes] from My children?" And they will reply, "They did not give us anything!"

"*Attend, House of Israel*"—[God will say to the House of Israel,] "Why did you not give the priests the twenty-four gifts that I prescribed in the Torah?" And they will reply, "Because of the house of the Patriarch, who took all of them!"[58]

> *"And give ear, royal house, for right conduct is your responsibility!"*—[God will say to the house of the Patriarch], "Was it yours? 'This then shall be the priests' due' [Deut. 18:3]. Therefore, upon you shall be the measure of judgment!"

Rabbi [Yehuda Nesiya, the Patriarch][59] heard and became angry.

That evening, Reish Lakish came to greet and appease [Rabbi Yehuda Nesiya] about [Yosei of Maon]. He said to him,[60] "We should be thankful to the nations of the world, for they bring in mimes to their theaters and circuses, and make fun of [the government], so that they won't sit and discuss [actual opposition to the government] among themselves. And Yosei of Maon said one word of Torah and you became angry with him?[61]

It is worth pausing at this point in the story to explain the method of peacemaking that Reish Lakish uses here. First and foremost, one must understand the analogy. As historian Moshe Herr notes, Roman theaters famously staged pantomimes that poked fun at or satirized the government, exactly as Reish Lakish explains.[62] The comedy served as a catharsis for the people who were frustrated with the government, and its goal was to obviate the need for actual revolt. Thus, what seemed to be a critique of the government actually served to support it and suppress opposition to it.

Reish Lakish attempts to recast Yosei of Maon's sermon as the very same thing: he critiqued Rabbi Yehuda Nesiya through a sermon ("one word of Torah"—a measly sermon!), but with the deeper intention of supporting him. As we will discover in the continuation of the story, this was not the case, and in fact Reish Lakish's claim that Yosei of Maon was trying to support Rabbi Yehuda Nesiya is exposed as a falsehood. Perhaps Reish Lakish invented the claim merely to lay the groundwork for a reconciliation encounter between the two.

In the next part of the story, Rabbi Yehuda Nesiya asks Reish Lakish to organize a meeting between him and Yosei of Maon, apparently to verify Reish Lakish's interpretation:

> [Yosei of Maon] went up to [Rabbi Yehuda Nesiya].
>
> [Rabbi Yehuda Nesiya] said to him: What is the meaning of the Scriptural verse (Ezek. 16:44), "Everyone who uses proverbs shall use this proverb against you ['As the mother, so her daughter']"?

[Yosei of Maon] replied: As the house [of the Patriarch, i.e., Rabbi Yehuda Nesiya] is,[63] so is the nation; as the generation is, so is the Patriarch; as the altar is, so are the priests."

When Rabbi Yehuda Nesiya and Yosei of Maon meet, the Patriarch tests him to see if Reish Lakish's claim is correct that Yosei did not intend to actually blame the Patriarch for the corruption and the catastrophes befalling the nation. He does so by asking him to explain a verse from the book of Ezekiel that likens the inappropriate behavior of a daughter to that of her mother.

This verse was originally intended to refer to the Israelites, the "daughter," worshiping idols like their "mother," the Canaanites who lived in the land beforehand. Rabbi Yehuda Nesiya most likely chose this particular verse since he knew it could be politicized and used to criticize political leaders, such as himself—similar to how Rabbi Yosei used the verse from the book of Hoshea in his synagogue. This is exactly what Yosei of Maon had intended, as he draws the same lesson from this verse in Ezekiel as he did from the verse in Hosea: "As the house of the Patriarch is, such is the nation." There is now no room for doubt that Yosei of Maon intended to criticize Rabbi Yehuda Nesiya, and thus Reish Lakish's attempt at making peace between the two through bending the truth has failed. In response, Reish Lakish turns to Yosei of Maon and says, "You have not yet appeased him over that one [sermon], and now you're bringing another?"[64]

The story concludes with Yosei of Maon being pressed further about his exposition of this and another verse, and each time he maintains his position. It is apparent that we have here a failed attempt at third-party peacemaking by means of telling a falsehood. Whereas we saw in the previous story of Rabbi Yaakov bar Iddi that it might be possible to transform an injured party's view of the other by means of a lie, in this case, we see that the rabbis were aware of the potential pitfalls of this method.

Reish Lakish's methods as a third-party peacemaker are similar to those of Aaron, as he too bends the truth in order to bring about a face-to-face meeting between the two parties. However, unlike Aaron, Reish Lakish is not a more distinguished figure than the two sides in conflict, and is unable to balance the power discrepancy and relate to the two parties equally. He focuses only on the distinguished, injured party. He fails to appreciate the complexity of the situation: Rabbi Yehuda Nesiya is upset that he has been dishonored in public, while Yosei of Maon is disgruntled with the office of the

Patriarch. Reish Lakish does not appear to have spoken with Yosei of Maon before the latter's meeting with Rabbi Yehuda Nesiya. The meeting fails to result in reconciliation, as Rabbi Yosei of Maon has not changed his opinion of the Patriarch in any way.

Rafram: Pursuing Peace through Clarifying the Truth
(Table 3.1, case 9)

A method that is the complete opposite of the one employed in the two previous stories can be found within rabbinic literature as well. In the next two stories (cases 9 and 10), instead of speaking only to the injured party, the less respected third-party peacemaker speaks specifically to the offending party in order to find out the truth about what motivated their behavior. Both legends revolve around a particular sage who misses the Sabbath *pirka*, the public lecture of a distinguished rabbi who is considered more honorable than both the offending party and the third side.[65] Not attending such a lecture could be seen not only as a lack of respect for the guest speaker but perhaps even as a form of protest against his authority.

The third-party peacemaker is a rabbi who takes it upon himself to help the offended distinguished rabbi "put out of his mind" the sage who failed to show up at his lecture. He does so, however, not by trying to recast the absence in a positive light, as the previous two peacemakers we read about would have done, but by first asking the absent rabbi himself why he missed the lecture and only then perhaps approaching the injured party. The peacemaker attempts to show the offending rabbi that he could have acted differently and indeed attended the lecture.

In the first story, the sage Ravina fails to attend the Sabbath *pirka* of the Exilarch, the leader of the Babylonian Jewish community[66] (akin to the Patriarch in the Palestinian Jewish community), which all local rabbis were required to attend:

> The Exilarch once came to Zabzonta.[67] Rafram and the rabbis came to the *pirka*; Ravina did not come.
>
> The next day, Rafram sought to put Ravina out of the mind of the Exilarch.
>
> He said to [Ravina], "Why didn't you come to the *pirka*?"
> He said to him, "My foot hurt me."

[Rafram:] "You should have put on a shoe and come."
[Ravina:] "The heel of my foot hurt me."
"You should have put on a sandal [a looser-fitting shoe] and come."
"There was a pool of water [in the way]."
"You should have crossed it with the sandal on."
[Ravina] said to him, "Do you not hold by [the ruling that] one should not [walk through water on the Sabbath] in sandals *ab initio*?"[68]

Here, Rafram presses the offending rabbi to clarify what motivated his absence. It is unclear whether he suspects that Ravina is lying about his foot or whether he simply doesn't understand why it ultimately prevented him from attending the *pirka*. He ultimately discovers that between the combination of Ravina's foot pain, requiring a loose-fitting shoe, and a body of water between his home and the *pirka*, Ravina was trying to avoid violating the Sabbath. We are not told, however, if these excuses are indeed truthful and whether Rafram transmitted this information to the Exilarch—and if so, whether he was appeased.

Like the other third-party peacemakers in this section, Rafram's status may be somewhat more elevated than that of Ravina, the offending party. He is certainly, however, not as distinguished as the injured party, but he holds his own high social status.[69] His method of peacemaking is the polar opposite of the method used in the previous cases; instead of manipulating the truth, he attempts to clarify it and bring it to light.

Abaye: Pursuing Peace through Clarifying the Truth
(Table 3.1, case 10)

The second story is very similar in structure to the previous one. A certain sage is absent from a prominent rabbi's Sabbath *pirka*. A third rabbi of intermediate social status seeks out the absent rabbi to find out the truth of the matter. He presses him to give a good reason why he did not make every effort possible to be present at the lecture. It comes to light that the offending rabbi felt that, under the circumstances, it would have been a violation of Jewish law for him to attend:

Rav Avya did not attend the *pirka* of Rav Yosef[70] [who became angry with him].[71]

> There are some who say Rav Yosef excommunicated him; others say he [cursed him]⁷² mentioned his name.⁷³
>
> The next day, when [Rav Avya] came, Abaye sought to put [him] out of the mind of Rav Yosef. He went to [Rav Avya] privately.
>
> [Abaye] said to him, "Why did you not come to the *pirka*?"
>
> [Rav Avya] said to him, "My heart was weak."
>
> He said to him, "Why did you not eat something and then come?"
>
> He said to him, "Do you not hold by what Rav Huna said, that one is not allowed to eat anything before the *mussaf* (additional) prayers?"
>
> He said to him, "You should have prayed the *mussaf* prayers by yourself and then eaten something and then come."
>
> He said to him, "Do you not hold by what Rabbi Yohanan said, that one should not offer one's personal prayers before the community offers theirs?"
>
> He said to him, "But did they not teach regarding that ruling that it applies [only when one is offering personal prayers] in the synagogue?" (Berakhot 28b)⁷⁴

Here too, we are not told what happened if and when Abaye returned to Rav Yosef after he attempted to clarify the truth, which might have appeased Rav Yosef. Rav Avya claims that he meant no offense; he was merely ill (it is written in some of the manuscripts at the beginning of the story that Rav Avya was ill, indicating he was indeed being truthful in his conversation with Abaye),⁷⁵ and he was trying to abide by Jewish law as he saw fit under the circumstances. Moreover, the intervention of the third party, like the behavior of the third party in the previous story, contrasts sharply with the methods of third-party peacemakers who manipulate the truth and suggest creative explanations for perceived insults. Here they speak directly to the offending party and clarify the truth. In both cases, it appears that the truth would have had the power to appease the offended party.

***

These four legends offer an important window into the range of possibilities for the third-party rabbinic intermediary in classical rabbinic literature who is considered to possess a lower status than one of the sides in an asymmetric conflict. As opposed to the Aaron legends, these peacemakers do not go back and forth between the two parties, relating to each as both victims and perpetrators. Rather, similar to the majority of traditional, non-Western conflict scenarios, such as in the *sulha* model, there is a clear side that is considered the offended party as well as the more respected and powerful one, and a side that is considered both the offender and the less respected and powerful entity.

In the first two cases (Table 3.1, cases 7–8) we explored, the third side acts similarly to Aaron, attempting to appease the injured, more powerful side through white lies—with varying degrees of success. In the second two cases (Table 3.1, cases 9–10), the third side, unlike Aaron, approaches the ostensibly offending and weaker party, attempting to clarify the truth as a means of reconciling them with the more powerful side. These third-party peacemakers are indeed well-respected rabbinic figures, but since, as opposed to Aaron or Rabbi Meir, they are not of higher status than the parties in conflict, they are forced to intervene in the dispute in a different manner.

Practical Implications for Third-Party Peacemaking Today

With regard to using these legends in educational training settings, while I have not presented the legends about Rafram and Abaye (cases 9 and 10), I have employed the first two about Rabbi Yaakov bar Iddi and Reish Lakish, often focusing on the role of a third party in facilitating anger management. Generally, I present the conflict scene of the legend before the interventions of Rabbi Yaakov bar Iddi and Reish Lakish, and ask participants to reflect on how they would respond if they were in the shoes of the third party. Then we explore how these two peacemakers actually responded. Next, we discuss to what extent participants agree with the rabbis' approaches and how they themselves might have responded differently, or understood the rabbis' responses differently. For example, some have seen Rabbi Yaakov bar Iddi's responses not as lying to simply placate Rabbi Yohanan, but rather as just an initial first step in defusing his anger. They surmise that Rabbi Yohanan would not initially be open to hearing anything opposed to his interpretation of reality, although perhaps at a later stage he would be amenable to hearing a more truthful, complex explanation of Rabbi Eliezer's behavior.

In the Pardes Rodef Shalom Schools Program middle school curriculum unit Unit 2, entitled "The Strategies of the Rodef Shalom," the legend of Rabbi Yaakov bar Iddi is included—with one major modification. The text presented to students ends immediately after Rabbi Yaakov bar Iddi tells Rabbi Yohanan that Babylonians show respect by not greeting those who are greater than they. Subsequently, the interpretation of Rabbi Eliezer's behavior is presented as being the correct one, thereby directly contradicting my entire argument here that Rabbi Yaakov bar Iddi was indeed lying! This issue was debated within my educational team designing the unit: I was uncomfortable changing what I felt to be the correct interpretation of the legend, while they argued that pedagogically the alternative reading carries a much better educational message of cultural sensitivity. I was outvoted.

The lesson in this unit therefore focuses on strategies third parties can employ to assist in changing conflicting sides' perspectives, especially regarding cultural misunderstandings. For example, participants learn that in different cultures people greet one another differently, and third parties working in such multicultural settings need to be versed, like Rabbi Yaakov bar Iddi, in basic cultural sensitivities in order to help bridge these differences.

Ironically, by not wanting to bring attention to the fact that Rabbi Yaakov bar Iddi lied in order to make peace, we are in essence lying for the sake of teaching peace by not giving participants the whole story—thus staying true to the essence of the legend!

Non-Rabbinic Peacemakers

Not all legends in classical rabbinic literature feature rabbis as third-party peacemakers. There are two legends that contrast rabbis with non-rabbinic peacemakers in an attempt to establish peacemaking models that even the most learned rabbis could learn from. These non-rabbinic peacemakers, similar to Aaron and Rabbi Meir, were, to a certain extent, held up as paradigmatic role models of peacemaking in later rabbinic literature. As noted in Chapter 1, in many indigenous cultural models the third-party peacemaker is not a religious figure but rather a layperson. This is prevalent in the *sulha* model, where the *jaha* delegation is composed of well-respected lay leaders and not religious figures. In Chapter 5, I will explore numerous examples of Jewish laypeople who served as peacemakers in historical Jewish communities.

The Exceptionally Distinguished Simpleton as a Peacemaker (Table 3.2, case 11)

This legend tells of a prominent sage, Rabbi Yanai (Palestine, 3rd cent. CE), who is incredulous that there is any significant merit worthy of respect other than accomplishment in Torah study. He eventually comes to learn that third-party peacemaking is equally, if not more, meritorious:[76]

> A story about Rabbi Yanai, who was walking on the road (*derekh*). An exceptionally distinguished[77] person happened upon him.[78] [Rabbi Yanai] said to him, "Would the rabbi [i.e., you] be inclined to be a guest at my house?" [The man] said to him, "Whatever pleases you."
>
> [Rabbi Yanai] brought him into his house and tested him in Scripture, and he did not find him [learned]. He tested him in Mishna [Jewish law], and he did not find him [learned]; in *talmud* [legal argumentation], and he did not find him [learned]; in *haggada* [lore], and he did not find him [learned]. He said to him, "Recite the blessing [over the meal],"[79] and [the guest] replied, "Yanai should bless in his own home." [Rabbi Yanai] said, "Can you repeat what I say to you?" [The guest] replied, "Yes."
>
> [Rabbi Yanai] said to him [that the stranger should repeat]: "A dog has eaten the bread of Yanai!"[80]
>
> [The guest] stood up and grabbed him. He said, "What, is my inheritance with you, and yet you mock me?"
>
> (Rabbi Yanai said to him: "What [do you mean] that your inheritance is with me?")[81]
>
> [The guest] said to him [explaining], "For the children say (Deut. 33:4): 'Moses commanded us a law [i.e., the Torah], an inheritance of the congregation of'—it does not then say 'Yanai' but 'Yaakov' [i.e., the Torah is the inheritance of the community of Yaakov, meaning all of Israel. Therefore, the two men share Israel's inheritance equally and are consequently of equal status, regardless of the guest's lack of Torah scholarship]."
>
> [Once they had reconciled with each other],[82] [Rabbi Yanai] said to him, "How did you merit to eat at my table?"[83]
>
> He replied, "In all my days, I never heard a bad word and then returned it to its owner, and I never saw two people quarreling and did not make peace between them."[84]
>
> [Rabbi Yanai] said to him, "You have so much *derekh eretz* [good manners, ethical behavior], and I called you a dog?[85] (Leviticus Rabba 9:3[86])

The hero of this story, as it were, is an unnamed but "exceptionally distinguished," seemingly well-respected individual who lacks all knowledge of Jewish learning beyond that of a young child. Nevertheless, his vigilance to intervene as a peacemaker sets him apart as a person worthy of great respect. While his methods of third-party peacemaking are not mentioned in the story,[87] his personal characteristics and interpersonal disposition are elaborated on in his interaction with Rabbi Yanai, the intention of which may be to describe some characteristics and methods of peacemakers worthy of emulation.

The story opens with Rabbi Yanai making immediate judgments about another person based on appearance, and later on accomplishment in Judaic learning. He assumes this unknown, respectable-looking individual must be a rabbi, and therefore invites him to his house for a meal.[88] Once there he begins quizzing the guest in his Jewish knowledge. It is possible that such a test was for the sake of assessing a newcomer's status as a scholar, as can be found in other legends in rabbinic literature.[89] When Rabbi Yanai understands that this man whom he called "Rabbi" is actually completely uneducated, and a simpleton, he asks him whether he can repeat what he (Rabbi Yanai) tells him.

At first it would appear that Rabbi Yanai's intention is to help the man lead the blessing after meals, as is customary.[90] Instead, though, it turns out that he is trying to poke fun at him and trick him into a crude prank, that of calling himself a dog, thereby demonstrating Rabbi Yanai's superiority in Torah knowledge over the defeated guest.[91] But that guest, who indeed lacked Judaic knowledge, is found to be not only *not* ignorant but actually very wise, as he presents a clever counter-riddle instead of falling prey to Rabbi Yanai's practical joke.[92] He grabs Rabbi Yanai and claims that he has taken his inheritance from him, in a way demanding that he return it to him.[93]

The guest's words and deeds seem inscrutable; Rabbi Yanai is perplexed. The guest has to solve his own riddle for Rabbi Yanai, and the solution turns out to be a simple midrash: the Torah is the inheritance of all Israelites; it does not belong solely to members of the intellectual elite such as Rabbi Yanai.[94] It turns out, then, that the one whom Rabbi Yanai regarded as a complete ignoramus manages to stump him in a clever Judaic riddle and to teach him a lesson in Torah that even little children already know. At this point Rabbi Yanai, surprised and caught off guard, attempts to reassess his guest, asking him how he merited eating at Rabbi Yanai's table. The guest answers by stating that he had never returned a bad word "to its owner" and had never seen two people in conflict with one another and not brought about peace between them.

The guest describes his meritorious acts in a general way here, but he may at the same time be hinting at his own encounter with Rabbi Yanai, in which the rabbi spoke ill of him (calling him a dog) and he did not respond in kind.[95] It was important to him to reconcile and make peace with Rabbi Yanai rather than engage in a confrontation with him. The story concludes with Rabbi Yanai appreciating his guest and giving him respect, not because of his knowledge of classical texts, of which he was nearly devoid, but because he was so imbued with good manners and consideration for others.

Over the course of the story, Rabbi Yanai undergoes a transformation due to the words and actions of his guest. This transformation is expressed through the story's chiastic structure:

A Rabbi Yanai respects the man on the road (*derekh*) since he assumes he is a rabbi;

   B Rabbi Yanai tests the man's level of Judaic knowledge, and the latter fails;

      C Rabbi Yanai plays a crude prank on the man, concluding with the implication that a person who possess no Judaic knowledge is a "dog";

      C The man poses a rabbinic riddle, the solution to which is that the Torah belongs to all, not only to the "congregation of Yanai";

   B Rabbi Yanai asks what merit the man has, and he answers that he makes peace between people and refrains from spreading evil speech;

A Rabbi Yanai respects the man for his *derekh eretz*.

The first and last lines here (A) parallel each other but include a significant difference:

Rabbi Yanai respects the man on the *derekh* (road) since he assumes he is a rabbi
Rabbi Yanai respects the guest for his *derekh eretz* (ethical behavior)

Whereas at first Rabbi Yanai expresses a positive attitude toward the man based on his outward appearance, which he assumed signified great Judaic scholarship, at the end of the story Rabbi Yanai expresses a positive attitude toward him based on his inner qualities and actions that have nothing to do with Judaic knowledge. Furthermore, the first line is a result of an immediate, unreflective judgment, while the last line illustrates judgment based on listening and learning from his guest.

Similarly, the second and penultimate parts of the story (*B*) dovetail but also oppose each other. Both involve Rabbi Yanai questioning his guest, but whereas at first he questioned him about his knowledge, at the end he questions him regarding what type of other merit he possesses.

The center of the story (*C*) involves a parallel that yields a transformation in each character:

> Rabbi Yanai plays a crude prank on the man, concluding with the implication that a person who possess no Judaic knowledge is a "dog"
> The man poses a rabbinic riddle, the solution to which is that the Torah belongs to all, not only to the "congregation of Yanai"

As soon as Rabbi Yanai insults the guest, the latter transforms from a passive, enigmatic figure to an active participant in their relationship ("He stood up," etc.) who reveals himself and his personal background to the rabbi (and to the readers). But the transformation that the rabbi undergoes is internal, and more significant. As soon as he hears what his guest has to say, his attitude toward both the man and the nature of personal merit is transformed. Rabbi Yanai realizes that at the very moment the guest was failing the test in Jewish knowledge, he himself was failing the more significant test of *derekh eretz*, ethical behavior.

These transformations are not incidental to the story; they are a significant feature of a peacemaker's characteristics. The guest, an uneducated, distinguished-looking layperson who is vigilant about intervening when he sees a quarrel, is someone who is capable of shifting the perspective of another person, even a great sage.

This legend, while not widely cited in later rabbinic literature, does serve as a form of proof text for the following statement in the Midrash in the name of Rabbi Yishmael, son of Rabbi Naḥman, which did become widely known and cited:

> *Derekh eretz* preceded [the giving of the] Torah by twenty-six generations. This is the meaning of what is written, "To keep the way [*derekh*] to the tree of life" (Gen. 3:24). *Derekh* refers to *derekh eretz*; afterward, [the verse mentions] "the tree of life," which is Torah.[96]

The expectation of *derekh eretz* in one's behavior was already made known to Adam, while the Torah was given twenty-six generations later, at the revelation at Mount Sinai. This statement, which expresses the moral of our legend, is the basis for the relationship between ethics and Judaism and has become a fairly common Jewish expression.[97]

From the story of Rabbi Yanai and his guest, several important conclusions can be drawn regarding the identity and methods of a person who describes himself as acting as a peacemaker.[98] The guest is not an important rabbi or scholar; instead, he seems to be a distinguished yet simple person who lights up his surroundings with his many good deeds. He is on the road (*derekh*) where the interactions of all sorts of people may be found, and he busies himself with *derekh eretz*, which implies ethically proper and sensitive behavior toward others: refraining from insulting others or from gossiping (which leads to discord among people), and bringing peace between people.

As mentioned earlier, the actual methods of peacemaking employed by Rabbi Yanai's guest are unknown.[99] However, from his interaction with Rabbi Yanai in which he succeeds in achieving reconciliation with his host, we can surmise which personal strengths he possessed that contributed to his peacemaking activities. First, he does not rebuke the side with whom he engages with harsh language. In our narrative, after patiently enduring various forms of humiliation by Rabbi Yanai, he responds by using clever language (a riddle). This leads his disputant to recognize his own error and discover a new perspective, which enables him to see the person opposite him in a new and different light.

Second, he uses metaphorical language anchored in values and terms familiar to the other side, which penetrates even more deeply into the identity of his interlocutor and causes him to think differently about his own behavior. Since he is speaking to a rabbi, despite his meager knowledge of Jewish subjects he draws on the simple level of Judaic knowledge to which he has access. He uses a verse that Jewish children memorize from a young age as the basis for his own hermeneutical interpretation—a distinctly rabbinic method of communication—to assert that the Torah is the inheritance of all Jews, regardless of their level of Jewish knowledge or any other source of merit.

This practice of speaking in terms of the other side's background and language has been noted as an important part of cultural conflict transformation and referred to as the "elicitive approach." As John Paul Lederach, the first to coin this phrase, writes, "The elicitive-oriented approach is built on drawing out and using what people bring you . . . it understands language, metaphor, proverb, and story as resources, mechanisms, and approaches to conflict resolution."[100]

The Simple Jesters Who Pursued Peace through Humor
(Table 3.2, case 12)

This story, like the previous one, helps establish the particular limitations of rabbinic knowledge and the value of deeper perception, specifically for the purpose of peacemaking and showing respect to peacemakers even when they lack Judaic knowledge. However, unlike the previous legend, where the non-rabbinic peacemaker was perceived as being distinguished and likely of high social status, in this legend the peacemakers are jesters, simple people lacking any apparent status. The story begins:

> Rabbi Beroka from Hoza'a was standing in the marketplace of Bei Lapat. Elijah [the prophet][101] came and appeared to him. [Rabbi Beroka] said to him, "Is there anyone in this marketplace who will enter the World to Come?" [Elijah] said to him, "No, not even one person."

At this point in the story Elijah identifies an individual who will indeed merit a portion in the World to Come. The individual reveals to Rabbi Beroka that he is a jailor who dresses as a non-Jew and does his best to keep the female prisoners separated and protected from the male prisoners, preventing Jewish girls from being raped.[102] He also warns the rabbis when the non-Jewish authorities are plotting evil decrees against the Jewish community. In fact, he works so hard at these righteous activities that at first he doesn't even have time to stop to answer Rabbi Beroka's question, and the conversation continues only the following day.

> Meanwhile, two others[103] passed by.
> [Elijah] said to [Rabbi Beroka], "These also [will enter] the World to Come.
> He said to them, "What is your occupation?"
> They said to him, "We are jesters. When we see someone who is sad we humor him [cheer him up]. Or when we see two people who have a quarrel we exert our efforts and make peace between them." (Ta'anit 22a)[104]

This legend is framed by a rabbi's conversation with Elijah, the mythical prophet, but the heroes of the story, the jailor and the jesters, are ordinary people. In fact, this story appears in the Talmud amid other stories about ordinary people whose actions earn them more merit even than certain rabbis.[105] Similar to the Rabbi Yanai story, here too a contrast is drawn between a great rabbi and ordinary people who earn special reward. While Rabbi Beroka stands in the marketplace looking, and failing, to see righteous and worthy people—like him—the individuals spotted by Elijah as worthy of eternal reward are far from being like him. While he stands passively judging others by their appearance, they actively pursue others whom they can help. This is exemplified by the jailer, who prioritizes helping others over responding to the initial call of Rabbi Beroka. This alone emphasizes a subtle theme in this story: the value of the proactive pursuit of justice and peace.[106]

A second subtle but carefully crafted contrast is drawn between Rabbi Beroka and both the jailor and the jesters: The laypeople who earn special reward for their active aid to people in distress have a particularly keen ability to perceive others and their situations. The three-letter Aramaic root *h.z.y.*, meaning "see," appears multiple times in this tale. In the first section of the story, it says that Elijah "was seen" by or "made himself seen" to (*it'hazeh*) Rabbi Beroka in order to help him see what he was unable to see.[107] The jailer says, "I saw [*hazina*] a Jewish girl," and then describes how he came to her aid. The jesters say, "When we see [*hazinan*] someone who is sad," and in several of the text witnesses of the story (found in early printed additions and manuscripts) the verb is also repeated with regard to seeing two people who are quarreling.[108]

Rabbi Beroka's very name may involve this same root, as he is introduced as Rabbi Beroka Hoza'a. It is not uncommon in the Talmud for rabbis' and others' names to be invoked as plays on words. Thus, instead of reading his name as Rabbi Beroka from the town of Hoza'a,[109] it can be read as an Aramaic description: *beroka* is Aramaic for *strong* and *hoza'a* can mean *seer* or *visionary*,[110] yielding: "Rabbi Strong Seer."[111] The intended irony, of course, is that Rabbi Beroka is blind to the true heroes in the marketplace, as he is to the people in need of help. This is again exemplified at the conclusion to the story of the jailor, as Rabbi Beroka had no idea there had been a decree against the Jews but the jailor was already busy taking care of it. A peacemaker, as portrayed in this rabbinic text and in contrast to the rabbi in the story, must be able to perceive people in need and actively pursue them in order to offer whatever help they can.

The jesters tell Rabbi Beroka that they do two things. The first is that they make sad people happy. Rabbenu Hananel b. Hushiel (Kairouan [Tunisia], 11th cent.) explains that this means, "We have a way with words that takes away sadness."[112] The second is that they worked hard to make peace between people who are fighting. They don't state how they do it, although Rashi explains that it was done "through words of humor between them," meaning they would use humor and joyfulness to dissolve tension.[113]

Humor has been acknowledged in the field of conflict resolution as a practical method for peacemaking in indigenous cultural models of conflict resolution. For example, Bruce Bonta writes in his study of conflict resolution in peaceful societies:

> Humor is undoubtedly a useful strategy for reducing tensions and resolving conflicts in many societies. . . . When a leader in a Paiyan community becomes involved in helping to resolve a conflict, he will often use joking or soothing to defuse the situation.[114]

Humor can also play a part in contemporary conflict resolution methods. Coleman and Deutsch write about the importance of creating a "serious but playful atmosphere":

> Humor, play, and a sense of fun can all contribute to releasing tension and opening up one's view of things, ultimately leading to development of a novel point of view. . . . But humor, playfulness, and fun are tricky endeavors when working with difficult conflicts. . . . If introduced, it must be done with sensitivity and artistry. To establish a climate that allows for play.[115]

The peacemaking jesters, who could not be more different from Aaron the high priest, become in their own way a model for third-party peacemaking in later rabbinic literature. This is evident from the way several medieval rabbis refer to the legend. The first is Rashi. He draws an important connection between these jesters, who merited a portion in the World to Come, and the mishna in tractate Pe'a (1:1), which lists making peace between people as one of "[the good deeds] of which a person 'eats of their fruit' in this world, yet the principal [reward] remains for that person in the World to Come."[116] Through the proof text he cites, Rashi establishes that indeed making peace between people is sufficient for meriting a portion in the World to Come. Moreover, by connecting the story with the mishna, the jesters are elevated to the status of those who have merited a portion in the World to Come, and thus they become important role models for third-party lay peacemaking.

Another example, from later rabbinic writings, of the high regard in which the peacemaking jesters in this legend were held is found in the comments of the Maharal of Prague:

> When those two would see a sad person they would joke with him. And this is humility and alacrity, for they would disgrace themselves in such humility in front of people in order to bring about peace between them. They wouldn't say, "What do they have to do with me?" And it has already been shown that [humility] is the characteristic of Hillel . . . and he would adjure others in this characteristic as well, saying, "Be a lover of peace and pursuer of peace." This is because the humility within Hillel would lead to this characteristic. . . . Moreover, this matter also requires great alacrity, for it is called "the pursuit of peace," and pursuit requires agility. It is fitting that because of this he would merit the World to Come.[117]

The Maharal associates the character traits of the peacemaking jesters with those of Hillel (and Aaron, as seen in the beginning of Chapter 2). He sees the jesters as people who would "clown around" ridiculously in public in order to make peace between quarreling people, and thus he sees them as extraordinarily humble people.

Rabbi Meir (Table 3.1, case 6) was depicted earlier in this chapter as undergoing humiliation in his encounter with one of the quarrelling parties, which parallels the sort of humiliation the jesters exposed themselves to, albeit at their own initiative. The humility the Maharal imagines peacemaking requires is akin to the humility Aaron displayed as a high priest who would tend to the marital disputes of ordinary people. Finally, the eagerness to actively pursue conflict in order to offer help as a third-party peacemaker recalls what we already noted in Chapter 2 regarding the importance of being proactive in pursuing peace.

Rabbenu Yona Gerondi (Spain, 1200–1263), as we shall see in the beginning of Chapter 5, held up these jesters as the paradigmatic lay peacemakers by citing this legend as part of his call for lay leaders to serve as third-party peacemakers in every community.[118] Rabbi Yosef ibn Al-Nakawa (Spain, 14th cent.) goes a step further in his use of this legend, calling not only for laypeople to "be of the students of the jesters," but even for rabbis and Torah scholars to learn from them as well:

> And a [Torah scholar] should be merciful with all creatures, compassionate to the poor, a salvation to the destitute, a friend to wise people, a brother to

the righteous, a companion to the simple, a friend to the *hasidim* (holy and righteous individuals), merciful to students, a father to the orphan, a husband to the widow, a reminder to the intellectual, a teacher to the simple, a joy to the person struggling through the day. And anyone who gladdens those who are in pain and suffering, and consoles the mourners, and speaks to the hearts of the poor and the unfortunate, it is certain that he will be of the World to Come. As we have learned in [tractate] Ta'anit about Rabbi Beroka Hoza'a. . . . And any Torah scholar who is careful in any of these, and acts appropriately in all aspects of what I wrote, he is called a [true] Torah Scholar. . . . And from the merit of Torah scholars God brings peace to the world, as it is taught, "Rabbi Elazar said in the name of Rabbi Hanina, Torah scholars increase peace in the world (Berakhot 19a)."[119]

Rabbi Yosef ibn Al-Nakawa here redefines "Torah scholar" as not simply someone who possesses a lot of textual and legal knowledge but as someone who in essence emulates the jesters in bringing joy to those who are suffering. Clearly the jesters' story resonated for centuries after it was recorded, and served as a model for later rabbis and laypeople interested in peacemaking.

These two stories (cases 11 and 12) of non-rabbinic peacemakers in classical rabbinic literature exemplify how the role of a third-party peacemaker is not limited to the saint or the religious leader. It can also be taken up by the respected layperson, as is common in the *sulha* model, and even by those who seemingly have very little social status such as the jesters. Indeed, these legends come to remind the scholars studying them to not be so detached from the "road" and the marketplace, and to learn from the simple, righteous peacemakers who are out there pursuing peace. Both narratives are reminiscent of the statement of Rabbi Yosei cited in Chapter 2: "If a person sits in his house and does not go out to the marketplace, how will he make peace between people?"[120]

Taking together the methods employed by the non-rabbinic peacemakers we have seen in the previous two stories, there are obvious divergences from the methods of the traditional peacemaking figures of Aaron (case 4) and Rabbi Meir (case 5). Yet there are also some important similarities. First, the third-party peacemaker would make peace of his own volition; both Rabbi Yanai's guest and the jesters describe seeing a quarrel and choosing to enter into it, just as Aaron and Rabbi Meir would. Second, they would relate to each of the two sides symmetrically, as equals (as opposed to cases 7, 8, 9, and 10 of those we have seen so far). Third, the legends of the non-rabbinic peacemakers do not mention any attempt to "solve" the dispute through signed compromise agreements; it would appear that their primary concern is rather improving the relationship between the two sides—which leads to the transformation of the perceptions of each side in the quarrel.

Practical Implications for Third-Party Peacemaking Today

With regard to using these legends in practice, I have employed both of them frequently in training and educational programs. I have used the first legend (case 11), that of the distinguished simpleton, similarly to the legend about Rabbi Yaakov bar Iddi discussed earlier, that is, to teach how knowing another person's cultural metaphors, proverbs, and stories can help facilitate peacemaking.

The legend of the jesters (case 12) is part of the Pardes Rodef Shalom Schools Program middle school curriculum, Unit 2, "Strategies of the Rodef Shalom" where students learn and role-play how humor can help de-escalate a conflict situation and transform relationships.[121] In other settings I have used this legend as a context for discussing the role humor can play in promoting peaceful relations in the most serious of conflicts. One example is the famous moment between Israeli prime minister Golda Meir and Egyptian president Anwar Sadat, caught on television, when they laughed about him calling her "the old lady." The moment of laughing together transformed both their relationship and those watching the dynamic between them.[122] Similarly, religious peacebuilders such as Rabbi Menachem Froman, Imam Ashafa, and Canon Andrew White have all been known to use humor in breaking the ice in extreme moments of interreligious conflict to help transform the situation. Another excellent example of this is the "Israeli Palestinian Comedy" group, whose motto is "If we can laugh together, we can live together."[123] This is a living example of humor being used the way the legend imagined it: to pursue peace.

I personally recall a challenging meeting once with an Islamic Movement sheikh, in which I, together with my partners at Mosaica, were trying to persuade him to agree to meet with a senior religious Zionist rabbi. The sheikh questioned, "but he's coming from the most extreme ideology, how can I possibly meet with him?!" To which I retorted, "No, he's of the 'Southern Branch'" (referring to the more moderate branch of the Islamic Movement in Israel, and as opposed to the more extreme Northern Branch). The sheikh paused, looked at me and then burst out in laughter. Applying the nuanced distinction, he was familiar with from within the Islamic community to that of the religious Zionist community was at first incongruent and then ultimately struck accord of familiarity and curiosity which led him to agree to the subsequent meeting.

There are, of course, risks and challenges in attempting to employ humor in sensitive issues such as religious peacebuilding in the context of the Israeli-Palestinian conflict. A good example of this came up for me while working on a short, animated video explaining the meaning of the Temple Mount/Al-Aqsa Mosque to Jews and Muslims, with versions in Arabic, English, and Hebrew.[124] In addition to the video's primary purpose, which was to educate the general public, I would also use this video as part of the trainings on cultural-religious sensitivity that I and our team at Mosaica were to present to Israeli security forces who serve on the Temple Mount/Al-Aqsa Mosque. This was supposed to be a short and simple project between Mosaica and journalist–film producer Elḥanan Miller's project People of the Book, which would nicely sum up the meaning of the most contested holy site on the planet in three minutes.

Well, that's what we thought. As it turned out, though, we each needed to get the approval of our own partners. Elḥanan, on the one hand, had an agreement with his partner, the animator, that all videos they produce together should have strong elements of humor in order to reach a broad audience in a professional manner. I, on the other hand, needed to get the approval of a senior Islamic sheikh who prays regularly at Al-Aqsa about how to make an animated video featuring the prophet Muhammad and other prophets without transgressing the strict Islamic prohibition against drawing of prophets! In addition, I needed the consent of rabbis I work with, including a very close family member of mine who goes up weekly on the Temple Mount. Funnily enough, I discovered during separate meetings with the sheikh and the rabbi that the only thing with which they were in agreement was that humor was certainly not welcomed with regard to this most sacred of spaces! After intense back-and-forth negotiations between all the various sides, we came up with a compromise that all parties were able to live with, despite the significant sacrifices each made. Now, if only we could figure out how to do that with the actual Temple Mount/Al-Aqsa Mosque!

Women Pursuing Conflict Prevention and Nonviolence

Identifying women as peacemakers in rabbinic literature is a significant challenge for several reasons. First, rabbinic literature, which was written by men for men, does not feature many legends about women. Second, as shown in studies on religious and traditional models of peacemaking, women acting as third-party mediators are far less common, as they were often considered "invisible" in the public sphere.[125] For example, it is almost unheard of today for a woman to be part of a *jaha* delegation in the *sulha* process.[126] Nevertheless, the same literature shows that women in these societies still acted, and act today, as influential peacemakers, but simply in different ways from men. In this final section of the chapter, I will present two legends of female peacemakers.[127] At first glance these legends may seem out of place in a book focused on third-party peacemakers, since the women in these stories, unlike the men in the previous legends, are not serving as mediators. Yet upon further examination, they indeed constitute appropriate examples of the role women often play in traditional societies.

The *Matronit*: Roman Noblewoman
(Table 3.2, case 13)

The first example of a woman acting as a peacemaker from behind the scenes can be found in the early commentary on *Megillat Ta'anit* (scroll of fasting). This early scroll (predating all other rabbinic works) records various dates of celebration marking joyful events that took place between the pre-Maccabean period up until shortly after the destruction of the Second Temple in 70 CE. The following version of the early commentary on *Megillat Ta'anit* is found in the Babylonian Talmud (Ta'anit 18a), and it tells of one of the commemorative events that took place on the twenty-eighth day of the Hebrew month of Adar:[128]

> "On the twenty-eighth [of Adar] came glad tidings to the Jews that they should not abandon the practice of the law."[129]
>
> For the government [of Rome] had issued a decree that they should not study the Torah and that they should not circumcise their sons and that they should profane the Sabbath.[130]
>
> What did Yehuda b. Shammu'a and his colleagues do? They went and consulted a certain noblewoman (matronit) whom all the Roman notables used to visit.
>
> She said to them, "Go and demonstrate (lit., cry out) at night."[131]
>
> They went and demonstrated at night, saying,

"Alas, in Heaven's name, are we not your brothers, are we not the sons of one father [and are we not the sons of one mother?]¹³² Why are we different from every nation and tongue that you issue such decrees upon us?"

[They did not move from there until]¹³³ the decrees were thereupon annulled.

And that day was declared a feast day."

Historians disagree over when exactly the events described in this legend took place, since Rabbi Yehuda b. Shammu'a was the student of Rabbi Meir and therefore lived in the second century CE. However, historically it had been understood that the commemorations on the dates *Megillat Ta'anit* mentions had been nullified much earlier than that following the destruction of the Second Temple, thereby leading some scholars to claim that this story explaining the events of the 28th of Adar was not historical at all.¹³⁴ Putting the historical conundrum aside, the legend presents an important case study of transforming a potentially violent situation into a nonviolent one through the critical advice of a woman acting as a third party.

The legend begins with the decrees by the Roman government forbidding the study of Torah, circumcision, and keeping the Sabbath, which placed the Jewish leadership in a difficult position regarding how best to respond. Similar decrees had been issued by Antiochus IV Epiphanes in 168 BCE, but in that case the Jewish response was the armed revolt of the Maccabees, celebrated to this day during the holiday of Hanukka.¹³⁵ In this legend, Yehuda b. Shammu'a and his colleagues do not call for rebellion at all. Rather, they seek the advice of a non-Jewish, Roman noblewoman, a "*matronit*,"¹³⁶ with whom Yehuda b. Shammu'a evidently had a trusting relationship and who also had a strong relationship with and understanding of the Roman leadership that had issued the decrees.¹³⁷ Her advice was not to take up arms or to give in to the decrees, but instead to go to the Romans at night and demonstrate. Rashi, in his seminal commentary on the Talmud, elaborates further on the *matronit*'s advice, commenting on the word *demonstrate*:

Scream out in the marketplaces and in the streets in order that the [Roman] ministers should hear and have compassion upon you.¹³⁸

Indeed, this is exactly what Yehuda b. Shammu'a and his colleagues did. They went out at night and called upon the Romans to recognize their shared humanity: "Are we not your brothers, are we not the sons of one father?"

Rabbi Shmuel Eidels, known as the Maharsha, notes in his commentary on this legend that the common father they are referring to here is Isaac, the father of Jacob and Esau, since the Jews are the descendants of Jacob (also known as Israel) and Esau is considered in rabbinic legend to be the precursor of Rome; the Jews and Romans therefore have a common father.[139] It is possible that the demonstrators, by mentioning the common lineage and identity they share with the Romans and protesting being discriminated against, were appealing to the Romans' own worldview (as understood by the rabbinic author of the legend), which was that the Jews should be like all other Romans. This view was embodied by decrees forbidding unique Jewish customs. Ironically, the Jews point out that such decrees are indeed discriminatory, and if the Romans really believe in equality then the right thing to do is to allow the Jews to continue to be different.

Three important principles of conflict resolution can be identified in this story. First, it serves as an important precedent for the argument made by later rabbis for better interreligious relations between Jews and non-Jews. Rabbi Dr. Moses Rosensohn (Vilna, 19th cent.) comments, after citing this legend in the very beginning of his book, *Shalom aḥim* (brotherly peace):

> It is an obligation from the Torah and the books of the Talmud and the rabbis to love all people as brothers and friends, without distinction with regard to which nation or religion they belong to.[140]

The second principle is the use of what Gene Sharp, in his famous book *The Politics of Nonviolent Action*, defines as the category of "nonviolent protest and persuasion" as a means of changing political and social norms. The nonviolent demonstration described in this legend is successful because it transforms the heart of the Romans. It constitutes what Sharp describes as the process of "conversion," through which "the opponent has been inwardly changed so that he wants to make the changes desired by the nonviolent actionists."[141] This story, therefore, may be seen as an important legend of such nonviolent action, especially if one takes into account the possibility of the use of force in the form of another Jewish rebellion (similar to what happened with the Maccabees).

The third important lesson for conflict resolution studies that can be applied from this legend pertains to the role of the *matronit*, the Roman noblewoman. The *matronit* does not serve as a visible public mediator, shuttling back and forth between the Romans and the Jews with the goal of brokering a peace agreement. She acts as a wise and trusted advisor who works behind the scenes, recommending a way for one side to adjust the perceptions of the other side. According to some versions of the story, she not only advised the Jews to go out and demonstrate at night, but also told them exactly what to say.[142] We can conclude from this version that the *matronit* possessed a deep understanding of the needs and values of both parties and was therefore able to advise the Jews how to speak to the core values of the Romans in a way that would not only not threaten them but would actually transform them. It is possible that she actually helped create a situation in which both sides are satisfied: The Jews are grateful the decrees have been canceled, and the Romans are pleased that the Jews, by following their own way, are being true to the Roman value of national homogeneity.

The image of the *matronit* in this legend evokes certain similarities to the role elderly, distinguished women have played in traditional third-party peacemaking. For example, the respected elderly woman in traditional Central African societies played an important role as a mediator:

> The elderly woman was respected by all, and played a key role in crisis management and conflict resolution. Thus, when a conflict degenerated into armed violence, an appeal would usually be made to a third party of mature years to calm the tension and reconcile the combatants. Such an appeal for mediation was usually made to a woman who enjoyed the consideration and respect of all who knew her.[143]

If an external enemy came to attack a village and refused to lay down their arms after initial attempts to de-escalate the situation, it was the elderly women who would go out naked, crawling on their knees, and say to the combatants:

> *We are your mothers.*
> *We do not want war.*
> *We do not want bloodshed.*
> *Do not fight with your brothers.*
> *They have sent us to sue for peace.*

This description raises certain questions regarding our legend, such as: it possible that Rabbi Yehuda b. Shammu'a and his colleagues visited the *matronit* not only to ask her advice but also with the hope that she would

132 THIRD-PARTY PEACEMAKERS IN JUDAISM

play the role of the trusted, respected mediator? On some level, the *matronit* gave her own script to the rabbis and had them play her role in pleading in the streets for mercy. Also notable are the similarities between the *matronit*'s words of advice and the description of the pleading elderly women: both invoke the familial connection between the two sides in conflict.

Beruria: Rabbi Meir's Wife and Counsel
(Table 3.2, case 14)

The second legend I have identified in classical rabbinic literature regarding a woman pursuing nonviolence showcases one of the most famous women in the Talmud, Beruria, the scholarly wife of Rabbi Meir. It is only fitting to conclude this chapter with a legend that presents Rabbi Meir as one of the sides in a conflict after having opened the chapter with legends of Rabbi Meir serving as a paradigmatic third-party peacemaker:[144]

> There were certain outlaws in Rabbi Meir's neighborhood.
> [And they would trouble him very much.[145] He excommunicated them.][146]
> He prayed that they should die.
> [Beruria][147] said to him, "What do you think:
> It is written, 'Let hata'im (sins) cease' (Ps. 104:35).
> Is hotim (sinners) written? [No;] hata'im (sins) is written![148]
> Rather, pray for them that they should repent!
> And once they repent, 'the wicked will be no more' (Ps. 104:35)."
> [Rabbi Meir prayed for them and they repented.][149]

This legend says almost nothing of the nature of the relationship between Rabbi Meir and the neighborhood outlaws or bullies who, at least according to some versions, were giving him a hard time. It is a story of how he changes his approach to them, from thinking only of himself and praying for them to die; to praying for them to repent, thereby reaffirming their humanity as not just as outlaws and recognizing their potential to change.[150] The shift in his approach happens thanks to his knowledgeable wife, Beruria, who proves her point with the help of a verse from Psalms. It is she who is able to maintain an open mind to the complexity of the situation.[151]

The verse from Psalms quoted in this legend in its simplest translation and interpretation reads, "Let *sinners* cease from the earth, and let the wicked be no more." Yet Beruria reinterprets the verse based on a different vocalization of the word. Thus, the verse is not about putting an end to sinners, which would be vocalized as *ḥotim*, but rather about putting an end to *sins*, which would be vocalized as *hata'im*. The latter is indeed how it appears in Scripture, which is written without vowels (the vowels were added much later), implying that wicked people can transform and repent.

According to some versions of the story, Rabbi Meir listens to Beruria's sage interpretation of the verse and wise advice, and prays for the outlaws to repent—and indeed they do. Without his wife's advice, the famous Rabbi Meir, who knew how to preach Torah, pursue peace between others, and even teach students how to do both, was unable to apply these values and skills to his own personal conflicts.[152]

In this story, Beruria, like the *matronit* in the previous legend, is clearly not acting as a neutral, third-party mediator. She is rather a close relative of one of the sides in conflict, and she does not attempt to lead the sides to make peace with one another directly. However, she plays an important role in de-escalating her husband's violent approach (i.e., praying for them to die) with a nonviolent alternative (praying that they repent). Beruria, who in rabbinic literature was understood to be very knowledgeable of Torah, speaks to her husband from within his own textual, linguistic world of meaning, leading him to ultimately draw the right conclusion as to how to proceed—and in such a way that he does not feel attacked. By giving her husband levelheaded advice, Beruria is playing the classic role of female peacemaker in traditional, patriarchal societies.

This method of using a novel interpretation of a verse as a way of shifting the attitudes or perceptions of religious leaders is reminiscent of Lederach's elicitive approach, noted earlier with regard to the distinguished simpleton who also knew to quote a line from Scripture to shift Rabbi Yanai's perspective.[153] Likewise Ibtisam Mahameed, a well-known Muslim female peacebuilder, who persuaded the men and religious leadership of her village to allow her to run for mayor. Marc Gopin, commenting on her tactics, writes, "Notice the ingenious way in which she uses the sheikh's own words to persuade him. This is clever argumentation, but also a very effective form of nonviolent conflict resolution."[154]

Doron Pely, in his research on the role of women in the *sulha* process, notes that women do not play a visibly active role in *sulha*, but one of the members of the *jaha* whom he interviewed stated that women are often involved indirectly: "The men go home and come back to us the next day with a completely different idea or attitude, and we know that they had a discussion with their wives, and are now actually representing them in the discussion."[155] Female peacemakers in Burundi are also described as promoting peace by way of advising their husbands:

> Their role in relation to their husbands was an important one: they were to advise them and be a constructive influence on them in any decision that was to be taken. If there was a dissension in the neighborhood, or when conflict threatened to break out, a woman would act in her advisory role in order to prevent its coming to a head. She would counsel her peers, where the matter involved women, or act through her husband in a disagreement between men.[156]

These descriptions affirm Beruria's identity as a traditional female peacemaker. Like the modern examples noted earlier, she may not have mediated between the men in conflict, but she did succeed in convincing her husband, the famous Rabbi Meir with whom we begin this chapter, to transform his approach from a violent to a nonviolent one.

Practical Implications for Third-Party Peacemaking Today

With regard to practice, I have used both rabbinic legends, the one about the Roman noblewoman and the one about Beruria, in various contexts. In the United States I have used them to train social justice advocates—pursuers of justice—to be pursuers of peace, and to illustrate that there are nonviolent ways to advocate against injustice.

I have used the legend of the *matronit* recently in trainings for rabbis and college campus leaders, as many of them struggle with the current political environment in the United States. The legend serves as an important starting point for facilitating discussion around critical questions, such as: How do you respond when a harsh and discriminatory new law by your government is made against your identity group or others you identify with? Who are the trusted "third-siders" you can turn to for assistance in de-escalating the situation? When and how can nonviolent demonstrations succeed in nullifying such draconian laws? Similarly, I taught over this story about nonviolence as part of a talk I gave at an interfaith gathering on Martin Luther King Day in Jerusalem.[157]

I have also used the story of the *matronit* as part of a training I did together with Ibtisam Mahameed for Women Wage Peace, a grassroots movement including women across the political spectrum advocating for a "mutually binding non-violent accord, agreeable to both sides" of the Israeli-Palestinian conflict.[158] There we discussed the role of women specifically in advocating for peace and demonstrating nonviolently. We pointed out that the very first time the modern Hebrew word for a demonstration, *hafgana*, was used was in this story, given as the advice of the *matronit*. We then discussed the implications of this story with regard to what it means to attempt to persuade people through demonstrating nonviolently and the challenges and limitations in doing so.

These two rabbinic legends are not sufficient in capturing the role women most likely played behind the scenes in advancing nonviolent peacemaking in Jewish history and rabbinic literature; however, they are all I have found to date. As mentioned, this seems to be a direct result of the fact that in traditional societies, such as reflected in rabbinic literature over the generations, women were excluded from the peacemaking process.

I once had a Muslim Bedouin graduate student in my class who was also the principal of a school in her village. In the middle of analyzing the story of the *matronit* and the lack of inclusion of women in general in many traditional third-party peacemaking processes, she burst into tears. She shared with the class that just a few days before an elementary school student of hers had been killed as part of an ongoing conflict between two clans in her village. As the principal of the local school, she knew and felt connected to both sides, but, being a woman, she was nevertheless confined to only being in the room with the women (of the victim's family), while well-respected men served as the third-party peacemakers going back and forth between the two sides.

In the context of my work at Mosaica, I have had the honor to get to know several religious Jewish women serving as third-party peacemakers, among them, Rabbanit Hadassa Froman, wife of the late Rabbi Menachem Froman, and Rabbanit Adina Bar Shalom, daughter of one of the most famous ultra-Orthodox rabbis in Israel, the late Rabbi Ovadia Yosef. Both of these women, each in her own way, fearlessly work to make peace between Jews and Muslims, Israelis and Palestinians. Rabbanit Hadassa has continued her late husband's work and has expanded upon it by building bridges between religious Jewish settlers and Palestinians. Rabbanit Adina co-led Mosaica's women's group of senior religious and ultra-Orthodox Jewish women and senior religious Muslim women in Israel, which continued to meet and make personal connections even at times of harsh political climates.[159]

I hope this book serves as a source of inspiration for discovering more such legends and historical accounts, or at the very least as a source to inspire

136   THIRD-PARTY PEACEMAKERS IN JUDAISM

more women today to serve as third-party mediators and peacemakers, both within and between communities in conflict—thus producing new stories and historical precedents!

***

This chapter has demonstrated not only that there are third-party peacemakers within classical rabbinic literature, but that there are a significant amount of similarities between them and Aaron. For all of them, peacemaking primarily meant changing the perceptions and interpretations of the parties involved in conflict with regard to themselves and others. In other words, as opposed to "resolving" material conflicts through negotiated compromise agreements, the third-party peacemakers reconciled between the two sides. Indeed, I am unaware of any legend that tells of third-party peacemakers in this early body of rabbinic literature who bring sides to a signed agreement— which we will see extensively in the following two chapters.[160]

The differences between each of the peacemakers discussed in this chapter are their identities (i.e., rabbi or layperson) and methods of changing the perceptions of the parties in conflict. This reflects a fundamental understanding of how classic rabbinic literature interprets the very core of interpersonal conflict, which was not over scarcity of tangible material resources but over honor and relationships. With these intangibles at the heart of the conflicts, it follows that peacemaking efforts focused on restoring honor and transforming relationships through a change in perspective, as is characteristic of traditional religious peacemaking processes.

In this chapter, we explored peacemakers from the rabbinic period ranging from Rabbi Meir, the most respected religious public figure of the time, to the jesters, perhaps the least distinguished in the traditional hierarchy. What we discovered is that social or professional status was not an indicator of the degree to which these figures would later be regarded in rabbinic literature as peacemaking role models. Moreover, there was no clear correlation between their status and their described level of success—or lack thereof.

Rabbi Meir clearly succeeded in bringing peace between the two individuals fighting in their home on a Friday afternoon (case 5), but his peacemaking efforts between a married couple leave the reader with a degree of skepticism, especially since it is unclear whether or not the couple actually reconciled in the end (case 6).

With regard to the less respected rabbinic peacemakers, while Rabbi Yaakov bar Iddi succeeded in appeasing the offended Rabbi Yoḥanan bar

Nappaḥa (case 7), we do not know how that actually impacted his relationship with Rabbi Elazar b. Pedat. As we saw in the legend of Reish Lakish appeasing Rabbi Yehuda Nesiya (case 8), he too succeeds in pacifying him initially, but when there is an actual face-to-face encounter between Rabbi Yehuda and Rabbi Yosei of Maon, the offending rabbi, Reish Lakish's efforts are proven to be futile.

Both legends that tell of non-rabbinic peacemakers (cases 11 and 12) describe more their character and methods but not as much a particular case of third-party peacemaking that can be assessed as successful or not. In both cases of female peacemakers (cases 13 and 14), the end result was a successful de-escalation of the situation.

Finally, through training and educational programs, these legends can play an important role today in encouraging people to engage in peacemaking—but with one caveat: facilitators must constantly be mindful of the significant gaps that might exist between the cultural settings of these ancient legends and the cultural assumptions and sensitivities of contemporary participants (as in the case of Rabbi Meir pursuing peace between the husband and wife) or of the facilitators themselves (as is the case in our reworking of the legend of Rabbi Yaakov bar Iddi for our school educational programs).

Table 3.1 Legends of Third-Party Peacemakers in Classic Rabbinic Literature

Parameters for Comparison	Highly Respected Rabbinic Peacemakers			Less Respected Rabbinic Peacemakers			
Case Number	5. R. Meir	6. R. Meir	7. R. Yaakov bar Iddi	8. Reish Lakish	9. Rafram	10. Abaye	
The Conflict							
1. The case	Satan is exacerbating conflict between two equal individuals	• Husband suspects wife does not respect him. • Power inequality	• R. Yehuda suspects R. Eliezer does not respect him • Power inequality	• R. Yehuda Nesiya suspects R. Yosei of Maon does not respect him • Power inequality	• Exilarch suspects Ravina does not respect him • Power inequality	• R. Yosef suspects R. Avya does not respect him • Power inequality	
The Third-Party Peacemaker							
2. Number	1	1	1	1	1	1	

Continued

Table 3.1 *Continued*

Parameters for Comparison	Highly Respected Rabbinic Peacemakers		Less Respected Rabbinic Peacemakers			
Case Number	5. R. Meir	6. R. Meir	7. R. Yaakov bar Iddi	8. Reish Lakish	9. Rafram	10. Abaye
3. Social status	High	High	medium (<side in conflict)	medium (<side in conflict)	medium (<side in conflict)	medium (<side in conflict)
4. Connection to sides in conflict	Strong	Strong (the peacemaker in this conflict contributed to the initial conflict).	Strong	Strong	Strong	Strong
5. Initiative to intervene taken by	Third party	Third party	Third party	Third party	Third party	Third party
6. Meeting with sides in conflict	———	Separately	Separately	Separately	Separately	Separately
7. Bringing sides to a compromise agreement	———	———	———	———	———	———
8. Transforming perspectives, reconciling the relationship	• Calming presence • stays with sides for 3 Fridays	Bends the truth in order to allow wife to spit in his eye to placate husband	Tells lie that other side really respects him	Tells lie that other side really respects him	Clarifies intentions of offending side	Clarifies intentions of offending side
9. Personal self-sacrifice	• travels • invests time	offers to be humiliated	———	———	———	———
Result of Third-Party Intervention						
10. Success/failure of intervention	Success: Satan leaves the house	———	Success: R. Yohanan no longer suspects R. Eliezer	Failure: R. Yehuda Nesiya continues to suspect R. Yosei	———	———

FROM RABBI MEIR TO BERURIA 139

Table 3.2 Legends of Third-Party Peacemakers in Classic Rabbinic Literature

Parameters for Comparison	Non-Rabbinic Peacemakers		Female Peacemakers	
Case Number	11. Distinguished simpleton	12. Jesters	13. Roman noblewoman	14. Beruria
The Conflict				
1. The case	R. Yanai mocks distinguished simpleton (the peacemaker is one of the sides of the conflict)	Two people fighting	• Roman decrees against Jews • Power inequality	R. Meir bothered by local thugs
The Third-Party Peacemaker				
2. Number	1	2	1	1
3. Social status	Medium	Low	High	————
4. Connection to sides in conflict	————	————	Strong	Strong (wife)
5. Initiative to intervene taken by	Third party	Third party	Disputant	Third party
6. Meeting with each side in conflict	————	————	Separately	Separately
7. Bringing sides to a compromise agreement	————	————	————	————
8. Transforming perspectives, reconciling the relationship	Quotes biblical verse	Humor	• Advises nonviolent demonstration • Speaks within Roman value system	Advises to pray for opponent through quoting biblical verse
9. Personal self-sacrifice	————	Maharal: "Disgraced themselves"	————	————
Result of Third-Party Intervention				
10. Success/failure of intervention	————	————	Success: decrees canceled	Success: R. Meir prays and they repent

4
From Rabbi Yosef Syracusty to Rabbi Nissi al-Nahrawani

Historical Accounts and Stories of Third-Party Rabbinic Peacemakers in Medieval and Early-Modern Rabbinic Literature

The previous two chapters explored the identity and methods of third-party peacemakers in classical rabbinic literature, including the figure of Aaron as the ideal peacemaker within rabbinic literature as well as numerous other peacemakers beyond Aaron. Over the following two chapters I will focus on third-party peacemakers in later rabbinic literature, namely, medieval and early-modern (10th–19th cent.). In this chapter I will examine rabbinic peacemakers and their methods, and in the following chapter lay peacemakers operating in historical Jewish communities. The division between the clergy and the laity reflects the distinction between these two camps within traditional models of third-party peacemakers, as noted in Chapter 1 and in particular in the Arab-Islamic context. There, the imam or sheikh is the model of a religious leader serving as a third-party peacemaker, and well-respected laypeople participate in the *jaha* as part of the *sulha* process.[1]

The sources for this chapter and the next include responsa literature, travel diaries, historical chronicles, and other hagiographic rabbinic books describing the glorious actions of rabbis and lay leaders from previous generations, thus creating a form of late legend literature that can serve as sources of inspiration for future peacemakers.

Throughout Jewish history, local communal leaders and rabbis would send legal queries to the well-known sages of their generation asking for rulings. These inquiries and the rabbinic responses to them together form the genre known as "responsa literature." In addition to the importance of this body of work for its record of rabbinic rulings on legal issues, it also offers an important window into Jewish communal life, as the authors of the letters would describe the circumstances of their queries to the rabbi.[2] Individuals are often described anonymously or with pseudonyms in such letters, but for the most part these are not theoretical conflicts or questions; they describe real-life quandaries that require practical responses from a trusted authority.

It is in the responsa literature where we find the vast majority of our evidence regarding medieval and early-modern Jewish peacemakers, both rabbis and, even more so, lay leaders. Ironically, for the most part we find direct evidence only of failed peacemaking attempts, since people would write letters to rabbis recounting a peacemaking process only if it did not work—they needed further advice in order to resolve the conflict or question. Still, these queries and their responses are a window into the people, institutions, and methods that were trusted and employed throughout the Jewish world to serve as peacemakers.

Several other literary sources provide valuable evidence of medieval and early-modern Jewish peacemakers, though they are not necessarily collected and organized the way the responsa literature is, and they are certainly not as voluminous. The first is historical chronologies where authors retell events they witnessed directly or that were handed down to them from a previous generation. These may not always be considered accurate historical accounts, but they do serve as a source of inspiration for readers. The second are letters (*iggrot*), which sometimes survive in collections but are often preserved only individually in manuscript form. These may be correspondence between individuals or between communities and individuals. Third, rabbis occasionally composed travel logs or diaries, and later in this chapter we will make extensive use of one such eighteenth-century rabbinic travel log. Fourth, eulogies of prominent rabbis or communal figures offer valuable windows into their work and, with greater historical accuracy, into their reputation in the community. A peacemaker's influence and success depend at least in part on such reputations, so while a eulogy is not a particularly reliable source for stories of the deceased's peacemaking efforts, it does help us understand what a particular rabbi's reputation was and how it might have served him as a third party in conflicts. Finally, other types of sources are available occasionally such as historical accounts or communal records.

As we explore these individuals, we will see resonances of Aaron as well as departures from him, just as we saw in the rabbinic sources in Chapter 3. The following chapters concretize and flesh out the range of individuals and methods that make up the rich and, until now, little-known tradition of Jewish third-party peacemaking. As discussed in Chapter 1, religious peacemakers—Jewish, Muslim, Hindu, and Christian—rely heavily on role models, sacred texts, and traditions from the past. Uncovering the treasure trove of examples that the following two chapters contain, therefore, is significant historically and theoretically, but it is also practically significant for those with vested interest in reviving and developing an indigenous Jewish culture of peacemaking and mediation today.

This chapter will examine eight examples of rabbis, or a group of rabbis, serving as third-party peacemakers, and will be split into three subsections based on the identity and status of the third party—similar to how the previous chapter was divided. The first section will focus on successful third-party rabbinic peacemakers with high social status and the second on unsuccessful rabbinic peacemakers who possessed less social status. The assumption is that there is a direct correlation between the social status of the rabbinic peacemaker and the success of his peacemaking, as we have seen in both Chapter 1 and Chapter 3. The third section of this chapter will explore two exceptions to this assertion, one in which a rabbinic peacemaker of high social status is nevertheless unsuccessful and one that describes a third party of lower social status who succeeds in his peacemaking efforts.[3]

Each of the examples of third-party rabbinic peacemakers discussed in this chapter will require a certain degree of textual decoding, historical context, and theoretical analysis of the identity and methods of the third party. If relevant, I will then reflect on practical implications of the case for the field of conflict resolution today.

Before we begin to examine these examples, it is worthwhile to present the rabbinic sources that discuss the special imperative for rabbis to engage in third-party peacemaking.

The Jewish Imperative for Rabbis to Be Third-Party Peacemakers

Moses Maimonides, the renowned Jewish philosopher, legal scholar, and physician, wrote in his legal code, *Mishneh Torah*, that a Torah scholar must behave as "a lover of peace and a pursuer of peace,"[4] referring of course to the mishna (Avot 1:12) about Aaron that we examined in Chapter 2. In another context in *Mishneh Torah*, Maimonides writes that only a "seasoned scholar" (*talmid vatik*) is permitted to alter the truth somewhat for the sake of peacemaking: "If he brought peace between a person and his fellow, and he added to or attenuated [the truth] in order to bring about affection between them, then it is permitted."[5] The assumption behind this ruling is that one of the occupations of a "seasoned scholar" is to make peace between two individuals. Maimonides' ideal Jew is a Torah scholar (*talmid ḥakham*), so his descriptions of proper behavior are generally presented as instructions for such a person. It is therefore sometimes unclear if he is singling out a certain behavior as required specifically of a Torah scholar or required of any Jew.[6] Other sources in medieval rabbinic responsa literature do, however, specify that the practice of peacemaking should be undertaken by communal rabbis.

Rabbi Levi ibn Ḥaviv (Spain, Palestine; 16th cent.) alludes more strongly than Maimonides did, though not explicitly, to a special commandment incumbent on Torah scholars to work as third-party peacemakers. The context is a responsum he sent to two Torah scholars who were in conflict. After a fairly lengthy legal opinion, ibn Ḥaviv concludes (emphasis mine):

> And since the obligation of the commandment to bring peace is greater than all other commandments. . . . Before I conclude my words, I request from the parties in conflict, the aforementioned *scholars*, that each one should attempt to seek peace. . . . And since *they are commanded to pursue peacemaking between others*, all the more so [are they obligated to do so] in their own conflicts![7]

Ibn Ḥaviv's language recalls *Avot d'Rabbi Natan*, which we saw in Chapter 2, that peacemaking is equal to all other commandments, and he refers (where an ellipsis appears in the above quotation) to numerous sources that we will discuss in Chapter 5 for the Jewish imperative of laypeople to make peace. But in mentioning explicitly that the people he is addressing here are scholars, he is calling attention to their special responsibility toward peacemaking. He then explicitly states that "they" are commanded to make peace between others. The word choice is important and seems to assume that the reader shares his assumption. Ibn Ḥaviv does not state that the commandment itself—which he spent several sentences prior to our excerpt describing—obligates all Jews to make peace between others, or that "we are" or "one is" commanded to do so. He uses the third person plural to describe these Torah scholars specifically; *they* are commanded to intervene in other people's conflicts, so they had better seek peace with regard to their own conflicts.

We arrive at an explicit statement regarding a rabbi's obligation to serve as peacemaker in a responsum of Rabbi Ḥayim Shabtai (Thessaloniki,

16th–17th cent.). There he describes the role of a communal rabbi (called a *hakham* here) specifically as "to mediate peace" (*letavekh hashalom*). The case before him was from a community that had sworn an oath not to appoint a communal rabbi for fear that it would lead to too many disagreements in the community. But when they saw that without a rabbi the community was plagued with even more disagreements and infighting, they wished to nullify their oath in order to hire a communal rabbi who would "mediate peace among them: love and brotherhood, peace and friendship." The community wrote to Rabbi Shabtai to inquire as to whether this was sufficient legal grounds to nullify the communal oath. In his reply he nullifies the oath and provides numerous rationales. Among them is the following:

> Any oath that is dependent on a certain situation is nullified once that situation no longer exists. Since their oath not to take on a rabbi was in order [to avoid] divisiveness, and now that this is moot [since the absence of a rabbi has led to constant quarreling], we can plainly see that, on the contrary, the taking on of a communal rabbi is for the purpose of having one heart and one mind for everyone, to mediate peace between them, and love and brotherhood. So perforce the oath is nullified.[8]

Rather than occupy himself solely with the laws of oaths and vows, Rabbi Shabtai includes a striking statement about the role of a communal rabbi, echoing the language that the authors of the inquiry themselves used. He affirms that a communal rabbi's role is indeed to unite people generally, but more specifically to "mediate peace"—just as they themselves wrote. The fact that this is a reference specifically to resolving interpersonal conflicts as a third-party peacemaker is evident by the use of the term "mediate peace" and by the specific problem the community sought help in solving: "fights and hatred."

The most straightforward statement about the special relationship that Torah scholars have with the pursuit of peace can be found in the words of a renowned sixteenth-century rabbi, kabbalist, and poet, Rabbi Elazar b. Moshe Azikri (Safed, 1553–1600), who writes:

> All people of Israel should tremble in fear not to damage the unity of the Most High by means of the sin of baseless hatred or slander or argument. . . . One should have great love and peace and friendship with all Israel, and should also try to make peace in the world. And Torah scholars,

since they know this secret, are greatly cautioned about this, as the Sages said: "Torah scholars increase peace in the world" (Berakhot 19a).[9]

To specify that a group of people, in this case Torah scholars, is "greatly cautioned" (*nizharim*) about a certain precept is rabbinic parlance for that group having a special, additional obligation to uphold that precept. Rabbi Azikri believes that since Torah scholars possess a unique understanding of how important peace is and how problematic argument and baseless hatred are from a theological perspective, they therefore have a special obligation to serve as peacemakers. We will see that numerous rabbis indeed saw this as their role, whether motivated by mystical conceptions of the divine and of peace, or for other reasons. Rabbi Azikri goes on to cite his own personal rabbinic peacemaking role model, Rabbi Yosef Syracusty, who will be the first rabbinic peacemaker examined in this chapter.

Practical Implications for Third-Party Peacemaking Today

In practice, these texts—especially the responsum of Rabbi Hayim Shabtai—have played an important role in encouraging and training rabbis to see themselves as peacemakers and mediators.[10] In trainings exclusively for rabbis I often open with a text study of Rabbi Shabtai's responsum and then ask them to discuss the following in small groups: "If you were to write a response to this question, which character traits or abilities would you suggest the community look for in choosing a rabbi who can truly 'broker the peace' and be a *rodef shalom*?" This reflective exercise offers rabbis the opportunity to imagine what their own ideal yet realistic image of a communal rabbi as a peacemaker truly is, and who they would strive to be.

The Successful Third-Party Rabbinic Peacemaker of High Social Status

Rabbi Yosef Syracusty (Safed, 16th cent.): Pursuing Peace among the Poor and Non-Jews (Table 4.1, case 15)

Among the various rabbis I have found in later rabbinic literature who served as third-party peacemakers, Rabbi Yosef b. Avraham El-Syracusty (also known as Yosef Saragossi)[11] can be identified as the most similar to Aaron, Judaism's ideal third-party peacemaker. A talmudist and kabbalist, Rabbi Syracusty was born in 1460, most likely in Spain. He appears to have been expelled with the Jewish community of Sicily (Syracuse) in 1494 and lived temporarily in Sidon in Lebanon. Here he was offered a nice sum of money by the Jewish community and the local Muslim Mameluke ruler to stay and serve as the local rabbi. However, in 1495, Rabbi Syracusty chose instead to move to the city of Safed in the Galilee; he lived there until his passing in 1507. He was one of the first rabbis to arrive in Safed, which at the time of his arrival was a mixed community of primarily Muslims and Jews.

The only surviving text that can be partially accredited to Rabbi Syracusty himself is a letter sent from the rabbis of Safed to the rabbis of Jerusalem, who were engaged in a major dispute over which year should be decreed as the Sabbatical year.[12] The stated purpose of the letter was to attempt to make peace among the rabbis of Jerusalem, and Rabbi Syracusty, the eldest of the Safed rabbis, signed his name last at the bottom of the letter.[13] However, two posthumous texts attest to Rabbi Syracusty more directly as a peacemaker.

The first is from Rabbi Yosef Garson, who delivered a powerful eulogy for Rabbi Syracusty (referring to him as Rabbi Syracusy) in Damascus, where Rabbi Garson served as rabbi. He states:

> The *hasid* (holy and righteous person) who passed away, according to what we have heard about him, would labor in two types of peace. The first was making peace between people and between husband and wife. The second was placing peace between God and the poor. . . . For whoever supports the poor makes peace between God and the poor person, for then the poor person will not say accusatory words against God. . . . It is appropriate to refer to him as a disciple of Aaron, for he loved peace, for even if others would fight with him he always was of the insulted and not among the insulting.[14] . . . This *hasid* . . . has created a great void in the Land of Israel, as there won't be anyone who can make peace . . . and for us as well, as he was one of the pillars of the world and he sustained the whole world through his peace; now this pillar will be missing from the world. Therefore, it is worthy for us to mourn tremendously for the void he has left us.[15]

Rabbi Garson's eulogy compares Rabbi Syracusty to Aaron the high priest, who, as we have seen, was the rabbinic ideal of a pursuer of peace. He also notes (not included in our excerpt) that as opposed to Moses, when

Aaron passed away everyone mourned for him because they felt his absence keenly; there was no longer anyone to step in and make peace between people. Rabbi Garson's understanding of Mishna Avot 1:12 is in line with the opinion of Rabbi Shmuel de Uçeda of Safed, which we saw in the beginning of Chapter 2; he also understood "lover of peace" as living in peace with others and "pursuer of peace" as serving as the third side in other people's conflicts.[16] Moreover, Rabbi Garson mentions that Rabbi Syracusty would also seek peace between God and the poor, thereby expanding the scope of peacemaking to include attention to basic communal needs and social justice. This concept is based on the rabbinic notion that when the poor are not looked after they become angry and in conflict with God,[17] and may serve as an important precedent for including social justice work as part of the call to pursue peace.

The second testament to Rabbi Yosef Syracusty's pursuit of peace is found in Rabbi Elazar Azikri's *Sefer ḥaredim*. After his charge to be a pursuer of peace, which we read in the previous section, he cites Mishna Avot 1:12 that one should be a disciple of Aaron, a lover of peace and a pursuer of peace:

> Learn from Aaron, since [pursuing peace] was his craft; taking time away from his studies, going to place peace (*lasim shalom*) in his place and pursuing peace in other places when he would hear of a conflict. And so it was here in Safed, that Rabbi Yosef Saragossi (i.e., Rabbi Syracusty), the rabbi of Rabbi David b. Zimra, would always place peace (*masim shalom*) between people, between husband and wife, and even between the non-Jews, and he merited to see Elijah the prophet.[18]

Rabbi Azikri introduces a very important biographical fact about Rabbi Syracusty, who is almost entirely unknown to subsequent generations: Rabbi David b. Zimra (known as the Ridbaz; 1479–1573), who would later become the most significant rabbinic figure of Egyptian Jewry at the time and whom we shall meet later in this chapter, studied under Rabbi Syracusty during his time in Safed.[19] This establishes Rabbi Syracusty's credibility as a significant rabbi despite his near anonymity, allowing Rabbi Azikri to portray both him and Aaron as Torah scholars engaged in learning. Invoking Aaron's and the distinguished Rabbi Syracusty's legacies as peacemakers, Rabbi Azikri encourages people to not hesitate to proactively go out of their way to make peace rather than waiting passively for conflicts to come to them. It is also significant that Rabbi Azikri tells of Rabbi Syracusty's meriting to see Elijah the prophet, as Elijah is known in rabbinic literature to be the ultimate peacemaker in the future.[20]

Rabbi Syracusty's peacemaking efforts between non-Jews is not expanded upon here. Indeed, what is written in *Sefer haredim* can be read as an overstatement intended to emphasize the lengths to which he would go in order to pursue peace. Nevertheless, we can deduce from this brief historical anecdote that Rabbi Syracusty felt it was within his responsibility to make peace even among non-Jews, and that the non-Jewish community of Safed at the end of the sixteenth century respected him enough that they would accept him as a peacemaker for their conflicts.

Rabbi Azikri's description of Rabbi Syracusty's peacemaking methods was cited by later rabbis, albeit in varying ways. Rabbi Hayim Yosef David Halevi Azulai (known as the Hida; Hebron, 1724–1806), who was himself very engaged in intracommunal Jewish peacemaking through his many travels around the Jewish world (as we will see later in this chapter), cites Rabbi Azikri's words about Rabbi Syracusty in his encyclopedia of rabbis, *Shem hagedolim*, albeit in paraphrase. He says Rabbi Syracusty "made peace and merited to see Elijah the prophet," omitting the scope of his peacemaking.[21]

Other rabbis emphasized the scope of Rabbi Syracusty's activities, viewing it as an important precedent for extending the parameters of peacemaking to include non-Jews. Rabbi Pinhas Eliyahu Horowitz (Vilna, 1765–1821) cites Rabbi Azikri's description of Rabbi Syracusty in his book, *Sefer haBrit*, first published in 1797. Like Rabbi Azulai, he too quotes Rabbi Azikri a little differently, stating that "[Rabbi Syracusty] would always make peace between husband and wife, between people, among Israel, and also among *the nations*, and he merited to see Elijah the prophet."

For Rabbi Horowitz, it seems that the primary innovation of Rabbi Azikri's description of Rabbi Syracusty was that he would make peace not only within the Jewish community but also between non-Jews, which Rabbi Horowitz refers to as "among the nations." The context in which he quotes Rabbi Azikri is part of his attempt to prove that "there is no distinction . . . between Jews and non-Jews" regarding loving one's neighbor as oneself; to his mind, non-Jews are also considered "neighbors" and must therefore be treated completely equal in all interpersonal matters, including peacemaking.[22] Rabbi Syracusty therefore represents a significant example of a rabbinic peacemaking role model, with regard to his efforts both to pursue peace and to expand the scope of Jewish peacemaking to include non-Jews.

Practical Implications for Third-Party Peacemaking Today

Although the historical anecdotes that attest to Rabbi Syracusty as a peacemaker do not mention his actual methods, this vignette of him in *Sefer haredim* has become a staple component of all training and educational programs I have facilitated for Jews (as well as for non-Jews), as it is an important precedent for including non-Jews within the scope of Jewish peacemaking. I shall return to discuss this critical point in the Conclusion.

The Hasidic Peacemaker: Rabbi Dovid of Lelov (Ukraine, 19th cent.) —The Power of Shared Prayer
(Table 4.1, case 16)

In the mid-eighteenth century, a pietistic spiritual movement arose in Eastern Europe known as Hasidism. The movement was founded by Yisrael Ba'al Shem Tov, and legends soon abounded about both the Ba'al Shem, as he was called, and other hasidic masters and spiritual leaders. The movement placed a high emphasis on inner spirituality, and thus several hasidic masters taught that one must first attain inner peace before pursuing peace among others, and that the real cause of conflict and war in the world was people's lack of inner peace.[23] However, alongside this understanding of inner peace, there are also legends of Hassidic masters serving as third-party peacemakers between conflicting sides.

The first to connect hasidic legend literature with third-party peacemaking was Virgil Peterson, who in 1993 wrote a short article on a legend of a hasidic master's peacemaking methods, entitled "The Rabbi's Resolution and the Power of Stories."[24] In the article, Peterson cites a hasidic tale of two neighbors who had a monetary dispute with each other that snowballed into an all-out, hateful conflict between their two families. The two sides decide to take their case to the local hasidic master, presumably to adjudicate between them.

The wise rabbi listens intently to the two sides, allowing each party to tell their version of the story for as long as they want, and each side listens to the other's claim. The rabbi then proceeds to tell them that their stories remind him of the Israelites' exodus from Egypt and later journeys through the desert. He goes into a lengthy discourse about how there must have been many fights and conflicts during that time as well. Upon the rabbi's conclusion of his story, the two sides thank him profusely, embrace one another, and leave as renewed friends.

Peterson cites the tale to make the point that contemporary conflict resolution often places too much of an emphasis on rational, analytical problem-solving, what he refers to as "left-brain" methods, and not enough on "right-brain" methods such as storytelling, which can shift people's perceptions of the conflict and of their opponent. Peterson explains that the hasidic master in this story does not address the actual conflict at hand. Rather, he places it in a much larger context, one of ancient shared narrative, of greater challenges in a common identity of peoplehood. The tale emphasizes the transformation of the relationship between the two sides over "solving" the actual monetary dispute.

Peterson did not refer to the primary source within hasidic literature that he drew inspiration from, so the legend cannot be verified as authentic.[25] Nevertheless, the basic premise made about hasidic legends regarding third-party peacemaking does seem to be quite accurate.

The following hasidic legend, which is an authentic hasidic tale, indeed demonstrates Peterson's basic premise. The legend is preserved in the hasidic work *Derekh tzaddikim*, published in 1912 by Rabbi Avraham Yellin in Lvov (Lviv or Lemberg; in present-day Ukraine), and involves early nineteenth-century hasidic rabbis in Poland:

> I heard that the holy master Dovid of Lelov, of blessed memory, traveled with his student, Rabbi Yitzḥak of Vurka, to a certain place in order to make peace (*la'asot shalom*) there. He prayed there. And after the prayer he ordered his wagon to be made ready to travel. The holy student, Rabbi Yitzḥak of Vurka, asked him, "Rabbi, did you not come in order to make peace (*asot shalom*)? So why leave right now?" And he answered him, "I have already made peace in my prayers when I said, 'The One who makes peace (*oseh shalom*) in heaven shall make peace upon us and upon all of Israel.'"[26]

This tale of Rabbi Dovid of Lelov (1746–1814) and his student Rabbi Yitzḥak of Vurka (1799–1848) is reminiscent of several other stories explored so far in this book, as it begins with a highly respected third party intervening on their own volition in a conflict between two sides to whom they are presumably well connected, in order to make peace (*la'asot shalom*) between them. The hasidic master claims that his recitation of the well-known daily prayer about God making peace (*oseh shalom*) in heaven and on earth has succeeded in making peace between the two parties in conflict. He had apparently not engaged in any obvious problem-solving discussions involving the parties themselves, leading his student to be baffled as to why they would be leaving town before they made peace. The story, therefore, according to its author, is about the supernatural power of prayer.[27]

Martin Buber, the great twentieth-century philosopher who had a particular affinity toward hasidic tales, retells this legend in a manner that takes it out of the realm of supernatural miracle and into that of social-psychological peacemaking.[28] In Buber's interpretation or reworking of the tale, the rabbi and his student stay in the community for the Sabbath and the rabbi leads the prayers, *with* the parties in conflict praying together in the synagogue. Buber's version of the student's question, asked after the Sabbath is over, is, "Were we not sent here to broker a compromise between the two sides in conflict?"

The student assumes that peacemaking must include arriving at a specific, detailed-oriented compromise (*peshara*) agreement, such as those we shall see throughout the following chapter and the Conclusion. The rabbi's response is that both parties' praying together about making peace, at the same time and in the same place, and being led by their mutually beloved rabbi, connected the two sides in such a way that peace was made. Like the legend cited by Peterson, peace, *shalom*, is about healing relationships and transforming perceptions, creating common identity—not about merely signing peace agreements. The assumption inherent in these stories is that if the relationship has been healed and the parties reconciled, the material aspects of the conflict are easily solvable.

Practical Implications for Third-Party Peacemaking Today

Shared prayer between parties in conflict is a well-known method used often by religious and traditional third-party peacemakers such as those among the Navajo and Oromo peoples.[29] It is also commonly employed by interreligious peacebuilders, sometimes as a way of building connectedness before a formal peace agreement is reached and sometimes as a means of strengthening relationships after the signing of a formal agreement.[30] For an example within a Jewish context, the contemporary peacemaker who makes the most use of this method is Eliyahu McLean, who was actually ordained as a *rodef shalom* (pursuer of peace). For the past two decades, McLean, a devout Jew highly influenced by hasidic teachings, has organized numerous interfaith activities that bring together Jews, Muslims, and Christians in the Holy Land, often engaging them in religious peacebuilding rituals and prayers (some of which I have had the privilege to take part in).

McLean tells a story of how he and his late partner, Sheik Abdul Aziz Bukhari, once participated in a large conference of Jews and Muslims in Spain at a time when tensions were high in the Middle East. Noticing that the two groups were not interacting and the conference was beginning to fail, they decided to intervene and engage the two sides in spontaneous prayer and song. He describes how very cautiously one religious leader after another joined together in a shared circle of prayer and song until all members were sitting together:

> What unfolded for the next four hours was a chanting from the mystical and spiritual traditions of both communities and a connection from the heart. And this sharing of spirituality, of prayer, transformed the heart connection so that the next day they could then speak about all the other issues, and work on the more difficult political and humanitarian issues that were coming between the people there.[31]

Similar to Buber's interpretation of the hasidic legend of Rabbi Dovid of Lelov, here too, joint prayer can be of great assistance in establishing a peace whose goal is to transform perceptions and relationships prior to more substantive conversations regarding the detailed areas of dispute.

Today McLean is one of the leaders of a multiorganizational interfaith initiative taking place monthly in Jerusalem called "Praying Together in Jerusalem." The program features Jews, Muslims, and Christians each praying their own particular prayers side by side in the same common space, then concluding in a joint circle.[32] It is a very creative attempt at balancing the need for both particular and shared religious identities through engagement in prayer.

It should be noted, though, that joint prayer, or even prayer at the same time may not work with more conservative religious groups. For example, while planning the Iftar of Mediation event, which I discussed in Chapter 2, I raised the possibility that the Muslims and Jews conduct their evening prayers at the same time in different parts of the hall. The rabbis and sheikhs, who were not coming from a liberal religious orientation, both rejected the idea as being inappropriate. Yet when such parallel prayer does occur spontaneously, it can be a very powerful moment.[33] At the beginning of a meeting between rabbis and sheikhs I was facilitating, one of the rabbis shared how once in an airport he accidently mistook a Muslim standing in praying as a Jew and decided to pray next to him, only to soon realize that he was indeed a Muslim, yet the two continued in their prayers and waved goodbye to one another at the end. The moment stuck with the rabbi as a profound positive experience, even though it was out of a mistaken premise. In response, one of the sheikhs in the meeting shared how he actually was once mistaken as a Jew and included as the tenth man in a *minyan* (quorum of ten men needed for Jewish prayer)!

The hasidic legend of Rabbi Dovid of Lelov presents the notion of using prayer to heal relationships and transform perceptions in place of drawing up a detailed peace agreement. In this respect, the legend is very similar to many of those seen in the previous chapter as well as in the Aaron legends, which almost entirely ignore any discussion of compromise agreements. The following story describes almost the opposite process. It is primarily about how third-party rabbinic peacemakers make peace between the parties in conflict through a very detailed compromise agreement. Tellingly, it is found in the literature of the *misnaged* movement, which strongly opposed Hasidism.

The *Misnaged* Peacemakers of Nineteenth-Century Volozhin: Rabbi Shlomo Zalman Ze'ev Wolf, Rabbi Dovid Tevele, Rabbi Yosef Friemer, and Rabbi Yitzḥak Elḥanan Spector— Peacemaking through Detailed Compromise Agreements (Table 4.1, case 17)

Volozhin, Lithuania, was the center of traditional *misnaged* (opponents of Hasidism) Eastern European talmudic studies in the nineteenth century. The yeshiva, or rabbinic academy, in Volozhin was established at the beginning of the century by Rabbi Ḥayim of Volozhin. One of its significant innovations was that it was not dependent on the financial support of a local community, as were other academies and rabbinical study halls in Eastern Europe.[34] Volozhin's institutional structure depended on a more elaborate administrative staff than most *yeshivot*. Specifically, in addition to a single rabbi serving as head of the yeshiva, a deputy or assistant head of the yeshiva was appointed to run the academic side of the yeshiva when its head rabbi was away fundraising or was consumed with managing the institution.

For the first decades of the yeshiva, Rabbi Ḥayim and then his son Rabbi Yitzḥak led the institution, after which both the head of the yeshiva and his deputy were direct relatives of Rabbi Hayim. But in the 1840s, when Rabbi Yitzhak's nephew, Rabbi Eliezer Yitzhak Fried, became ill while serving as deputy head of the yeshiva, Rabbi Yitzhak appointed Rabbi Naftali Tzvi Yehuda Berlin (known as the Netziv) as an additional deputy. Rabbi Berlin was Rabbi Yitzhak's son-in-law, but he was not a blood relative of Rabbi Hayim as the other deputies had been. When Rabbi Yitzhak died in 1849, Rabbi Eliezer Yitzhak Fried took over as head of the yeshiva, but he died only four years later. At that point Rabbi Berlin became head of the yeshiva, and no deputy served under him.

Rabbi Berlin's appointment as head of the yeshiva was contested by, among others, Rabbi Yehoshua Heschel Levin, who was married to a great-granddaughter of Rabbi Hayim's. Rabbi Levin and Rabbi Berlin had different visions for the yeshiva: Rabbi Levin wanted it to become a rabbinical school for the training of professional rabbis, while Rabbi Berlin sought to maintain it as a study house strictly for "study for its own sake."

Within several months of Rabbi Berlin's appointment, the yeshiva was divided into two camps, Rabbi Levin's and Rabbi Berlin's. What distinguished this rift from those of this sort that might occur in other *yeshivot* was the absence of a communal body whose members, as the financial sponsors of the yeshiva, could serve as a third party in the dispute. As mentioned earlier, Rabbi Hayim had established this yeshiva as a uniquely independent Jewish institution, so the local community had no particular sway or power to settle this conflict.

Third-party peacemaking efforts eventually came from two prominent rabbis, Rabbi Shlomo Zalman Ze'ev Wolf, known as the Maggid (preacher) of Vilna, and Rabbi Dovid Tevele b. Moshe, the rabbi of Minsk. Rabbi Wolf was known as an outstanding preacher, a respected Torah scholar, and a modest and friendly person. Rabbi Dovid Tevele, a generation older than Rabbis Levin and Berlin, had served in the past as one of the administrators of the yeshiva and had been a student of Rabbi Hayim.

According to the 1900 account of Hillel Noah Steinschneider, Rabbis Wolf and Dovid Tevele were chosen by an unknown body from Volozhin that was split over the controversy. It is not clear why specifically these rabbis were chosen to settle the controversy, but they were definitely well-respected elder rabbis of that generation and both of them had a personal connection to the yeshiva. Their mandate was to "quiet the fight" and "mediate,"[35] not to rule as a rabbinic court (*beit din*) or even as traditional arbitrators (*borerim*). The fact that only two rabbis were chosen to mediate the dispute, as opposed to the traditional odd number of three or five rabbis required to rule on or arbitrate a legal dispute, is evidence of the extralegal intention of their role.[36]

Rabbis Dovid Tevele and Wolf led the two sides of the conflict to an agreement, which was then sent in writing to other great rabbis of the generation for their support and official signatures. While Steinschneider describes the agreement as a "ruling," he also notes that it was intended to be "pleasing to both sides." In other words, these rabbis served as third-party peacemakers working to achieve a compromise agreement that would settle the dispute between the two camps in an amicable way.

The compromise agreement included three primary points. First, Rabbi Berlin would remain head of the yeshiva. Second, Rabbi Levin would not be appointed to any formal position in the yeshiva but would nevertheless continue to receive payment from the yeshiva as part of the administration for a certain period of time. Third, Rabbi Yosef Dov Soloveitchik, a great-grandson of Rabbi Hayim of Volozhin, would be appointed deputy head of the yeshiva under Rabbi Berlin.[37]

The agreement was accepted, but it created another problem: there was now tension between Rabbi Berlin and Rabbi Soloveitchik. Numerous issues underlay this tension. To begin with, this was the first time that the deputy head of the yeshiva was not appointed by the head of the yeshiva. Furthermore, the deputy head had a more direct genealogical connection to the founder of the yeshiva, Rabbi Hayim of Volozhin, whose family Rabbi Berlin had only married into. Furthermore, Rabbi Berlin and Rabbi Soloveitchik had markedly different methods of study. Rabbi Berlin focused on the contextual, straightforward meaning of classical texts, while Rabbi Soloveitchik employed intense analytical methods to these same texts, often yielding conclusions that differed from those of Rabbi Berlin. The two rabbis also differed in their approaches to the management of the yeshiva.

These points of tension may have been intensified by the fact that there was no formal title for the deputy head of the yeshiva to distinguish him from his superior; they were both known as the *rosh yeshiva* (head of the yeshiva) despite their technically separate statuses.[38] Once again, the rift led to a division among the students, and two camps emerged.

This time, two additional rabbis joined Rabbis Dovid Tevele and Wolf to mediate the conflict: Rabbi Yosef Friemer of Slutzk and Rabbi Yitzhak Elhanan Spector of Novardhok. Rabbi Friemer, like Rabbi Dovid Tevele, had previously been involved in the administration of the yeshiva, as he had been a student of Rabbi Hayim of Volozhin, and was a generation older than both

Rabbi Berlin and Rabbi Soloveitchik. Rabbi Spector, on the other hand, was a contemporary of the two men. According to the account of Rabbi Spector's personal secretary Rabbi Yaakov Lifschitz, in his book *Zikhron Yaakov*, Rabbi Berlin traveled to Novardhok to personally request that Rabbi Spector join the delegation to Volozhin.

Lifschitz describes the rabbinic delegation of peacemakers and their mission:

> They were the greatest scholars of their generation who were called upon to increase peace between Torah scholars, who increase peace in the world,[39] using the wisdom of peace and truth which they employed out of their love of truth and peace. And they set the minds of the entire community to rest.[40]

Rabbi Berlin's trip to Novardhok notwithstanding, it is again unclear exactly who appointed these rabbis to intervene. Lifschitz describes the excitement among the entire student body, across the conflicting camps, upon the arrival of the greatest rabbis of the generation. As we have seen numerous times, the high regard in which the peacemaker is held is often a key element of his or her success.

The mediators labored over the compromise agreement in a room near the yeshiva for several days. According to the memoir of Rabbi Baruch Epstein, Rabbi Berlin's nephew, the agreement opens by stating: "The following has been agreed upon by both the parties. First and foremost, peace shall reign between the rabbis."[41] The agreement then establishes protocols in the management of the yeshiva regarding the punishment of disrespectful students, the acceptance of new students, the locations and sizes of the classes, and the management of the yeshiva's finances.

The details of the compromise minimized or eliminated some of the discrepancies between the two rabbis' roles and authority, while still preserving Rabbi Berlin's higher position of authority. For example, the first clause of the agreement stated that it was forbidden to disgrace either of the heads of the yeshiva, and Rabbi Berlin and Rabbi Soloveitchik were equally required to punish any student who did so. The third clause included a prohibition incumbent upon both rabbis against setting up classes or prayers outside the yeshiva. The fourth clause stipulated that all contributions to the yeshiva had to be reviewed by both rabbis and mutually recorded, and the seventh clause stipulated that no fundraising emissaries of the yeshiva could be fired without the consent of the two. These stipulations clearly established symmetry between Rabbi Berlin and Rabbi Soloveitchik.

The second clause of the agreement gave expression to Rabbi Berlin's superior status, as it granted him authority over the process of accepting new students—as he had had before. Still, it also stated that Rabbi Soloveitchik was allowed to accept students on his own if their application included a letter directed personally to him. The fifth clause stipulated that "money shall be kept locked up in a box in the home of [Rabbi Berlin]," and that "all expenditures on food, lighting, and so on shall be made by [Rabbi Berlin]."[42] This was explained as an effort "to avoid the need of constantly troubling [Rabbi Soloveitchik]."[43] The ninth clause set Rabbi Berlin's salary at 13 rubles per week, while Rabbi Soloveitchik would earn 8 rubles per week, but this was a relatively narrower wage gap percentage-wise than they previously had (10 for Rabbi Berlin, 5 for Rabbi Soloveitchik).

The statuses of the two rabbis were thus not equal, and while there appears to be some attempt to equalize their roles and authority, the symmetry was not to be absolute. The strategy of the peacemakers was to establish a new status quo in the yeshiva. Rather than having an authoritative head of the yeshiva with a deputy beneath him, there would be two almost equal heads of the yeshiva who would complement one another, and differences between them would be minimized.[44]

The third-party rabbinic peacemakers in Volozhin were careful to avoid appearing as though they were coming to rule for one side over and against the other. Rather, they facilitated a collaborative and consensual process involving a team of mediators as well as the actual parties in conflict. They physically came to the place of the dispute, which showed respect for the two sides, and, due to the peacemakers' own status, generated excitement and awe among the students, as well as positive feelings. They dealt with almost every aspect of the conflict in detail, and included concrete solutions in the written compromise.

Rabbis Epstein and Lifschitz both add additional components to their shared description of the third-party peacemaking that took place in Volozhin, which sheds additional light on the identity and methods of these peacemakers. Moreover, their personal understanding of how they perceived their own task and their relationship with the parties in conflict is noteworthy. In Rabbi Epstein's memoir, he quotes Rabbi Wolf, the Maggid of Vilna, who was one of the third-party peacemakers in both conflicts, shortly before his departure to Volozhin:

> This invitation reminds me of a recurring problem I encounter at the same time every year ... my problem is this. You know, as the official Maggid of Vilna, one of my functions is to sermonize every Sabbath on the Torah portion of the week. One of the secrets to being a preacher is to highlight the conflicting sides in every story. First I find the "good side," and in an eloquent way I show how good, kind, and righteous that side is. Then I take the "bad side," and I show how terrible and evil it is. Every possible good is emphasized about the hero of the weak and every possible evil attributed to the villain.

Rabbi Wolf goes on to explain that he would apply this method to biblical conflicts, such as those between Adam and the serpent in the Garden of Eden, Noah and the generation of the Flood, Abraham and the people of Sodom, and Jacob and Esau. But when he arrives at the story of Joseph and his brothers, he explains that both sides "are holy, both [sides are] righteous," making this method difficult to apply. He continues:

> I feel exactly the same way about the mission that lies before me. . . . I have been called to mediate between two holy people—between holy and holy—between Rav Naftali Tzvi [Berlin] and Rav Yosef Ber [Soloveitchik], between a gracious spirit and a precious soul. I feel lost. I can't use my normal method, because I love them both and hold them both in equal esteem. The Jewish people desperately need both of them and the different talents and approaches with which God has blessed them. . . . But, still, there was no way I could refuse an invitation to a meeting of such crucial importance to the Torah's honor and for peace among the students who carry its banner. My heart is lifted to heaven that God should show me the proper path to mediate between these two giants, for their benefit and for the good of all Jews, to enhance the glory of the Torah![45]

Rabbi Wolf's analogy to biblical conflict narratives is instructive. Textual paradigms can shape a textual community's understanding of the nature of conflict as well as conflict resolution. The very practice of approaching a conflict as though it were a textual narrative in need of exegesis can shape the approach of the peacemaker as well as the parties in conflict.

Lifschitz's account includes an additional story about these rabbinic peacemakers that, while seemingly tangential, may have played an important role in their success. Lifschitz notes the long-standing tradition in Volozhin to offer a well-respected visiting rabbi the opportunity to deliver the weekly, school-wide Talmud lecture, and in this case Rabbi Yitzhak Elhanan Spector, one of the four peacemakers, was invited to do so. According to Lifschitz, the entire student body prepared for days in advance, hoping to stump Rabbi Spector with their sharp questions. Not only did they fail to do so, they found themselves awed by his knowledge and talmudic acumen, as well as with the behavior and comportment he modeled for them:

> Of all the greatness [he demonstrated], he amazed them by far the most with his patience in the face of the sharp students. They competed to stump him and interrupt him with their objections to the analytical structure he was building, but he did not become emotional at all, and he did not become angry. He responded gently and pleasantly to every questioner and objector, until he completely satisfied the questioner.[46]

In the common lecture hall of the yeshiva, the students actively engaged with an esteemed scholar who, they knew, came for the purpose of making peace. His manner with them not only affected their studies, it impressed upon them the importance of being peaceful and patient with those who challenge you. This was a student body in the midst of a significant rift. He modeled patience, listening to the other side, and proper, respectful conduct in a dispute—behaviors that at that time the yeshiva was clearly lacking.

This image of all sides studying Talmud together in a shared space and from a respected instructor, who traveled a long way to make peace, has an interesting parallel with the previous hasidic legend, where the rabbinic peacemaker, Rabbi Dovid of Lelov, traveled to pray with the two sides in a shared space. These activities reconnect the sides of the conflict based on their common values and shared love and respect for the peacemaker, the difference being that within the hasidic context prayer plays the core role of promoting shared identity and communal gathering, while in the *misnaged* world analytical Talmud study plays that role.

Practical Implications for Third-Party Peacemaking Today

The words of Rabbi Wolf, the Maggid of Vilna, connecting the way he interpreted biblical conflicts as either holy and profane or holy and holy, as well as the way he interpreted the conflict he was called upon to mediate, have played a central role in my work. In Israel, I quoted these words as part of my address to several hundred people at an event held in 2019 at the home of Israel's president, Reuven Rivlin. The participants included the directors of the forty mediation and dialogue centers throughout Israel, as well as Esther Hayut, president of the Israeli Supreme Court. The talk was part of the launch of a program I helped initiate, in my role as the director of Mosaica's Religious Peace Initiative, which was in conjunction with Project 929.[47] The goal of the program was to engage people in studying biblical conflict stories through the eyes of a mediator, with the aim of understanding the conflicting sides in text and in life today as "holy/holy."[48]

In the United States and Europe, through the Pardes Center for Judaism and Conflict Resolution, which I directed, Rabbi Wolf's words were used to ground a project called Mahloket Matters: How to Disagree More Constructively, the Beit Midrash Way.[49] In this five-part educational workshop series, participants are challenged to read contradictory interpretations of five biblical conflict stories through the lens of "holy and holy." The goal here is to gain a deep understanding of the conflicting narratives as a means of strengthening their ability to engage more constructively in political disputes in their community and country today.

In addition to these educational projects, I personally used Rabbi Wolf's words (and Rabbi Spector's method of shared text study) once as part of a mediation I was asked to facilitate between two rabbis in a conflict that included both financial and personal elements. I opened the mediation with all three of us studying and discussing Rabbi Wolf's words about "holy and holy." Part of the implied message was that even the most distinguished rabbis of the nineteenth century, whom I knew these rabbis held in very high regard, were receptive to third-party mediation. In addition, the words served as an important framework for the rabbis to begin to once again see the other as also *kadosh* (holy), and not to perceive the conflict as a binary of one side being holy and the other profane.

Once, during a discussion of the role of the third-party peacemakers in Volozhin, an ultra-Orthodox student of mine pointed out a somewhat similar contemporary controversy. Two heads of a well-known ultra-Orthodox *yeshiva* were entangled in a deep conflict resulting in a split and tremendous animosity among the students. However, in that case, instead of third-party rabbinic peacemakers successfully stepping in to mediate the peace, the police were breaking up physical brawls among the students and lawyers were representing each side in court, in an ongoing lawsuit. It is critical that the role of the rabbinic peacemakers in Volozhin, which is not well-known enough, serve as an important inspiration today for highly respected rabbis to proactively go and serve as third-party peacemakers in such conflicts.

While the hasidic legend of Rabbi Dovid of Lelov related to peacemaking as transforming relationships and perceptions, and the third-party *misnaged* peacemakers in Volozhin primarily emphasized bringing the sides to a detailed compromise agreement, the following rabbinic peacemaker is a strong example of combining the two.

Rabbi Hayim Yosef David Azulai (the Hida): Italy, France; Eighteenth Century (Table 4.2, cases 18–23)

Rabbi Hayim Yosef David Azulai (Jerusalem, 1724–Livorno, 1806), known as the Hida, was among the greatest Torah scholars of his generation.[50] In addition to being a great Jewish legal scholar, a mystic, and a philosopher, he also traveled widely to raise money for the Jewish community of Hebron in the late eighteenth century, which was considered a very distinguished role for a rabbi to fill in those days.[51] He believed that infighting and baseless hatred among Jews, traditionally the cause of the destruction of the Second Temple, was also delaying the redemption of the Jewish people and the world. It was therefore of highest priority to constantly pursue peace: between communities, different factions within a community, families, and spouses.[52]

Rabbi Azulai was a prolific writer, producing well over one hundred books—many of which are still in manuscript form. But the source that sheds the most light on his peacemaking efforts is his personal travel diary, *Ma'agal Tov*.[53] In it he recounts his visits to Egypt, Tunisia, Italy, France, Germany, Holland, and England.[54] He does not merely keep an account of his various fundraising efforts, he also describes his thoughts about the places he visited and the experiences he had there. He shares numerous stories of the interactions he had with Jewish communal leaders, as well as the many positive interactions he had with Christian scholars and noblemen.[55] This section will outline Rabbi Azulai's peacemaking methods by exploring some of the key events he wrote about in his diary. These include four examples of intracommunal conflicts (cases 18–21) and two marital conflicts (cases 22–23).[56]

Rabbi Azulai was especially proud of his communal peacemaking success in northern Italy, particularly in three cities: Ferrara, Lugo, and Ancona. In fact, he saw such significance in his activities in those cities that he associated his success with the verse in Isaiah 25:1: "Lord, You are my God. I will exalt You, I will give thanks to Your name, for You have done wonders, [i.e.,] counsels from afar, steadfast and sure."[57] Rabbi Azulai noted that the three letters of the Hebrew word *peleh*, "wonder"—*peh, lamed, aleph* (פלא)—are the first letters of each of those three cities: Ferrara (פ),[58] Lugo (ל), and Ancona (א). On July 3, 1776, he wrote:

> "For You have wrought a *peleh*":[59]—Ferrara, Lugo, Ancona—for the Holy One, blessed be He, in His mercy, helped me establish peace among them.[60]

I will therefore explore the conflicts pertaining to these cities first (cases 18, 19 and 20), in chronological order, and what Rabbi Azulai did to broker peace within them. I will then discuss the two other examples of his peacemaking efforts.

Ancona (case 18)

Rabbi Azulai's peacemaking efforts in Ancona began before he arrived there. He was still in Pesaro on August 17, 1775, when he received a letter from the local rabbi of Ancona, Rabbi Ḥayim Avraham Israel of Rhodes, who had served as the rabbi of Ancona since 1774.[61] Rabbi Ḥayim Avraham Yisrael informed Rabbi Azulai that when the latter arrived in Ancona he would be residing at the estate of the wealthy Signore Pinḥas Cohen.[62] S. Pinḥas was the uncle of the man who had been his host in Pesaro at that time, Avraham Halevi. The letter also stated that S. Pinḥas happened to be in Pesaro.

Rabbi Azulai is then introduced by the deliverers of the letter to an enormous dispute plaguing that family. S. Pinḥas was in conflict with his sister Giudecca (Judith), Avraham's mother, who lived in Pesaro. Rabbi Azulai immediately went to meet S. Pinḥas for the first time, pleading with him to make peace with his sister, but Cohen at first refused. However, he quickly relented and went to his sister's home, saying he had come out of respect for the rabbi.

The conflict was broader than merely between S. Pinḥas and his sister Giudecca. Giudecca insisted that if her brother was ready to make peace, and if he truly respected her, he would go and make peace with her daughter-in-law. This daughter-in-law, from the prominent Morpurgo family, was of course the wife of the Rabbi Azulai's host Abraham. S. Pinḥas made peace, and his sister kissed his hand.[63] Little did S. Pinḥas know at the time that this was only the beginning of Rabbi Azulai's peacemaking efforts, as Cohen was in a much more complicated conflict with his other sister, as well as with two brothers-in-law, in Ancona.

On August 18, 1775, Rabbi Azulai arrived in Ancona to stay at the home of Pinḥas Cohen.[64] During his first weeks in Ancona he was raising money for the community of Hebron, which was, after all, his primary mission. At the time of his arrival, there was a great amount of apprehension and financial uncertainty within the Jewish community of the city, which was one of the Papal States, in anticipation of what the newly elected Pope Pius VI's policies toward the Jews would be.[65] Only on September 13, after receiving a long-awaited, positive response from the pope, did the communal leaders gather together to discuss the sum of money to be granted to Rabbi Azulai. Rabbi Azulai notes that he miraculously succeeded in negotiating them up to 500 Italian *scudi* (silver coins).[66] After receiving this official communal gift, Rabbi Azulai turned to soliciting particular wealthy individuals within the community.

On September 17, Rabbi Azulai visited the home of David and Isaac, whose last name was also Cohen, and who were the brothers of Pinḥas's wife—apparently to solicit them.[67] Upon the rabbi's arrival he discovered that David and Isaac, as well as David's wife, Reina, who was Pinḥas's sister, had been in a major conflict with Pinḥas; his wife, Giudecca (Judith; not to be confused with Pinḥas's sister Giudecca/Judith from Pesaro); Pinḥas's other sister, Sapira; and her husband, Samuel Cagli, for some twelve years.[68]

> I went to the noblemen, David and Isaac Cohen. . . . And for twelve years they had been in a tremendous *makhloket* (conflict) with S. Pinḥas and his wife, their sister. . . . And they had a lawsuit for almost 30,000 Italian *scudi*. And Cardinals, Bishops, and other senior Christian clergy, as well as rabbis, all tried over time to make peace between them but to no avail, as the hatred between them was too great.

The conflict included a lawsuit entailing some 30,000 Italian *scudi* (as well as multiple land disputes and damages, as will be discussed). Due to the family's social and economic status, rabbis and even senior Christian clergy had all tried to make peace between them but, as Rabbi Azulai notes in his diary, "to no avail, as the hatred between them was too great."

This did not deter Rabbi Azulai. On the contrary, he writes, "And a spirit came over my young self [to make peace]."[69] He immediately understood that the conflict was not only financial but also, or perhaps primarily, about the hatred between the sides and a breakdown in the relationship. His understanding of the two aspects of the conflict led him to advance two parallel tracks of peacemaking, as we will see: one of conflict resolution to bring the parties to a financial settlement and the other of reconciliation to heal the broken relationships of this deeply splintered family.

Upon hearing the details of the conflict, Rabbi Azulai immediately admonished David Cohen to make peace (*shalom*) with everyone. He even persuaded him to cancel an upcoming trip to Venice he had already scheduled. He noted in his diary that David's brother Isaac, who was with them during this initial visit, assisted him in persuading David that they should make peace with the other side. However, both brothers insisted on two conditions: that the financial part of the conflict be decided upon by Rabbi Azulai and the local rabbi, Rabbi Ḥayim Avraham Israel of Rhodes; and that the decision of the rabbis be in accordance with the strict letter of Jewish law (*din*) and not through compromise agreement (*peshara*).[70]

Rabbi Azulai then went to the home of Rabbi Israel, who rejoiced upon hearing the news, and together they approached each side separately, making them swear to be committed to both the process and the ultimate ruling of the two rabbis. Rabbi Azulai describes the moment as a "great and awesome wonder." His decision to work closely with Rabbi Israel as his peacemaking partner in this process will prove to be critical, as he understood that it is imperative to have local third side who knows the personalities of the players in the dispute and the background of the conflict, and who will continue to accompany the sides after the peace process is completed.

A few days later, on September 22, Rabbi Azulai began the reconciliation process of healing the relationships, which he refers to simply as *shalom* (peace). Rabbi Azulai gathered together all the family members involved in the dispute, both the men and the women, at the local yeshiva (which also served as the synagogue), which apparently was jointly funded by their families and was located close to their homes inside Ancona's Jewish ghetto. There, Rabbi Azulai writes, "*Shalom* was made."[71] The family members would no longer be officially estranged from one another and normal relations would be renewed between the two sides—even though the financial dispute was still far from being resolved at this point. Rabbi Azulai's decision to gather the disputants together at this neutral, shared, and holy ritual space was essential to his reestablishing their sense of common identity and familial relationship, similar to the *jirga* process mentioned in Chapter 1.[72] As Lisa Schirch writes, "Creating a ritual space may help people feel more comfortable and open in a peacebuilding process. Peacebuilding planners should design physical and temporal spaces for peacebuilding that are liminal, safe spaces that symbolically support the desired transformation of perceptions and relationships."[73]

The following day, September 23, which was the Sabbath, Rabbi Azulai walked with Pinhas to the synagogue, and after services walked with him to greet the other disputants, including David and Isaac. Then they all went together to visit Samuel and Sapira Cagli's home, and from there they went to the home of Pinhas and his wife, Giudecca—David and Isaac's sister.[74] Rabbi Azulai was thus continuing the process of reestablishing normal relations between the parties by having them greet one another in the shared sacred space, after which they would walk together around the community visiting each other's homes—all the while being escorted by the highly respected rabbi on the holy Sabbath. This was another step in the long journey of reconciling the relationship, and another example of Rabbi Azulai's understanding of the importance of ritual in creating peace.[75]

The next day, Sunday, September 24, was the eve of Rosh Hashana, the Jewish New Year. Rabbi Israel was eager to continue communal peacemaking efforts, this time between two other respected members of the community seemingly not connected to the Cohen dispute. He suggested that Rabbi Azulai accompany him, but the latter turned down his offer, choosing instead to meditate in solitude at his temporary residence as part of his spiritual preparation for the holiday. Rabbi Israel's peacemaking efforts were not successful that day; those involved felt it was because Rabbi Azulai was not present.[76] This is a powerful example of the peacemaker drawing boundaries around his own well-being and spiritual needs, choosing to focus on his inner peace even when it came at the expense of the peacemaking process.[77]

Over the following months of October and November 1775, Rabbis Azulai and Israel examined together close to seventy different legal claims between the sides, which ranged from property damage to inheritance, and which were in addition to the financial dispute of the 30,000 *scudi*. Rabbi Azulai tells how he carefully balanced the amount of time he spent working with Rabbi Israel on the case with the amount of time he invested in writing his own book. He also describes the dynamics between the partners, writing, "and we had many arguments between us, but it was all with respect and great love."[78]

During this time of examining the legal aspects of the dispute, Rabbi Azulai recalls that sometime toward the end of the year, a particular event occurred that was a testimony to the success of his peacemaking efforts. The niece of Pinḥas, his sister Giudecca's daughter Sarah, and her husband came from Pesaro to Ancona for a visit. The extended Cohen family, all of whom apparently felt very close to her, decided to use this as an opportunity to throw a massive, lavish banquet full of liquor, singing, and general merriment. Over the course of the evening, several members of the family stood up and spoke, including Sapira, Pinḥas, and David, each one adding something great (presumably about the previous speaker)—and doing so while apparently slightly intoxicated. Rabbi Azulai describes this particular event as "causing *shalom* to further increase," as he understood that the sides were becoming closer and closer to each other without his prodding.

It is worth mentioning that while Rabbi Azulai was very happy to see the warming of relations between the family members, he personally felt deeply awkward and out of place at such a lavish event, remarking that he stayed close to Rabbi Israel the whole evening, speaking only words of Torah and eating almost nothing.[79] This too adds to Rabbi Azulai's heroism as a pursuer of peace, as despite his own discomfort with attending such an affair, he saw his presence as an important phase in his peacemaking efforts and a critical part of the evening's success.[80]

Sometime between December 1775 and January 1776, Rabbis Azulai and Israel concluded their legal investigation into the dispute and came up with their ruling in accordance with their understanding of the strict letter of the law (*din*), which the brothers David and Isaac Cohen had insisted upon. But they felt that sharing their verdict with the parties in dispute would lead only to the dismantling of still-tenuous relations between family members and greater animosity. They therefore decided to change course and make a valiant effort to persuade the parties to come to a compromise agreement (*peshara*) in all aspects of the dispute, except for the issue of the 30,000 *scudi*—with regard to which the ruling would stay as already adjudicated according to the strict letter of the law.[81]

Rabbi Azulai writes that no words can describe how incredibly difficult this effort was, and it was only with God's help that they had the wisdom, patience, and creativity to succeed in convincing the sides to engage in a process of compromise as opposed to strict law. This process of bringing the sides to a compromise agreement would take Rabbi Azulai an additional several months of work.[82] His success likely had to do with the high regard in which both sides held him. For example, on March 5, 1776, during the holiday of Purim, he writes that both sides gave him very generous gifts, as part of the holiday tradition. He interpreted this as a show of continued respect and trust.[83]

On March 21, Rabbis Azulai and Israel delivered their ruling with regard to both the monetary dispute over the 30,000 *scudi*, which was in accordance with the strict letter of the law, and the compromise agreement covering the rest of the disputed property, which had been reached according to the will and opinions of the disputants.[84] However, two days later, Rabbi Azulai learned that Isaac, and even more so David, were "exceedingly sullen and annoyed, 'out of [David's] mouth go burning torches' (Job 41:11)"—apparently over the amount of money the rabbis ruled the two brothers were obligated to pay.[85] On March 29, Rabbi Azulai went to David's home. He describes in his diary how he "spoke at length 'to his heart.'" Isaac Cohen then came to the house and assisted in calming down his brother further until he accepted the ruling.[86]

This left only the final stage in the process of resolving this complex and long conflict, namely, the ceremonial taking of the oath by the two parties indicating that they accept the final ruling and compromise agreement.[87] This too was a major challenge, as the exact order, language, and timing of the oath had to be just right and agreed upon by each party. Finally, on April 2, David and Isaac Cohen and Pinḥas Cohen, after listening to the court scribe read off the oath, simultaneously swore to uphold it. Rabbi Azulai describes the moment as nothing short of a miracle.[88]

On April 18, 1776, after the holiday of Passover, Rabbi Azulai writes that the agreement was brought before the official papal court scribe, who recorded the agreement in Italian and added a note of his own on the document out of amazement:

> The quarrel among the *g'virim* [distinguished members of the community] had been going on for years and the Pope, the Cardinal, and [other] nobles had all tried without success until along came one from Jerusalem.[89]

Rabbi Azulai describes this moment as the ultimate *kiddush Hashem*, the sanctification of God's name, by means of casting the Jews, and therefore God, in a positive light in public by making peace.[90]

On April 21, 1776, eight months after his arrival in Ancona, Rabbi Azulai finally left the city, with hundreds of residents bidding him farewell and with Pinḥas, Isaac, and David escorting him together some eleven miles until he arrived at the next town.[91] On May 23, 1776, after traveling to several smaller

Jewish communities and making peace there as well, Rabbi Azulai returned to Pesaro together with Pinḥas, and this time the whole family stayed together at Pinḥas's sister Giudecca's house.[92]

Lugo (Table 4.2, case 19)

On May 1, 1776, Rabbi Azulai arrived in Lugo, where there was an ongoing dispute between members of the city's three most prominent Jewish families in the eighteenth century: the Senigallia, Finzi (or Pinto), and del Vecchio families.[93] In this case, several of the same features of Rabbi Azulai's peacemaking practices emerge. One important difference, however, is that in this case, as well as in that of Ferrara (case 20), the next city he visited, instead of intervening on his own initiative he is called upon by others to intervene. Rabbi Azulai's reputation and status preceded him, especially after his success in Ancona, and one must assume that this goes a long way toward explaining his further peacemaking successes where others had failed. His description of the Lugo conflict begins:

May 5–6, 1776 (16 Iyar): During the day we visited S. Gedalia Senigallia, for he was sick. And he asked [of us] for the "release of curses" [he had made] and [also] to recite the [deathbed] Confession. All those present had grown sick of trying to make peace between him and the [community] officials, the elder S. Joseph del Vecchio and S. Barukh Solomon Pinto: and they told me to try.[94]

It seems that Rabbi Azulai was asked to intervene in this conflict both by one of the parties in conflict and by other well-respected community members with whom he had been in deep discussion the previous night. While Rabbi Azulai spent many months dealing with the conflict in Ancona, his intervention in Lugo took less than a week. During this week he dedicated many hours to the dispute, repeatedly sitting with the parties in conflict. He expresses how difficult this was in several entries:

May 6–7, 1776 (17 Iyar): [On Sunday night], I spent four hours with the aforem.[entioned] elder [Joseph del Vecchio]. His head is "iron mixed with miry clay" (Dan. 2:43)—I achieved nothing. In the morning he was waiting for me by the door of the synagogue and he said to me that during the night he had thought about my words. But I did not [even] turn my face toward him since I was wrapped in in my *tzitzit* and wearing my *tefillin*;

and he thought that I was angry with him. He was very much affected [by this] . . . after the prayers, he came to my house and brought his colleagues with him. And they agreed to make peace under certain conditions, which were written down; and they donated some small amounts, on [that] Monday and on Tuesday, for my mission.[95]

Here Rabbi Azulai understood the turning point in his peacemaking efforts to be when S. Joseph thought the rabbi was too angry with him to even greet him, while in reality Rabbi Azulai was simply in the middle of his prayer at a time when one is forbidden to speak. The mere possibility that Rabbi Azulai would be so upset caught S. Joseph off guard and was enough to get him to change his attitude toward the conflict, and indeed he switched from being sought by Rabbi Azulai to seeking the rabbi's good graces and then offering terms for peace (and a gift toward his mission). It appears that Rabbi Azulai did not bother to clarify the misunderstanding between him and S. Joseph, choosing instead to intentionally use it as a tactic to shake up the nobleman by exposing a risk to their own relationship if S. Joseph failed to follow through with making peace.[96]

That evening, Rabbi Azulai went to read the terms of the peace agreement to S. Gedalia's son, S. Abraham. He writes that "[S. Abraham] was extremely difficult indeed!" but "with the help of the Almighty" he succeeded, and Abraham accepted all the terms.[97] The following day, the compromise agreement was written up in Italian and signed by Rabbi Azulai and the local rabbi. Once again, Rabbi Azulai considered this a miraculous compromise, especially since the matter had already been sent to the pope to rule on. Rabbi Azulai writes that S. Gedalia "was almost nearly dead—but out of his joy he rose up and became cured of his illness. I went to see him, and he was walking around in the house—blessed is God!"[98]

Rabbi Azulai's diary entries during that week indicate the long hours spent and the great efforts and patience he exerted, arranging private conferences with each party as he did in the Ancona case. His commitment to the peacemaking process is a salient feature of his description. Also as in the previous case, the rabbi notes at various points that many community members and prominent people had already attempted to make peace between the parties in conflict, but to no avail; again this does not deter Rabbi Azulai. As in Ancona, he succeeds, and calls the peace a miracle.[99]

In Lugo, he uses a new tactic to influence the two sides to make peace with each other: He pretends to have been upset with one of the sides for failing to make peace, while later neglecting to tell them that he had simply been praying. This tactic, of course, can work only if the party in conflict places great value on their relationship with the highly respected third-party peacemaker, which was, as we have seen, the case with S. Joseph del Vecchio.

Interestingly, Rabbi Azulai does not mention in this case any description of an actual reconciliation encounter between the two sides. He does allude to the fact that the local rabbi was involved in the process, as both he and Rabbi Azulai signed on the compromise agreement. This attests once again to Rabbi Azulai's prescience to engage a local third side to assist in solving disputes.

Ferrara (Table 4.2, case 20)
From Lugo Rabbi Azulai traveled to Ferrara, where he was greeted with his third communal conflict:

> May 13, 1776: And there in Ferrara was a flaming fire between the entire holy cong.[regation] and the noble S. Moses Hayim [Vita] Cohen concerning the tax; and the Pope[100] and Cardinal Borghese had entered [the dispute] as well as many ministers and sages and emissaries, including S. Amron and S. Morpurgo—"and they hauled up but a shard."[101] And they urged me pressingly to intercede.[102]

Here too, the community members invite Rabbi Azulai to intervene in a long-standing conflict that others before him had not succeeded in resolving. The request was most likely due to Rabbi Azulai's reputation of peacemaking success.

The Ferrara case introduces us to an additional peacemaking method of Rabbi Azulai's, namely, secret meetings:

> I went to the noble S. Moses Hayim [Vita]; and we sat arguing how to compromise between him and the whole holy congregation, in utmost secrecy.[103]

Rabbi Azulai does not explain why it was necessary to meet in secrecy with S. Moses Vita, but it is nevertheless noteworthy and most likely has to do with an attempt to keep the conversation, which included many arguments, constructive. It eliminated external distractions and the pressure of others' knowing that he was working on making peace.

Rabbi Azulai continued meeting secretly with each side, until he eventually brought the parties to a compromise agreement.[104] On July 3, 1776, a document was written and taken to each of the parties separately to sign and take an oath at the same time, as in the Ancona case. Afterward, all the parties involved gathered together as Rabbi Azulai signed the compromise agreement and spoke words of Torah about peace and "He [meaning God] who makes Peace."[105] A few days later, on the Sabbath of July 6, Rabbi Azulai describes how he invited senior community leaders to visit him in the home of S. Moses Vita Cohen. He writes, "And they all came and the agreement became public knowledge." Later that evening, after the Sabbath ended, S. Moses Vita and others came to visit Rabbi Azulai in the home of one of the community leaders who had paid a visit earlier that day.[106]

This case is perhaps the closest replica of the *sulha* process from any of Rabbi Azulai's cases. It begins with one of the sides asking him to intervene to make peace. It continues with the rabbi meeting with each side separately, until the disputants finally meet to sign the formal compromise agreement that resolves the financial dispute between them. The third-party peacemaker speaks about the great value of making peace, and then, as a symbol of reconciliation, has each disputant pay a visit to the home of the other.

Bordeaux (Table 4.2, case 21)
Rabbi Azulai's range of methods unfolds in several other cases he describes. In the winter of 1777, he was in Bordeaux, France, when he was again approached by community members seeking his intervention in a conflict. In this case, Rabbi Azulai was able to not only restore a former *gabbai* (synagogue manager) to his position, but also to request the forgiveness of two members of the community on the *gabbai*'s behalf:

> 29 Heshvan (November 29, 1777): [On Sabbath morning], after prayers, the Avignoises came to plead with me that I should speak peace to [Jacob Naquite],[107] who was their *gabbai*, but [who] had resigned through some pique some 6 months previously; Moses and Solomon Petit had been filling this office [in the meantime]. And he came to see me that evening. Even though I was in a black mood, and also feeling a little unwell, I controlled myself and spoke to him until he agreed to return to being *gabbai*; and everyone was happy.[108]

Here we see the extent of Rabbi Azulai's sacrificing his personal comfort and actual pain for the sake of furthering the peace. He succeeds in persuading Naquite to return to his previous communal role. This in turn opens up the possibility of Rabbi Azulai's requesting forgiveness on Naquite's behalf. And indeed a few days later, on December 2, Rabbi Azulai met with Moses and Solomon Petit, discussing peace with them. He ultimately secured their forgiveness of Jacob Naquite, whose apology they accepted.[109]

Rabbi Azulai's role of third-party peacemaker is of course reminiscent of the role the *jaha* play in the *sulha* process. It also recalls the Aaron legend (case 4, according to most versions of the story), although it might contradict the opinion of Rabbi Yaakov ibn Ḥaviv, who, as we saw in Chapter 2, ruled that it is a mistaken custom for the third party to ask forgiveness on behalf of an offending side.[110]

After brokering this peace, Rabbi Azulai was supposed to depart from Bordeaux, but due to strong rain was persuaded to stay on until the following Sunday. He writes that this delay was probably in order to do some kind of good, and indeed it was. The following Sabbath morning, he took an additional step in attempting to strengthen the reconciliation between the sides he had worked with the previous Sabbath. As he writes:

> In the morning Ss. Solomon and Moses Petit came [to the synagogue; and I went up to the *teiva* (reading dais)] together with S. Jacob Naquite, and I told him the formula he should recite for the pardon and afterward I gave a blessing to the whole holy cong[regation]. After Minha, at the yeshiva of S. Daniel, I preached for about a half hour about peace.[111]

While staying that extra Sabbath in the community, Rabbi Azulai seized the opportunity to take the reconciliation process an important step further and have Jacob Naquite himself ask forgiveness of Moses and Solomon in front of the entire community, with the rabbi at his side overseeing the public ritual. This aspect of his peacemaking efforts, i.e., engineering a public apology at the synagogue in front of the community, aligns with what is said in Jewish law about how one is required to ask forgiveness.[112] It is also especially appropriate in this case, as the conflict had to do with the actual management of the synagogue. Rabbi Azulai then continues to teach on the subject of peace to the community later that day, in a continued effort, before he departed, to strengthen the spirit of reconciliation in the community.

Paris (Table 4.2, case 22)

The examples of Rabbi Azulai's peacemaking efforts so far have all been in the context of intracommunal disputes, although he also invested a significant amount of time and effort in pursuing peace between spouses. Much can be learned from how he describes his peacemaking methods in two such conflicts.[113] The first case takes place in 1777, during his visit to Paris. On Saturday, December 27, the third day of the Jewish holiday of Hanukka, he writes:

> 27 Kislev [December 27, 1777]: I dined with R. David [Naquite]. Dining with us were S. Elia Perpignan—a brother of the mistress of the house—and his wife between whom there was a great quarrel: they were still "leaning" and they had asked me, in Bordeaux, to make peace between them.[114]

It seems likely that Jacob Naquite of Bordeaux, whom Rabbi Azulai had helped reconcile to Moses and Solomon Petit, was a close relative of David Naquite of Paris, and had already asked Rabbi Azulai to try to make peace between the Perpignans when he would be in Paris. In other words, it was no coincidence that Rabbi Azulai was at the Sabbath meal with this couple.

The next morning, Rabbi Azulai attempted to make peace between the couple:

> 28 Kislev (Sunday, December 28, 1777): S. Elia Perpignan and his wife came to me. And I gave the woman a "Hear, O Israel" to swallow, a talisman—as used by the Rema z"l (Rabbi Menaḥem of Fano; Italy, 1548–1620)—for they were in fear that she contemplated apostasy, Heaven forfend! I spoke to them to make a lasting peace.[115]

Here Rabbi Azulai used a supernatural remedy to reconcile the couple. He was told that the problem was primarily a theological one, as the wife was considering converting to Christianity. He therefore thought the solution was to have her swallow a tiny parchment of paper on which it was written, "Hear, O Israel, the Lord is our God, the Lord is One,"[116] with a liquid potion which he had learned about a year prior during his travels in Italy.[117]

With this, Rabbi Azulai might have assumed that he had succeeded in restoring peace between the couple. However, a few days later, he returns to the issue in his journal, emphasizing a different aspect of the couple's conflict:

First day of the New Moon of Tevet (Wednesday, December 31, 1777): I then went with R. Mordecai Ventura to the home of Elia Perpignan and talked with his wife. I spoke to her, at some length, persuasively. Then her husband came home. I arranged that he should give *into her hand* sufficient [funds] for all the household expenses that they needed, so that she should be the mistress of the house. And I strove with all my might to make peace between them.[118]

This time Rabbi Azulai makes no mention of the woman's theological issues; rather, it seems that he has learned after sitting in discussion with the woman herself, accompanied by a respected, local third party (Mordekhai Ventura), that the issues between her and her husband pertained to how much control she had over household finances. Therefore, Rabbi Azulai's solution for peace between the couple was for the husband to hand over more financial control to his wife. Here we see Rabbi Azulai's willingness to change his peacemaking methods when the original approach turns out to be insufficient and as his understanding of the conflict evolves. It is noteworthy that his perspective evolved because he spoke directly, and additionally, with the parties in conflict.

Bayonne (Table 4.2, case 23)
A similar course of events took place a few months earlier, in September 1777, in Bayonne, France, in the community of Parnassel, but with different results. Rabbi Azulai was staying with the wealthy Abraham Nounez and soliciting donations for the community of Hebron. While there, he decided to try to make peace between Nounez and his wife, who had been in conflict for eight years.[119]

12 Tishrei (October 13, 1777): Before Rosh Hashana (September 25) I learned of an 8-year quarrel between the said Abraham [Nounez] and his wife. I rebuked him strongly [to make up the quarrel]. He accepted on the condition that his wife would make an oath on the Sefer Torah. And so it was done—his wife took an oath before me and before R. Jacob Attias and R. Abraham de Leon on a Sefer Torah, and the conditions were signed on a document. But his heart "was going in blackness and without light" as will be explained.[120]

Rabbi Azulai does not hesitate in his pursuit of peace even when it concerns his host and benefactor. As a first step, he encourages Nounez to make peace with his wife after being separated from her for eight years. He asks Nounez to set the conditions for their reconciliation, which the rabbi approves, and has the wife, in addition to signing on the written contract of conditions, swear on a Torah scroll as a sign of her own acceptance of these conditions. This she proceeds to do in front of him and other local rabbis.

But Rabbi Azulai still saw that something was not right, and he writes a few days later:

> 20 Tishri (October 21, 1777): Now, I already thoroughly understood his mind and his trickery and his lies. He came to see me, and his mother followed him in. She had never come to me before, and I understood that now it was for the purpose of talking against her daughter-in-law. I told him that he was committing a great sin in "bringing forth against her an evil name"—[namely,] that she wanted to poison him! And, furthermore [I told him]: that she went hungry and thirsty, but that she [nevertheless] "stood in her faith and righteousness"; and that he used to beat her; and that he had [even] hired [people] to kill her—and similar abominations of his; and that he had deceived me and had caused her to swear on the Sefer Torah in vain. I told him that God would "avenge her vengeance." He answered me that I [should] look upon him as an embittered soul. I replied that I look upon him as a hypocrite showing saintliness but underneath deceit—but I had recognized it and proved it; he had deceived [previous] emissaries, but I had seen through him. And I shouted at him and at his mother. Then he became meek, and began asking for new conditions. And I instructed him and persuaded him, and he gave his word that on [the Sabbath of the Torah portion of] Noah, when his son would be [ready for] "completing the count" [toward his bar mitzva], he would take her back into his house. Then I sent for his wife and warned her; and she accepted everything.[121]

Here Rabbi Azulai reports that he uncovered the true nature and character of his host and benefactor, who had no intention of reconciling with his wife and was more interested in humiliating her and perhaps physically harming her. Again, when the rabbi learned more information about their relationship, he altered his peacemaking method. He harshly rebukes and scolds Nounez and dictates new conditions upon which he must reconcile with his wife. Under the new conditions, she will return to his house in time for their son's bar mitzva.

However, it is unclear how effective this approach of rebuking and yelling at Nounez was, as just a day later, Rabbi Azulai received a letter from Nounez stating that he will not take his wife back and that Rabbi Azulai should speak no more of it.[122] A few days later, Rabbi Azulai tells senior community leaders of what he has discovered about Nounez—much to their surprise.[123]

Ten days later, Rabbi Azulai relates that he returned to pray in the community of Parnassel on the Sabbath of the bar mitzva.[124] Notably, he writes that he "did not see their faces," which implies that he did not greet Nounez, since he did not fulfill his promise of returning his wife to the house. After the Sabbath, Nounez sent a message asking if he could visit with the rabbi before the latter left town the following morning and offering to donate 12 *litra* to the community of Hebron. Rabbi Azulai refused to see him, and suggested he give the money to a different fundraiser for the Land of Israel but not to him.[125] Rabbi Azulai did not succeed in restoring peace between the Nounezes, despite his valiant efforts and despite remaining in the area until after the bar mitzva of their son. Moreover, he refused to be "bought off" by the wealthy husband's offering him a large sum of money to get back into his good graces.

***

Much can be learned from these long and complicated case studies about Rabbi Azulai's peacemaking methods (see Table 4.2). First and perhaps most important, everywhere he traveled he was held in extremely high regard, which served as a critical component of his peacemaking efforts. Yet he realized he was a well-respected rabbinic "outsider," and therefore on several occasions worked together with less distinguished, local rabbinic "insiders," who would serve together with him as third-party peacemakers, thus contributing to Rabbi Azulai's goal of establishing trust and lasting peace within the community. He sometimes took the initiative in making peace and did not wait to be invited to do so, in other cases he was invited by another party to intervene, and in still other cases he was approached by one of the sides in the conflict. He would initially meet with each side separately, bringing them to commit to the process and its outcome, only after which he gathered them together.

He understood that conflicts are often both financial and relational, and therefore he distinguished between *shalom*, reconciling relationships, and *peshara*, a formal compromise agreement that addressed all financial aspects and power dynamics under dispute. While Rabbi Azulai was clearly committed to the systems of strict law, known as *din*, he preferred bringing the sides to a compromise agreement instead, which sometimes required heroic efforts from him in order to accomplish this (case 18).

He advanced reconciliation between warring sides by creating ritual spaces of reconciliation such as in the synagogue, or going with one side to visit the other with the objective of participating in their joint family gathering. He worked tirelessly to make peace, often sacrificing his own personal well-being in the process. He often sacrificed his time, such as by extending his trips (case 18), as well as his personal comfort, such as when he participated in the family banquet (case 18), and his health (case 19). Yet he also protected his own spiritual needs by meditating before the Jewish New Year, not speaking while praying, and writing his book.

While Rabbi Azulai often brought disputing parties together to reconcile *after* a compromise agreement was reached, as is the accepted practice in the *sulha* process, he also understood that at times the hatred between the parties was so great that reconciliation had to come *beforehand* in order for the financial aspect of the conflict to be properly resolved (case 18). He was open to the possibility that he had misread a conflict and a relationship, and was not afraid to change course as necessary, despite the immense challenges this might have posed (case 23). Yet despite his being a masterful peacemaker, even he appears to have failed on at least one account. Finally, peacemaking was a deeply religious endeavor for him, which is evident by the fact that in every diary entry of his in which he describes overcoming another hurdle on the path to making peace, he constantly gives thanks to God for assisting in his efforts.

Practical Implications for Third-Party Peacemaking Today

I have used the entries in Rabbi Azulai's diary, in particular the first story of his peacemaking efforts in Ancona (case 18), in various trainings for rabbis from all denominations, initially as part of my center at Pardes and more recently as part of the Religious Peace Initiative of Mosaica. The rabbis study various entries in small groups and reflect upon Rabbi Azulai's decisions as a peacemaker at different critical junctures. We encourage them to ask themselves what they would have done at each turn had they been in his situation. At the end of their study time they are asked to write a short diary entry in which they reflect upon some of the key lessons they learned from

Rabbi Azulai that they would like to take with them in their own efforts to pursue peace in their rabbinical positions. This case has also played an important role in opening up critical conversations about what should come first: reconciliation of relationships or a formal agreement which resolves the conflict—a question critical to the understanding of different strategies for engaging in the Israeli-Palestinian conflict.

I have also used the case of Rabbi Azulai in Bordeaux (case 21), which tells of how he facilitated a process of forgiveness within the community, as part of a training for Mosaica's restorative justice facilitators. These facilitators meet every few months to share and analyze the cases they have recently worked on, which generally pertain to convicted felons by the Israeli courts and their victims. As part of this peer learning, I was asked to present a workshop on forgiveness in Judaism. In addition to presenting the core Jewish sources on this topic,[126] I had them analyze this case of Rabbi Azulai, just as they analyzed their own cases. The experience was absolutely illuminating to all, both those who identify as religious and those who identify as secular, as they each shared what was similar and different between what Rabbi Azulai did and what they do, and what can be learned from this ancient Jewish process of restorative justice for today.

Of all the third-party peacemakers discussed in this book, it is the role of Rabbi Azulai serving as a peacemaker that has been the greatest source of inspiration for me to serve as a mediator and peacemaker, and to share my enthusiasm with other rabbis. In one of my first meetings of religious leaders in my role at Mosaica, I was sitting next to one of the most senior ultra-Orthodox rabbis in Israel. During the break, he asked me about myself. I took a deep breath, and decided not to begin by talking about religious peace between Jews and Muslims, but instead shared my research of Rabbi Azulai as a rabbinic mediator. This immediately established a point of connection between us. The other rabbi's face lit up, and he began sharing his love for Rabbi Azulai and other rabbis like him, as well as his own work as serving as a mediator within his community.

The next story I shall examine is that of an anonymous, itinerant rabbinic peacemaker in Ağriboz who fails in his peacemaking efforts. One of the outstanding differences between him and Rabbi Azulai is the level of esteem in which these third-party peacemakers were held. Rabbi Azulai's reputation was outstanding, both as a rabbinic scholar and as a peacemaker, which as we shall see is not easy to replicate successfully and still not a guarantee of success.

The Less Respected, Unsuccessful Third-Party Rabbinic Peacemaker

The four examples of third-party peacemakers we explored in the first part of this chapter (cases 15–23) are for the most part successful third-party peacemaking interventions in which the peacemaker was a noteworthy rabbinic figure highly respected by all sides in the conflict. In this second part of the chapter I will bring two examples of interventions conducted by less respected third parties, whose stature in the eyes of the community seems to have contributed to the failure of their peacemaking interventions.

It should be noted that the sources for these stories are also of a different ilk from the ones already described. All the sources cited in the first part of the chapter are taken from students of the rabbinic peacemaker or from the rabbinic peacemaker himself and are far more likely to preserve successful interventions (except for the last case discussed). By contrast, the first three examples in this section are taken from the responsa literature, which, almost by definition, would showcase examples of failed interventions, as otherwise the case would never have been brought as a query to the leading rabbis of the generation to rule on the matter.

The Anonymous Visiting Rabbi: Ağriboz, Sixteenth Century (Table 4.3, case 24)

The first of these stories takes place in the Ottoman province of Ağriboz, today the Greek city of Khalkis (Chalcis). In the beginning of the sixteenth century, the small Jewish community of Ağriboz did not have its own Jewish court system or rabbinic leadership. The community was led solely by elected lay leaders, who would send all their questions to rabbis in nearby cities. The community enacted several *haskamot* (communal agreements) that were designed to help regulate the numerous communal conflicts taking place at the time. These agreements would be recited before the entire community once a month. Four such agreements from the beginning of the sixteenth century are known: it was forbidden for any elected official to serve as judge in a case involving a family member, no individual was allowed to separate themselves from the community and establish a separate community, no one individual was allowed to force their will upon another individual without the consent of the elected officials, and no one was allowed to form a group of ten men to force the rest of the community to excommunicate another community member.

The situation that led to the involvement of a non-local rabbinic peacemaker involved a group of Ağribozan Jewish merchants who tried to break the long-standing communal agreement (*haskama*) against excommunicating or banning any individual from the community without the permission of the appointed officials. There was a financial dispute involving a certain Reuben (a pseudonym[127]), a broker among the merchants, which turned verbally violent. Two merchants, Simon and Levi (also pseudonyms), gathered a group of relatives together to enact a ban against Reuben. The group signed a document saying that they would have nothing to do with Reuben, whether in business or in personal matters.

The elected leaders of the community sent a query to Rabbi Shmuel b. Moshe de Medina, an influential rabbi in Thessaloniki:

> After about a year (since the initial dispute took place), a certain <u>h</u>akham (rabbi) passed through here to give a lecture in the community, and he heard about the clashes and fighting and the baseless hatred between [the people of the community] and Reuben, and so he lectured to the community on the matter of peace, and about making peace between [the parties], and that there should not be any [baseless] hatred with Reuben at all anymore.
>
> Then they all said as with one mouth: "Reuben the broker should ask forgiveness, and we will all, as with one heart, release him from the ban and forgive him, and the document that we made will no longer apply to him, and will be torn up, so that it will not be brought up ever again, and so there will be peace between us as was before."
>
> Then, Reuben got up and asked forgiveness wholeheartedly and with a humbled soul, as is the practice of forgiveness in accordance with all the conditions of the community, from all of them, from the "smallest" to the "biggest," exactly as is appropriate. And the rabbi was appeased and satisfied with what Reuben the broker did. Afterward, the rabbi went on his way in peace.[128]

While it would seem from this description that the anonymous itinerant rabbi stayed in Ağriboz only briefly, it goes on to indicate that he stayed long enough to compose a new written agreement that released Reuben from the ban. The account also implies that the itinerant rabbi gave a successful lecture and then brokered an immediate peace between Reuben and the others, resulting in forgiveness and reconciliation between the sides in conflict.

The authors of the query to Rabbi de Medina go on to describe how this quickly unraveled:

> But when they heard about the document that the rabbi had written (freeing Reuben from the ban), they stalled and avoided making peace and doing away with the document that they had made against Reuben, and they regretted what they had said, and they took an oath to rip up the [new] document . . . and they did not want to forgive. And they were not concerned about the rabbi's words, as if his words were broken pottery or something without substance. Rather, they held to their position and trusted in their own strength.

The itinerant rabbi then wrote a new document, freeing Reuben from the ban, and then left that document with the community while he went on his way. Although the other merchants and the rest of the Jewish community of Ağriboz were involved in the public apology and forgiveness in the presence of the rabbi, the latter neglected to oversee the acceptance of the new document or deal with its fallout. His early exit seems to have played a significant role in the peace agreement's unraveling.

The event described in the query attests to the lack of weight the itinerant rabbi, who unlike Rabbi Azulai was neither well known nor highly respected, held in the eyes of the community members. They "trusted in their own strength" far more than that of the visitor, whom they easily dismissed as speaking words of no greater substance than "broken pottery."

While there is no guarantee that a local, more trusted authority would have succeeded in resolving this conflict, we can safely assume that a rabbi who was well known to the community, and all the more so who had a relationship with all the disputants, would not have been subject to this kind of dismissal. The itinerant rabbi did not know the history of the community's communal agreements or the details of the conflict, which from the perspective of the elders who wrote the query both sides contributed to, though it was the weaker party who was forced to ask forgiveness. This played right into the interests of the more powerful side of Simon and Levi, who may have actually manipulated the naïve peacemaker into accepting their peace terms in order to further humiliate Reuben.

Rabbi de Medina responded with outrage to the situation described in the query. He responded unequivocally that the merchants had no right to draw up a document banning anyone from the community, as this was a clear violation of a binding communal agreement. He had, in fact, harsh words for the "sinful people" who had done this.

The visiting rabbinic peacemaker's methods are very similar to those employed by the other rabbinic peacemakers discussed in this chapter so far. During his communal lecture in the Ağriboz synagogue, which both parties attended, he too drew on traditional sources that stress the importance of peace and peacemaking within Judaism, perhaps even citing some of the same primary sources Rabbi Azulai, for example, may have used in his peace promoting sermons about peace.

At first, the community members quickly obeyed the itinerant rabbi's call: they reconciled their relationship with Reuben and accepted (at least from the rabbi's point of view) some kind of written agreement that resolved the areas in dispute. The question is, Why did he fail where others in similar circumstances succeeded? It is of course possible that a similar event took place the day after Rabbi Dovid of Lelov or Rabbi Azulai left a community in which they had just made peace. It is also true that sometimes nothing more can be done by a third party if at least one of the sides is not interested in making peace. However, there are a few important differences between this story and the ones discussed previously in this chapter that could explain why the anonymous rabbi failed and others succeeded.

To begin with, the visiting rabbi was anonymous, meaning he was no Rabbi Dovid of Lelov or Rabbi Azulai, both of whom were already well known and respected rabbis in their time. In addition, he had no previous knowledge of the conflict and the communal agreements, as well as no long-term relationship with the sides in conflict. It is also not clear whether he attempted to cultivate local third-party peacemakers who would have continued to hold the sides accountable, as Rabbi Azulai did in several cases. As a result, the visiting rabbi not only did not bring the sides to real, sustainable peace, he might even have contributed to the further deterioration of the community whereby they succumbed to power imbalances and injustice.

This story serves as an important reminder that sometimes good intentions are insufficient when it comes to third-party peacemaking. It brings to mind the parable of the professional doctor versus the amateur practitioner we saw in Chapter 2.[129] The wrong person using the same medicine might well hurt the patient instead of saving him.

Practical Implications for Third-Party Peacemaking Today

Despite the Ağriboz story's being about an anonymous, unsuccessful third-party rabbinic peacemaker, it can still play an important role in educational programs and trainings in which participants learn to become skilled third-party peacemakers themselves. For example, it is the primary text used in the Pardes Rodef Shalom Schools Program middle school curricular unit Unit 5, on bullying prevention and the power of the community.[130] In this unit students are asked to reflect on various parts of the story, beginning with the community *haskama* (agreement) that forbade any group of ten people from banding together and excommunicating others. Students are asked to reflect upon what a class *haskama* similar to the one described in the beginning of the Ağriboz story might look like that could assist in preventing bullying.

After reading about the initial conflict in the Ağriboz Jewish community and the excommunication of the weaker side, students are asked if one or more of the contemporary methods for preventing bullying (which they learned about earlier in a preparatory lesson with their teacher) could have prevented this situation from happening. In light of the failed intervention of the visiting rabbi, they are asked to write feedback for him in which they tell him in a constructive and respectful manner that while his intentions might have been good, he may have misread the situation as a result of not knowing the history of the conflict.

Rabbis Moses Benjamin and Moses Dammuhi: Cairo, Sixteenth Century (Table 4.3, case 25)

The previous story of the itinerant, anonymous rabbi demonstrates the need for local third-party peacemakers who know the background of a community's conflicts and players, and who will continue to oversee the peace process and its aftermath from within the community. However, as we will discover in the following story, having local third-party peacemakers is not in itself sufficient—especially when they are not considered to be of the highest status.

In the middle of the sixteenth century, a bitter dispute erupted in the Jewish community of Cairo over a seemingly trivial incident. At the end of a festive wedding celebration, when the time came for reciting grace after meals, Rabbi Yaakov ibn Tibbon was asked to lead the blessing. Rabbi ibn

Tibbon, originally from Alexandria, had been appointed to serve as the rabbinic head of the Cairo Jewish community. As he began, Rabbi Yitzḥak de Molinio, the head of the local yeshiva, who was not considered a great Torah scholar—or at least not on par with Rabbi ibn Tibbon—became insulted that he had not been asked to lead the grace, and therefore stood up to leave.

When Rabbi ibn Tibbon saw this, he cursed Rabbi de Molinio in front of the members of the Jewish community, most of whom were in attendance and many of whom were sages in their own right, saying, "Wicked of wicked! Lover of abominations—he and the one who supports him!"[131] His words were directed not only at Rabbi de Molinio but also at his primary financial supporter, Shlomo Alashkar, known as the *mualem*, who besides being a wealthy community leader was also well connected to the government.[132] Alashkar supported the local yeshiva in Egypt as well as a yeshiva in Safed in the Land of Israel; he also sponsored the first publication of the famous *Shulḥan arukh* of Rabbi Yosef Karo.[133]

As a result of Rabbi ibn Tibbon's outburst, Rabbi de Molinio's students from the yeshiva excommunicated Rabbi ibn Tibbon, and in return Rabbi ibn Tibbon, with the support of other rabbis, excommunicated Rabbi de Molinio, his students, and Alashkar. With each side excommunicating the other, the conflict quickly became public and proceeded to spread like wildfire, as described in the following responsum of Rabbi Moshe di Trani:

> The dispute was like a hot fire, burning without anyone to extinguish it.... No one remained uninvolved.... No brave person could be found who would fulfill the *mitzva* of mediating peace and cooling the fire of the dispute.[134]

Ultimately, the *mualem*, Alashkar, wrote to the three most prominent rabbis of the generation, who were living in Safed: Rabbi Yosef Karo, Rabbi Moshe b. Yosef di Trani (known as the Mabit), and Rabbi Yisrael b. Meir di Curiel. Alashkar requested they take sides and rule on the matter. The rabbis refused Alashkar's request, and instead instructed the two camps to make peace by employing what they refer to as "explicit rebuke and implicit love":[135]

> We mandate by Torah decree that the two rabbis who have a dispute should gather together with the rest of the sages within three days, or on the first Sabbath after the *mualem* shows them this letter. They should stand before

God in the synagogue, which belongs to everyone equally, and the rabbi who [led the grace after meals] should stand before everyone and say, "I regret what I said against the *ḥakham* (de Molinio) and his supporter (Alashkar), and I seek their peace and well-being." And the *ḥakham* should stand up and say, "I, too, seek your peace and your well-being, and the peace of your fellows, the rabbis." And they should go to their homes "in peace and uprightness" (Mal. 2:6).

And they should not refrain from any of this, God forbid, or transgress our words. The weak side will say, "I am mighty: 'Who is mighty? The one who conquers his inclination' (Mishna Avot 4:1)." And it is upon the *mualem* to not stand on principle but to pursue peace, and to pursue it as is his good custom. For all of his ways are ways of strengthening the Torah (and peace). And [concerning] the rabbis, we know the uprightness of their intellects and the pleasantness of their characters . . . and they will seek peace and pursue peace.[136]

While we do not know what the Cairo community did in response to this letter, the letter itself is instructive of the peacemaking efforts and methods of these rabbis: (1) The rabbis compliment the players on each side of the conflict, showing confidence in their character and their interest in pursuing peace; (2) they call for a public reconciliation to take place within three days (or on the first Sabbath) in the shared sacred space of the synagogue, requiring both sides to reach out in peace to the other; and (3) they see their role not as judges or arbiters at this point in the conflict, but rather as facilitators of a reconciliation process that must be undertaken by those involved themselves.

It should be noted that Rabbis Karo, di Trani, and di Curiel, who were supported by Alashkar and to whom this letter is directed, do not include him as one of the sides of the conflict at all. On the contrary, they require Rabbi ibn Tibbon to be the first to speak and apologize for his offensive words. Earlier in their letter they had written, "[The scholars of Egypt] should have shown honor to the *mualem*, who supports the study of Torah throughout the land, and concerning him who blessed (i.e., Rabbi ibn Tibbon), we are angry at how he offered in front of them on that day a blessing juxtaposed to a curse; it is none other than the work of Satan, the accuser [of the Jews, who was present] during the festive meal."[137] In other words, while these rabbis encourage mutual reconciliation between the two rabbis, they do seem to favor Alashkar, who is directly connected to Rabbi de Molinio, over Rabbi ibn

Tibbon, and do not, for example, scold equally Rabbi de Molinio for standing up and leaving at the beginning of grace.

While the rabbis of Safed called for peace from afar, two local yet far less respected rabbis, Rabbi Moshe Benjamin and Rabbi Moshe Dammuhi, took it upon themselves to pursue peace between the parties in this conflict. It seems probable that they were motivated to serve as third-party peacemakers as a result of the letter from the rabbis in Safed. Rabbi Benjamin describes their efforts in a letter to yet another rabbi, Rabbi David b. Zimra, known as the Ridbaz (who was mentioned earlier as the student of Rabbi Syracusty), who was then living in Jerusalem after having lived in Egypt for many years. He writes that Alashkar was amenable to making peace, and that he had in fact taken upon himself a year of repentance including fasting every Thursday, lashes, and confessing his wrong behavior in front of ten men.

After this year of repentance, the two sides were to meet and reconcile. However, when Rabbis Benjamin and Dammuhi came to Rabbi ibn Tibbon's home, the conflict only spun further out of control. Rabbi Benjamin writes:

> And everyone knows how hard I strove to mediate peace between them.... And all eight days of Passover I had no tranquility or quiet and did not rest day and night, but I did not succeed. And one time I went together with the distinguished Rabbi Moshe Dammuhi to the wise and distinguished Rabbi Yaakov Tibbon, to mediate peace (*letavech shalom*).... And we rebuked him in order to lower him a bit so that he would enter into a covenant of peace, because the *mualem*, Rabbi Shlomo (Alashkar), had already been appeased (i.e., was ready to make peace).[138]

Several features of these rabbis' peacemaking methods emerge from this letter. First, Rabbi Benjamin worked tirelessly to pursue peace, even at the expense of enjoying the Passover holiday. Second, the rabbinic peacemakers apparently met with each side separately. Third, Rabbi Benjamin says of the meeting with Rabbi ibn Tibbon that the peacemakers "rebuked him in order to lower him a bit." In other words, he understood that ibn Tibbon's high opinion of himself was preventing him from the humility required to make peace with his adversary. Rabbi Benjamin tried to instill humility in Rabbi ibn Tibbon for the sake of peace by rebuking him. This, however, did not work, he reports.

At this point, while it seems that Alashkar was ready to reconcile, Rabbi ibn Tibbon rejected Alashkar's sincerity and the efforts of the peacemakers.

He further escalated the conflict by cursing and stating that Alashkar should be deemed an unfit witness in a rabbinic court—a grave demotion not only in prestige but in simple credibility as a citizen. When the peacemakers heard him cursing, they left, and apparently ceased their efforts to bring peace between the two parties. Rabbi Benjamin, the erstwhile peacemaker, then took it upon himself to investigate matters and issue a ruling with regard to whether Rabbi ibn Tibbon's excommunication or the counter-excommunication of the students of Rabbi de Molinio should take precedence.

The legal question of the validity of the excommunications became the subject of much debate among the sages of the generation.[139] Rabbi ibn Tibbon wrote a long responsum to the rabbis of Safed trying to prove that his excommunication should take precedence over that of de Molinio's students. The rabbis of Safed were divided on the matter. Rabbi di Trani disagreed with Rabbi ibn Tibbon, and held that the students' excommunication stood;[140] Rabbi Yosef Karo, on the other hand, claimed that it didn't, siding with Rabbi ibn Tibbon.[141] Rabbi Benjamin argued that the students' excommunication was valid, but the Ridbaz agreed with Rabbi ibn Tibbon that it was not.[142]

Despite the efforts of local third-party rabbinic peacemakers, together with the support of highly respected, non-local third-party peacemakers calling upon the parties to make peace, the reconciliation process failed in this case. One can only speculate as to why. Perhaps the local peacemakers were simply not considered more distinguished than the disputants themselves. Perhaps if the great rabbis from Safed, or the Ridbaz, had come in person to Egypt to facilitate the process, as what happened in Volozhin (case 17), the results would have been different.

It is also possible that the actual peacemaking methods of Rabbis Benjamin and Dammuhi, pleading with and rebuking Rabbi ibn Tibbon (the way Moses is described as doing in Chapter 2 and the way Rabbi Azulai did in case 23), were not effective in transforming the dynamics of the dispute. This might be because Rabbis Benjamin and Dammuhi neither allowed Rabbi ibn Tibbon to express his frustrations and needs nor listened to his feelings and perspective with great humility and persistency in the spirit of Aaron. It is also possible that they did not address the power dynamics between the two sides appropriately, and the various third-party peacemakers may have been perceived as favoring one of the parties, namely, Alashkar. And finally, it is also possible that Rabbi ibn Tibbon was intransigent in his refusal to reconcile with the other side.

Whatever the cause of failure might have been, this story represents another important case study of efforts of third-party rabbinic peacemakers attempting, albeit unsuccessfully, to reconcile two sides and avoid resolving a conflict through the strict letter of the law.

Practical Implications for Third-Party Peacemaking Today

While I have not had occasion to use this story in educational programs or trainings, I have drawn inspiration from the words of Rabbi Moshe di Trani, who describes the dispute as "a hot fire, burning without anyone to extinguish it.... No one remained uninvolved.... No brave person could be found who would fulfill the *mitzva* of mediating peace and cooling the fire of the dispute."[143] This is very powerful imagery of what a community in conflict looks like when there are no third-party peacemakers. Rabbi Michael Melchior, chairman of the board of Mosaica, quoted these words in his address to some six hundred mediators from all sectors of Israeli society attending Mosaica's annual conference on mediation and dialogue at Bar-Ilan University in 2019. He then added, in his own words, that in the Cairo dispute there was no one there to mediate; no mediation center and no mediators. Everyone took a side in the conflict and there was no one left to put out the fire! How special it is to be in the company of hundreds of volunteer community mediators, from all over the country, who do their best to ensure that a situation such as this doesn't happen within their own communal conflicts.[144] (I have not used Table 4.3, cases 26, and 27 as part of educational programs or trainings, and therefore do not have reflections on practice to share.)

Exceptions to the Rule:
The Unsuccessful Third-Party Rabbinic Peacemaker of High Social Status and the Successful Third-Party Rabbinic Peacemaker of Lower Social Status

In this final section of the chapter I will explore two stories of third-party rabbinic peacemaking, the first by a rabbi of higher social status than the parties in conflict who was unsuccessful, and the second by a rabbi of lower social status than the parties in conflict who ends up succeeding in making peace. The contrast between the stories demonstrates that while the identity and status of the third party plays a notably significant role, their peacemaking methods are often equally important.

The Unsuccessful Intervention of Rabbi Avraham b. Moshe b. Maimon: Cairo, Thirteenth Century (Table 4.3, case 26)

The following story describes the unsuccessful attempt of Rabbi Avraham b. Moshe b. Maimon (commonly known as Rabbenu Avraham ben haRambam; 1186–1237), a highly respected rabbinic figure, to intervene as the third party in a dispute. Rabbi Avraham succeeded his father, the famous Maimonides, as the *nagid*—leader—of the Jewish community of Egypt. First, however, some background is in order.

As part of his official communal role, Rabbi Avraham would appoint local judges and rabbis to their positions. One such appointment was of Rabbi Yosef b. Gershom, a rabbi from Egypt's French-Jewish community. In 1234, Rabbi Avraham appointed him *rosh yeshiva*, judge, and head of the rabbinical court in Alexandria. Soon afterward, this appointment met with strong opposition from Hodaya b. Yishai, who was known as the *nasi*, Patriarch, in Alexandria, and was assumed to be of royal lineage dating back to King David. Hodaya had initially supported the appointment of Rabbi Yosef, but subsequently became strongly against it, and the two became bitter enemies.[145]

The larger context of this conflict was the ongoing tensions between the native Jewish community of Alexandria, represented by Hodaya, and the immigrant Jewish community from France, represented by Rabbi Yosef.[146] The conflict touched upon personal jealousies, theological differences between the two communities, questions of communal authority based on lineage as well as education, and most likely financial issues as well. The case of third-party peacemaking on the part of Rabbi Avraham is preserved in the responsa of Rabbi Avraham, which contain a letter from Rabbi Yosef to Rabbi Avraham and the latter's response.

Rabbi Yosef opens his letter with the accusation that Rabbi Avraham took Hodaya's side in their conflict. Rabbi Yosef accuses Rabbi Avraham, therefore, of either flattery or cowardice in the face of Hodaya's political power. It appears that he interpreted Rabbi Avraham's visit to Hodaya as a sign of favoring Hodaya, while from Rabbi Avraham's perspective it was an attempt to mediate peace between them, as we shall see.

Rabbi Yosef then proceeds to explain the conflict from his perspective. According to his testimony, the issue began with the case of a woman whose divorce or widowhood needed to be confirmed before she could remarry. Hodaya accused Rabbi Yosef of taking a bribe to confirm her status as a single woman, and he cursed Rabbi Yosef and called him and his ancestors *mamzerim*, illegitimate children (alluding to Rabbi Yosef's permission for the woman to remarry and have children, who themselves would be *mamzerim* if the woman had not been truly single when she remarried). In addition, Hodaya declared the entire immigrant community of French Jews heretics (*kofrim*) and apostates (*minim*), claiming they believed God has a physical form, which according to Maimonides would define them as heretics.[147]

Hodaya had also demanded some ten Egyptian dinars in order to release the community from a particular oath they had taken upon themselves, despite the fact that the community was able to pay only eight dinars. When he insisted on their paying all ten, several members of the community began simply transgressing the oath. Rabbi Yosef, who was head of the rabbinic court, saw this as a profanation of God's name and decided to release them of the oath without the payment of any fee. Hodaya subsequently excommunicated not only Rabbi Yosef but the entire French and Byzantine Jewish community in Alexandria, forbidding any economic ties with them. He claimed that since he was the *nasi*, all of Israel must adhere to his edict.[148]

The letter continues to set out Rabbi Yosef's response to this. First, he rejects all Hodaya's claims. Moreover, he denies ever speaking disrespectfully to Hodaya, despite the testimony of Hodaya's witnesses; to whatever extent he was disrespectful, Rabbi Yosef claims, it was in response to Hodaya's insults. He claims that Hodaya does not have the legal authority of a *nasi* in the first place, which means that his excommunication is null and void. Rabbi Yosef, in turn, excommunicates Hodaya for decreeing an unjust and unlawful excommunication.[149] Rabbi Yosef's letter concludes with a series of legal questions, in essence pushing Rabbi Avraham to clarify his position on the conflict, on Hodaya's status as *nasi*, and with regard to which party has more authority to excommunicate the other.

Rabbi Avraham begins his response to Rabbi Yosef by rejecting the accusation that he had taken Hodaya's side, and that such an act of taking sides is clearly against Jewish law. He then explains the course of events from his perspective: He had initially wanted both sides to come together before him in Cairo, which would have allowed him to clarify the situation and rule on the matter appropriately. With each side claiming that the other insulted him,

Rabbi Avraham had no way of determining what actually happened. Both parties had apparently refused to appear together with the other, insisting that Rabbi Avraham rule on the matter using strict justice. He then tried to meet with each side separately to broker the peace.

His approach to Hodaya, Rabbi Avraham continues, was "the left [hand] should push away while the right [hand] should draw close," an allusion to the sages' suggestion for dealing with difficult situations or people.[150] It means that on the one hand, he wanted to show respect and honor toward Hodaya, who was after all an elderly man of distinguished lineage. But on the other hand, he did whatever he could to rebuke and scold him for both his position and his behavior in this conflict, since Hodaya had shown that he did not want to make peace with Rabbi Yosef. Rabbi Avraham writes:

> As is my way in ethical behavior (*derekh eretz*) and benevolence (*gemilut ḥasadim*), and the way of my father in whose way I walk, and I ignored his character traits, and I said, "Perhaps [Hodaya] will leave [Cairo] in peace and honor, as so many respectable people had done in the past." And when he came here to [Cairo], I went to him and received him before your honor (Rabbi Yosef) came. And I saw his heart burning and with great anger, and he would not keep his tongue from cursing good people in God's name and speaking about you and the sages of France (in Egypt), just as you had said. And I silenced him to the best of my ability, but he would not hear my advice. And if he had heard my advice it would have been good for him and for the honor of his home.
>
> And when you came, I took with me sages (*hakhamim*), elders (*zekeinim*), and distinguished people (*hashuvim*) and I went to him at his home to make peace (*lahatil shalom*) between you and to silence the words of strife. But he did not want to. Rather, he stood firm in his position and his anger increased, and words of blasphemy came from his mouth, and curses and oaths and matters that are not appropriate to write, for it is not my desire to publicize his anger.[151]

Rabbi Avraham explains here that the purpose of the visit to Hodaya was genuinely for the sake of persuading Hodaya to make peace. Clearly, the attempt was unsuccessful.

As a result of this failure, Rabbi Avraham changes his approach to the conflict once more. He instructs Rabbi Yosef to *manage* the conflict instead of trying to *resolve* it. He admits that Hodaya began the insults because Rabbi Yosef was French. He advises Rabbi Yosef to take the high road and to be "of those who are insulted and not of those who insult."[152] He further tells Rabbi Yosef that "it should be sufficient for you to be my friend." In other words, there is no reason for Rabbi Yosef to be intimidated by Hodaya's threats, since Rabbi Avraham will stand by him.

Rabbi Avraham then answers all of Rabbi Yosef's legal questions about the case, taking Rabbi Yosef's side unequivocally. He rules that Hodaya is not an actual *nasi*, that he has no authority to excommunicate Rabbi Yosef, and that Rabbi Yosef acted appropriately in excommunicating Hodaya. The French and native Egyptian Jewish populations, as a result of Rabbi Avraham's rejection of Hodaya's excommunication, can therefore return to function as one community again.

At the very end of his legal response to Rabbi Yosef, Rabbi Avraham writes:

> It is difficult for my eyes and painful for my heart that you do not receive great honor, as befits your wisdom and stature and the stature of your forefathers, and that [Hodaya] should not have double the honor, as befits his lineage and the honor of his great family. But anger and other ideas are confusing him. If he had only listened to my advice and the advice of those of reason and wisdom, he would have had his and his family's honor. And since he has not listened, what can we do? We cannot and we did not want to bring down the honor of his household.[153]

Rabbi Avraham here expresses his genuine desire for matters to have concluded otherwise, along with his realistic acceptance of the situation and the limitations of third-party peacemaking in this situation.

Reviewing the conflict and Rabbi Avraham's peacemaking efforts, we find a multi-step strategy. At first he attempts to resolve the conflict by inviting the two sides together to stand before him to rule on the matter. When this fails, he attempts to meet with each side separately to make peace between them as a mediator. Finally, when these peacemaking efforts fail as well, he comes out in unequivocal support of Rabbi Yosef and the French community, to the detriment of Hodaya and his position. Rabbi Avraham describes his own method of peacemaking as a balancing act; he shows great honor and respect to Hodaya, while simultaneously reprimanding him.

This story is very similar to the previous one that took place in sixteenth-century Cairo (case 25). Both stories tell of struggle between two powerful communal leaders and the failed attempt of a third party to intervene, despite valiant efforts. However, while Rabbis Benjamin and Dammuhi are virtually unknown rabbinic figures, Rabbi Avraham is and was then a very well-known and respected one. Yet despite this difference, Rabbi Avraham failed in his peacemaking attempts. There can be many reasons for this. From his perspective, it was due to the anger and folly of Hodaya, similar to how Rabbis Benjamin and Dammuhi blamed Rabbi ibn Tibbon's stubbornness for the failed peace process.

Rabbi Avraham's failure may run deeper than that, however. It is unclear to what extent he attempted, or whether he even tried, to address the needs and concerns of Hodaya and those he represented—in particular regarding their relationship with the French immigrants, which had become fraught.[154] Rabbi Avraham shares no detail of his conversation with Hodaya, nor does he outline his compromise proposal—if there even was one. Rather, he states only that he tried to settle the fight between them. Hodaya then became only more enraged, and Rabbi Avraham became angry in return.

This vignette provides a stark contrast to both Aaron's and Rabbi Meir's methods of pursuing peace between individuals (Table 2.1, case 4; Table 3.1, case 5). Aaron, according to one version of the legend, would humbly sit with each side until they were able to release all their anger and jealousy, and only then would he shift their perception of the conflict. With regard to Rabbi Meir, his mere presence went a long way toward making peace. But Rabbi Avraham's presence does not calm Hodaya at all.

Furthermore, Rabbi Avraham is far from a neutral third party in this conflict, unlike our perception of Rabbi Dovid of Lelov (Table 2.3, case 16), Rabbi Azulai, and the rabbinic peacemakers of Volozhin (Table 2.3, case 17). As Rabbi Avraham had appointed Rabbi Yosef in the first place, Hodaya may have seen him as a permanent supporter of Rabbi Yosef. On the other hand, Rabbi Avraham's show of respect to Hodaya backfired, as it convinced Hodaya that Rabbi Avraham was on his side after all, and led to Rabbi Yosef's accusing Rabbi Avraham of this injustice.

I can only speculate as to what would have been the outcome of this bitter dispute if Rabbi Avraham's peacemaking delegation of "sages, elders, and important people" had included members of the native Egyptian Jewish community who were closer to Hodaya and shared his concerns. We may also wonder whether transparency about the nature and goals of the separate meetings with each side would have been more effective than trying to hide the fact that these meetings took place—which then allowed the goals of the meetings to be misinterpreted by the other side.

It is also possible that this story represents another important reminder that sometimes even the most respected, righteous, and talented third-party peacemaker does not succeed in making peace due, as claimed by Rabbi Avraham, to the stubborn refusal and anger of one of the sides in the conflict.[155] On the other hand, the following story, which also tells of a major power struggle between two very respected leaders with one side refusing to make peace with the other, may challenge this simple assumption, as it tells of third-party peacemaker who was of lower social status than the parties in conflict yet nevertheless succeeded in transforming perspectives and making peace between them.

The Successful Intervention of Rabbi Nissi al-Nahrawani: Baghdad, Tenth Century (Table 4.3, case 27)

The following story is found in *Seder olam zuta*, the mid-tenth-century chronicles of Natan b. Yitzhak the Babylonian (also known as Natan b. Yitzhak HaBavli), and is the earliest post-talmudic story of third-party rabbinic peacemaking within medieval rabbinic literature that I have found.[156] Rabbi Natan tells the story of a rabbi who serves as a third-party peacemaker in a conflict between a Gaon (head of one of the two major Babylonian rabbinic academies) and an Exilarch (the religious and political leader of the entire Babylonian Jewish community). Particularly in this case, the historicity of Rabbi Natan's account is not necessarily reliable. But whether as history or legend or some combination of the two, the value of Rabbi Natan of Babylonia's account is akin to that of the earlier talmudic accounts of rabbinic peacemakers (Chap. 3) and the hasidic legend we explored previously. Here, the author describes rabbinic peacemaking in what became a popular book that was read by many Jews then and later. However, like all the cases discussed in this chapter, is for the most part unknown beyond scholarly circles today.

The rabbinic peacemaker in Rabbi Natan's account is Rabbi Nissi (in the version of the story I will cite he is referred to as Nissim)[157] al-Nahrawani, a well-respected leader who held the distinguished position of *reish kalla*[158] in the rabbinic academy of Baghdad; he was also blind. He took the initiative to make peace between the head of the rabbinic academy of Pumbedita, Kohen Tzedek Gaon, and the Exilarch, David b. Zakkai (whom we will meet again in the next chapter in a different conflict with another Gaon).

The roots of the conflict, according to Rabbi Natan, can be traced back to the time when Kohen Tzedek Gaon ousted the previous Exilarch, Mar Ukva, and expelled him from Babylonia. As a result, the position of Exilarch was left unoccupied for several years, until the rabbis of Sura, another major rabbinic center in Babylonia, appointed David b. Zakkai as Exilarch. Kohen Tzedek rejected the appointment, because David b. Zakkai was the nephew of the ousted Mar Ukva. For three years, Kohen Tzedek Gaon and the rabbinic academy of Pumbedita refused to recognize David b. Zakkai as the Exilarch, resulting in a significant rift in the leadership of the Babylonian Jewish community.

According to Rabbi Natan, Rabbi Nissi had attempted to intervene over the course of these three years, but the focus of his story is on the culmination of that process, which appears to hinge on elements of the supernatural and surprise:

> There was a certain blind man (Nissi) known for his miracles (*nissim*), Nahrawani the *reish kalla*. And he would enter between them (i.e., Kohen Tzedek Gaon and David b. Zakkai) in the way of peace, [thinking that] maybe he would be able to make [David b. Zakkai] the leader over the rabbinic academy of Pumbedita, which would mollify Kohen Tzedek the *rosh yeshiva*. One night he went and opened all the locks in Babylonia by [pronouncing aloud] the [Ineffable] Name of God. He opened four (other versions: fourteen)[159] locks until he arrived at [Kohen Tzedek's] home and stood above him. He found [Kohen Tzedek] studying in the middle of the night. When Kohen Tzedek saw him he trembled before him and asked him about his coming. [Nissi answered:] "By your life, sir! I opened four(teen) locks in order to arrive at your home." [Kohen Tzedek] said, "And what do you want now?"
>
> [Nissi] replied, "That you bless the Exilarch (i.e., David b. Zakkai) and make him the leader over you."
>
> He replied that he would do as [Nissi] said. Nissim [Nissi] left there and went to the Exilarch [David b. Zakkai] and informed him, and he set a time during the day that [Kohen Tzedek] would come. He returned to Kohen Tzedek and informed him of the time.[160]

The beginning of the story appears to paint Nissi as a classic, traditional third-party peacemaker, intervening and shuttling back and forth between the two sides in the hope of making peace. But Rabbi Nissi was at a clear disadvantage, as he was of lower social status compared to the two most powerful leaders of Babylonian Jewry who were in conflict. To overcome this significant hurdle, Rabbi Nissi employs a supernatural tactic of mentioning the Ineffable Name of God,[161] thereby temporarily changing the power dynamics between him and Kohen Tzedek Gaon in order to make peace.

Invoking the Name of God is a very significant act in Judaism, and is generally strictly forbidden.[162] Traditionally, God's Ineffable Name was invoked only when the priests (i.e., the *kohanim*, from the family of Aaron) would offer their blessing of peace to the people in the Temple of Jerusalem,[163] and when the high priest would enter the Holy of Holies in the Temple on Yom Kippur, the Jewish Day of Atonement.[164] Thus, Rabbi Nissi's invoking this specific Name of God demonstrates significant supernatural powers, reminiscent of the peacemaking saints discussed at the end of Chapter 2. This act also catches Kohen Tzedek Gaon completely off guard, which serves as a critical step in Nissi's successful peacemaking efforts.

A legend of a peacemaker using supernatural powers to surprise and then gain the trust of one of the sides in a conflict is reminiscent of Deganawida, the Great Peacemaker mentioned in Chapters 1 and 2. According to the legend, he convinced the Mohawk council to join in his intercommunal peace alliance only after he was able to demonstrate supernatural powers:

> The Peacemaker climbs a great tree, perched precipitously over a deep gorge. The Great Warrior's men then cut down the tree. Deganawida plunges into the river's turbulent waters below and disappears. The next morning, a young man sees smoke rising from the edge of the cornfield, which turns out to be where the Peacemaker is encamped, and the chief, Great Warrior, and deputy are now convinced of the Peacemaker's power to accomplish his mission.[165]

By employing such supernatural powers in peacemaking, these peacemakers are demonstrating the lengths to which they are willing to go to persuade the sides in conflict to make peace, and that there are greater powers governing human interactions than may meet the eye which can shift the perspectives and power dynamics of those in conflict.

The need for supernatural or miraculous intervention is also significant for what it communicates about both Kohen Tzedek Gaon as a party in the conflict and Rabbi Nissi as a peacemaker. In order to gain access to

Kohen Tzedek Gaon's home, Rabbi Nissi had to invoke the Ineffable, secret Name of God and magically open several locks. This demonstrates both how distant and reserved Kohen Tzedek Gaon had become from others and from engaging in peacemaking, and how much of an effort Rabbi Nissi was willing and able to make in order to draw him out. The elements of surprise and supernatural tactics appear to shock Kohen Tzedek Gaon into recalculating the power dynamics. Moreover, he becomes unable to continue avoiding his social problem by hiding inside his private quarters. He finds himself suddenly vulnerable with Rabbi Nissi standing above him both literally and figuratively, and immediately agrees to the latter's demands.

It is also possible that Rabbi Nissi's blindness was an asset to him as a peacemaker in this case; it certainly adds to the element of surprise when he suddenly appears. Furthermore, Rabbi Natan writes that when the *rosh yeshiva* of Sura passed away twenty years later, David b. Zakkai consulted with Rabbi Nissi about whom to appoint in his stead. David b. Zakkai had two candidates in mind, but he first offered the position to Rabbi Nissi—as a gesture of good will, knowing very well that he wouldn't accept. Rabbi Nissi responds that it would not be appropriate for him to be the *rosh yeshiva* because of his blindness.[166] But being unfit for the formal role of *rosh yeshiva*, he was able to play the role of a trusted, communal rabbinic leader. The fact that he dared not seek the highest leadership position would serve as an assurance to the community that he never acted out of personal ambition or political interests. This, of course, also made him the ideal peacemaker.

The story concludes with the description of a classic coronation, symbolizing the reconciliation between the disputants. The two sides publicly meet and reconcile as David b. Zakkai is finally inaugurated as the new Exilarch. It is similar to the ceremony performed at the end of a *sulha* process:

> Kohen Tzedek then instructed all of his students and the members of his academy who were on his side to gather and stand upright and to go out toward the Exilarch. They went out to the place called Zarzar, a half-day's journey from Babylon. There they met the Exilarch, and behold he too was coming with his own very significant camp, all of his students and escorts. . . . And when [both parties] arrived at the gates of Babylon [together] they sang pleasant songs and lovely choruses until they arrived at the courtyard that was prepared for [David b. Zakkai]. And he entered and

dwelled in Babylon, he and all his men and women and the members of his household.[167]

The story of Rabbi Nissi serves as an example of how third parties of somewhat less elevated social status can actually be even more effective peacemakers than the most powerful leaders in the community.[168] Rabbi Nissi, despite his relative lack of status, is able to surprise—nay, shock—the entrenched side in the conflict, thereby successfully changing both the power dynamics and that side's perception of the dispute, ultimately leading to reconciliation. The story stands in contrast to the previous one about Rabbi Avraham, as there the third party was highly respected but nevertheless unable to shift the dynamics of the conflict or the different parties' perceptions of it.

***

This chapter explored eight cases of rabbis serving as third-party peacemakers as described in medieval and early-modern rabbinic literature. Some of these rabbis, such as Rabbi Yosef Syracusty, Rabbi Dovid of Lelov, the rabbis in Volozhin, and Rabbi Azulai, were highly respected, successful peacemakers. They served as role models of third-party rabbinic peacemakers for their students and for subsequent generations, in a similar manner to the third-party peacemakers discussed in the previous two chapters. Other examples of third-party peacemakers in this chapter examined the stories of rabbis of lower social status who were unsuccessful in their peacemaking efforts, such as the anonymous visiting rabbi who came to Ağriboz (case 24) and Rabbis Benjamin and Dammuhi (case 25).

Yet we also saw that there was not always a direct correlation between the social status of the rabbinic peacemaker and his successes. Sometimes even the most respected rabbi failed in his efforts, such as Rabbi Azulai's last case (23) and Rabbi Avraham's attempt (case 26); other times, even a far less respected rabbinic figure was able to succeed in making peace, such as Rabbi Nissi (case 27).

The peacemaking these rabbis so diligently sought to accomplish can be defined in one of two ways. The first is transforming perspectives, healing relationships, restoring honor, and reconciling the sides (category 8 in the tables at the end of this chapter), similar to what Aaron and the other peacemakers mentioned in classical rabbinic literature were described as doing. This was often referred to in the various cases as *la'asot shalom bein* (to make peace between), such as in the case of Rabbi Dovid of Lelov (case 16), the various cases of Rabbi Azulai (such as cases 18, 20, and 21), and the anonymous visiting rabbi (case 24). In many of the cases the conflict was described as a serious breakdown in the relationship between the two parties, often resulting in one or both sides formally or informally excommunicating the other. In such conflict scenarios, the peacemaker needed to address the relationship through reestablishing shared identity between the sides and restoring damaged honor.

Another core aspect of peacemaking these rabbis employed was bringing the sides in conflict to a formal, written (*ktav*) compromise (*peshara*) agreement that would allegedly resolve the financial and/or power dynamics between them (category 7 in the tables at the end of this chapter), as was done in the Volozhin case (17), as well as by Rabbi Azulai (cases 18, 19, 20, and 22) and the visiting anonymous rabbi (case 24). This aspect of peacemaking was entirely absent from the earlier legends of third-party peacemakers addressed in Chapters 2 and 3, which focused exclusively on the transformation of the relationship between the disputants. However, we shall see that this is the core component of the lay peacemakers in the coming chapter.

The rabbinic peacemakers we studied in this chapter often took the initiative to intervene without being asked to do so (cases 16–18, 23–27), although some intervened upon the request of others in the community or the sides in conflict themselves (cases 19–22). In many instances they invested a tremendous amount of time and self-sacrifice to move the process forward; still, resolution of the dispute sometimes took months or even years.

While the peacemaking rabbis were highly respected in their own right, some of them took other rabbis or respected elders with them to be part of a peacemaking delegation (category 2 in the tables at the end of this chapter). Two examples are Rabbi Azulai, who took Rabbi Israel (case 18), and Rabbi Avraham, who was accompanied by well-respected elders of the community (case 26). Those who went alone, such as the anonymous visiting rabbi (case 24), might have been less successful as a result.

The peacemaking rabbis in this chapter usually met with each side separately and only afterward brought the parties together (category 6 in the tables at the end of this chapter). At the stage of separate meetings, they are often portrayed as giving *tokhaḥa* (rebuke) as part of their attempt to persuade one side to make peace with the other. Using *tokhaḥa* as a means of peacemaking was generally unsuccessful, as is evident with regard to Rabbis Benjamin and Dammuhi (case 25), and perhaps with regard to Rabbi Azulai as well (case 23). When the rabbinic peacemakers did bring the sides together, they employed different methods of reconciling between them. Joint prayer and study were used, as well as gathering the sides in shared spaces such as a synagogue. These methods were all employed to reestablish common identity and friendship between the sides. Sometimes, the reconciliation encounter included one side publicly and formally asking forgiveness from the other, such in the case of Rabbi Azulai in Bordeaux (case 21) and in the case of the anonymous visiting rabbi (case 24). This is also what was supposed to take place in the sixteenth-century Cairo case upon the request of the rabbis of Safed (case 25).

Taken as a whole, this chapter serves as a small sample of what might have been a much broader phenomenon of rabbis serving as third-party peacemakers in historical Jewish communities. This echoes the findings in other traditional and religious models of peacemaking in which religious leaders, such as the imam as noted in Chapter 1, see peacemaking as part of their communal responsibility.

The cases enumerated in this chapter can also serve as important sources of inspiration for rabbis today to embrace as part of their identity as mediators and peacemakers between individuals and groups, both within and beyond the Jewish community. Upon entering my role at Mosaica, I was shocked by how little connection there was between rabbis and their local mediation and dialogue centers that Mosaica supports throughout Israel. Many rabbis and sheikhs have begun training through basic mediation courses, but what they learn there is insufficient. There is a great need to ground modern-Western mediation courses in religious texts and stories of famous religious leaders serving as third-party peacemakers. As noted, several of the sources analyzed in this chapter are being used as part of training rabbis to serve as mediators and work with local community mediators as well as part of Mosaica's "Rabbis as Mediators Program."[169]

I have often noticed the difference it makes if the representative of one of the sides in the conflict, or the third-party peacemaker himself, is a religious leader, such as a rabbi or a sheikh, as opposed to a lay leader. Even though I personally no longer serve in a formal rabbinic position, the mere fact that I am an ordained Orthodox rabbi has helped me at times gain credibility and respect as a mediator between rabbis and sheikhs.[170]

Table 4.1 Historical Accounts and Stories of Third-Party Rabbinic Peacemakers in Medieval and Early-Modern Rabbinic Literature

Highly Respected Rabbinic Peacemakers			
Case Number	15. R. Syracusty	16. R. Dovid of Lelov	17. Rabbis in Volozhin
The Conflict			
1. The case	Husband and wife, individuals, non-Jews	Two individuals	Two highly respected rabbis
The Third-Party Peacemaker			
2. Number	———	2	2–4
3. Social status	High	High	High
4. Connection to sides in conflict	———	Strong/outsider	Strong/outsider
5. Initiative to intervene taken by	Third party	Third party	Third party
6. Meeting with each side in conflict	———	Together	Together
7. Bringing sides to a compromise agreement	———	No	Yes
8. Transforming perspectives, reconciling the relationship	———	• Supernatural power of prayer • Is physically present with the sides in conflict • Gathers sides in ritual space (synagogue) • Joint prayer (according to Buber)	Gathers sides in joint Torah study
9. Personal self-sacrifice	———	Travels far	———
Result of Third-Party Intervention			
10. Success/failure of intervention	———	Success	Success: written compromise agreement

Table 4.2 Historical Accounts and Stories of Third-Party Rabbinic Peacemakers in Medieval and Early-Modern Rabbinic Literature

	Highly Respected Rabbinic Peacemakers						
Case Number	18. R. Azulai (Ancona)	19. R. Azulai (Lugo)	20. R. Azulai (Farrera)	21. R. Azulai (Bordeaux)	22. R. Azulai (Paris)	23. R. Azulai (Parnassel)	
The Conflict							
1. The case	Family/business dispute with personal hatred and lawsuits	Communal conflict between wealthy families	• Community and wealthy banker • Power inequality	Two community lay leaders insulted by another leader	Husband and wife	Husband and wife	
The Third-Party Peacemaker							
2. Number	2 (R. Azulai and local rabbi)	2 (R. Azulai and local rabbi)	1 (R. Azulai)	1 (R. Azulai)	2 (R. Azulai and layperson)	3 (R. Azulai and 2 local rabbis)	
3. Social status	High	High	High	High	High	High	
4. Connection to sides in conflict	Strong/outsider	Strong/outsider	Strong/outsider	Strong/outsider	Strong/outsider	Strong/outsider	
5. Initiative to intervene taken by	Third party	Community	Community (disputant)	Community	Relative of disputant	Third party	
6. Meeting with each side in conflict	Separately/together	Separately (pretends to be upset with one of the disputants)	Separately (and secretly)	Separately	Together/separately	Separately/together	
7. Bringing sides to a compromise agreement	Yes	Yes	Yes	——	Yes	——	

Continued

Table 4.2 Continued

	Highly Respected Rabbinic Peacemakers					
Case Number	18. R. Azulai (Ancona)	19. R. Azulai (Lugo)	20. R. Azulai (Farrera)	21. R. Azulai (Bordeaux)	22. R. Azulai (Paris)	23. R. Azulai (Parnassel)
8. Transforming perspectives, reconciling the relationship	• Rebukes one of the sides in conflict • Gathers both sides in ritual space (yeshiva) • Escorts sides to each other's home	Surprises disputant by pretending to be angry with him	• Preaches about peace (after agreement signed) • Facilitates reciprocal visits to each side's home	• Serves as emissary of forgiveness • Facilitates public forgiveness ceremony • Preaches about peace	• Uses supernatural potion against heresy • Changes approach: brings to financial agreement	• Takes husband's side: rebukes him to reconcile with his wife, has her swear on Torah and sign contract • Takes wife's side: rebukes husband
9. Personal self-sacrifice	• 8-month process • Participates in lavish family banquet • Sets boundaries	Works very hard	—	Goes to meeting despite being ill	—	Might have prolonged trip to ensure agreement was kept

The Result of Third-Party Intervention

Case Number	18. R. Azulai (Ancona)	19. R. Azulai (Lugo)	20. R. Azulai (Farrera)	21. R. Azulai (Bordeaux)	22. R. Azulai (Paris)	23. R. Azulai (Parnassel)
10. Success/failure of intervention	Success: reconciliation and written compromise agreement	Success	Success	Success: • reconciliation ceremony where offending party publicly asks forgiveness from victims in Synagogue on the Sabbath • preaches about peace	Success: new distribution of power between husband and wife	Failure: wife does not return

Table 4.3 Historical Accounts and Stories of Third-Party Rabbinic Peacemakers in Medieval and Early-Modern Rabbinic Literature

Parameters for Comparison	Less Respected		Exceptions	
Case Number	24. Anonymous visiting rabbi	25. R. Moshe Benjamin and R. Dammuhi	26. R. Avraham b. Moses	27. R. Nissi
The Conflict				
1. The case	• Merchant and broker in business dispute • Power inequality	Two highly respected rabbis/communal leaders	Two highly respected religious and communal leaders	Two highly respected religious and communal leaders
The Third-Party Peacemaker				
2. Number	1	2	2+	1
3. Social status	Medium	Medium	High	Medium
4. Connection to sides in conflict	Weak/outsider	Strong/insider	Strong/outsider	Strong/insider
5. Initiative to intervene	Third side	Third side	Third side	Third side
6. Meeting with each side in conflict	———	Separately	Separately	Separately
7. Bringing sides to a compromise agreement	Yes	———	———	———
8. Transforming perspectives, reconciling the relationship	• Preaches in public about peace • Facilitates public forgiveness ceremony (weaker side asking from stronger side)	Third side rebukes one disputant	Third side advises one disputant to not be angry and other disputant how to manage conflict in absence of peace	• Third side utters Ineffable Name of God to approach disputant by surprise • Facilitates public reconciliation/coronation ceremony
9. Personal self-sacrifice	———	Holds meetings through all of Passover	———	———
Result of Third-Party Intervention				
10. Success/failure of the intervention	Failure: conflict returns after third side leaves	Failure: angry side in conflict becomes angrier	Failure: angry side in conflict becomes angrier	Success: reconciliation and coronation ceremony

5

Rodfei Shalom, Metavkhei Shalom, Pashranim, and *Nikhbadim*

Historical Accounts and Stories of Third-Party Lay Peacemakers in Medieval and Early-Modern Rabbinic Literature

Now that I have examined in the previous chapter several historical accounts and stories of rabbis who served as third-party peacemakers, I will continue our exploration of peacemakers within the vast body of medieval and early-modern rabbinic literature, but this time focusing on lay peacemakers. As opposed to the rabbis of whom the identities of almost all were known, lay leaders who served as third-party peacemakers are almost entirely anonymous. They were, however, often referred to with quasi-titles to signify their role as third-party peacemakers. I have therefore divided this chapter into four primary sections based on these titles: *rodfei shalom* (pursuers of peace); *metavkhei shalom* (mediators of peace); *pashranim* or *mefashrim* (compromisers); and finally, well-respected lay leaders, often referred to simply as *nikhbadim* (well-respected individuals) or *hashuvim* (distinguished individuals).

In each of these sections I will first survey the use of the title employed to describe these third-party lay peacemakers. I will then analyze in greater depth select case studies of their methods. At the conclusion to this chapter I will discuss the similarities and differences between these third-party lay peacemakers and other traditional cultural peacemakers. I will also share reflections of the possible implications of these historical accounts for promoting third-party peacemaking today.

Yet beforehand, as in the previous chapter, I will address the Jewish imperative for lay leaders to be peacemakers.

The Jewish Imperative for Laypeople to be Peacemakers

In the previous chapter we saw that one of the primary early rabbinic sources on which medieval and early-modern rabbinic writers relied to encourage rabbis to serve as peacemakers was the mishna (Avot 1:12) "Be of the disciples of Aaron: a lover of peace and a pursuer of peace." Yet as we saw in Chapter 2, the identity of those who can be considered "disciples of Aaron" was not understood to be limited to religious leaders such as rabbis but was to include laypeople as well.[1] An explicit example of this can be found in a medieval midrashic source, which applies the epithet "lover of peace and pursuer of peace" to an additional biblical character besides Aaron, namely, his non-priestly brother-in-law, Nachshon, the son of Aminadav:

> "Aaron took (for a wife) Elisheva, the daughter of Aminadav, the sister of Nachshon" (Ex. 6:23). Why does the text indicate "the sister of Nachshon"? Because just as Aaron was a lover of peace and a pursuer of peace, so too, Nachshon was a lover of peace and a pursuer of peace.[2]

Nachshon was chief of the tribe of Judah and was therefore essentially a well-respected lay leader.[3]

A second early rabbinic source which was understood to encourage laypeople to serve as third-party peacemakers can be found in the first mishna in tractate Pe'a, which states:

> These are the things of which a person eats of their fruit in this world, yet the principal remains for that person in the World to Come: honoring one's father and mother, acts of loving-kindness, and bringing peace between man and his fellow. But the study of Torah is equal to them all.

According to this mishna (which is customarily recited by all prior to the daily morning prayers[4]), a person who brings peace between people is similar to one who honors their parents and does acts of loving-kindness, meriting reward both in this world and in the afterlife. In both the Babylonian Talmud and the Jerusalem Talmud it is stated that "bringing peace between man and his fellow" in this mishna is learned from the verse in Psalms (34:15): "Seek peace, and pursue it."[5] The commentaries understood this mishna to include third-party peacemaking and not just peace made between the disputing parties themselves.[6] In Chapter 3, we saw that Rashi cites this mishna in his commentary on the legend of the non-rabbinic jesters acting as third-party peacemakers (case 12) as the proof text for his assertion that they received a portion in the World to Come. Rashi is emphasizing that third-party peacemaking encouraged in this mishna applies to simple, non-scholarly laypeople as well.[7]

Yet despite these early sources, finding references to the imperative for third-party peacemaking, whether lay or rabbinic, in a legal (halakhic) context in medieval and early-modern rabbinic literature is surprisingly difficult.[8] This may partially be due to the fact that the verse containing the directive to pursue peace is found not in the Torah but in the book of Psalms. While Psalms, like the rest of the Hebrew Bible, is considered a sacred and central text, only the Five Books of Moses carries legal weight. Thus peacemaking, while appreciated and sometimes even stressed in early rabbinic sources, is not usually viewed as one of the core biblical commandments.

Still, a few medieval and early-modern rabbis considered peacemaking a legal imperative, whether of biblical or of rabbinic origin. This is evident in their works; some of them found creative ways to include peacemaking as one of the 613 commandments.[9] Rabbi Yitzhak of Corbeil (France, 1210–1280), in his book of *mitzvot*, connects the pursuit of peace with the commandment in Leviticus to love one's neighbor as oneself:

> To love one's fellow [person], as Scripture says: "You shall love your neighbor as yourself" (Lev. 19:18). And included in this is bringing peace between man and his fellow, and judging him favorably... and King David wrote in his book, "Seek peace, and pursue it" (Ps. 34:15).[10]

"Bringing peace between man and his fellow" is the exact language of the earlier mishna in tractate Pe'a cited earlier, and seems to imply the obligation of a third party to bring peace between conflicting sides.[11] Rabbi Yitzhak of Corbeil's interpretation imposes the obligation to fulfill the commandment of bringing peace upon all individuals, not just upon Torah scholars.[12] It is important to note that he did not write his book for purely scholastic purposes; it was intended to be both practical and accessible to the general public, and indeed it was widely popular.[13]

Rabbi Yitzhak was associated with the Jewish pietistic movement known as Hasidut Ashkenaz. For the members of this ascetic, mystical movement, founded in twelfth-century Germany, the pursuit of peace might have been of special importance. Additional evidence of this interest in peacemaking is found in the writings of Rabbi Eliezer of Worms (Germany, 1165–1240), one of the movement's leaders. In his *Sefer haroke'ah*, he advocates that a *hasid* (pious one) should "seek peace between a person and his fellow."[14] He even dedicates a section of this work to "The Root of Good Character Traits: Bringing Peace." There he writes:

> It does not say "seek" except with respect to peace, seeking peace in your city, pursuing it outside of your city. "But to the counselors of peace is joy" (Prov. 12:20), because [the person engaged in] bringing peace eats of its fruits in this world, yet the principal remains for him in the World to Come: seek peace.[15]

Rabbi Eliezer of Worms is not describing a Torah scholar's or a rabbi's activities, but those of a *hasid* (holy and righteous person), and appears to be encouraging this practice broadly across the community.

A third rabbi deeply rooted in and connected to the Ashkenazic pietistic movement who promoted the value of pursuing peace was Rabbi Yona Gerondi, known as Rabbenu Yona (Spain, 13th cent.), one of the greatest medieval Spanish scholars of his day.[16] In his ethical treatise, *Sha'arei Teshuva* (Gates of Repentance), he writes, "Whoever does not engage in doing good and bringing peace transgresses [the commandment of] fearing God, and is considered one of the wicked, for he does not fear God."[17]

Rabbenu Yona called upon the Spanish Jewish communal leaders to institutionalize peace as a value. These selected or elected communal leaders in thirteenth-century Spain were known as *berurim* ("selected individuals"). They often held specific communal responsibilities, such as handling finances or dealing with civil disputes between members of the Jewish community.[18]

Rabbenu Yona invokes the legend of the jesters introduced in Chapter 3 (case 12), who were not Torah scholars and who merited the World to Come, in his other popular ethical work, *Iggeret hateshuva* (letter of repentance):

> [the people of] Israel are obligated to choose people who can bring peace between a husband and wife, between a person and his fellow, who have the power to coerce and force people regarding peace. And these selected individuals (*haberurim*) should be *gavrei bedihu*: joyful people who know how to reconcile individuals and render peace. And they should not be angry and irritable people.... And it is said in the Talmud about those who make peace: "We are *gavrei bedihu* (joyful people)[19] and we make peace." And our

sages have said regarding these people who make peace with joy that it is promised to them that they shall merit the World to Come.[20]

Rabbenu Yona appears to be fusing the importance of peacemaking touted by the Ashkenazic pietists with the existing Sephardic convention of *berurim*. He emphasizes that these lay peacemakers need to be "joyful," not "angry and irritable." He charges them with the task of peacemaking, ostensibly granting them the power to coerce people to make peace.[21] Whether this involved forcing both parties to be part of a peacemaking process or obliged them to accept a judgment is unclear. Whatever the case, Rabbenu Yona's writings suggest an attempt to transform peacemaking from the grassroots effort it may have previously been in the Ashkenazic pietest movement to a formal communal function in the Sephardic community.

This call upon the *berurim* to serve as communal pursuers of peace was echoed by the slightly later Sephardic scholar Rabbi Yitzhak bar Sheshet (known as the Rivash; Barcelona, Algeria; 1326–1408):

> [The *berurim*] should be wise, intelligent people, knowledgeable in communal matters, [the community's] customs and enactments, lovers of justice, *rodfei shalom* (pursuers of peace), and accepted by the majority of the community.[22]

Here Rabbi Sheshet delineates the character traits necessary for a person to be elected as one of the communal *berurim*. Included in this list is *rodfei shalom*, pursuers of peace. Thus, while third-party pursuit of peace is not found in most medieval and early-modern rabbinic legal works, several scholars do indicate its ethical significance. Moreover, a number of distinct commandments or directives clearly place responsibility for its implementation on communal lay leaders, requiring that they take the initiative and engage as third-party peacemakers within their community.

Without a doubt, the clearest call for communal laypeople to serve as third-party peacemakers can be found in the words of Rabbi Hayim Palagi (Turkey, 1787–1868) in his book *Tzeva'ah mehahayim* (*lit.* A Living Will), who was the chief rabbi of Izmir and well known for being a pursuer of peace himself:

> May God in His mercy give me the strength to make a special charity fund (committee) that should comprise special individuals who will serve as

rodfei shalom, as is the case for other holy committees (*ḥevrot kedushot*), in order that as soon as they hear of a conflict between two individuals or within the community, they should be able to dedicate all of their efforts to make peace between them. Their membership in this committee is conditional on their taking a formal, strict oath that they will not become angry at all, even if [people] curse them and hit them. And they should be careful not to speak harshly, and to be patient. And there is no doubt that if they do this they bring Redemption closer. And it goes without saying that they themselves should not be engaged in conflicts at all and should be forgiving. And a great benefit comes out of such a "gathering for the sake of Heaven" (Mishna Avot 4:11). And there is no need to spend money at all (on this) except for a community official [who will be responsible] for gathering [the *rodfei shalom* together].[23]

Rabbi Palagi is in essence calling to institutionalize third-party lay peacemaking by having a special fund that would be used to support a community official whose task it would be to gather together appointed third-party lay peacemakers when there is a conflict in the community. The peacemakers themselves, whom he refers to as *rodfei shalom*, are community volunteers. He emphasizes that these laypeople need to take a special oath before serving as *rodfei shalom* that calls upon them to be very patient and not aggressive even when people are cursing and hitting them as they pursue peace. This directly connects to category 9 ("Personal self-sacrifice") in the tables showcasing the various cases we have examined in this book. Moreover, *rodfei shalom* must exemplify these values in their own personal lives by not engaging in conflicts and being forgiving of others. While I am unable to determine if Rabbi Palagi ever got his wish of having such a communal *rodfei shalom* committee, the very call to have such an institution can inspire others to do so.

Practical Implications for Third-Party Peacemaking Today

I have used several of these texts at the beginning of various constructive controversy workshops I ran as part of the Pardes Center for Judaism and Conflict Resolution for Jewish professionals and lay leaders, such as Federation leaders in the United States. I begin the workshops with the above quote of Rabbenu Yona, and ask participants to discuss the obligation to appoint communal leaders to pursue peace within the community. Then I have them study the quote from Rabbi Yitzhak bar Sheshet, cited earlier, and ask them to discuss and write down the ideal character traits of the Jewish community leader. We then discuss their own lists and the list of traits mentioned by Rabbi Sheshet, which includes lay leaders being *rodfei shalom*. Finally, I present them a selection of key quotes from some of the cases about lay third-party peacemakers cited in the following sections, and ask them to discuss what can be learned from these examples of Jewish community leaders acting as *rodfei shalom* within their communities.

I commissioned a close friend, Micah Selya, who is, among other things, a Torah scribe, to copy on special parchment paper, in the manner in which Torah Scrolls are written, the beautiful quote of Rabbi Hayim Palagi in which he envisions having community volunteer *rodfei shalom* take a special oath and be brought together by a paid communal official. The words were written vertically down the middle of the parchment paper to symbolize being a mediator and third-party. I then had this parchment reproduced, framed, and given as a gift to the dozens of community rabbis throughout Israel participating in a new Mosaica project called "Rabbis as Mediators" (which has a separate, parallel Islamic project called "Sheikhs as Mediators"). The idea is for these rabbis to see themselves both as those who are fulfilling Rabbi Palagi's dream and as third-party rabbinic peacemakers who also support the local community mediation and dialogue center that Mosaica supports within their own city.[24] These centers activate community volunteer mediators. I have referred to this text as being a kind of Jewish Hippocratic Oath for mediators and peacemakers. Having this old rabbinic text hanging on the walls of rabbis' offices and modern mediation and dialogue centers in Israel is meant to offer a cultural grounding and inspiration for those doing the labor of love of third-party peacemaking and mediation today. It is for this reason that I chose to have the image of Rabbi Palagi's words on the parchment be the image on the cover of this book, as it truly embodies third-party peacemakers in Judaism, in text, theory and practice.

I now turn to address four different terms used to refer to such third-party lay peacemakers as found in rabbinic responsa literature and other historical sources.

Rodfei Shalom (Pursuers of Peace)

The term *rodfei shalom* can be found throughout the responsa literature. It describes a group of laypeople who worked together to make peace between two conflicting parties within the Jewish community. *Rodfei shalom* always worked as a group or a delegation; no mention of the singular *rodef shalom*, an individual who tried to make peace between two conflicting parties, is found anywhere in responsa literature.[25] In this sense, and with regard to many other characteristics that we will encounter in the cases in this chapter, pursuers of peace are akin to the *jaha* who facilitate the *sulha* but very different from modern third parties such as those described in the Interactive Problem-Solving Workshops model (see Chap. 1).

To the extent that this term evokes the tradition of the biblical Aaron as a "lover and pursuer (*rodef*) of peace," those who used this term apparently saw a connection between the identities and practices of their own "pursuers of peace" and the prior traditions found in rabbinic literature relating to the pursuit of peace generally and to the legends of Aaron specifically.[26] A close look at how the term is used makes that connection more apparent.

Groups known as *rodfei shalom* in responsa literature, as we shall see, always actively interfered in conflicts at their own initiative rather than at the invitation of the parties in conflict. When the pursuers of peace are described as having "entered between them (i.e., the parties in conflict)," this points more explicitly to the pursuers' initiative rather than to that of the disputants. Both the term "pursuer of peace" and the phrase "entered between them" parallel what we learned in Chapter 2: they evoke the rabbinic traditions concerning Aaron as well as connect directly with the statement of Rabbi Yosei, who encouraged the third side to "enter between them and [effect a] compromise between them."[27] A "pursuer of peace" is thus distinguished in the tradition from a "lover of peace," which denotes a love of peace but no active engagement.

Rodfei Shalom Interceding in a Conflict between a Husband and Wife: Spain, Eleventh Century
(Table 5.1, case 28)

The earliest source in which *rodfei shalom* are mentioned is the responsa of Rabbi Yosef ibn Migash of eleventh- to twelfth-century Spain, commonly known as the Ri Migash. The context is the failed attempt of peacemakers to resolve a certain marital conflict, which leads the local authority to write to the Ri Migash for his input and guidance. The husband had rented a home for the first year of the marriage, at the end of which time a conflict began between him and his wife regarding their future permanent residence. The husband wanted to live in an extension of his parents' home because it would cost him nothing and because all his assets were there and he was eager to oversee them. The wife did not want to move to her in-laws' property for fear that her mother-in-law would harass her. Instead, she wanted to live on *her* parents' property, or at least in a rented home somewhere else. This conflict includes both a delicate relationship (or multiple relationships, if we include the relationship between the wife and her mother-in-law) and financial/material interests (the oversight of the husband's assets).

The original compromise solution was to continue renting and not to live with either side's parents. As explained in the letter written to the Ri Migash, "*Rodfei shalom* intervened and [the husband] stayed with her in the rented home for another five years.... And every day conflicts arise between them."[28] The writer of the letter asks the Ri Migash which claim was justified: that of the wife, who wanted to continue renting or live near her parents, or the that of the husband, who wanted to live near his parents and assets. In his responsum, the Ri Migash favors the husband and writes that the *rodfei shalom* did not act appropriately in supporting a preservation of the original situation (the husband renting a home for the couple):

> And what the *rodfei shalom* did to mediate between them (*lefasher beineihem*), [namely that] he rented her a home, should only have been done if he had already been renting a home with her mother-in-law, such that her claim that the mother-in-law would harass her was verified. But in actuality, this woman had not yet lived with her mother-in-law and had not been harassed, as you noted (in your query), and we should not force her husband to rent her a house based on her speculation alone, which was not verified in practice. In such a case, a claim on the part of a wife who says, "Lest your father and mother harass me," is not an appropriate basis on which to prevent [the husband] from residing in his own lot (near his assets).[29]

We do not know who the *rodfei shalom* were in this case. Most likely, they were composed of members of the community, neutral enough and respected enough that both parties were willing to accept their directive. It is no accident that without the backing of a spiritual authority to shore up one's peacemaking efforts, lay peacemakers would have to work as part of a group. Consequently, in lieu of a religious peacemaker, having a group of lay peacemakers instead of just one bolstered people's confidence in the third party.

The original letter to the Ri Migash from the community authorities uses the term "entered between them," indicating that the pursuers of peace took their own initiative in helping the couple, which we saw was a key component of the Aaron model and many others. But it is impossible to reconstruct exactly what these *rodfei shalom* did in their meeting or meetings with the couple. Like many such sources whose goal is not to record the identities and methods of peacemakers, we are limited in what we can learn from them.

The Ri Migash uses Jewish legal language when he refers to the issue of making a decision based on speculation alone,[30] and his primary concern appears to be the lack of a firm basis on which to discount the husband's material interests. We have no direct evidence regarding if or how the *rodfei shalom* related to the social-emotional issues in the relationships involved, which are, as we saw, a central concern of traditional models of peacemaking (Table 5.1, category 8). However, their interests clearly included resolving the material and financial issues under dispute.

Rodfei Shalom Interceding in a Conflict between Two Rabbis: Prague, Fifteenth Century (Table 5.1, case 29)

A second case of *rodfei shalom* that survives through letters and responsa took place in Prague in 1456, where lay peacemakers attempted to resolve a dispute between two rabbis.[31] The conflict was between Rabbi Eliyah of Prague, who had been the sole rabbi and the elder of the community, and a young and relatively new rabbi in Prague, Rabbi Eliezer of Passau. Several similar conflicts were taking place in the area at this time, reflecting shifting Jewish communal leadership structures. For one, various communities were transitioning from having unofficial and unpaid local rabbis to employing institutional, paid rabbis brought in from other communities and appointed as communal rabbis.[32]

The intervention of the *rodfei shalom* is described in a letter sent to Rabbi Eliezer of Passau from a scholar named Rabbi Peretz.[33] Apparently, Rabbi Eliezer ignored the agreement brokered by the *rodfei shalom* and therefore Rabbi Peretz demands that Rabbi Eliezer leave the city of Prague immediately, since he is transgressing the prohibition of competing with one's neighbor (*hasagat g'vul*). He threatens to have Rabbi Eliezer of Passau excommunicated if he does not comply:

> And it has been over two years since this iniquity of yours began. And truthful people, *rodfei shalom*, inserted themselves, attempting to make peace between you. And they produced a *ktav* (written agreement) between you, firmly bound up and written with strong prohibitions [against transgressing the agreement].[34]

The agreement itself allowed both rabbis to remain working in Prague, but regulated their relationship and the division of roles between them. Soon after the agreement was signed, a conflict arose over its interpretation, and the brokered peace was upended.[35]

As in the previous case, the anonymous *rodfei shalom* were apparently not rabbis themselves (there is no evidence of any other rabbis in the city of Prague at the time besides than Rabbi Eliyah and Rabbi Eliezer), but respected members of the Prague Jewish community. They might have been the same community leaders to whom Rabbi Peretz wrote other letters about this subject, addressing them as "nobles of the land of the holy community of Prague."[36] Likewise, these peacemakers also functioned as a group and took the own initiative in resolving the conflict (they "inserted themselves"). The Prague case is striking, however, in that the initiative is not merely to intervene in a conflict between, say, an ordinary married couple, but to intervene and attempt to resolve a conflict between two rabbis in their town. In addition, this case points both to the practice of using written agreements for peacemaking and to the limitations of this practice, since the implementation of such an agreement hinges on its interpretation and the willingness of the parties to adhere it.

Rabbi Peretz's letter also makes clear that the *rodfei shalom* did not or could not force an agreement or a peaceful solution on the two rabbis. This is evident both from the phrase "attempting to make peace" and from the fact that they were apparently unable to enforce the document. Furthermore, Rabbi Peretz states: "At the end of the document, it is written that you accepted it upon yourselves," that is, it would not have been effective had they not included this declaimer.

A similar conflict had taken place in Regensburg, Germany, ten years earlier. The dispute there was between Rabbi Anschel Segal and Rabbi Yisrael of Bruna (known as Mahari Bruna). In a letter addressed to the leaders of the community from Rabbi Yaakov Weil, a leading rabbi at the time, Rabbi Weil criticizes the lay leaders of the community for not intervening and pursuing peace:

> I am astonished that you see and yet are silent. You should have taken the necessary efforts to make peace between them so that no destruction should come of it, God forbid! And already several communities have been destroyed as a result of disputes. Seek justice, seek peace.[37]

Rabbi Weil's expectation was that the leaders of Regensburg's Jewish community would initiate some sort of resolution. Here again the lay leaders are considered, in their non-rabbinic capacity and as a group (rather than as individuals), responsible for actively pursuing peace in their community. The communal leaders of Prague may have indeed learned from the mistake of the leaders of Regensburg.

In another case during the same period, a settlement was reached in a conflict between two rabbis in the city of Posen, Germany. In that case as well, the people who mediated between the rabbis were respected lay leaders and not rabbinic authorities. The document that settled the conflict there was signed by two mediators, one of whom is described as "distinguished" but neither of whom bear rabbinic titles or honorifics.[38]

There is one aspect of the peacemakers' role that could be misconstrued as force. They serve, as it were, as guarantors to the written agreement. We know this from the fact that after one of the peacemakers in the Posen case died the agreement had to be renewed. However, it was not renewed by an additional peacemaker but by Rabbi Yisrael Isserlein, a leading rabbi at the time. He stated that the renewal was distinct from the original agreement in that he was forcing them to comply. He writes, "I am mixing compromise (*peshara*) with law (*din*), and I am clarifying for you how the document shall be renewed."[39] The rabbinic and legal prerogative he took was unlike the original process, which produced the agreement through communal *rodfei shalom* without force.

All of these cases involve a group of non-rabbis who function as peacemakers, actively inserting themselves in a conflict or being reprimanded for not having done so. In Prague and in Posen the peacemakers had the parties in conflict agree to a resolution and sign a document, not through coercion but through a process of peacemaking of which we unfortunately have no details. But we can be certain that there were personal, emotional, and social aspects involved relating to each party's honor. In his letter to Rabbi Eliezer of Passau, Rabbi Yisrael of Bruna criticizes the two rabbis for having insulted each other. He rebukes Rabbi Eliezer for calling Rabbi Eliyah "Eliyah" several times, without his rabbinic title. Turning to Rabbi Eliyah, he writes, "I ask and plead that you also forbear and behave in a manner appropriate to the dignity of rabbi and a congregation, and its members and teachers."[40] The concern to protect the honor of an individual of high social status is similarly a salient concern common among traditional peacemaking efforts, as we have seen throughout this book.

Rodfei Shalom Interceding in a Family Conflict over Inheritance: Italy, Fifteenth Century (Table 5.1, case 30)

Whereas most of the cases of lay *rodfei shalom* involve anonymous groups of peacemakers, a fifteenth-century responsum from northern Italy written by Rabbi Yosef Colon b. Shlomo Trabotto[41] recounts a conflict in which a group of peacemakers intervened, identifying one of the peacemakers as Hayim Halfan. Based on a different responsum of Rabbi Trabotto, Halfan appears to have been the treasurer of the community.[42]

Only part of the responsum has survived, and the original question is missing. What we do know is that there was a conflict over inheritance after the death of a certain man. On one side of the conflict was the man's brother and on the other side were the man's widow and *her* brother, to whom the deceased owed a substantial amount of money. The conflict was settled by "distinguished [individuals], *rodfei* shalom, and truth." The agreement stated that the deceased man's brother would pay the full value—rather than merely the base value—of the *ketuba* payment to the widow,[43] and nullified the additional debts he would have had to pay the widow's brother. In addition, the widow and her brother agreed to swear they would not harm the deceased's brother.

After the agreement was reached, the deceased's brother attempted to appeal, claiming that what he gave "beyond the base value of her *ketuba* was given under duress, since the wife's brother had threatened to take him to non-Jewish courts." At this point, Rabbi Trabotto responds to the question. He dismisses the deceased's brother's claim, ruling in favor of the widow. This is due in part to a letter sent to him by one of the *rodfei shalom*, Hayim Halfan. Halfan attests that the deceased's brother had agreed to add on to the value of the marriage contract in exchange for all his other debts to the widow (and her brother) being nullified. He furthermore affirms that the deceased's brother had not been the subject of threats.

This source fills in with certainty some of the issues that other sources merely implied. First, although the peacemakers function as a group and are described as "distinguished" in other sources, here we have an example of the composition of such groups—in this case, Ḥayim Ḥalfan, a well-known member of the community, apparently its treasurer, and a leader whose word and perspective carries weight with a prominent rabbi. Second, while the question of whether the *rodfei shalom* (referred to here as *rodfim shalom*, which bears the same meaning) acted on their own initiative is less clear in this case—possibly due to the fragmentary nature of the evidence—the lack of coercion in the process of peacemaking is clear, and in fact central to the query. Ḥayim Ḥalfan, a neutral party, attests to the fact that the deceased's brother willingly accepted the agreement and that no threats were involved.

Acting in "the Way of Pursuers of Peace": Italy, Sixteenth Century (Table 5.1, case 31)

The source for this case is a sixteenth-century responsum written by Rabbi Meir Katznellenbogen of Padua (Maharam Padua), who was mentioned earlier in Chapter 3 (as part of case 5). The rabbi describes his own approach as being "the way of the *rodfei shalom*" with regard to a particular conflict that took place between two local rabbis from 1535 to 1542 in the city of Candia (then part of the Republic of Venice, today Heraklion on the island of Crete). Even though this is not a direct description of third-party lay leaders, since our goal here is to unpack the meaning of the phrase *rodfei shalom*, which has been found only in the context third-party lay peacemakers, it is appropriate to explore his words in this context.[44]

Rabbi Katznellenbogen describes his approach to this conflict in a letter to Rabbi Moshe Alashkar, who had also been involved as a third party in the dispute but who had chosen to take clear sides:

> [T]o rule between two celestial lions who have been warring against one another now for many days. I chose to flee from ruling between them, even though they sent their letters and explanations to me multiple times, once

I became aware that this disagreement was not for the sake of Heaven; only jealousy and competition have brought them to this place. I thought if I wrote them my absolute opinion—I would agree with one of them—then one would raise up his hand over his fellow and say, "Behold, I have won!" and the hatred would only increase between them.... So I wrote to both of them that they should not hope to receive any absolute ruling from me with regard to their dispute. And I asked them to make peace several times, and I showed each of them ways in which the other side could win, since neither are farfetched opinions. For this is the way of the *rodfei shalom*, who change [the truth] for the sake of peace, and for this reason I did not write to them my absolute opinion at all.[45]

Rabbi Katznellenbogen is of the opinion that this is not a disagreement "for the sake of Heaven"—the Mishna's term for a proper, well-intentioned, healthy disagreement.[46] Rather, he sees it rooted in jealousy, competitiveness, and the desire to win. He refuses to rule in favor of one side over the other and instead emphasizes to each party the truth and justice of the other's view. His goal, apparently, is for both sides to realize they do not have an absolute monopoly on the truth. He describes this method of slightly manipulating the truth for the sake of peace as being "the way of the *rodfei shalom*," apparently referring to what he understands to be the methods used by third-party lay peacemakers, who would go back and forth between each side, telling them things that would encourage them to ultimately compromise and make peace with their antagonist. If my suppositions about Rabbi Katznellenbogen are correct, then this source provides an important insight into at least his perception of the methods of the lay *rodfei shalom*.

It is not exactly clear what Rabbi Katznellenbogen is referring to when he mentions changing the truth for the sake of peace. It does not seem to be similar to what we saw with regard to Aaron (case 4) or to the cases described in Chapter 3 (cases 7 and 8), where the peacemakers were inventing stories. It is possible that Rabbi Katznellenbogen is acting somewhat like Rabbi Azulai did in Ancona (case 18), when he knew which way the verdict would go yet nevertheless persuaded the sides to compromise. Here too, Rabbi Katznellenbogen may know which way a strict ruling will go but is intentionally keeping that from the disputants, as he prefers to heal the situation and not just rule on the legal issue. It is also possible he is acting like a contemporary mediator who "reframes" the conflict slightly in order to enable each side to ultimately see the other's point of view.

Rodfei Shalom in Early-Modern Morocco (Table 5.1, case 32)

The descriptor *rodfei shalom* (as well as *metavkhei shalom*, mediators of peace, as we shall see) is found numerous times in the responsa literature of eighteenth- and nineteenth-century Moroccan rabbis with regard to various interpersonal conflicts, including but not limited to those between spouses. These peacemakers are usually anonymous, though one responsum concerning a conflict between a husband and wife recounts that "*rodfei shalom* stepped in, the honorable Moshe Elbaz and the honorable Shlomo b. Maimon."[47] Moshe Elbaz and Shlomo b. Maimon appear on a list of community leaders (*yechidei hakahal* or *rashei hakahal*) of the city of Sefrou in 1799.[48] Together they were considered the most authoritative, if informal, community members managing Jewish communal matters.[49]

Moshe Elbaz was a wealthy philanthropist, one of the heads of the community and among its most important representatives.[50] Shlomo b. Maimon was likewise among the heads of the community and involved in numerous communal matters.[51] In other words, these Moroccan *rodfei shalom* were not authoritative rabbis or judges but prominent communal lay leaders with considerable social status.

They did, however, have a strong relationship with the formal Jewish justice system, and consistently collaborated with it. This is evident by the signatories to the written compromise agreements the *rodfei shalom* worked with the conflicting parties to produce; they were signed not by the *rodfei shalom* themselves but by the judges of the city's Jewish court of law. This conferred full legal authority on these documents. For example, one responsum recounts: "*Rodfei shalom* stepped in and mediated (*pishru*) . . . and they had proof in their hands . . . and it was signed by [the esteemed teacher and rabbi] Shaul Yeshua Abutbul and by [the esteemed teacher and rabbi] Shlomo Abutbul."[52]

Another time, after having issued a certain judgment, Sefrou's chief judge Rabbi Shaul Yeshua Abutbul (1739–1809) decreed that if the community leaders felt that adhering strictly to the Torah's judgment (that is, to his own rabbinic judicial decision) would lead only to destruction, then it would be preferable for people to interfere "in order to mediate peace between them however they see fit."[53] He concludes:

> And what can a "hyssop on the wall" (a talmudic reference to an unimportant person)[54] such as I do other than pursue peace? The respected ones of

this glorious city want to pursue peace, as they signed [the agreement] in a manner agreeable to the sages noted above. So too, my hand should be set with theirs. Signed . . . Shaul Yeshua Abutbul.[55]

We learn from this case that *rodfei shalom* intervened in disputes in order to reconcile the two parties even *after* they had concluded the formal legal process,[56] and that judges and rabbis worked amicably with them in such cases. This connects directly back to the distinction we saw in Chapter 2 regarding Aaron pursuing peace, where some of the commentaries on the Talmud understood that since he was not acting as a judge in court, he was therefore allowed not only to bring the sides to a compromise agreement but even to do so after a judge had ruled on the matter.[57]

Additional examples help fill out our picture of *rodfei shalom* in Morocco and the cases they dealt with. In one case, which concerned a certain business conflict, "Rabbi Shimon Elasri had to put him before the judges of the city and they found him guilty . . . and the *rodfei shalom* stepped in and mediated between them."[58] In another conflict, this time between a son and his mother regarding the father's inheritance, after the judge wrote, "I have ruled that justice is with the widow and the other inheritors,"[59] a responsum recounts that "the son, on the advice of lawyers, stubbornly kept looking for different rabbinical courts, but he was not successful, and *rodfei shalom* stepped in and mediated between him and his mother."[60]

The same occurred in conflicts between spouses. For example, one responsum recounts: "He was required by law to pay her the customary fine, but *rodfei shalom* intervened and mediated between them."[61] Similarly: "After he won in court and was permitted to pay her *ketuba* payment and release her with a *get* [Jewish bill of divorce] before me in court, *rodfei shalom* intervened."[62] Another example: "I therefore ruled in favor of the husband that she may be divorced without receiving the *ketuba* payment, and after the holiday they invited us to write the bill of divorce. But after we had begun preparing the *get*, *rodfei shalom* intervened."[63] And finally: "And after I ruled on their case, *rodfei shalom* stepped in."[64]

Rabbi Yeshua Shimon Ḥayim Ovadia of Sefrou (d. 1872) wrote regarding the timing of the intervention of *rodfei shalom*:

We have seen many times, when a man and his wife are in dispute and are committing to divorce with oaths and severe vows, or he pays her the entire sum of the *ketuba* with the intention of divorcing her after thirty days in accordance with the terms, that in the meantime *rodfei shalom* step in and make peace between them, and sometimes this will be at the time of the writing of the *get*, before it is given.[65]

The *rodfei shalom* functioned in one of two ways: mediation with the goal of a written compromise agreement, or reconciliation with the goal of improving the relationship between the conflicting parties. With regard to mediation, the *rodfei shalom* would sometimes gently pressure the parties to compromise: "We urged him to add to her *ketuba* payment."[66] But the document had to be accepted by both sides, and not forced upon either side: "They accepted the compromise upon themselves."[67]

Written compromise agreements took into consideration the interests of both sides, sometimes creatively. For example, in a business dispute in which a man borrowed money in order to purchase a plot of land but was unable to repay the loan, instead of the borrower having to sell the land in order to repay the loan, as a judge would require, the parties reached a compromise with the help of *rodfei shalom*. The borrower absented himself from the land and transferred ownership to the lender, which was preferable to the borrower in this case.[68] Likewise, in a conflict between a man and his wife's heirs, whereby the man wanted to divorce his ailing wife in order not to have to share his assets with them, after the intervention of *rodfei shalom* the man agreed that he would not divorce his wife, that she would recuperate in his home, and that her heirs would relinquish their rights to anything beyond her *ketuba* payment; it would then be upon the man himself to add to that sum.[69]

Another creative solution orchestrated by *rodfei shalom* involved a conflict between the families of a betrothed bride and groom. The bride's family claimed the groom's family did not abide by its obligations under the betrothal agreement. Instead of the latter paying a fine, as they were legally required to do according to Jewish law, the two sides compromised with the aid of *rodfei shalom*. The groom's family would recommit to fulfilling its obligations under the betrothal agreement but within a new time frame. If they did not fulfill their obligations, for example by sending the betrothal gifts but not arranging the wedding on time, or by not sending the betrothal gifts on time, the bride would be free to marry someone else and would be entitled to keep the betrothal gifts as a penalty to the erstwhile bridegroom's family.[70]

Rodfei shalom engaged in reconciliation with the aim of improving relationships primarily in conflicts between spouses. One responsum recounts that they pleaded with the husband to forgive his wife and take her back to his house;[71] another mentions that they asked the husband to put off the date of the divorce so that they would have time to persuade the young woman to reconcile with him (*ledaber al lev hana'ara*).[72] It should go without saying that all the cases mentioned in this book that relate to making peace between a husband and wife (cases 1, 2, 3, 6, 22, 23, to 28) reflect a very different reality and value system than what is accepted in contemporary modern liberal societies today.

Rabbi Menahem Serero of seventeenth-century Fez, Morocco, is credited in one responsum with advice to the *rodfei shalom* regarding how to reconcile a husband and wife in a case where the wife left the husband:

> And you, the *rodfei shalom*, speak to the husband soft and good words, so that he will appease her to her satisfaction. . . . And as long as he verbally abuses her and tells her she will be forced to stay with him, she will become increasingly angry and hateful toward him. Therefore, he should be quiet in response to whatever she says, until she calms down. For we have seen many women like this. And when the husband leaves her, and he forgets about it, she returns on her own and longs for him, and they make peace between them. And they are in greater love and good friendship than those who never longed for each other.[73]

The essence of Rabbi Serero's advice is that the husband should remain quiet and not force his wife to return to him, so that she will ultimately return to him of her own free will. Notably, it seems from this source that the *rodfei shalom* would meet with each spouse separately.

Another source provides a more detailed account of the involvement of *rodfei shalom* as they attempt to reconcile a couple:

> The cries of Yehuda ibn Shalem La'arbi over the issue of his wife, Balaida, the daughter of Yitzhak ibn Shetrit, who rebelled against him (i.e., she left him), came before me many times. Time after time she would act as though she was not rebelling, giving a pretext for the [supposed] rebellion. And the *rodfei shalom* would return her to her husband by pressuring him to eliminate the reasons she gave for rebelling. When she said it was because he hit her, they made him swear not to hit her anymore. When she said that he spoke ill of her relatives they made him swear about that. And when she said it was because of their location he left his home and rented another in a place where she wanted to live.

And this time she [left her husband] for a long time and the *rodfei shalom* tried to return her [to her husband] but were unable to do so, so they stood her before me in court. And this time too she did not desist from giving reasons for her rebellion, hanging it on empty jars full of nothing (as it were). She said he would turn away from her when they lay together in bed, and when they sat together to eat he would not tell her to eat but would himself eat first of the fruits ... and leave only the leftovers for her. And sometimes he would clap his hands together in irritation and anger. And he replied that on the contrary, he appeased her the way [everyone appeases his wife], but she would not be appeased, and [wouldn't allow him to have intercourse with her].

And after we spoke at length about the ways of peace and appropriate behavior, she was reconciled, and agreed to return after her husband swore a severe oath regarding the details she had mentioned, one by one. And she too swore not to delay her ritual immersion (required before intercourse), and would behave toward him as befitted a proper daughter of Israel.

But when she left [the court], instead of going to her husband's house with the *rodfei shalom* who accompanied her, she went to the house of her father and told them to leave her there for a day or two, since she had a certain ailment. And that day [the husband] sent with the neighbors some food for her to eat, but she did not want to accept it from him. And the next day, when she was feeling better, the *rodfei shalom* returned to her, but she did not want to return [to her husband's house]. And he stood before me to issue plain judgment.[74]

This example, which clearly took place over an extended period, demonstrates the degree of dedication of these laypeople to the pursuit of peace. As in most cases that survive in the responsa literature, the *rodfei shalom* did not succeed entirely, resulting in the case coming before a Jewish court for judgment (hence, its preservation in the responsa literature). Nevertheless, from this source we learn the extent to which the *rodfei shalom* were involved throughout the duration of the spousal conflict, endeavoring to restore peace in the marriage. We can divide their involvement into three stages.

First, they enter into the conflict repeatedly in an effort to reconcile the wife to her husband by extracting promises from the husband that he will stop doing whatever is causing his wife to rebel against him. Second, after seeing that their efforts until now have been unsuccessful, they bring the couple to a rabbinic court of judges, apparently not in order for them to receive a legal judgment but to involve the judges in their efforts to reconcile the couple. The judges and the *rodfei shalom* help the couple arrive at an agreement that each party swears to uphold. This is clear evidence of the *rodfei shalom* working together with the formal Jewish legal system. Third, the *rodfei shalom* escort the wife back to her husband's home, even coming back for her after she spends the night at her father's.

To summarize, in early-modern Moroccan Jewish communities there were respected community members, not judges, who were known as *rodfei shalom* (or *metavkhei shalom*, as we will see in the next section). Although they included prominent individual communal leaders, as a group they were referred to most commonly as an anonymous collective, indicating that their authority and effectiveness did not rest on the position or name recognition of one or two well-known figures. The group appears to have had an identity of its own. They would enter of their own initiative into disputes between individuals and between spouses to help the conflicting parties arrive at a compromise agreement or a reconciliation that would return the relationship to its former state.

The *rodfei shalom* worked closely with the established Jewish legal system and maintained positive, cooperative relationships with rabbinic judges. The parties were not forced into any agreements, but would enter freely into compromises and reconciliation as a result of the involvement of the *rodfei shalom*. They helped conflicting parties come up with creative compromises that would suit each party's needs. They might hold separate meetings with each side, and would maintain their involvement even over a long period if a conflict persisted or if their efforts were unsuccessful. The evidence of their activities in early-modern Morocco makes it clear that the *rodfei shalom* as a communal institution were widely known and active.

It is only fitting to conclude this section of third-party peacemakers in Morocco with a quote by Rabbi David Ovadia (Sefrou, 1913–Jerusalem, 2010). Rabbi Ovadia was the son of the chief rabbi of Sefrou, and then served as the chief rabbi himself for several years before serving as the chief rabbi of other cities in Morocco, including Rabat and Fez. He moved to Israel in 1963, where he served as a rabbi in Jerusalem.

Rabbi Ovadia compiled five volumes of sources and documents that go back hundreds of years, which attest to the history of the Jewish community of Sefrou. Included in these documents are several instances where the term *rodfei shalom* or *metavkhei shalom* is mentioned in the context of entering into a conflict and attempting to mediate between the two sides.[75] In the section of his book in which he describes the relationship between neighbors within the Jewish community of Sefrou, Rabbi Ovadia recalls how the proximity of the homes to one another at times led to extremely tense and violent clashes between neighbors. But then he concludes:

> Once matters calmed down a bit, *metavkhei shalom* would enter in and make peace between them, then they would do a *"sulha"* and a party to celebrate the peace. The friendship [between them] after peace [was achieved] was often tighter than before the fight.[76]

Rav Ovadia testifies that third-party peacemakers in the Jewish community of Morocco would facilitate a festive ceremony, which he refers to as being like a *sulha*, as a symbol of reconciliation and restoration of relationship.

Metavkhei Shalom (Mediators of Peace)

A second term used to describe those trying to make peace between rival parties, without force or recourse to formal legal authority, is *metavkhei shalom* (mediators of peace). The term *metavkhei shalom* can be reasonably understood as interchangeable with *rodfei shalom*, as both terms describe not judges but respected laypeople in a community who engaged in the same sorts of activities. They would intervene in an interpersonal conflict before the disputing parties took their cases to court. They would not force a compromise between the parties, but would "mediate between them" (*mefashrim beineihem*).[77]

For example, the following query was sent to Rabbi Shaul Yeshua Abutbul with regard to a complicated family business dispute in eighteenth-century Morocco:

> *Metavkhei shalom* ... intervened ... and mediated between them concerning oaths, without any mention of force or compulsion at all, and [the disputants] accepted upon themselves the compromise with a commitment and a severe oath, by their own simple will. ... [The *metavkhei shalom*] mediated between them with words of love and fellowship concerning the oath.[78]

Part of the dispute in this case was that one of the *metavkhei shalom* was a Torah scholar from the local court and therefore one of the sides accused him of forcing the compromise upon them, and thus the responsum emphasized that the compromise was only done through "words of love and fellowship," without any coercion or force.

In another dispute, this time between business partners in eighteenth-century Morocco who had decided to dissolve the partnership, we read in a query written to Rabbi Refael Bardugo, that "after some time, *metavkhei shalom* stepped in and restored their partnership regarding the aforementioned fields to the way it had been."[79] In an eighteenth-century financial dispute in Syria between a father and a son, we read that "the *metavkhei shalom* entered and mediated between them (*ufishru beineihem*)."[80]

Another dispute was settled by *metavkhei shalom* as late as mid-twentieth century Egypt. A husband found a blemish in his wife and was about to divorce her. Then "the *metavkhei shalom* intervened to return her to her original state, and if by that [predetermined] time the blemish or defect was remedied they would stay together, and if not he would divorce her and pay her the sum of her *ketuba*."[81] Similarly, in the case of a man who discovered only after his wedding that his wife was not a virgin and therefore wanted to divorce her, "the *metavkhei shalom* stepped in between the spouses . . . and with pleading and appeasement the husband became willing to live with her."[82] This case, from the 1950s in Egypt, is the latest example I have found that describes laypeople as *metavkhei shalom* (or any of the other terms discussed in this chapter).

As noted, the *metavkhei shalom* were supposed to always mediate in a noncoercive manner, however, the concern that they may not always do so may have always existed. A good example of this can be found in the words of Rabbi Joseph Molkho (1688–1760, Thessaloniki) in his comment on the rabbinic legal question discussed in Chapter 3, of whether or not an offending party must go themselves to ask forgiveness of their victim, or can they send a third-party peacemaker to do so on their behalf.[83] Rabbi Molkho, after citing the words of Rabbi Yackov Ibn Haviv (discussed in Chapter 3), who held that such a custom of sending a third-party was mistaken, writes:

> Also in this time, this custom has become wide spread, when one person sins against another, *metavkhei shalom* are entered in between them in order to mediate the peace, not out of the will of the one forgiving and not out of the will of the one asking to be forgiven. And this is not the correct path. For since the forgiveness is forced upon the one forgiving, he only forgives in front of the *metavkhei shalom*, "but in his heart he lies in wait

for him" (Jeremiah 9:7). And all the more so, when the one asking for forgiveness doesn't go to the one forgiving on his own and of his own will, but rather they bring him against his will, for in such an instance for sure the forgiveness is not (regarded as) forgiveness. Rather (forgiveness is only) when the one asking for forgiveness goes on his own and of his own will to reconcile with (his) words, and the one forgiving forgives from his heart and soul.[84]

Rabbi Molkho equates here the offending party going on their own to ask forgiveness from their victim with going of free will and no coercion. It is assumed that if the *metavkhei shalom* are involved in going back and forth between the sides that there is a coercive and insincere process which is not regarded as authentic forgiveness.[85] Below are two examples where third-party lay peacemakers are referred to as *metavkhei shalom*. The first is a letter sent from an immigrant to the Land of Israel in the early seventeenth century containing a near mythical description of *metavkhei shalom*, and the second is a query describing how a *metavekh shalom* found himself in an extremely vulnerable situation as a result of his good will in trying to make peace.

The Custom of Metavkhei Shalom in Seventeenth-Century Safed (Table 5.2, case 33)

This case was reported by Rabbi Shlomo Shlumiel Minstrel, who was born in Moravia and moved to Safed in 1602 at the age of 28. Between the years 1607 and 1609 he wrote several letters to friends and relatives describing the greatness of the Land of Israel, including the community of Safed. The following is from a letter he wrote to his brother-in-law in 1607:

[T]here are good customs practiced in the Land of Israel, such that there are no disputes or fights between people, even among the laypeople. And sometimes when they do dispute with each other, a bystander would think that at any moment they are going to kill each other in their anger. But I testify by heaven and earth that the bystanders (who take the role of *metavkhei shalom*) do not move from there until [the parties in conflict] become like brothers and friends, together, and they hug and kiss each other. The younger of the two asks forgiveness from the other, and he hugs and kisses him on his face and on his neck. And all of the curses and insults that they had said about each another are forgotten as if they had never been said. And the bystanders near the fight are the *hametavkhim shalom* between them, and they do not let them move from one another until they make peace and eternal forgiveness between them.

And if they have a dispute over an unjustified loss of money, they mediate between them (*mefashrim beineihem*). And if one of the parties in the argument preempts and swears that he does not owe the other anything, in just a moment the other forgives him, saying: "Why would I take you to court if you've preempted and sworn?"

And if one of them scorns a rabbi or a great scholar, the fine is great, for the rabbi would decree upon him excommunication. [But the scorner] immediately removes his shoes and sits on the ground for (merely) the time it takes to roast an egg, and immediately the rabbi says to him, "Stand up." He immediately gets up and kisses the sage on his knees or on his legs, and the sage says to him three times, "It is released: there is no ban and there is no excommunication. Your transgression is removed and your sin will be forgiven," and he sends him off in peace.[86]

This remarkable text attests to the widely practiced and highly successful conflict resolution mechanisms in Safed in the early seventeenth century, even if in a somewhat exaggerated fashion (characteristic of this author). To understand exactly what Rabbi Minstrel is describing, however, requires careful examination of the many telling phrases he employs.[87]

First, Rabbi Minstrel introduces his description as "good customs practiced in the Land of Israel," which is to say that he is not describing a onetime event that he happened to witness—or even a handful of occurrences. Describing these as "customs" indicates he understands this to be (or at least wants to portray it as) a widespread *model of peacemaking*. Furthermore, he describes these customs as common "even among the laypeople" (*amei ha'aretz*); in other words, these practices are employed within the entire Jewish community. The term *amei ha'aretz*, translated here as "laypeople," generally refers to those who are particularly unsophisticated or even coarse in their behavior, which is why Rabbi Minstrel writes, "*even* among the laypeople."

This peacemaking model is apparently employed even at the most heated stages, early in a conflict, when "a bystander would think that at any moment they are going to kill each other in their anger." One might think that a moment such as this would not lend itself to mediation but would be more suited to formal legal intervention, but Minstrel makes clear that the mediators, whom he refers to as *hametavkhim shalom*, do not shy away from stepping in at this point.

Later in the letter, Rabbi Minstrel refers to "curses and insults" that had been exchanged before the *metavkhei shalom* intervened. In light of such an intense conflict, the earlier phrase, "[the mediators] do not move from there," points to the corresponding intensity of the mediation process, which continues until the entire process of peacemaking is complete. Rabbi Minstrel adds that the mediators "do not let them move from one another until they make peace and eternal forgiveness between them." The active expression, "do not let them move," makes it even clearer that even if they meet resistance at some point from the parties in conflict, they pressure them to continue working through the process of peacemaking until it is complete. Minstrel also makes clear that this is a process of reconciliation, where the goal is not only to reach a practical agreement to resolve the conflict, but to repair the relationship between the two parties as well, "until they become like brothers and friends." We have already seen that there are multiple ways to accomplish this.

The Safed model, in contrast to the legend of Aaron (case 4) and the *sulha* model in which the peacemakers meet separately with each party, seems to involve both parties working together with the mediator—as is the norm in modern-Western models such as Interactive Problem-Solving Workshops (see Chap. 1). This is what Rabbi Minstrel appears to mean when he writes, "until they become like brothers and friends, *together*." What this model does share with the legend of Aaron and the *sulha* model is the conclusion of the process in which the parties "hug and kiss each other." However, reconciliation between the sides is not enough if the dispute is financial; the *metavkhei shalom* "mediate between them," meaning they presumably bring about some type of formal compromise agreement that resolves the financial aspects of the conflict.

When Rabbi Minstrel identifies the third-party peacemakers as *hametavkhim shalom*, he is describing none other than the "bystanders." That is to say, the people who engage in this work are not rabbis and judges, nor are they professional or quasi-professional peacemakers. In fact, they are not even a consistent group of individuals, but comprise whoever has witnessed the conflict unfold. One can assume that this implies they know the people who are fighting, or minimally that they saw what transpired so far in the conflict with their own eyes. This aspect of the model points to how widely it was known and practiced; even people who only happened to be bystanders were able and willing to interfere in this way and play the role of the peacemakers.

The issue of power imbalance appears in this text in two contexts. First, the younger party must take the initiative in asking for forgiveness. Second, in the last paragraph Rabbi Minstrel stresses the severity of entering into a conflict with a rabbi or Torah scholar, as the other party must physically demonstrate remorse and respect for the offended side. This is because of the cultural importance of personal honor, apparent in the Jewish community of Safed described here and of course in other traditional societies such as in the Arab communities who practice the *sulha*. The party with lesser social status must return the greater party to its former social status and reestablish the honor that had been sullied. In turn, the party of higher status is willing to forgive and reconcile immediately. The issue of personal honor is generally not part of the equation in modern-Western models.

Although we have only Rabbi Minstrel's description of the *metavkhei shalom* of seventeenth-century Safed, it gives us window into a third-party peacemaking model that shares a great deal in common with those we have surveyed until now—its own idiosyncrasies notwithstanding. This model presents laypeople, referred to here as *hametavkhim shalom*, engaging in what must have been an elaborate process of mediation and peacemaking at times, yet in the end proves successful.

The Vulnerability of a Nineteenth-Century Metavekh Shalom (Table 5.2, case 34)

In the previous example enumerating the peacemaking custom of Safed, power dynamics were acknowledged (younger/older, layperson/rabbi), all sides acted appropriately in accordance with their social status, and peace was quickly restored with the help of the *metavkhei shalom*. But it was not always so simple. A second example of third-party lay peacemakers referred to as *metavkhei shalom* appears in a nineteenth-century responsum from Baghdad, and tells of power discrepancies between the sides that exposed the vulnerability of the third side.

In the legends of Aaron (case 4) and Rabbi Meir (case 6), and occasionally in the *sulha* model as well, we saw that a third-party peacemaker would be willing to sustain personal humiliation if it would aid in the peacemaking process, but this was not indicated in the examples of lay peacemakers in medieval and early-modern Jewish communities. Likewise, we read that Rabbi Palagi called upon lay peacemakers to remain patient even as they are being cursed or beaten, but we have not yet seen an actual example of peacemakers taking on personal risk in their peacemaking efforts. The following case shows how a lay peacemaker put himself at personal financial risk in his role as a *metavekh shalom*. The names given, as is common in responsa literature, are pseudonyms. The query was sent to Rabbi Yosef Hayim (Iraq, 1835–1909), generally known as the Ben Ish Hai, after his book of the same name, and reads as follows:

> Reuben, who is among the respected, important men of the city, had a big dispute with Simon, and the *metavkhei hashalom* came to make peace between them. Reuben, due to his power and strength, did not agree to make peace with Simon until Simon agreed to pay him such and such a sum as a gift. And he set a time of thirty days, and Simon accepted the obligation fully and completely to pay Reuben the set amount by a certain time, and he gave him a receipt signed by witnesses. And Reuben wanted a guarantor, so in order not to undermine the peace, Levi (one of the *metavkhei shalom*) agreed to serve as the guarantor. . . . And when the time arrived for payment of the gift, Simon was unable to give Reuben the set amount that he owed him. So Reuben went to retrieve the sum from Levi, the guarantor. Can Reuben take this sum from Levi based on the contract he signed, even though Levi was one of the *metavkhei hashalom* and (only) tried to make peace, and it would be harsh to obligate him to pay money also?[88]

In his concern to establish and maintain peace between Reuben and Simon, Levi, who served as one of the *metavkhei shalom*, agreed to serve as a guarantor for the weaker, more vulnerable party (Simon), despite the fact that the original conflict presumably had nothing to do with money. The phenomenon of a third-party peacemaker stepping in financially with the aim of resolving the conflict on behalf of one of the sides can be found in other traditional cultural models of third-party peacemaking.[89] Here, the question is whether in practice Levi has to actually pay the money he agreed to guarantee.

The Ben Ish Ḥai answers that according to every opinion in the legal (halakhic) literature, the *metavekh shalom* is not obligated to pay, since "he did this *mitzva* in order to make peace between them."[90] It is difficult to say with certainty what the Ben Ish Ḥai had in mind by referring to this as a *mitzva*, since he does not elaborate on this point. However, based on his legal ruling, Levi is freed from what otherwise appears to be a straightforward legal obligation for having intervened in order to make peace. We can also assume from his ruling that the Ben Ish Ḥai considers laypeople serving as *metavkhei shalom* to be an exceedingly admirable activity.

In his response, the Ben Ish Ḥai goes on to denounce the very need for the weaker side to offer a financial gift to the more powerful side in order to make peace, insisting that "certainly strict law obligates Reuben to make peace with Simon for free; why should he take money?"[91] While this claim is made within the context of trying to free the peacemaker from his financial obligation, what arises from it is a challenge against the accepted practice in peacemaking whereby the stronger side overly leverages and thus abuses his power against the weaker side. Thus the rabbi is calling upon the community to whom he is responding to do more to serve as third-party "equalizers" and not to succumb to the more powerful side always getting their way—a demand perhaps easier said from afar than practically implemented from up close.

Pashranim and *Mefashrim* (Compromisers)

A third term used to refer to third-party lay peacemakers, similar to *rodfei shalom* and *metavkhei shalom*, is *pashranim* or *mefashrim* (compromisers). Both were used to refer to well-respected laypeople in the Jewish community[92] who entered into disputes on their own initiative, with no authority to force a compromise agreement on the parties.[93]

Sometimes these terms can be found being used interchangeably with *metavkhei shalom*. For example, both terms are used in a query addressed to Rabbi Ḥayim Palagi regarding a dispute over inheritance between the heirs of the deceased and the trustees of his assets earmarked for the community:

> If the *pashranim* enter into this matter in order to make peace ... when they see that each side holds its own opinion and has committed itself to sitting

passive-aggressively, and [the disputants] have not yet reached common ground, and for that reason *metavkhei shalom* come and seek to facilitate a compromise . . . are [we] permitted to accept this and be appeased with the compromise that they facilitate?[94]

Similarly, a query addressed to the Ben Ish Ḥai regarding a business dispute notes that "the *pashranim, metavkhei shalom*, stood between them without a judge or judgment."[95] Here the term *metavkhei shalom* is used as an enumeration of the term *pashranim*. The term *pashranim* can also be used to refer to arbitrators (*borerim*), meaning judges who were chosen by both sides to issue a ruling that would serve as a compromise. Once the parties accept the authority of an arbitrator they are legally bound to abide by the arbitrator's decision.[96]

Sometimes multiple meanings of the same term are used in a single letter. For example, a query sent to Rabbi Yitzḥak bar Sheshet tells how *mefashrim* attempted numerous times to bring peace between a couple in a complicated marital dispute that took place in 1398 in Ancona, Italy:

> *Mefashrim* entered between them, so that [the couple] would stay together in a different house for four months, because perhaps the marital problem is caused by the location, and they did this, and they stayed together approximately two months. And [as in Genesis 32:26, when Jacob wrestled with the angel] "he saw that he could not prevail," and he ran away to a different place; and their claims against each other multiplied. After that, *mefashrim* entered between them, so that they would remain [together in their home] another twelve months.[97]

These *mefashrim* are clearly well-intended third-party lay peacemakers who attempt over and over to reconcile between the couple.[98] Later in the same letter it is related that the husband sent his own well-respected "*mefashrim*" with the demand that he would agree to divorce his wife only if her rich brother paid him a large sum of money.[99] Further on, it is told that the judges who served as agreed-upon rabbinic arbitrators attempted to compromise between them ("*mefashrim*" *beineihem*) in order that they would stay together.[100] Thus in the same letter, the term *mefashrim* is used to describe three different groups of third-party interveners: mediators like the *rodfei shalom* and *metavkhei shalom*; rabbinic arbitrators, who functioned as *borerim*; and messengers on behalf of one of the sides in the conflict. Scholars searching for additional examples within the literature should be attuned to these terms and their nuances, as the vast corpus of rabbinic responsa does not always reflect consistent usage of these terms.

It is sometimes possible to identify the type of *pashranim* or *mefashrim* by the actions ascribed to them. When they are described as having "stepped in"[101] or as "entered into" a dispute on their own initiative, the term is referring to lay third-party peacemakers, as we have seen above in the context of *rodfei shalom* or *metavkhei shalom*. The following is one example of respected lay leaders referred to as *pashranim* that describes both a context and a method of peacemaking not yet seen in this book.

Intercommunal *Pashranim* in the Sixteenth Century: Symbolically Burning the Causes of Conflict
(Table 5.2, case 35)

All the conflicts presented so far in this book have been interpersonal, whether between two leaders, two individuals, or husband and wife. A good example of a third party making peace between groups of people and not only individuals can be found in a query sent to the Maharshdam (Rabbi Shmuel b. Moshe de Medina, whom we met in Chapter 4 in connection with case 24). According to the author of the query, whose identity and location are unknown, there were two separate Jewish communities in the same city, as was quite common in the immediate generations after the expulsion from Spain at the end of the fifteenth century. Over time, tensions between the two communities grew, each one taking upon itself certain communal agreements of oaths and bans against the other, which subsequently led to further tension and conflict between the two communities.[102] That is, until one day:

> *Anashim nikhbadim* (well-respected people) from a different city came to the city, and when they saw the conflict between [the two communities], and the desecration of God's name that was made by them, they had courage to make peace between the two sides, for "great is peace," etc. And so they did. And the communities made a

compromise that all the agreements (*haskamot*) and bans (*ḥaramot*) that they made against one another would be nullified and considered like broken clay, and that [those documents] would be handed over to these *pashranim* to be burned and destroyed from the world, and this is what they did.[103]

The author describes here how a group of peacemakers referred to as *pashranim*, which was composed of several well-respected lay leaders from a nearby city and therefore neutral, pursued peace between two Jewish communities in dwelling in the same city. They took the initiative to intervene during their visit to the city when they saw the profanation of God's name. Their visit did not seem to be for the purpose of pursuing peace, although they do appear to have stayed in the city long enough to resolve the various deep community conflicts.[104]

According to the author of the query sent to the Maharshdam, the group of *pashranim* spoke to both sides about the importance of peace, even though their exact words are not preserved. Then they proceeded to resolve the conflict between the two communities by physically burning and destroying the communal agreements that had been made by each community against the other, thereby symbolizing an end to the hostile era between the two. It is also reasonable to assume that the fact that the author refers to them as *pashranim* indicates that they indeed brought the community to a compromise agreement, which was symbolized by the burning of the old agreements. However, no such agreement is mentioned explicitly in the letter.

Several important lessons can be learned from this historical account regarding the identity and methods of these intercommunal peacemakers. First, they were referred to as both *pashranim* and also simply as *nikhbadim* (well-respected individuals), a term that will be explored in the following section. Second, they were "outsiders" who took the initiative to make peace between the communities. Third, and particularly striking, is their method of ritually burning and destroying the physical community agreements that were at the heart of the conflict.[105] Notably, certain African nations today symbolically demonstrate the end of a civil war through a public ritual of burning the weapons that were used to hurt one another.[106] There is a powerful lesson here regarding using such public rituals in intergroup disputes to represent the end of conflict and reestablish relations between the sides.

Nikhbadim and Hashuvim
(Well-respected and Distinguished Lay Leaders)

In this chapter we have seen three quasi-titles used to refer to third-party lay peacemakers in medieval and early-modern rabbinic literature. In addition to these, there are also cases in which no particular title is ascribed to the peacemakers, but the descriptions of their activities fit the same or a similar mold as that of a well-respected, third-party lay peacemaker. Sometimes these people were referred to with a more generic terms such as *nikhbadim* (well-respected individuals) and *hashuvim* (distinguished individuals). One example is in a responsum of Rabbi Aharon b. Yosef Sasson (Thessaloniki, Kushta; 1550–1626), where he attempts to encourage a father and son who had sued one another in court:

> It is appropriate that the father and son not say, "Let the law pierce through mountains";[107] rather, they should reconcile with one another on their own, or at least *nikhbadim* should enter in between them to mediate the peace between them, for great is peace![108]

Another example in which the title *nikhbadim* is used to refer to third-party lay peacemakers is found in a sixteenth-century letter addressed to Rabbi Yosef Karo in Safed, which describes a dispute in the city of Manissa (modern Turkey).[109] The dispute, which was primarily between two communities, included a personal conflict between the local *hakham* (sage or rabbi) and "one of the *kohanim* (priests)—though not of the seed of Aaron in his actions."[110] On the holiday of Sukkot, in front of the entire community in the synagogue, the *kohen* cursed and disgraced the *hakham*, and in response the *hakham* excommunicated him. At this point there is a description of an intervention of the *nikhbadim*:

> Official representatives of the communities came to appease the *hakham*, so that [the *kohen*] could come and ask forgiveness from him. The *hakham* conceded to the request of the *nikhbadim*, so that "the left [hand] should push away while the right [hand] should draw close."[111] And [the *kohen*] came and asked forgiveness from the *hakham* and kissed his hands.

In this case the *nikhbadim*, who are described here as official representatives of the different communities, facilitated a classic asymmetric reconciliation ceremony, reminiscent of the one described by Rabbi Minstrel in case 33 and of the *sulha* ceremony, in which the less respected side asks forgiveness and kisses the hands of the more respected side. As it turns out, in this case the feelings of hatred were not sufficiently attended to, and consequently the *kohen* did not asked to be released from the *hakham*'s excommunication and the *hakham* in turn did not initiate nullifying the ban![112]

Sometimes these well-respected laypeople were simply referred to as *hashuvim*, distinguished people. For example, in the previous chapter we saw Rabbi Avraham b. Moshe b. Maimon (case 26) describe how he took with him "sages (*hakhamim*), elders (*zekeinim*), and distinguished people (*hashuvim*)" to try to make peace between the sides in conflict.[113] Another example in which the third party is described as a *hashuv* is that of Bishr b. Aharon. It is the earliest historical account of a lay peacemaker found in medieval rabbinic literature and is extremely rich with details of the peacemaking process.

Bishr b. Aharon, the Paradigmatic Lay Peacemaker: Baghdad, Tenth Century (Table 5.2, case 36)

The story of Bishr b. Aharon appears in the tenth-century Babylonian historiographical work, *Seder olam zuta* of Rabbi Natan b. Yitzhak the Babylonian, the same source that preserved the story of Rabbi Nissi discussed at the end of the previous chapter (case 27). The conflict in question developed against the background of a larger conflict between Rabbi Sa'adya Gaon, essentially the chief rabbinic leader in Babylonia, and the Exilarch, David b. Zakkai, the chief political leader of the Babylonian Jewish community and one of the sides in the conflict examined in the previous chapter.[114] As a result of a dispute regarding a judicial decision, they each attempted to depose the other and install an alternative leader in the other's stead. The conflict had already persisted for seven years when one of the supporters of the Exilarch, Khalaf Sarjado, bribed the Muslim authorities to depose the Rabbi Sa'adya, and thus an open conflict between Rabbi Sa'adya and the Exilarch ensued. This took place roughly in the year 937 in Baghdad.

Two people sought an arbitrator to deal with a certain dispute between them. One chose David b. Zakkai, while the other chose Rabbi

Sa'adya Gaon. The Exilarch was so furious at the litigant who chose Rabbi Sa'adya Gaon, whom the former had deposed, that he ordered the litigant to be physically beaten. The beating nearly killed the litigant. As a result, the community began to take action, hoping to reconcile the Gaon and the Exilarch, under the guidance of Bishr b. Aharon, a wealthy Jewish banker who was an extremely prominent figure at the time.[115] The full text of the Natan the Babylonian's description of the process is worth presenting:

> And everyone gathered before Bishr b. Aharon, who was the father-in-law of Khalaf Sarjado (who had bribed the authorities to depose Rabbi Sa'adya seven years prior), and a prominent figure in Babylonia and among the distinguished people of his region (*ḥashuvei mekomo*), and they told him of the extent this dispute (*makhloket*) within Israel had reached and how awful the events were. They said to him, "Arise, for the matter is upon you, and we are with you, and perhaps we can remove the dispute, which is only about your son-in-law Khalaf Sarjado." And Bishr went to the prominent men of the generation and gathered them in his house. And the Exilarch was with them, and [Bishr] spoke to [the Exilarch] in front of them: "What is this thing that you have done? How much longer will you 'hold on to this dispute'[116] and not protect yourself from punishment? Fear your God, and remove yourself from the dispute, for you know how great the dispute has become. So now, look into how you can repair your ways with Rabbi Sa'adya and make peace with him, and lay to rest whatever is in your heart about him."
>
> The Exilarch answered him with peace that he would do as he said.
>
> And he arose and went to Rabbi Sa'adya and brought him to [Bishr's] house, he and his entourage, and [Bishr] said to him all the same things he had said to the Exilarch, and [Rabbi Sa'adya] too answered with peace.
>
> And the Exilarch was in one house along with his entourage, and Rabbi Sa'adya, along with his entourage, was in another house opposite that one. And both houses were in the courtyard of this Bishr, who went between them with words of peace. And the men from among the heads of the community arose and divided into two groups; one group held the hands of the Exilarch and the other held the hands of Rabbi Sa'adya. And one group came from one side, and the other group came from the other side, until they met each other, and they kissed each other and embraced each other. And this took place on the Fast of Esther (the day before the

festival of Purim, on which the scroll of Esther is read). And when this was complete, Bishr was happy that they had made peace through his efforts.

And he had them and all those who were standing there with them swear that they would sleep that night in his house, and that they would read the scroll (of Esther) in his house. Neither the Exilarch nor Rabbi Sa'adya wanted to do so. Rather, the Exilarch said that either Rabbi Sa'adya would feast at [the Exilarch's] house or he would feast at Rabbi Sa'adya's house. They drew lots between them, and the lot fell to the Exilarch, such that Rabbi Sa'adya would go to his home, which he did. He went to his house and feasted with him the feast of Purim, and he stayed there for two days. On the third day he left happily and in good spirits.

And when the compromise (*hapeshara*) was made between them, Rabbi Yosef b. Yaakov, whom the Exilarch had appointed to replace Rabbi Sa'adya as head of the academy all those years of the dispute between them, now that the dispute was nullified, this Rabbi Yosef (who was the) head of the academy, would sit in his home, yet nevertheless, the salary that he was earning as head of the academy, would not be denied from him, rather they would send it to his home.[117]

This story begins with "everyone," an anonymous entity indicating the larger community, approaching the highly respected Bishr b. Aharon—who had a direct connection to the conflict through his son-in-law—to intervene in the dispute between the two powerful leaders once it had become violent. Bishr then gathers other respected communal leaders well connected to the disputants to assist him in facilitating a successful reconciliation process between the Exilarch and Rabbi Sa'adya Gaon. He first holds separate meetings with each party at his large estate, communicating the same message and encouraging each one to let go of the dispute and reconcile. This, of course, is highly reminiscent of the legend of Aaron (case 4) and the *sulha* process, but quite different from modern-Western models of third-party reconciliation such as Interactive Problem-Solving Workshops.

Bishr uses language and metaphors that would have resonated with both parties.[118] His message to each disputant includes a subtle reference to a talmudic passage that presumably both of them would have been familiar with. When he says, "How much longer will you hold on to this dispute," he invokes the following Talmudic passage:

"Moses rose up and went to Dathan and Abiram" (Num. 16:25). Reish Lakish said, "From this we learn that one should not hold on to a dispute, as Rav said, Anyone who holds on to a dispute transgresses a prohibition of the Torah, as it is stated (Num. 17:5): 'That he fare not as Korah, and as his company.'" Rav Ashi said, "[One who does so] deserves to suffer."[119]

The continuation of this Talmudic passage makes it particularly appropriate to this situation, as various rabbis discuss the severity of engaging in conflict with a rabbi (such as Rabbi Sa'adya Gaon) or with the house of David (such as the Exilarch, David b. Zakkai, who was understood to be a descendant of the royal house of David):

> Rabbi Yosei said, "Anyone who engages in a dispute with the kingdom of the house of David deserves to be bitten by a snake. . . ." Rav Hisda said, "Anyone who engages in a dispute with his rabbi is as one who engages in a dispute with the Divine."[120]

Bishr installs each side in a separate house within his courtyard and goes back and forth, meeting with each party alone. Both sides are separately and lavishly escorted by an entourage to a festive reconciliation encounter in the courtyard culminating with the sides kissing and embracing. The depth of the reconciliation is indicated by David b. Zakkai's insistence that they feast not at Bishr's home, a neutral space, but at one of their own homes. They further solidify their renewed relationship with a two-day stay together, which ends peacefully and happily. There is evidence that this was in fact a lasting reconciliation between the two; after David b. Zakkai died two years later, followed shortly thereafter by the death of his son, Rabbi Sa'adya Gaon took it upon himself to take care of the Exilarch's grandson, who was only twelve years old at the time he inherited his grandfather's position.[121]

The timing of the reconciliation between Sa'adya Gaon and David b. Zakkai around the holiday of Purim and the fast day that precedes it may not be a coincidence. Purim symbolizes Jewish unity in the face of external threats, and its observance culminates in a festive meal that marks the transformation of calamity into joy. Moreover, the concluding words of the scroll of Esther describe the hero Mordecai as "speaking peace to all his people."[122] Purim is also marked by reciprocal gift-giving (specifically of food) within the Jewish community. Both this gesture and the festive meal symbolize the strengthening of communal peace and harmony, which in essence the disputants in our story were symbolically fulfilling by each offering to host the other. In addition, the casting of lots to determine in whose home the meal would be eaten recalls one of the major themes of the scroll of Esther (Est. 3:7, 9:24). Facilitating this reconciliation process within the sacred time of the holiday of Purim establishes a larger perspective of the events, the strengthening of a common identity, and an atmosphere of peace.

The reconciliation process described by Natan the Babylonian is a near-exact parallel to the Arab-Islamic *sulha*. A well-respected third party consisting of several notables shuttles back and forth between each side in the conflict. The two sides come together in a public gathering in a neutral place, full of displays of reconciliation. They then visit each other's homes (in our case, they went to David b. Zakkai's home only) and partake in a festive meal.

What is distinct in this case is the absolute symmetry between the two sides in conflict. Neither Bishr nor the community appears to favor one side over the other; the power each wields and the respect each commands appear to be equal. This comes on the heels of shifting and contentious power struggles between the two, each, as noted, having attempted to depose the other. While the Exilarch had formal political power and connections to the Muslim authorities, the community's respect for him may have diminished after he had a man beaten nearly to death. Rabbi Sa'adya Gaon, as the former head of the academy, had at the time no formal political power, but his influence within the community had increased considerably during the years of his conflict with the Exilarch. A reconciliation that leveled the playing field in a clear, visible way was particularly suited to this conflict.

After the reconciliation, the account concludes with a brief report about the compromise the two sides agreed upon. This appears to refer to a formal agreement that resolved the political and financial aspects of the dispute. Since the Exilarch had deposed Rabbi Sa'adya from his position as head of the academy (an appointment always made by the Exilarch), Rabbi Yosef b. Yaakov was serving as head of the academy and being paid in this capacity. Now that Sa'adya would, by all accounts, be reinstated as the sole head of the academy, they had to decide what to do with Rabbi Yosef b. Yaakov. There are no details as to how the agreement came about or regarding any formal processes associated with it (such as a written agreement), or even at which point in relation to the reconciliation ceremony they reached the compromise. The upshot, however, is that Rabbi Yosef b. Yaakov is removed from office, but he continues to be paid his salary.

The addition of this brief section highlights the goals of the reconciliation process facilitated by Bishr. This process aimed to both solve the practical problems of who exactly should serve in what capacity within the community through a compromise agreement, as well as conduct a transformation of the relationship between the sides and facilitate reconciliation.

***

In this chapter we saw several cases of third-party lay peacemakers. For convenience's sake, I grouped the cases based on the title used to describe the peacemakers: *rodfei shalom*, *metavkhei shalom*, *pashranim/mefashrim*, and *nikhbadim/ḥashuvim*—although no evidence points to any substantive difference between them. All titles represent a group of lay leaders (as opposed to religious leaders) whose peacemaking role is characterized by the fact that they always acted in groups and not as individuals, as is clear from the consistent usage of the plural forms of their titles (i.e., *rodfei shalom* and not *rodef shalom*; see category 2 in the tables at the end of this chapter). They almost always are described as "entering into" a dispute and generally do not wait to be invited in by others, in particular by the sides themselves (category 5).

The conflicts these lay leaders intervened in included disputes between neighbors, business partners, spouses, family members, and occasionally two factions in the same community (category 1). The goals of these peacemakers depended in large part on the nature of the conflict. If it involved a monetary dispute, they strove to facilitate a compromise agreement that was noncoercive (category 7). If the conflict involved damage to one side's honor or to the relationship, they would help facilitate reconciliation between the disputants, thereby restoring honor and reestablishing healthy relationships between the sides (category 8).

Exploring these cases of lay peacemakers is valuable on multiple levels. From a historical perspective, we see precedents for groups of Jewish laypeople serving as third-party peacemakers from as far back as the tenth century and as recently as the nineteenth century. These laypeople came from the ranks of dignitaries, wealthy leaders, communal appointees, and occasionally even humble bystanders. They also span geographic location, with cases coming from Baghdad, Prague, Spain, Italy, and Morocco, to name just a few, therefore including both Sephardic and Ashkenazic Jewish communities (although there are many more sources found among Sephardic communities in Arab-Islamic lands, particularly in Morocco).

From a theoretical, cross-cultural perspective, there are clear affinities between the values and concomitant peacemaking practices of these Jewish lay peacemakers and those found in numerous other traditional and indigenous third-party peacemaking processes—as opposed to modern-Western models of third-party peacemakers. One particular example is the *jaha* in the Arab *sulha* model, where third-party lay peacemakers also play a central role in the process.[123] However, many other indigenous third-party lay peacemakers also emphasize brokering a compromise agreement regarding the monetary aspects of the dispute, as well as restoring the honor of those whose social or religious status was infringed upon.

One potential unique aspect of Jewish lay peacemakers that may set them apart from traditional third-party lay peacemakers in other cultures and religions is their characteristic of "entering in" to the conflict on their own initiative, literally "pursuing" peace between the sides, without waiting for one of the disputants to approach them and ask them to intervene on their behalf. This accords with one of the interpretations of the difference between loving peace and pursuing peace we saw in Chapter 2. However, this is speculative, as clearly in most traditional "collectivist" societies, when two parties are stuck in conflict, a third side will take the initiative to intervene.

Practical Implications for Third-Party Peacemaking Today

We can draw several important, practical lessons relevant to peacemaking and mediation today from the core characteristics of the Jewish lay peacemakers we explored in this chapter. These include:

1. The importance of working as part of a network of "pursuers" and not alone, thereby bringing together various relationships and connections;

2. The importance of taking the initiative and not waiting to be invited in to a conflict;

3. The significance brokering a practical, agreed-upon, noncoercive compromise;

4. The importance of being mindful of the breakdown in the relationship between the disputants and the need to reestablish it through processes and ceremonies of reconciliation—which need to be authentic and not simply lip service;

5. The value of using symbols and rituals to mark the end of conflict and to reestablish relations, for example by burning damaging documents and eating a festive meal together; and finally,

6. The ever-significant fact that it is the responsibility of laypeople to engage in peacemaking, and it must not be left solely to rabbis and judges.

All of these characteristics have played a critical role in informing my current work a director of Mosaica's Religious Peace Initiative, which serves as a network of "insider religious mediators" often mitigating crisis situations in the context of the Israeli-Palestinian Conflict. For example, Mosaica's senior Jewish and Islamic insider mediators helped mediate between Israeli security forces and Palestinian-Islamic leadership during the Tempe Mount Crisis of 2017.[124] Toward the very beginning of my directorship, in February 2019, I found myself, together with Mosaica's senior Jewish and Islamic mediators, once again attempting to mediate between the sides over a similar crisis involving the Temple Mount/Al-Aqsa Mosque in Jerusalem. Mosaica, however, this time seemed to not be the only nongovernmental insider mediators attempting to help negotiate between the two sides. I became aware of this fact several days into the crisis, and immediately insisted on setting up a joint meeting of the two teams. This was not simple. Mediating in such situations is extremely sensitive, and the issues of who has what connections and who trusts whom is critical for such peacemaking interventions to succeed—and sharing this information with others can be complicated.

As the mediators of the two teams sat in the room together, I opened the discussion by saying that there never was such a thing as a *rodef shalom*, in the singular; only *rodfei shalom*, in the plural. If we truly wanted to pursue peace and save lives, I continued, we needed to work together. We did not succeed that day in what we set out to do, but the experience did help build deeper working relationship between us that did not previously exist.

Perhaps the most significant implication from the cases discussed in this chapter is the fact that throughout Jewish history, there were people known in their communities as *rodfei shalom*, *metavkhei shalom*, and *pashranim*. This served as the basis for the various *rodef shalom* educational programs and trainings I have run for schools and communities through the Pardes Center for Judaism and Conflict Resolution.

It is interesting to note that when Israeli lawmakers looked to introduce mediation into Israeli law in 1992, they were not sure what term to call this brand-new phenomenon.[125] They reached out to the Academy of the Hebrew Language, whose scholars suggested mediation be referred to as *tivukh*, from the same root as *metavkhei shalom*. However, since this term had already become popular in the context of the real estate industry, it was suggested that the term for mediation be *pishur* (compromise). This was an attempt to draw a connection to and yet a distinction from *peshara* (from the same root as *pishur*), which already referred to court-ruled compromise (which is what we saw the rabbis of the *Tosefta* disagree over in Chap. 2).

The term for mediator that ultimately caught on in Israeli society was *megasher* (lit., bridger), while the term for mediation became *gishur* (lit., bridging). The latter ultimately took the place of *pishur*. Today *gishur* and *pishur* are both defined as a process in which a third party facilities a discreet, noncoercive process between two sides in conflict through the option of separate meetings, with the aim of achieving an agreement.[126]

I would like to claim that in light of the evidence presented in this chapter (as well as the discussion in Chapter 2 with regard to *Tosefta* Sanhedrin), the concept of third-party mediation and peacemaking was actually not a new concept at all to the Jewish culture and the Hebrew language, and the appropriate term for a "mediator" should have been *rodef shalom*, like Aaron, the first mediator; *metavekh shalom*; or *pashran*. I believe that the terms *rodfei shalom* and *pashran* did not become the terminology to describe the modern profession of mediator because they have become associated with political peacemaking and compromising, and thus could not be used strictly to mean contemporary mediation. As for the term *metavkhei shalom*, I believe it was unknown in the modern lexicon, and even if it had been, the word *shalom* may have felt too presumptions for contemporary mediators to want to be defined in this manner.

Yet precisely because these terms never made their way into contemporary discourse, they can serve as powerful historical precedents and sources of inspiration for people today not only to work as third-party peacemakers in the context of professional mediation, but to see themselves as *rodfei shalom* engaging in a *mitzva* and reviving an ancient Jewish communal tradition within their personal, communal, and national-civil lives.

Table 5.1 Historical Accounts and Stories of Third-Party Lay Peacemakers in Medieval and Early-Modern Rabbinic Literature

I. *Rodfei Shalom* (pursuers of peace)

Case Number	28. *Rodfei shalom*, 11th cent. Spain (*Shut Ri Migash* 101)	29. *Rodfei shalom*, 15th cent. Prague (*Shut Mahari Bruno* 78)	30. *Rodfei shalom*, 15th cent. Italy	31. Acting in the way of *rodfei shalom*, 16th cent. Italy*	32. *Rodfei shalom*, 18th–20th cent. Morocco
The Conflict					
1. The case	Husband and wife: financial/marital dispute	Two rabbis: R. Eliezer of Passau and R. Eliyah of Prague	Inheritors of a husband's brother's will	Two rabbis	• Husband and wife • Inheritance • Business partners
The Third-Party Peacemaker					
2. Number	2+	2+	2+	1	2+
3. Social status	Respected laypeople	Respected laypeople	Respected laypeople (Hayim Halfan, community treasurer)	Well-respected rabbi acting in the way of a *rodef shalom*	Respected laypeople
4. Connection to sides in conflict	Strong/insider	Strong/insider	Strong/insider	———	Strong/insider
5. Initiative to intervene taken by	Third party	Third party	———	———	Third party
6. Meeting with each side in conflict	———	———	———	———	Separately/together
7. Bringing sides to a compromise agreement	Yes	Yes	Yes	———	Yes (even after court ruling)
8. Transforming perspectives, reconciling the relationship	———	———	———	Bends the truth so that each side understands how the other side could be right	Yes (primarily in marital disputes, swears sides to uphold the peace)

Continued

Table 5.1 Continued

I. *Rodfei Shalom* (pursuers of peace)					
9. Personal self-sacrifice	——	——	——	——	Invests a lot of time
Result of Third-Party Intervention					
10. Success/ failure of intervention	Failure	Failure	Failure	-----------	n.a.

* Not a case of lay peacemaking, but of a rabbi describing himself as acting like a pursuer of peace.

Table 5.2 Historical Accounts and Stories of Third-Party Lay Peacemakers in Medieval and Early-Modern Rabbinic Literature

	II. *Metavkhei Shalom* (mediators of peace)		III. *Pashranim* (compromisers)	IV. *Nikhbadim/ hashuvim* (well-respected and distinguished individuals)
Case Number	33. The custom of *metavkhei shalom* in 17th cent. Safed	34. The vulnerability of a 19th cent. *metavekh shalom*	35. Intercommunal *pashranim* in the 16th cent.	36. Bishr b. Aharon, 10th cent. Baghdad
The Conflict				
1. The case	• Business disputes in the marketplace • Asymmetrical relationships/ power inequality	• Conflict between a highly respected and a less respected individual • Power inequality	Conflict between two communities	Two highly respected rabbis/ communal leaders: R. Sa'adya Gaon and Exilarch David b. Zakkai
The Third-Party Peacemaker				
2. Number	2+	2+	2+	2+
3. Social status	Lay bystanders	Respected laypeople (less respected than one side)	Respected laypeople	Highly respected layperson (wealthy banker)
4. Connection to sides in conflict	Medium/insider	——	Medium/outsider	Strong

Table 5.2 *Continued*

	II. *Metavkhei Shalom* (mediators of peace)		III. *Pashranim* (compromisers)	IV. *Nikhbadim/ḥashuvim* (well-respected and distinguished individuals)
Case Number	33. The custom of *metavkhei shalom* in 17th cent. Safed	34. The vulnerability of a 19th cent. *metavekh shalom*	35. Intercommunal *pashranim* in the 16th cent.	36. Bishr b. Aharon, 10th cent. Baghdad
5. Initiative to intervene taken by	Third party	Third party	Third party	Third party (community)
6. Meeting with each side in conflict	Together	————	————	Separately/ together
7. Bringing sides to a compromise agreement	Yes	Yes	Yes	Yes
8. Transforming perspectives, reconciling the relationship	Yes	————	Symbolically burns old agreements	• Convinces sides to make peace also using religious quotes • Facilitates symmetrical reconciliation ceremony in Bishr's courtyard • Ritual day of Purim
9. Personal self-sacrifice	————	Financial guarantor of peace	————	————
Result of Third-Party Intervention				
10. Success/ failure of intervention	Success: sides hug and kiss	Failure	Failure	Success: sides reconcile at joint festive holiday meal

Conclusion

The Text, Theory, Practice, and Scope of Third-Party Peacemakers in Judaism

In this book I have presented numerous cases of third-party peacemakers found in the vast body of rabbinic literature spanning between the third and nineteenth centuries CE. The criteria for including a particular legend or historical account as one of the case studies was a description of a third side intervening or known to have intervened in a conflict between two sides with the intent of de-escalation of the conflict and ultimately bringing peace between the sides. This broad definition allowed me to include diverse identities and approaches to peacemaking. Yet in reflecting back upon these diverse cases, several common features may be identified.

As I discussed in Chapter 1, identifying common features is particularly important for advancing the theoretical study of religious and traditional cultural models of third-party peacemaking. We may now look back at the thirty-six case studies of third-party peacemaking found in rabbinic literature that were discussed in this book, and reflect on some of the key similarities and differences between them and other cultural models of third-party peacemaking, based on the ten categories of theoretical comparison through which they were all analyzed (Tables 1–5).[1]

Common Characteristics of Third-Party Peacemakers

Identity and Number

Third-party peacemakers can be divided into three primary typological identities based on parallel traditional cultural models of peacemaking:

1. Aaron the high priest as the paradigmatic peacemaker (Table 2.1, cases 1–4); similar to other religious, paradigmatic peacemakers as discussed in

Chapter 1. The rabbinic portrayal of Aaron is also similar to the descriptions of how the saints of the Atlas Mountains are supposed to serve as peacemakers. For example, they do not fight with others, and they pursue peace alone.

2. Rabbis as peacemakers; similar to imams and sheikhs. Members of this category sometimes make peace alone (Table 3.1, cases 5–10; Table 4.2, cases 20–21; Table 4.3, cases 24, 27) and other times as part of a group (Table 4.1, cases 16–17; Table 4.2, cases 18–19, 22–23; Table 4.3, cases 25–26).[2]

3. Lay peacemakers; similar to the third-party lay peacemakers in the Arab *sulha* process known as the *jaha* (Table 1.1). This group almost always makes peace as part of a group and never alone (Table 3.2, case 12; Table 5.1, cases 28–30, 32; Table 5.2, cases 33–36).[3]

In addition to these three primary typologies, we also saw two cases of women serving as peacemakers in rabbinic literature (Table 3.2, cases 13–14) and compared them with other traditional cultural models of female peacemakers.

Social Status and Connection to the Sides in Conflict

Consistent with other religious and traditional cultural models of peacemaking, and in contrast to modern-Western models, third-party peacemakers were most commonly individuals of high social status with strong connections to both sides in the conflict. The more distinguished and connected they were, the higher the likelihood of their intervention being successful. This was especially true, for example, in the legends of Aaron (Table 2.1, cases 1–4), Rabbi Meir (Table 3.1, cases 5–6), Rabbi Dovid of Lelov (Table 4.1, case 16), and Bishr b. Aharon (Table 5.2, case 36). Each was described as a highly respected and connected individual, and very successful in his peacemaking efforts.

By contrast, in cases where the third party was of lower social status than one of the disputing sides, or generally less influential—such as in the cases of Reish Lakish (Table 3.1, case 8), the anonymous traveling *hakham* (Table 4.3, case 24), and the vulnerable *metavekh shalom* (Table 5.2, case 34), the peacemaking intervention failed. This is consistent with the findings of other research into traditional cultural third-party peacemaking processes.

Despite our findings, we also saw several exceptions to the correlation between the status of the peacemaker and their success. For example, the legends of the simple jesters (Table 3.1, case 12) and Rabbi Nissi al-Nahrawani (Table 4.3, case 27) illustrate that peacemakers of lower social status can be highly successful, while the accounts of Rabbenu Avraham ben haRambam (Table 4.3, case 26) and Rabbi Azulai (Table 4.2, case 23) prove that highly respected peacemakers can be unsuccessful.

Initiative to Intervene

The third-party peacemakers presented in this book almost always intervene of their own initiative and do not wait to be invited in. Just about every case explored in this book is consistent with this finding, from the legends of Aaron to the historical accounts of lay peacemakers who are described as "entering into" the conflicts of others. Sometimes members of the larger community approach specific individuals to serve as peacemakers, which we saw in some of the cases involving Rabbi Azulai (Table 4.2, cases 19, 21–22) and the case involving Bishr b. Aharon (Table 5.2, case 36).

In only two cases in this book, one of the disputants initiated contact with the third side, requesting them to get involved (Table 3.2, case 14; Table 4.2, case 20); they are the rare exceptions, as in most cases the intervention comes as a result of the third party's initiative. This too reflects a strong and consistent cultural value of collectivism, where the conflicts of others are not just the disputants' problem but the problem of each member of the community. This notion of communal collectivism is consistent with other traditional cultural models of peacemaking, and is in contrast to modern-Western models of mediation.

Meeting with Each Side in Conflict

As opposed to modern-Western approaches, third-party peacemakers of the traditional cultural school are often described as meeting with each side in the conflict separately, especially in the early stages of the peacemaking process. This was done in almost every case study discussed here (Table 2.1, cases 1–4; Table 3.1, cases 6–10; Table 3.2, cases 13–14; Table 4.3, cases 25–27; Table 5.1, case 32; Table 5.2, case 36). There are, of course, exceptions to this rule (Table 4.1, cases 16–17), but it is difficult to determine whether the exceptional cases in which the third party is described as meeting both sides together reflect an intrinsic difference in approach from the general rule, or merely the manner in which these cases were recorded.

Bringing Sides to a Compromise Agreement

In all the cases of historical accounts describing third-party lay peacemaking (Table 5.1, cases, 28–30, 32; Table 5.2, cases 33–36), and in many of the historical accounts of rabbis serving as peacemakers (Table 4.1, case 17; Table 4.2, cases 18–19, 22–23; Table 4.3, case 24) in medieval and early-modern rabbinic literature, the peacemaker is described as attempting to bring the conflicting sides to a formal, noncoercive compromise agreement (*peshara*) that would resolve the monetary aspects of the dispute. However, in all cases describing third-party peacemakers in the earlier, classical rabbinic literature (cases 1–14 in Tables 2.1, 3.1, and 3.2), this aspect is entirely absent. The authors of these cases chose instead to tell only of conflicts revolving around the breakdown of a relationship that did not require a compromise agreement to repair.

It should be noted that Aaron did indeed engage in bringing the sides to a compromise agreement (*peshara*)—at least according to the commentaries on the early rabbinic source *Tosefta* Sanhedrin; he just did so either before the sides came to him for judgment, in a noncoercive manner, or as a peacemaker and not as a judge.[4] In some of the later cases as well, the contractual component of the third-party intervention was either intentionally dismissed as being less important as the relational aspect (such as in the case of Rabbi Dovid of Lelov; Table 4.1, case 16) or simply not the focus of the story despite the fact that a formal agreement had been achieved (such as in the case of Bishr b. Aharon; Table 5.2, case 36). This too, reflects traditional cultural models of peacemaking, which often emphasize the reconciliation between the parties, relegating the financial aspects to a place of lesser importance.

Transforming Perspectives, Reconciling the Relationship

Many of the third-party peacemakers attempted to transform the perceptions of the sides in conflict and thereby reconcile the relationship, and they employed an array of methods:

CONCLUSION 257

- Being a calming influence simply by being present with the sides in conflict (Table 2.1, case 4; Table 3.1, case 5; Table 4.1, case 16; Table 4.2, case 18)
- Coaching or advising at least one of the sides in conflict to choose a peaceful approach to its resolution (Table 2.1, case 2; Table 3.2, cases 13–14; Table 4.3, case 26)
- Serving as a guarantor of the peace (Table 2.1, case 1; Table 5.1, case 29;[5] 34[6])
- Offering to be humiliated as an anger absorber (Table 2.1, case 3; Table 3.1, case 6)
- Bending the truth (Table 2.1, cases 3–4; Table 3.1, cases 6–8; Table 5.1, case 31)
- Clarifying the intentions of the offending side to the other side (Table 3.1, cases 9–10)
- Rebuking one of the disputants (Table 4.2, cases 18, 23; Table 4.3, case 25)
- Making disputants swear to uphold the peace between them (Table 4.2, case 23; Table 5.1, case 32)
- Speaking from within a disputant's value system, such as by quoting a verse (Table 3.2, cases 11, 13–14; Table 5.2, case 36)
- Using humor (Table 3.2, case 12)
- Surprising one of the sides in conflict (Table 4.2, case 19; Table 4.3, case 27)
- Gathering the sides in joint prayer or study (Table 4.1, cases 16–17)
- Preaching publicly about peace (Table 4.2, cases 20–21; Table 4.3, case 24)
- Serving as an emissary to ask forgiveness on behalf of one of the parties (Table 2.1, case 4; Table 4.2, case 21)
- Gathering the sides in a ritual space or on a ritual date (Table 4.1, case 16; Table 4.2, case 18; Table 5.2, case 36)
- Facilitating a public forgiveness ceremony (Table 4.2, case 21; Table 4.3, case 24)
- Using supernatural powers (Table 4.1, case 16; Table 4.2, case 22; Table 4.3, case 27)
- Facilitating a public, festive reconciliation ceremony (Table 4.3, case 27; Table 5.2, case 36)

As has been noted repeatedly, many of these methods can be found in other traditional cultural models of third-party peacemaking, but are completely foreign to contemporary modern-Western models of peacemaking and reconciliation (see Table 1.1).

Personal Self-Sacrifice

Many cases discussed in this book tell of the immense efforts and personal sacrifice third-party peacemakers endured as part of their efforts to make peace. This is also characteristic of traditional cultural peacemaking processes. The most extreme cases in this book were those of Rabbi Meir and Aaron allowing a wife to spit in their eye in order to placate their jealous husbands (Table 2.1, case 3; Table 3.1, case 6), and that of a lay peacemaker agreeing to be a financial guarantor to keep the peace—only to find himself owing a large sum of money to a community strongman (Table 5.2, case 34). Other, less extreme cases also testify to the humility and self-sacrifice of some peacemakers. This could be expressed through the peacemakers' going to the homes of the sides in conflict (Table 2.1, case 4; Table 3.1, case 5; Table 4.2, case 20), traveling great distances for the sole purpose of making peace (Table 4.1, cases 16–17), or being very generous with their time (Table 2.1, case 4; Table 3.1, case 5; Table 4.2, case 18). Other manifestations of self-sacrifice can be seen in Rabbi Azulai's sacrificing his own personal comfort for the sake of making peace, such as when he participated in a lavish banquet that seemed to have offended his sensibilities (Table 4.2, case 18) or took part in a peace meeting despite being ill (Table 4.2, case 21). Yet Rabbi Azulai also wrote about his ability to set boundaries and protect his own interests and well-being, such as by meditating or working on his book instead of focusing all his time on peacemaking (Table 4.2, case 18).

Success/Failure of Intervention

Many of the case studies of third-party peacemakers had a "happy ending" (Table 2.1, cases 1, 4; Table 3.1, cases 5, 7; Table 4.1, cases 16–17; Table 4.2, cases 18–22; Table 4.3 case 27; Table 5.2, cases 33, 36). In most of these cases success was expressed through various symbols of reconciliation, such as a hug and kiss or a public ceremony. However, several of the cases presented enumerated the unsuccessful intervention of a third party (Table 3.1, case 8; Table 4.2, case 23; Table 4.3, cases 24–26; Table 5.2, cases 28–29, 39).

CONCLUSION 259

Throughout this book I have argued that we can learn much from both successes and failures of third-party interventions, and I believe this fact should imbue a certain degree of caution and humility among all those intending to intervene as a third party in other people's conflicts. As we have seen, sometimes the third party made mistakes, or was simply the wrong person to intervene. Sometimes, even the appropriate third party that did everything correctly was still unable to succeed, as there are perforce always at least two other parties engaged in the conflict that making peace depends on.

Core Contributions to and Further Research for Text, Theory, and Practice

Now that I have summarized and analyzed the specific findings of the various cases discussed throughout this book, it is possible to reflect more broadly on the three key layers of analysis that this book sought to contribute to: The text, theory, and practice of third-party peacemaking in Judaism. I have also attempted identify further areas of research I hope to encourage.

Text

While several conflict resolution scholars in the past have pointed to Aaron as the ideal Jewish peacemaker (Table 2.1, case 4), and Marc Gopin doubled this list of one to include the legend of Rabbi Meir making peace between a husband and wife (Table 3.1, case 5), none of the other thirty-four cases of third-party peacemakers discussed in this book had ever been previously identified and researched.[7] As I noted in the Preface, after having read Gopin's section on Aaron and Rabbi Meir in his book, *Between Eden and Armageddon*, I recall wondering if there even existed other cases of third-party peacemakers in rabbinic literature. This book, therefore, comes to introduce and analyze numerous other legends, historical accounts, and stories of third parties intervening in conflicts to make peace. Several of these examples have never previously been the subject of any scholarly analysis within Judaic studies.

Moreover, my research has revealed historical evidence testifying to the fact that within certain Jewish communities throughout the ages, there were dedicated terms used to describe third-party lay peacemakers, such *rodfei shalom, metavkhei shalom,* and *pashranim* or *mefashrim*. To cite one example, in the Jewish community of Morocco during the eighteenth through twentieth centuries, there seems to have been a recognized, quasi-communal role of the lay peacemaker. It is possible that this communal custom ceased to exist once the ancient Jewish communities of Morocco were dismantled in the mid-twentieth century.

While I have spent many years searching for the various cases examined in this book, I am certain they are only the tip of the iceberg and many more such examples of rabbis and laypeople serving as peacemakers and mediators exist. I hope this book will stimulate further research in this area. Such research should also be expanded to include more recent examples from the last century, which I did not touch upon at all. With more cases we might be able to draw more substantial historical conclusions about the evolution of peacemaking practices within various Jewish communities over time.

Theory

The second layer of analysis of these cases was as theoretical models of conflict resolution, and in particular as religious and traditional cultural models of third-party peacemaking. Here the primary question was, How do the various cases of third-party peacemaking found in rabbinic literature compare with and contrast to one another and to other religious and cultural models? The cases examined comprised a combination of religious and cultural models of peacemaking. Some serve as clear examples of religious models, as the legends and stories describing these model peacemakers seek to instruct adherents how one *should* act. This pertains to Aaron, of course, as the paradigmatic peacemaker in Judaism, whom we identified as being the Jewish equivalent of other paradigmatic religious peacemakers noted in Chapter 1, such as Muhammad, Krishna, Deganawida, and Jesus. It also applies to the other paradigmatic Jewish peacemakers whose stories were interpreted throughout the generations by the rabbis, such as those of Rabbi Meir (Table 3.1, cases 5–6) and those of the non-rabbinic peacemakers (Table 3.2, cases 11–12). These legends were held up as models of inspiration and instruction by later rabbinic writers. Rabbis Yosef Syracusty and Dovid of Lelov can be added to the list, as they too were identified by subsequent generations as religious models of peacemaking.

Other cases researched in this book, primarily the historical accounts discussed in Chapters 4 and 5, constitute more of a window into traditional cultural or indigenous peacemaking models with regard to how Jewish communities *would* act. And yet other examples fall someplace in between, as they are historical yet can serve as role models for peacemaking. These include the peacemakers in Volozhin (Table 4.1, case 17) and of course, Rabbi Hayim Yosef David Azulai (Table 4.2, cases 18–23).

With regard to the three primary conceptual models of third-party peacemaking that I have mentioned, Aaron the high priest, as portrayed in rabbinic literature, was identified as being most similar to the traditional peacemaking model of the saint. The various cases of rabbis serving as peacemakers found in Chapters 3 and 4 constitute examples most similar to religious leaders such as the Islamic imam or sheikh. And finally, the examples of third-party lay peacemakers found in Chapters 3 and 5 exhibit strong parallels to the lay delegation of peacemakers in the *sulha* process known as the *jaha*.

Every case explored in the book has been analyzed through the filter of the same conceptual questions designed to understand the conflict, identify the methods of the third-party peacemaker, and discover the result of the intervention. It is my hope that this analytical framework within which I worked conducting the theoretical research can serve as a basis for conducting further parallel research of peacemakers in other religious and cultural contexts, whether they be historical or contemporary.

One theoretical question with very practical implications for today that arises from this study is the relationship between brokering a formal compromise agreement that resolves all matters under dispute on the one hand, and facilitating the transformation of perceptions and the reconciliation of disputants on the other. Obviously, the need for these components differed with each case, depending on the nature of the conflict and to what extent there was a financial component to the conflict as well as a relational one. In the cases where both components were featured, sometimes a formal compromise agreement resolving the financial and power relationship between the sides needed to be reached *prior* to the sides meeting directly and reconciling (Table 4.2, case 20; Table 5.2, case 36). This is in line with the accepted sequence of stages within the Arab *sulha* process of reconciliation (and with modern-Western models of reconciliation such as Interactive Problem-Solving Workshops, Table 1.1). In other cases, however, efforts aimed at reconciliation and normalization of relationships preceded and greatly contributed to the later, formal compromise agreement (Table 4.2, case 18).

This raises a very important practical question for religious peacebuilding today, for example within the context of the Jewish/Israeli–Muslim/Palestinian conflict. What should precede what? Is there a need first for shifts in the perceptions of each side toward the other and a reconciliation of the relationship, which will then allow for an amicable compromise agreement that both sides support? Or do the disputants need to achieve a formal agreement first, through the help of third-party peacemakers shuttling back and forth, resolving power dynamics and distribution of the scarce resources under dispute, only afterward normalizing relations and exploring the potential for reconciliation?

This distinction may be referred to as the difference between "cultural peacebuilding" and "structural peacebuilding." Yvonne Wang, in her study of religious peacebuilding NGOs operating in the context of the Israeli-Palestinian conflict, defines structural peacebuilding organizations as those that advocate for a just and amicable political peace agreement first, and only afterward encourage normalization and reconciliation between the two sides. Cultural peacebuilding organizations, on the other hand, promote first strengthening social relations and mutual understanding, as well as reducing hatred between the two sides; only then can political peace agreements become more attainable and sustainable.[8]

Through my work as the director of Mosaica's Religious Peace Initiative, we attempt to do both simultaneously. This means both to work at cultivating stronger relationships between Jews and Muslims and, through connecting with senior influential religious Jewish and Islamic leaders, to discuss the possibilities of peace agreements that would be acceptable to these leaders and their constituents and to actually resolve crisis situations as they arise.

More extensive historical and contemporary research is needed to determine whether there are cultural components that impact how those engaged in the conflict might respond differently to this highly disputed question.

Practice

The third layer of analysis enumerated in this book pertains to the extent to which these textual-historical cases of peacemaking can be applied in practice today. I have shared several reflections throughout the book on the possible implications and ramifications of the practice of conflict resolution in general and in the context of educational programs for youth and trainings for rabbis and laypeople in particular. I highlighted several particular cases that played an instrumental role in establishing *rodef shalom* programs for schools and synagogues. For example, the very existence of communal *rodfei shalom*, discussed in Chapter 5, can inspire the entire spectrum of those committed to peacemaking, from children to communal leaders, to see themselves in the same role.

I also shared several examples of how particular cases in this book were used in educational experiences. I have had participants reflect on their own personal *rodef shalom* role model, using some of the cases (e.g., Table 3.1, case 5; Table 3.2, case 12; Table 4.2, case 18) for role-playing. Sometimes this was a challenge for participants due to the vast cultural gap between them and the texts (Table 2.1, case 4; Table 3.1, cases 6–7). I have also shared several reflections throughout the book of some of my own experiences serving as a third-party peacemaker in the context of my role as director of Mosaica's Religious Peace Initiative, and how my own thinking has been influenced by my research on third-party peacemaking in Judaism.

Further research needs to be conducted in two primary areas. The first concerns the concept, "From theory to practice," meaning how can these cases of third-party peacemakers found in rabbinic literature be used and accessed in the context of conflict resolution education and training across diverse Jewish identity groups? The second concerns the concept, "From practice to theory," meaning what can be learned from rabbis and Jewish communal leaders engaged in the practice of third-party peacemaking and mediation today? This would necessitate, for example, interviewing rabbis and lay leaders serving various communities today and examining to what extent they serve as third-party peacemakers both within their own communities and between various communities across diverse identity groups. What are the various methods they employ in their peacemaking efforts? How equipped do they feel they are to engage in such communal and intercommunal peacemaking efforts? To what extent are their efforts grounded in Jewish text and tradition? Have they studied contemporary mediation and conflict resolution tools? What stories and texts inspire them to do the work they do? And finally, what is the scope of their peacemaking efforts; is it primarily interpersonal and intracommunal, or is it also intercommunal and even beyond the Jewish community?

The Scope of Third-Party Peacemaking in Judaism

As noted in Chapter 1, one of the greatest questions facing religious models of peacebuilding pertains to the ambiguity of religious texts and traditions, many of which can be interpreted in different ways.[9] Almost without exception, all the cases of third-party peacemaking found within rabbinic literature examined in this book have been intra-Jewish, primarily relating to conflicts between individuals, spouses, or rabbis (see Tables 2–5, category 1). In Chapter 2, we saw that Aaron would pursue peace between individuals, husband and wife, and—according to one source—even between tribes. However, he did not pursue peace between Israelites and non-Israelites. This raises the question, To what extent can the legends of Aaron, and the many other accounts and stories investigated in this book, serve as models of inspiration to pursue peace beyond the Jewish community today?

To further illustrate this ambiguity, I will share a personal story. Several years ago I had a long and fascinating conversation with a young relative of mine through marriage. The young man's first and middle names are Ari (or Aaron) Ohev-Shalom (lover of peace). He was born not long before the assassination of the prime minister of Israel, Yitzhak Rabin, by a fellow Jew in 1995. His parents decided to call him by this special name as a symbol of building bridges between the divided Jewish Israeli communities on the "secular left" and the "religious right," and for this child to be "of the disciples of Aaron." Toward the end of the conversation I asked him how he understands the scope of his name, meaning, can Aaron serve as a pursuer of peace also between Jews and non-Jews, perhaps even between Israeli Jews and Palestinian Muslims? His reaction to my question was an unequivocal No. For Ari, who grew up in a right-wing, religious-Zionist home in a Jewish settlement in Samaria, in the West Bank, and who had personally witnessed numerous acts of violence against fellow Jews, this possibility was quite simply beyond the mandate of his namesake. Aaron was a pursuer of peace strictly between the tribes of Israel; let the Messiah one day make peace between the nations.

I would nevertheless argue that if every Jewish child, including those similar to Ari, were to grow up being educated and trained to be a *rodef shalom* within his or her classroom, and if every rabbi and lay leader were to be challenged to see themselves as a *rodef shalom* within their own communities first, this would ultimately contribute to and increase the likeliness of their applying this identity and skill set to those beyond their own core identity groups. My confidence in this claim stems partially from the fact that the scope of Jewish peacemaking has expanded and contracted over time in accordance with changing historical circumstances. One example of this is Rabbi Yosef Syracusty, who was apparently inspired to be a peacemaker by Aaron; yet he expanded the scope of his peacemaking to include his non-Jewish neighbors in Safed with whom he clearly had a close relationship (Table 4.1, case 15). He in turn served as an important source of inspiration for future Jewish peacemakers looking to expand the scope of their own efforts.

The most significant source that both reflects and impacts the scope of Jewish peacemaking is a statement attributed to the prominent rabbi, Rabban Yohanan b. Zakkai, shortly before the destruction of the Second Temple in the year 70 CE. During the siege of Jerusalem, Rabban Yohanan b. Zakkai risked his life by escaping, in a coffin, from the grasp of Jewish zealots controlling Jerusalem. His purpose was to make his way to the Roman army camp in order to negotiate a peace with Vespasian between the warring Jews and Rome. He stated:[10]

> The person who makes peace between fellow individuals, between husband and wife, between city and city, between nation and nation, between family and family, between government and government . . . there shall not come upon him any harm.[11]

Roughly 1,000 years later, the medieval biblical commentator, Rabbi Shlomo Yitzhaki (known as Rashi; France, 1040–1105), cites Rabban Yohanan b. Zakkai in his commentary on Exodus. However, the citation is only a partial one: it glaringly omits Rabban Yohanan's references to peacemaking between nations and between governments.[12] This omission does not seem to be coincidental, as noted by Rabbi Hayim Hirschensohn (Palestine, United States; 1857–1935), one of the founders of religious Zionism. He writes in his commentary on Rashi:[13]

> Rabban Yohanan b. Zakkai who was of the people of peace, who tried hard to make peace between Israel and Rome . . . trusted that he would not endure suffering when he pretended to be dead [in order] to be taken to the fortress of the Romans for the sake of peace. . . . However, in Rashi's generation, there was not a Jew in such a situation that could make peace "between city and city, nation and nation, government and government." Rashi omitted this part from his moral teachings, and left what could be a lesson for our brethren in his generation: "between fellow individuals, between husband and wife, between family and family."[14]

Rabbi Hirschensohn makes an important distinction between the circumstances of the Jews in Rashi's generation and those in the generation of Rabban Yoḥanan b. Zakkai. Living in the time of the First Jewish Revolt against Rome, Rabban Yoḥanan b. Zakkai felt it was relevant to attempt to make peace between nations and governments as well as between individuals. Living in France at the time of the First Crusade, Rashi considered the pursuit of peace relevant only in an intracommunal context: between individuals and families within the Jewish community. In the absence of Jewish national sovereignty or any kind of national entity, medieval Jews had no means of effecting peace between nations or governments.

This historical distinction between medieval and first-century Judaism raises a critical question regarding twenty-first century Judaism. Namely, to what extent should the scope of Jewish peacemaking today go beyond interpersonal and intra-Jewish conflicts to include once again, as in the days of Rabban Yoḥanan b. Zakkai, "nation and nation, government and government"?

I believe the answer to this question can be found in the remarks of Rabbi Yosef Nissim ibn Adhan (Morocco, d. 1925) on Rabban Yoḥanan b. Zakkai's statement:

> [Rabban Yoḥanan b. Zakkai's statement] provides an answer to the nations of the world who say that the people of Israel do not seek their peace and well-being. . . . For it explicitly wants to state to the nations of the world that the nation of Israel loves peace and pursues peace (with) all peoples. . . . And may we be granted the ability to make peace between warring kings and for there to be peace in the world, for then we would sell all our household possessions, so that it would be declared "and the land had rest [from war]" (Judges 3:11) and "nation shall not lift up sword against nation, neither shall they learn war anymore" (Is. 2:4).[15]

Notes

Preface

1. Kevin Avruch, *Culture and Conflict Resolution* (Washington, DC: United States Institute of Peace Press, 1998); David W. Augsburger, *Conflict Mediation across Cultures* (London: Westminster John Knox Press, 1992).
2. https://faculty.biu.ac.il/~steing/conflict/Conferences/religionandconflictresolution.html.
3. https://faculty.biu.ac.il/~steing/conflict/infoaboutprogenglish.html.
4. Marc Gopin, *Between Eden and Armageddon: The Future of World Religions, Violence, and Peacemaking* (Oxford: Oxford University Press, 2000), 186.
5. Ibid., 137.
6. Ibid., 181–82.
7. The rabbinic dictum "Torah scholars increase peace in the world" is found in several places throughout rabbinic literature, including at the very end of several tractates of the Babylonian Talmud: Berakhot, Ḥagiga, Yevamot, Sukka, Nazir, and Keritut, as well as at the very end of JT Berakhot; *Sifrei*, Deut.; *Avot d'Rabbi Natan*; et al. This dictum will also be cited as part of various rabbinic quotes found throughout this book. See Chap. 4, ns. 9, 23, 39, 119.
8. Daniel Roth, "The Tradition of Aaron, Pursuer of Peace between People, as a Rabbinic Model of Reconciliation" [in Hebrew] (PhD diss., Bar-Ilan University, 2012).
9. Howard G. Kaminsky, "Traditional Jewish Perspectives on Peace and Interpersonal Conflict Resolution" (EdD diss., Teachers College, Columbia University, 2005).
10. Ibid., 307.
11. Raphael Ahren, "Using an Old-new Formula in the Search for Peace: New Pardes Program Combines Judaic, Conflict Studies," *Haaretz*, September, 17, 2010, https://www.haaretz.com/1.5114327.
12. Lauren Gelfond Feldinger, "Jewish Peacemaking Program in Jerusalem Creates a Niche," *Haaretz*, July 13, 2012, https://www.haaretz.com/conflict-resolution-with-a-jewish-twist-1.5299093. See also https://www.pardes.org.il/program/pcjcr/pardes-center-for-judaism-conflict-resolution/; Sidney Slivko, "Pursuing Peace in the Classroom: Israeli Center Promotes Conflict Resolution as a Core Jewish Value," *New York Jewish Week*, February 5, 2014, https://jewishweek.timesofisrael.com/pursuing-peace-in-the-classroom/.
13. https://elmad.pardes.org/topic/critical-issues/pcjcr/rodef-shalom/online-courses/.

14. Jeremy Sharon, "Pardes Institute Encourages Jews to Engage in 'Constructive Conflict' for New Adar Holiday," *Jerusalem Post*, February 8, 2014, https://www.jpost.com/Jewish-World/Jewish-News/New-holiday-encourages-Jews-to-engage-in-constructive-conflict-340786; Jeremy Sharon, "150 Organizations Worldwide Prepare to Mark Adar 9 as Jewish Day of Constructive Conflict," *Jerusalem Post*, February 26, 2015, https://www.jpost.com/Diaspora/150-organizations-worldwide-prepare-to-mark-Adar-9-as-Jewish-Day-of-Constructive-Conflict-392343; Renee Ghert-Zand, "9 Adar Encourages Conflict, Constructively," *Times of Israel*, February 9, 2014, https://www.timesofisrael.com/9-adar-encourages-conflict-but-in-a-constructive-way/.
15. Ron Kronish, "The Pursuit of Religious Peace in the Israeli-Palestinian Conflict," *Times of Israel*, May 24, 2020, https://blogs.timesofisrael.com/the-pursuit-of-religious-peace-in-the-israeli-palestinian-conflict/.
16. https://resolution.tau.ac.il/course-7.
17. https://law.biu.ac.il/en/node/3871.
18. http://coexistencetrip.net/file/Syllabus_Religion_in_the_Holy_Land.pdf.

Introduction

1. For an outline of different roles a third party can play, see William Ury, *The Third Side: Why We Fight and How We Can Stop* (New York: Penguin Books, 2000); Augsburger, *Conflict Mediation across Cultures*, 194.

    The modern-Western definition of the scope of third-party intervention is often more limited. See Ronald J. Fisher, "Methods of Third-Party Intervention," *Berghof Handbook for Conflict Transformation* (Berlin: Berghof Research Center for Constructive Conflict Management, 2001), http://edoc.vifapol.de/opus/volltexte/2011/2579/pdf/fisher_hb.pdf. The use of the term "peacemaker" is therefore not intended to differentiate it from, say, the term "peacebuilder," but rather as a broad term for how third parties can bring about peace between two sides in a conflict.
2. Some scholars have distinguished between Western and non-Western cultural models of conflict resolution. I prefer to distinguish between modern-Western and traditional, non-Western cultural models, as often these "cultural" differences reflect the differences between urban and rural societies.
3. Scholars interested in further textual analysis of these examples are referred to my doctoral dissertation, "The Tradition of Aaron, Pursuer of Peace between People, as a Rabbinic Model of Reconciliation" [in Hebrew].
4. See above, Preface, n. 6, regarding Gopin's call for religious conflict resolution education and training. See also Susan Hayward and Katherine Marshall, eds., *Women, Religion, and Peacebuilding: Illuminating the Unseen* (Washington, DC: United States Institute of Peace Press, 2015), 11, who write, "Religious teachers and leaders can teach conflict resolution skills and values to communities, instructing through classes, sermons, or media the religious values that support reconciliation, love of neighbors, and peace."

Chapter 1

1. The term "conflict resolution studies" is meant to include the broader field, from interpersonal and communal mediation and alternative dispute resolution, to international peace and conflict studies.
2. For a conceptual mapping and overview of the field, see Katrien Hertog, *The Complex Reality of Religious Peacebuilding: Conceptual Contributions and Critical Analysis* (Lanham, MD: Lexington Books, 2010). See also Atalia Omer, "Religious Peacebuilding: The Exotic, the Good, and the Theatrical," in *The Oxford Handbook of Religion, Conflict, and Peacebuilding*, ed. Atalia Omer, R. Scott Appleby, and David Little (Oxford: Oxford University Press, 2015), 3–32; S. Ayse Kadayifci-Orellana, "Ethno-Religious Conflicts: Exploring the Role of Religion in Conflict Resolution," in *The SAGE Handbook of Conflict Resolution*, ed. J. Bercovitch, V. Kremenyuk, and I. W. Zartman (London: SAGE, 2009), 264–80.
3. For list of academic programs and courses in the field as well as an updated bibliography of literature from the field, see Cassandra Lawrence, Sara Singha, Najla Mangoush, and Douglas Leonard, "Demystifying Religion in Mediation: Identifying Gaps in Training, Knowledge, and Practice," *Al Amana International*, 2017, https://www.peacemakersnetwork.org/our-work/network-publications/.
4. Hertog, *Complex Reality of Religious Peacebuilding*, 1–38.
5. R. Scott Appleby, *The Ambivalence of the Sacred: Religion, Violence, and Reconciliation* (Lanham, MD: Rowman & Littlefield, 2000). See also Hertog, 18–19, where she writes that a "fundamental characteristic of the studies [on religion and peacebuilding] is the fact that they all start from the implicit or explicit acknowledgment of the ambivalence."
6. See Hertog, *Complex Reality of Religious Peacebuilding*, 74: "This analysis is mainly informed by disciplines such as sociology and religious studies, although it could be further complemented with approaches from psychology, philosophy, or political science."
7. Hertog, 74–77, writes that her conceptual mapping of the field is primarily informed by sociology and religious studies. She distinguishes between "Religion as Organization" and "Religion as Social Actor." Today, both fall into the study of religious individuals.
8. David Little, "The Settler Who Spoke with Arafat: Rabbi Menachem Froman," in *Peacemakers in Action: Profiles of Religion in Conflict Resolution*, ed. David Little (New York: Cambridge University Press, 2007), 341–56; Yehezkel Landau, *Healing the Holy Land: Interreligious Peacebuilding in Israel/Palestine* (Washington, DC: United States Institute of Peace Press, 2003); Marc Gopin, *Bridges across an Impossible Divide: The Inner Lives of Arab and Jewish Peacemakers* (New York: Oxford University Press, 2012), 47–75; Rabbi Michael Melchior, "Establishing a Religious Peace," in *Coexistence & Reconciliation in Israel: Voices for Interreligious Dialogue*, ed. Ronald Kronish (Mahwah, NJ: Paulist Press, 2015), 117–28. See also Marc Gopin, *Holy War, Holy Peace: How Religion Can Bring Peace to the Middle East* (Oxford: Oxford University Press, 2002); Yvonne Wang, "Strategic Engagement and Religious

Peace-Building: A Case Study of Religious Peace Work in Jerusalem," *Approaching Religion* 4, no. 2 (2014): 71–82, https://doi.org/10.30664/ar.67551.

9. Hertog, *Complex Reality of Religious Peacebuilding*, 77–78, refers to this area as "Religion as Living Tradition."
10. Gopin, *Eden and Armageddon*, 80.
11. Robert Eisen, *The Peace and Violence of Judaism: From the Bible to Modern Zionism* (New York: Oxford University Press, 2011). See also Reuven Firestone, *Holy War in Judaism: The Fall and Rise of a Controversial Idea* (Oxford: Oxford University Press, 2012).
12. Gopin, *Eden and Armageddon*, 13–14.
13. Hertog, *Complex Reality of Religious Peacebuilding*, 77.
14. Mohammed Abu-Nimer, "An Islamic Model of Conflict Resolution: Principles and Challenges," in *Crescent and Dove: Peace and Conflict Resolution in Islam*, ed. Qamar-ul Huda (Washington, DC: United States Institute of Peace Press, 2010), 73–88; Mohammed Abu-Nimer, *Nonviolence and Peace Building in Islam: Theory and Practice* (Gainesville: University of Florida Press, 2003).
15. According to *Encyclopedia Britannica*, the hadith is the "record of the traditions or sayings of the Prophet Muhammad, revered and received as a major source of religious law and moral guidance, second only to the authority of the Koran."
16. Abu-Nimer, "An Islamic Model," 88.
17. In addition to these three, there are other scholars who have focused on one particular Jewish model of conflict resolution. Solomon Schimmel, *Wounds Not Healed by Time: The Power of Repentance and Forgiveness* (Oxford: Oxford University Press, 2002), compared the Jewish concept of *takanat hashavim* (an enactment to assist criminals to be rehabilitated back into society) with the contemporary model of restorative justice. Ariel Burger, *Hasidic Nonviolence: R. Noson of Bratzlav's Hermeneutics of Conflict Transformation* (Boston: Boston University Press, 2008), presents a fascinating historical example of nonviolence within the Hasidic movement. In addition, Rabbi Amy Eilberg, *From Enemy to Friend: Jewish Wisdom and the Pursuit of Peace* (Ossining, NY: Orbis Books, 2014), is an important example of how many of these types of models can be applied in a variety of conflict settings today, from interpersonal to interfaith.
18. Gopin, *Eden and Armageddon*, 167–95. A similar chapter written by Gopin, entitled "Judaism and Peacebuilding," was published in *Religion and Peacebuilding*, ed. Harold Coward and Gordon S. Smith (Albany: State University of New York Press, 2004), 111–27. See also Marc Gopin, "Judaism and Peacebuilding in the Context of the Middle East Conflict," in *Faith-Based Diplomacy: Trumping Realpolitik*, ed. Douglas Johnston (New York: Oxford University Press, 2003), 91–102.
19. Gopin, *Eden and Armageddon*, 167–68.
20. Ibid., 195.
21. Gopin, "Judaism and Peacebuilding" (Coward and Smith), 111.
22. Gopin, *Eden and Armageddon*, 173. Within the context of his discussion on mourning, Gopin writes that as opposed to the accepted rationalist approach in conflict resolution studies, which generally advises not to dwell on the painful memories

of the past, the Jewish model encourages dealing with them and not ignoring them. When Gopin mentions Aaron as a pursuer of peace, he contrasts him with the mediator, whose rationalist approach encourages direct dialogue between the sides, as opposed to Aaron, who would meet with each side separately. Furthermore, in the context of his discussion on *teshuva* as a process of transformation, Gopin claims that formal, rational agreements between conflicting sides is often insufficient (187).

23. Gopin, *Eden and Armageddon*, 171–74; "Judaism and Peacebuilding" (Coward and Smith), 114–15. Gopin returns to discuss this topic in his *Holy War, Holy Peace*.
24. Gopin, *Eden and Armageddon*, 186. He also relates to this model at 77–79. See also "Judaism and Peacebuilding" (Coward and Smith), 120–21.
25. Gopin, *Eden and Armageddon*, 187–91; "Judaism and Peacebuilding" (Coward and Smith), 121–23. Gopin returns to discuss the topic of *teshuva* in *Holy War, Holy Peace*, 117–24.
26. Gerald M. Steinberg, "Conflict Prevention and Mediation in the Jewish Tradition," *Jewish Political Studies Review* 12, nos. 3–4 (Fall 2000), special edition of *Jewish Approaches to Conflict Resolution*, Jerusalem Center for Public Affairs, http://jcpa.org/wp-content/uploads/2000/10/conflict-prevention.pdf.
27. Steinberg, 3n1, refers to literature on culture and conflict and resolution in general, and in n. 2 mentions Mohammed Abu-Nimer, "Conflict Resolution in an Islamic Context: Some Conceptual Questions," *Peace and Change* 21, no. 1 (January 1996): 22–40; George E. Irani, "Islamic Mediation Techniques for Middle East Conflicts," *Middle East Review of International Affairs (MERIA)* 3, no. 2 (June 1999).
28. Steinberg, "Conflict Prevention," 3.
29. Ibid., 7–8.
30. Gerald M. Steinberg, "Jewish Sources on Conflict Management: Realism and Human Nature," in *Conflict and Conflict Management in Jewish Sources*, ed. Michal Roness (Ramat Gan, Israel: Conflict Management and Negotiation Graduate Program, Bar-Ilan University, 2008), 10–23, http://pconfl.biu.ac.il/files/pconfl/shared/conflict_handbook.pdf.
31. Steinberg, "Jewish Sources," 10–11. In n. 10 he cites Gopin, *Eden and Armageddon*.
32. Regarding these two definitions, see Avruch, *Culture*, 24–26.
33. Steinberg, "Jewish Sources," 10.
34. Gerald M. Steinberg, "The Limits of Peacebuilding Theory," in *The Routledge Handbook of Peacebuilding*, ed. Roger MacGinty (Abingdon: Routledge, 2013), 36–53. This is also apparent through his work at the NGO Monitor (https://www.ngo-monitor.org/).
35. Steinberg, "Jewish Sources," 13–15. It is interesting to note that Gopin, *Eden and Armageddon*, 177–78, also associates constructive conflict with disagreement for the sake of Heaven.
36. Steinberg, "Jewish Sources," 15–17. The reference to Joseph in the title seems to be an error, and should probably be read as Jacob.
37. Ibid., 19.
38. Ibid., 19–20.
39. Ibid., 17–19.

40. Ibid., 20.
41. For a discussion on the disagreement between Gopin's "idealistic" approach and Steinberg's "realist" approach, see Kaminsky, *Fundamentals of Jewish Conflict Resolution: Traditional Jewish Perspectives on Resolving Interpersonal Conflicts* (Boston: Academic Studies Press, 2017), 455–57, who argues that both approaches can be found within Jewish sources.
42. See previous note.
43. I do refer to Kaminsky's book, *Fundamentals of Jewish Conflict Resolution: Traditional Jewish Perspectives on Resolving Interpersonal Conflicts*, in several places throughout the book.
44. Abu-Nimer, *Nonviolence*, 63. Abu-Nimer also cites the quranic verse that calls upon believers to be peacemakers (Al-Hujurat 49:9): "And if two parties among the Believers fall into a quarrel, make peace between them."
45. Ibn Ishaq, *Sirat Rasonl Allah*, https://archive.org/stream/Sirat-lifeOfMuhammadBy-ibnIshaq/SiratIbnIahaqInEnglish#page/n13/mode/2up. Ibn Ishaq refers to his book as the earliest biography of Muhammad.
46. Abu-Nimer, *Nonviolence*, 63.
47. Abu-Nimer, *Nonviolence*, 67. He cites there *Sahih al-Bukhari* 5:59:603.
48. Little, *Peacemakers in Action*, 262.
49. Abu-Nimer, "An Islamic Model," 83. For more examples and analysis of how Muhammad served as a third-party peacemaker, see S. Ayse Kadayifci-Orellana, Mohammed Abu-Nimer, and Amjad Mohamed-Saleem, *Understanding an Islamic Framework for Peacebuilding* (Birmingham: Islamic Relief Worldwide, 2012), 28. See also Y. Yetkin, "Peace and Conflict Resolution in the Medina Charter," *Peace Review: A Journal of Social Justice* 18 (2006): 109–17; Doron Pely, *Muslim/Arab Mediation and Conflict Resolution: Understanding Sulha* (New York: Routledge, 2016), 10–34.

    One can find other important examples not noted by these scholars. In the section of the *hadith* called "Peacemaking," there are several other important examples of the Prophet acting as a peacemaker himself which these scholars have not cited:

    Narrated by Sahl bin Sad: There was a dispute among the people of the tribe of Bani 'Amr bin 'Auf. The Prophet went to them along with some of his companions in order to make peace between them.

    Narrated by Sahl bin Sad: Once the people of Quba fought with each other till they threw stones on each other. When Allah's Apostle was informed about it, he said, "Let us go to bring about a reconciliation between them." (*Hadith Sahih al-Bukhari* 3:49: "Peacemaking," 855, 858, https://sunnah.com/bukhari/53).
50. Aalok Sikand, "ADR Dharma: Seeking a Hindu Perspective on Dispute Resolution from the Holy Scriptures of the Mahabharata and the Bhagavad Gita," *Pepperdine Dispute Resolution Law Journal* 7, no. 2 (2007): 323–72, http://digitalcommons.pepperdine.edu/cgi/viewcontent.cgi?article=1095&context=drlj. Some Hindi students of mine have pushed back against referring to Lord Krishna as a third-party mediator. They point out that Krishna was inclined toward the Pandavs due to family ties and to the fact that the Kauravs were vilified in the Mahabharata and Krishna as a God incarnate was born to wipe evil from the world. It has been suggested that there

are better examples of third-party peacemakers in the Udyog Parva book (Book of Efforts), which is the fifth book of the Mahabharata.
51. Anthony Wanis-St. John, "Ancient Peacemakers: Examples of Humanity," in *Peacemaking: From Practice to Theory*, vol. 2, ed. Susan Allen Nan, Zachariah Cherian Mampilly, and Andrea Bartoli (Santa Barbara, CA: Praeger, 2011), 578–89.
52. Christopher Buck, "Deganawida: The Peacemaker," in *American Writers*, supplement 26, ed. Jay Parini (n.p.: Charles Scribner's Sons: 2016), 81.
53. See, for example, Jean Houston, *Manual for the Peacemaker: An Iroquois Legend to Heal Self and Society* (Wheaton, IL: Quest Books, 1995).
54. John Paul Lederach, *Reconcile: Conflict Transformation for Ordinary Christians* (Harrisonburg, VA: Herald Press, 2014), 45–46.
55. Ken Sande was the founder of Peacemaker Ministries: http://peacemaker.net/. For other examples of Christian conflict resolution literature and programs, see *Musalaha: A Curriculum of Reconciliation* (Jerusalem: Musalaha Ministry of Reconciliation, 2011), 66, 266.
56. Ken Sande, *The Peacemaker: A Biblical Guide to Resolving Personal Conflicts*, 3rd ed. (Ada, MI: Baker Books, 1997), 32.
57. Little, *Peacemakers in Action*, 324.
58. Hamdesa Tuso and Maureen P. Flaherty, eds., *Creating the Third Force: Indigenous Processes of Peacemaking* (Lanham, MD: Lexington Books, 2016), 14.
59. Katrien Hertog writes that the interest in religious peacebuilding also stems from the interest in cultural models. She adds: "The elicitive approach of Lederach, which supports the concepts and mechanisms for conflict management and transformation that can be found in the local cultures, implies a call upon religious traditions as a constituent element of each culture, to explore, engage, develop, and realize their potential for peacebuilding" (Hertog, *Complex Reality of Religious Peacebuilding*, 13).
60. John Paul Lederach, *Preparing for Peace: Conflict Transformation across Cultures* (Syracuse, NY: Syracuse University Press, 1996). Hartog, *Complex Reality*, 73–74, describes Lederach's approach as aiming "to evoke from within local religious traditions the conceptual and theological-ethical resources which are relevant to the culture-specific task of fostering peaceable relationships within and across divided communities."
61. Avruch, *Culture*, 80–85.
62. Augsburger, *Conflict Mediation across Cultures*, 191–92.
63. See above, n. 58.
64. Tuso and Flaherty, *Creating the Third Force*, 530.
65. Some scholars have suggested common characteristics of these models. Graham Kemp and Douglas P. Fry, in their book, *Keeping the Peace: Conflict Resolution and Peaceful Societies around the World* (New York: Routledge, 2004), examine nine peaceful societies from around the world, noting several core characteristics consistently found in all of them. See 194–98 in their book.
66. Augsburger, *Conflict Mediation*, 225–26; Avruch, *Culture*, 80–81.
67. E. E. Evans-Pritchard, *The Nuer* (Oxford: Oxford University Press, 1940), 163–76.

68. Goh Bee Chen, *Law without Lawyers, Justice without Courts: On Traditional Chinese Mediation* (Aldershot, England: Ashgate, 2002), chap. 1. Chinese students of mine have also pointed out that in rural Chinese areas, and old man with a good reputation, known as Xiangxian, will mediate between conflicting families, promoting compromise and avoiding a breakdown in relations.
69. Kadayifci-Orellana, Abu-Nimer, and Mohamed-Saleem, "Understanding an Islamic Framework," 33–35.
70. Ali Gohar and Lisa Schrich, "Ritual and Symbol in Justice and Peacebuilding: Lessons from Pukhton Tribes on the Jirga," in Tuso and Flaherty, *Creating the Third Force*, 460.
71. Ibid.
72. Yitbarakh Nagat, "The *Schmagluch* Establishment's Conflict Resolution Methods in the Ethiopian Jewish Community: Self-Perceptions of Interveners Regarding the Decision Management Process" [In Hebrew] (master's thesis, Bar-Ilan University, 2006).
73. Ibid., ii.
74. Cathie J. Witty, *Mediation and Society: Conflict Management in Lebanon* (New York: Academic Press, 1980); Elias Jabbour, *Sulha: Palestinian Traditional Peacemaking Process* (Montreat, NC: House of Hope, 1996); Joseph Ginat, *Blood Revenge: Family Honor, Mediation, and Outcasting* (Portland, OR: Sussex Academic, 1997); Nizar Hamzeh, "The Role of Hizbullah in Conflict Management within Lebanon's Shi'a Community," in *Conflict Resolution in the Arab World: Selected Essays*, ed. Paul Salem (Beirut: American University of Beirut, 1997), 93–121; Richard T. Antoun, "Institutionalized Deconfrontation: A Case Study of Conflict Resolution among Tribal Peasants in Jordan," in *Conflict Resolution in the Arab World*, 140–75; George E. Irani and Nathan C. Funk, "Rituals of Reconciliation: Arab-Islamic Perspectives," *Arab Studies Quarterly* (ASQ) 20, no. 4 (Fall 1998): 53–72; Laurie King-Irani, "Rituals of Forgiveness and Processes of Empowerment in Lebanon," in *Traditional Cures for Modern Conflicts*, ed. I. William Zartman (Boulder, CO: Lynne Rienner Publishers, 2000), 129–40; Abu-Nimer, *Nonviolence*, 91–110; Kadayifci-Orellana, Abu-Nimer, and Mohamed-Saleem, "Understanding an Islamic Framework"; George E. Irani, " 'The Best of Judgments': Rituals of Settlement (Sulh) and Reconciliation (Musalaha) in the Middle East," in Tuso and Flaherty, *Creating the Third Force*, 55–76; Pely, *Muslim/Arab Mediation*.
75. Irani and Funk, "Rituals of Reconciliation," 64. Abu-Nimer, *Nonviolence*, 92, uses the terms *sulh* and *musalaha* to refer to reconciliation; *sulha*, in certain geographical areas, refers to the specific reconciliation ceremony at the end of the process, but not to the whole process. Jabbour, *Sulha*, 31, and King-Irani, "Rituals of Forgiveness," use only the word *sulha*.
76. Abu-Nimer, *Nonviolence*, 96; Jabbour, *Sulha*, 26; King-Irani, "Rituals of Forgiveness," 22. Antoun, "Institutionalized Deconfrontation," 163, writes that the *sulha* does not come to solve the ethical and psychological issues of the sides, but rather functions as a mechanism for restoring social harmony. Pely, *Muslim/Arab Mediation*, 77, emphasizes the aspect of "re-integrative honoring" in the reconciliation process of *sulha*.
77. Jabbour, *Sulha*, 26; King-Irani, "Rituals of Forgiveness," 21.

78. Jordan: Antoun, "Institutionalized Deconfrontation"; Lebanon: King-Irani, "Rituals of Forgiveness," Hamzeh, "Role of Hizbullah"; Witty, *Mediation and Society*; Israel/Palestine: Jabbour, *Sulha*; Ginat, *Blood Revenge*; Pely, *Muslim/Arab Mediation*.
79. On the values at the heart of the conflict, see Pely, *Muslim/Arab Mediation*, 54–75. See also Abu-Nimer, *Nonviolence*, 98; and similarly, Jabbour, *Sulha*, 17; Irani, "'The Best Judgments,'" 59; King-Irani, "Rituals of Forgiveness," 133.
80. Jabbour, *Sulha*, 23; King-Irani, 132; Ginat, *Blood Revenge*, 76. However, Irani and Funk, "Rituals of Reconciliation," 65, and in particular 72n24, write that the *sulha* today is performed primarily in cases of murder and not in less severe cases. Out of the twenty-two cases Ginat brings in *Blood Revenge*, fourteen deal with cases of murder or manslaughter. Other cases include disrespecting women (cases 15, 25), physical injuries (cases 13, 24, 31), land dispute (case 14), and dispute over a political position (case 27). Ginat also notes, at 80–81, that in recent years there has been a decrease in the *sulha* process among the Bedouin of the Negev in cases that do not involve homicide, as they are increasingly turning to the Israeli law enforcement to resolve their disputes.
81. King-Irani, "Rituals of Forgiveness," 132, writes that the first step of the *sulha* is to establish who is the victim and who is the perpetrator.
82. Abu-Nimer, *Nonviolence*, 102. At 107 he writes that the *sulha* functions as a mechanism for social control.
83. Ibid., 103; Irani and Funk, "Rituals of Reconciliation," 69; Pely, *Muslim/Arab Mediation*, 39.
84. Jabbour, *Sulha*, 27–28, and Pely, *Muslim/Arab Mediation*, 3, 90–92, both use this term to refer to Arabs living in the upper Galilee, explaining that the word signifies these people are well respected in the area. See also Antoun, "Institutionalized Deconfrontation," 153.
85. King-Irani, "Rituals of Forgiveness," 132, uses this term to refer to mediators in the *sulha* process in Sunni Lebanon. Irani and Funk, "Rituals of Reconciliation, 65, use *jaha* and *muslihs* interchangeably, with *muslihs* referring to the mediators and *jaha* to the respected delegation.
86. Kadayifci-Orellana, "Understanding an Islamic Framework," 6–27. Ginat, *Blood Revenge*, 57, uses the term *wasita*.
87. Jabbour, *Sulha*, 28, writes that in the upper Galilee, the number of *jaha* in a *sulha* depends on the severity of the case. In simpler cases two or three mediators may be sufficient, while in more severe cases the number of *jaha* may reach as many as twenty mediators, at which time they might need to arrive at decisions by majority. See also Abu-Nimer, *Nonviolence*, 104.
88. Abu-Nimer, 105. Irani and Funk, "Rituals of Reconciliation," 65, also describe the mediators as respected elders of the village. For a case where the mediator was too many years younger than the parties in conflict, see Ginat, *Blood Revenge*, 62–63 (case 14).
89. Ginat, *Blood Revenge*, 84.
90. Ginat, *Blood Revenge*, 82, writes with regard to the Bedouins of the Negev desert that one whose family boasts other mediators, or whose father is a mediator, is accorded increased respect when he himself functions as a mediator.

91. See Ginat, *Blood Revenge*, case 13 (60–69), in which the mediator was the mayor of a city. Case 19 (68–69) involved a mediator who was a member of parliament. Case 22 (71) involved a mediator who was politically well connected.
92. Ginat, *Blood Revenge*, 84. Antoun, "Institutionalized Deconfrontation," 149, describes in detail that the mediator in a conflict in Jordan was both very wealthy and a member of the Jordanian Senate.
93. Kadayifci-Orellana, "Understanding an Islamic Framework," 29. Hamzeh, "Role of Hizbullah," 110–11, notes that in Shi'a communities in Lebanon there has been a shift in recent years from the model of respected lay leader as peacemaker to the model of religious leader associated with the Hezbollah as peacemaker. Abu-Nimer, *Nonviolence*, 105, also notes that in Gaza, the peacemaker is often a religious leader, such as an imam who may be "the most trusted person in the community because of his strict observance of Islamic values and traditions."
94. Jabbour, *Sulha*, 33.
95. Abu-Nimer, *Nonviolence*, 105.
96. Ginat, *Blood Revenge*, mentions several cases in which the reputation of the third-party peacemakers was damaged as a result of their failed attempt to make peace (case 16, 64; case 24, 73–74; case 25, 74–77).
97. Ginat, *Blood Revenge*, also mentions several cases in which the social status, and occasionally political power, of the mediators rose as a result of successful *sulha* processes (case 23, 72–73).
98. See Irani and Funk, "Rituals of Reconciliation," 59, Table 2.1, regarding the neutrality of the third-party. See also Jabbour, *Sulha*, 27–29.
99. Kadayifci-Orellana, "Understanding an Islamic Framework," 30.
100. Ginat, *Blood Revenge*, 98, describes a conflict that continued for fifteen years and yet the third-party peacemakers did not despair in their attempts to bring the sides to *sulha*. Ginat also writes (case 17, 66) about the immense patience of the mediators in their attempts to make peace in a conflict that continued for so long.
101. Pely, *Muslim/Arab Mediation*, 85, and Jabbour, *Sulha*, 48.
102. Jabbour, 27, describes how the family of the murderer needs to go from house to house and plead with the distinguished members of the community to join the delegation of the *jaha*. Only in extreme cases do the mediators intervene on their own initiative, as the family of the victim may question whether they were indeed sent on behalf of the murderer's family. A similar description is found in Irani and Funk, "Rituals of Reconciliation," 65, and Pely, *Muslim/Arab Mediation*, 80. According to Abu-Nimer, *Nonviolence*, 104, and Pely, 82, occasionally the third-party intervenes on their own initiative, or the community elders. See a similar discussion in King-Irani, "Rituals of Forgiveness," 132.
103. Jabbour, *Sulha*, 42, tells how the mediators cannot go to sleep until they go to the victim's family. Ginat, *Blood Revenge*, 67, tells of the importance of the delegation's visiting the home of the victim's family within the first twenty-four hours.
104. Jabbour, *Sulha*, 42, and Ginat, *Blood Revenge*, 59, write that the side of the perpetrator may communicate with the side of the victim only through the mediators. Jabbour also describes the importance of the two sides not meeting one another

during the *sulha* process (33–36). Ginat distinguishes between the Bedouin in the Negev, where it is accepted that the perpetrator and his family go into exile—at least temporarily, and Arabs of the Galilee, where exile is not possible. In the latter case, there are other clear rules regarding how to separate between the sides so that they do not see each other until an agreement is achieved.

105. Pely, *Muslim/Arab Mediation*, 80–89.
106. Ibid., 89–92.
107. King-Irani, "Rituals of Forgiveness," 132.
108. Regarding the *hudna* (temporary ceasefire) and *'atwa* (payment for achieving the ceasefire), see Jabbour, *Sulha*, 33–36, and Pely, *Muslim/Arab Mediation*, 95–99. Ginat, *Blood Revenge*, 67–68, writes that among the Arabs of the Galilee a ceasefire is almost always achieved, the only question being the amount of the *'atwa*, while among the Bedouin of the Negev most of the time there is a ceasefire, although sometimes there are attempts at blood revenge. See also Hamzeh, "Role of Hizbullah," 111, who states that sometimes among the Shi'ite tribes in Lebanon there are attempts at blood revenge after the third day, and the Hezbollah steps in to stop them, sometimes through using force (see Chap. 2, 79–81, for more about third-party peacemakers using force).
109. On the negotiations and *sulha* agreement, see Pely, *Muslim/Arab Mediation*, 99–111. Regarding the *diya*, which is the reparations or blood money paid to the victim's side, see Jabbour, *Sulha*, 40–42. Ginat, *Blood Revenge*, 72, writes that the average *diya* paid for a murder case is NIS (new Israeli shekels) 500,000, although payment can be as low as NIS 50,000 (case 23, 72) and as high as NIS 1,500,000 (case 25, 75).
110. Hamzeh, "Role of Hizbullah," 113, quotes a Hezbollah mediator who said that usually the family of the victim demands that the murderer be exiled in addition to paying reparations. Ginat, *Blood Revenge*, cites a case among the Bedouin of the Negev where the murderer had to be exiled for seven years (case 18, 66–67) and one among the Arabs in the Galilee where the murderer was exiled for six months (case 25, 75). However, he notes that exile is considered the exception in these cultures, and that usually blood money is sufficient.
111. Jabbour, *Sulha*, and Pely, *Muslim/Arab Mediation*, refer to the ceremony itself as *sulha*, while Irani and Funk, "Rituals of Reconciliation," refer to it as *musalaha*.
112. Jabbour, *Sulha*, 51, writes that usually the *sulha* ceremony takes place between 10 A.M. and 12 P.M. in order that everyone can attend the reconciliation. See also Irani and Funk, "Rituals of Reconciliation." King-Irani, "Rituals of Forgiveness," writing about Sunni Lebanon, reports that the ceremony begins in the home of the victim and then moves over to a neutral public place.
113. Jabbour, *Sulha*, 56, and Irani and Funk, "Rituals of Reconciliation," 69, call this stage of shaking hands *musafaha*.
114. Jabbour, *Sulha*, 52, writes that on a rare occasion one of the members of the victim's family may refuse to shake hands, thereby expressing their refusal to forgive—which can then cause the continuation of hostilities. Ginat, *Blood Revenge*, 79, case 16, reports a situation where the brother of the victim stabbed to death the brother of the murderer during the hand-shaking ceremony in the Southern hills of Hebron in the 1970s.

115. Abu-Nimer, *Nonviolence*, 99, writes that in a *sulha* he witnessed in the Gaza Strip, a representative of the murderer's family emphasized regret and requested forgiveness for his family through expostulating on verses from the Quran (42:43). After him, a representative from the victim's family spoke and also incorporated quotes from the Quran (42:37) that stress the granting of forgiveness in times of anger. He also cited a tradition of the Prophet Muhammad that one must forgive like Joseph forgave his brothers (Abu-Nimer, n. 9). For other examples of speeches given at the reconciliation ceremony see Witty, *Mediation and Society*, 58; Hamzeh, "Role of Hizbullah," 114; Jabbour, *Sulha*, 54–55.
116. Jabbour, *Sulha*, 56–57, refers to this stage as *mumalaha*, and writes that sharing the meal expresses friendship and peace.
117. Jabbour, *Sulha*, 43; Hamzeh, "Role of Hizbullah," 114; Ginat, *Blood Revenge*, 93, case 32.
118. Jabbour, *Sulha*, 57, writes that there are five components of the *sulha* ceremony: forgiveness, shaking of hands, reciprocal home visits, drinking bitter coffee, and eating a joint meal together. Ginat, *Blood Revenge*, 76, case 25, describes one case that took place in the West Bank: After the *sulha* ceremony, the family of the perpetrator visited the home of the victim, as is the custom. However, they did not say they would immediately visit the home of the perpetrator, and the visit was postponed until the next morning. As a result, the whole process ceased to be considered *sulha* and instead turned into a process of "conflict management" with a prolonged ceasefire, since the honor of the perpetrator's side had been damaged.
119. Jabbour, *Sulha*, 52–56, and Pely, *Muslim/Arab Mediation*, 111–18, describe the ceremony of the white flag, which is customary in *sulha* ceremonies in the Galilee. At the beginning of the ceremony, a representative of the murderer's family makes a knot in the white flag, which was delivered to his family from the family of the victim; afterward, the murderer holds the white flag and begins to walk toward the main square of the town, escorted by his family and the delegation of mediators together with other distinguished people. These symbols represent the taking of responsibility by the murderer's family and the acknowledgment of guilt by the murderer himself. After this the family members stand in straight lines facing one another and shake hands, and a few people tie additional knots in the flag to symbolize their commitment to guaranteeing that the peace will be upheld. Witty, *Mediation and Society*, 58, tells of a ceremony in Sunni Lebanon in which the victim would give a haircut to the perpetrator, which represented his forgiveness. King-Irani, "Rituals of Forgiveness," 133, describes a Shi'ite ceremony in Lebanon in which the murderer had to approach the home of the victim's family wearing a red scarf around his neck symbolizing his guilt and the handing over of his fate to the hands of the victim's family.
120. Augsburger, *Conflict Mediation*, 39–40.
121. Paul Salem, "A Critique of Western Conflict Resolution from a Non-Western Perspective," *Negotiation Journal* 9, no. 4 (1993): 361–69.

122. Mohammed Abu-Nimer, "Contrasts in Conflict Management in Cleveland and Palestine," in Zartman, *Traditional Cures for Modern Conflicts*, 141–52. See also Mohammed Abu-Nimer, "Conflict Resolution in an Islamic Context," 22–40.
123. Irani and Funk, "Rituals of Reconciliation," 53–72. This article was republished with minor changes as George E. Irani, "'The Best of Judgments': Rituals of Settlement (*Sulh*) and Reconciliation (*Musalaha*) in the Middle East" (mentioned above in n. 80). See 55–76 there.
124. Similarly, Augsburger, *Conflict Mediation*, 204–5, writes that traditional models promote reconciliation while North American models promote "reaching an agreement on issues." Tuso, *Creating the Third Force*, 524, writes in the context of contrasting Western models with traditional models: "[I]ndigenous systems of peacemaking are different from ADR [alternative dispute resolution] in the sense that the goal of ADR is to reach an amicable agreement regarding some expressed issues in a dispute between the conflicting parties, whereas in indigenous forms of peacemaking, peacemakers seek to restore the damaged relationships between the parties in conflict and the families and the larger communities where the conflict occurred."
125. Jeanmarie Pinto, "Peacemaking as Ceremony: The Mediation Model of the Navajo Nation," in Tuso and Flaherty, *Creating the Third Force*, 171.
126. Doron Pely and Golan Luzon, "The Muslim/Arab Sulha and the Restorative Justice Model: Same Purpose, Different Approach," *Cardozo Journal of Conflict Resolution* 19 (2018): 289–307.
127. Pely, *Muslim/Arab Mediation*, 47.
128. Ibid. Tuso and Flaherty, *Creating the Third Force*, 12–13, note the connection between restorative justice and indigenous models of peacemaking.
129. In particular, that of the *sulha* process.
130. Ronald J. Fisher, *Interactive Conflict Resolution* (Syracuse, NY: Syracuse University Press, 1997), 19–76. One of the founding books on this model is John Burton, *Conflict and Communication: The Use of Controlled Communication in International Relations* (London: Macmillan, 1969).
131. Ronald J. Fisher, "Social-Psychological Processes in Interactive Conflict Analysis and Reconciliation," in *Reconciliation, Justice, and Coexistence: Theory and Practice*, ed. Mohammed Abu-Nimer (Lanham, MD: Lexington Books, 2001), 25. For a fuller, more recent discussion of reconciliation and basic psychological needs, see Felicia Pratto and Demis E. Glasford, "How Needs Can Motivate Intergroup Reconciliation in the Face of Intergroup Conflict," in *The Social Psychology of Intergroup Reconciliation*, ed. A. Nadler, T. E. Malloy, and J. D. Fisher (New York: Oxford University Press, 2008), 117–44.
132. All reconciliation scholars characterize the conflict they are coming to address in this manner. See, for example, R. J. Fisher, "Social-Psychological Processes," 25; Walter G. Stephen, "The Road to Reconciliation," in *The Social Psychology of Intergroup Reconciliation*, 373–75.
133. The following studies all relate directly to the model of the problem-solving workshops in the context of reconciliation: Joseph Montville, "The Healing Function in

Political Conflict Resolution," in *Conflict Resolution in Theory and Practice*, ed. D. J. D. Sandole and H. van der Merwe (Manchester: Manchester University Press, 1993). See 112-27, where Montville calls this model "Problem-Solving Workshops"; Herbert C. Kelman, "Informal Mediation by the Scholar/Practitioner," in *The Handbook of Interethnic Coexistence*, ed. Alan B. Slifka (New York: Continuum, 1998), 310-31; Blake M. Riek et al., "A Social-Psychological Approach to Postconflict Reconciliation," in *The Social Psychology of Intergroup Reconciliation*, 255-73, where the model is called "Interactive Problem-Solving"; Fisher, "Social-Psychological Processes," 25-45, where the model is called "Interactive Conflict Resolution"; Stephen, "The Road to Reconciliation," 369-94, where the author uses the term "Problem-Solving Groups."

134. Fisher, "Social-Psychological Processes," 33. On the specific effects that come as a result of such reconciliation encounters such as "decategorization," "positive functional relations," and "common group identity," see Riek et al., "Social-Psychological Approach," 255-73. On the social-psychological approach of "reconciliation" in conflict resolution studies in general as distinguished from the "realist approach of conflict resolution," see Yehudith Auerbach, "Conflict Resolution, Forgiveness and Reconciliation in Material and Identity Conflicts," *Humboldt Journal of Social Relations* 29, no. 2 (2005): 41-80; Herbert C. Kelman, "Reconciliation from a Social-Psychological Perspective," in *The Social Psychology of Intergroup Reconciliation*, ed. A. Nadler, T. E. Malloy, and J. D. Fisher (New York: Oxford University Press, 2008), 15-32.

135. On the identity and role of the third side in this model, see Fisher, "Social-Psychological Processes," 32, 34, 35-36; Montville, "The Healing Function," 114-15; Stephen, "The Road to Reconciliation," 371; Kelman, "Informal Mediation," 312.

136. Kelman, "Informal Mediation," 312, writes that there should be three permanent and five rotating advisors.

137. The presentation of the third-party as a psychologist is found in Montville, "The Healing Function," 115.

138. This point is emphasized by Kelman, "Informal Mediation," 310.

139. Fisher, "Social-Psychological Processes," 29; Kelman, "Informal Mediation," 312; Stephen, "The Road to Reconciliation," 381.

140. For example, Fisher, "Social-Psychological Processes," 28, writes: [T]he conditions and outcomes of successful dialogue and conflict analysis lay the groundwork for the reciprocal enactment of the necessary elements of reconciliation: acknowledgment of transgressions, apologies for these, forgiveness of these, and assurances that such acts will not occur in the future."

141. Kelman, "Informal Mediation," 311.

142. See Avruch, *Culture*, 85-100; Gopin, *Eden and Armageddon*, 40-51.

143. As part of the network of community mediation and dialogue centers that Mosaica supports through the Tochnit Gishurim Project, more and more are opening in the Arab sectors of Israeli society. For example, in the south of Israel in the Bedouin city of Rahat, the senior sheikhs—the Islamic community leaders—took a contemporary mediation course and now incorporate traditional *sulha* practices with modern mediation.

Chapter 2

1. On the transformation of Aaron's image from biblical literature to rabbinic literature, see Henry Bamberger, "Aaron: Changing Perceptions," *Judaism* (Spring 1993): 201–13.
2. Bamberger concludes his article explaining that through this rebranding of Aaron as a peacemaker, the rabbis were able "to claim that they, rather than their priestly opponents, were the true heirs of Aaron. Of course they recognized that biological descent from Aaron belonged to the ... priests. However, those priests were seen—or, at least portrayed—as arrogant, overbearing, and often ignorant. Thus by praising Aaron for the very qualities which they saw in their leaders, and which they strove to attain, the Pharisees (i.e., the rabbis [DR]) could put forward their claim to be Aaron's spiritual children. In emphasizing spiritual rather than biological descent, thus distancing the Sadducees (i.e., the priestly class [DR]) from their original priestly ancestor, the Pharisees established their right to be the recognized judges and interpreters of the law." Similarly, Gopen, *Eden*, 182, writes regarding the rabbinic identification of Aaron as "Judaism's ideal peacemaker": "there are a variety of motivations for the rabbis to do this, some involving the inner logic of biblical hermeneutics and others involving a contemporaneous antiviolence critique of priestly Judaism embedded in the counterexample of Aaron." It is, however, important to note that these claims of the historical motivation of the rabbis is somewhat speculative, as Nathan Still Schumer mentions as a general statement about historical readings of rabbinic texts relating to priests: "[I]n general, this set of assumptions about the function of the priesthood in rabbinic literature leans heavily on its own historiographic bias that all mentions of priests are meant to contrast unfavorably with the rabbis. It is not always so clear that this set of interests is reflected in the texts themselves." See Nathan Still Schumer, "The Memory of the Temple in Palestinian Rabbinic Literature" (PhD diss., Columbia University, 2017), 8–9.
3. This translation is based on the Hebrew *talmido* (a disciple), found in MS Kaufman (Budapest: Magyar Tudomanyos Akademia, A50), considered the best manuscript of the Mishna according to Ma'agarim, the Historical Dictionary Project. However, in the standard printed editions of the Mishna, the wording is *mitalmidav* ("of the disciples [of Aaron]"), in the plural. Unless otherwise indicated, all translations of classical rabbinic literature will be based on the preferred manuscript of the Academy.
4. It should be noted that the commentators, especially the later ones, often had the printed edition of the texts in front of them. I have therefore chosen to use the more common translation based on the printed editions when discussing the commentaries of the Mishna.

    The Hebrew word is *briyot*, which may literally mean "creatures," and is sometimes translated as "humanity."
5. I will address the question of why specifically Aaron was considered the seminal pursuer of peace and how we know he was a pursuer of peace later in this chapter.
6. Stuart A. Cohen, *The Three Crowns: Structures of Communal Politics in Early Rabbinic Jewry* (Cambridge, UK: Cambridge University Press, 2007), 80.
7. Shmuel de Uçeda, *Midrash Shmuel* [commentary on Mishna Avot] (Venice, 1585).

8. Yosef b. Hayim Yaavetz, *Pirkei Avot im peirush haYaavetz* (Tel Aviv, 1998). A similar statement is found in the commentary of Rabbi Yosef b. Shushan, *Peirushei Rabbenu Yosef b. Shushan al masekhet Avot*, on this mishna. After citing the story of Aaron pursuing peace between a husband and wife by allowing the wife to spit in Aaron's eye (Table 2.1, case 3), he writes: "And if Aaron would do this.... How much greater is the sin of the person who acts arrogantly [and refrains from making peace] if we sense hatred between our brethren, the children of Israel—even if they be simpletons, and of the less [respectable] families—if we don't try to place peace between them with all our ability."
9. Marc Gopin, *Eden and Armageddon*, 182. Michal Roness also refers to Aaron as the "prototype of a mediator and peacemaker." See Michal Roness, *Conflict and Conflict Management*, 140, http://pconfl.biu.ac.il/files/pconfl/shared/conflict_handbook.pdf.
10. Later in this chapter I will cite an additional distinction between the lover of peace and the pursuer of peace brought in hasidic literature.
11. *Avot d'Rabbi Natan* Version B, chap. 24.
12. Many of the early rabbinic sources appear to be based on or inspired by Ps. 34:15: "Seek peace, and pursue it." Both the Jerusalem (Pe'a 1:1 [15d]) and Babylonian (Kiddushin 40a, b; Yevamot 109a–b) Talmuds identify this verse as the source of the mishna in Pe'a, which encourages people to "bring peace between people." The verse may also have been an inspiration for Hillel's statement in Mishna Avot 1:12.
13. A similar statement can be found in *Avot d'Rabbi Natan* A, chap. 12: "Pursuer of peace"—how so? It teaches us that one should pursue peace between every one of (the people of) Israel in the same manner that Aaron would pursue peace between every one of (the people of) Israel, as it says, "Seek peace, and pursue it" (Ps. 34:15). Rabbi Shimon b. Elazar said: If a person sits in his house and is quiet, how does he pursue peace between all the people of Israel? Rather, he must leave his place and go throughout the world in order to pursue peace among Israel. As it says, "Seek peace, and pursue it." How so? "Seek it"—in your place; "Pursue it"—in another place.
14. It is important to note that other commentaries seem to have understood that the idea of "lover of peace" as passive and "pursuer of peace" as active is not referring to the realm of third-party peacemaking but rather to interpersonal relations. To be a lover of peace means to avoid engaging in conflict with others; to be a pursuer of peace means to proactively pursue making peace if you are engaged in conflict. See, for example, Rabbi Shmuel de Uçeda's commentary on this mishna in *Midrash Shmuel*, where he mentions the possibility of interpreting "lover of peace" as one devoid of strife and "pursuer of peace" as one who, if peace is running away from him, chases after his adversary to appease him. With regard to the latter, he explains: "For if your fellow does not want to make peace with you, pursue after him to reconcile with him." Rabbi de Uçeda also connects the mishna to Ps. 34:15, as above.

Rabbi Ḥayim of Volozhin (Belarus, 1749–1821), in his commentary on the Mishna, *Ruaḥ Ḥayim*, similarly understands loving peace and pursuing peace to be in the context of interpersonal relations and not third-party peacemaking: "And that which is said, 'Seek peace' (Ps 34:15), means that you should want there to be peace between you, and even if in your opinion [someone] sinned against you, nevertheless 'pursue [peace]'; be the *rodef shalom*, and do not hope that your [adversary] will reconcile with you [first]" (*Ruah Hayim*, Avot 1:12).

Rabbi Hayim uses a different term, "*matil shalom*" (placer of peace), to denote third-party peacemaking. He writes: "When there is conflict between two people, and a third wants to place peace between them, he must appease and go against the will of each side, saying, 'Yes, it is true that even if you are innocent and your fellow sinned against you, nevertheless you should be the pursuer of peace.' For if he tells him that he sinned against his fellow and he is obligated by law to go and appease him, he will not heed him. Rather, he will fight with the placer of peace over this, [as] 'every way of man is right in his own eyes'" (Prov. 21:2).

15. The exception to this would be community mediation centers, which often do proactively intervene in conflicts.
16. Maharal, *Derekh hayim: Peirush lemasekhet Avot* [commentary on tractate Avot], Hayim Halevi Pardes edition (Tel Aviv, 1975), chap. 1.
17. For an overview of the theories of conflict prevention, see Alice Ackermann, "The Idea and Practice of Conflict Prevention," *Journal of Peace Research* 40, no. 3 (2003): 339–447.
18. *Peirushei Rabbenu Yitzhak b. Shlomo miToledo al masekhet Avot* (1:12).
19. It is unclear to me from Rabbi Yitzhak's commentary whether there is any independent value to being a lover of peace, and if there would be something missing if the mishna had stated only to be a "pursuer of peace."
20. *Midrash Shmuel*, Avot 1:12.
21. It is notable that Rabbi Menahem Meiri (Provence, 13th cent.), commonly known as "the Meiri," similarly connects the obligation to pursue third-party peacemaking with the obligation to develop one's own character. In his commentary on the mishna we have been discussing, however, he interprets these two characteristics conversely to *Midrash Shmuel*: "lover of peace" concerns third-party peacemaking, whereas "pursuer of peace" pertains to one's own interpersonal relationships as well as personal character development. See Meiri, *Beit haBehira*, Avot 1.
22. See, for example, Phyllis Kotite, "Education for Conflict Prevention and Peacebuilding: Meeting the Global Challenges of the 21st Century" (Paris: UNESCO, 2012), http://unesdoc.unesco.org/images/0021/002171/217106e.pdf; Connie Peck and Eleanor Wertheim, eds., "Strengthening the Practice of Peacemaking and Preventive Diplomacy in the United Nations: The UNITAR Approach," https://unitar.org/pmcp/sites/unitar.org.pmcp/files/sppd.pdf.
23. Peter T. Coleman, Morton Deutsch, and Eric C. Marcus, eds., *The Handbook of Conflict Resolution: Theory and Practice*, 3rd ed. (San Francisco: Jossey-Bass, 2014), xi–xii.
24. The language of *Midrash Shmuel* is *ohev shalom le'atzmo*, loving peace for oneself. This unquestionably refers to one's own relationships with others. Whether or not it can also be taken to include one's relationship with oneself in the pursuit of inner peace is unclear. For a discussion on the need for inner peace before attaining "outer peace," see Chap. 4, n. 23. For further discussion on non-Western peacemakers emphasizing the connection between peace in the home and pursuing peace among others, see

Gopin, *Bridges*, 224n14, who reflects on how each of the Palestinian peacemakers he interviewed always emphasized the concentric levels of peace: beginning with inner peace, segueing to peace in the home, and then working for peace on a larger scale. He writes that "love and peace in the home and love and peace in the world are inseparable."

25. For further discussion on the meaning of peace/*shalom* in rabbinic Judaism, see Kaminsky, *Fundamentals*, 36–56.
26. Rabbi Don Yitzḥak Abarbanel, *Naḥalat Avot* 1:12. Abarbanel's wording and ideas strongly echo those of Rabbi Yitzḥak b. Moshe Arama of fifteenth-century Spain in his philosophical commentary on the book of Numbers, *Akeidat Yitzḥak*, chap. 74 (*Naso*). For the connection between the two, see Kaminsky, *Fundamentals*, 42.
27. For a different yet somewhat complementary meaning of *shalom*, see Rabbi Yosef Albo (Spain, 1380–1444), *Sefer ha'ikkarim hashalem* (Jerusalem: Horev, 1995), vol. 4, part 2, chap. 51, 493. Rabbi Albo understands *shalom* to be "the unity of opposites" and not uniformity. For more on this understanding of *shalom*, see Alick Isaacs, *A Prophetic Peace: Judaism, Religion, and Politics* (Bloomington: Indiana University Press, 2011), 138.
28. Royce Anderson, "A Definition of Peace," *Peace and Conflict: Journal of Peace Psychology* 10, no. 2 (2004): 101–16.
29. Anderson, 105–6. Kaminsky, *Fundamentals*, 53–54, also connects the concept of "positive peace" to the peace Aaron would pursue.
30. For further sources connecting the meaning of *shalom* to positive peace, see Kaminsky, 53–56.
31. Similarly, Rabbi Amy Eilberg writes with regard to the above commentary of Abarbanel, as well as in light of the comments of participants in a *rodef shalom* training she facilitated on the meaning of *shalom*: "We sometimes speak of peace in its minimal sense, as in the absence of violence or the absence of conflict between people. . . . But I am convinced that prayers for peace offered by people all over the world every day express more far-reaching yearnings—for wholeness, balance, acceptance, and ease." See Eilberg, *From Enemy to Friend*, 21.
32. For more on the distinction between elite and cultural religious peacebuilding, see Wang, "Strategic Engagement and Religious Peace-building," 71–82.
33. The *iftar* meal is the break-fast held at the conclusion of each day of fasting during the Islamic month of Ramadan.
34. Elhanan Miller, "'Those Wishing to See the Face of God Must See the Face of the Other,'" *plus 61j Media*, June 6, 2019, https://plus61j.net.au/panel5/wishing-see-face-god-must-see-face/.
35. Gil Hoffman, "Sheikh, Rabbi Hope Baseless Love, Joint Fast Will Stop COVID-19," *Jerusalem Post*, July 27, 2020, https://www.jpost.com/israel-news/sheikh-rabbi-hope-baseless-love-joint-fast-will-stop-covid-19-636492. See also Yaniv Sharon, "To Realize How Alike We Are," published in Hebrew 29, July 2020, https://www.davar1.co.il/238991/ and in Arabic 2, August, 2020, https://ar.davar1.co.il/239700/.
36. Peter Schäfer, "Rabbis and Priests, or: How to Do Away with the Glorious Past of the Sons of Aaron," in *Antiquity in Antiquity: Jewish and Christian Pasts in the Greco-Roman World*, ed. Gregg Gardner and Kevin L. Osterloh (Tübingen: Mohr Siebeck, 2008), 168. It is possible that the mishna is also doing a literary play on words between

"draw them closer," *mikarvan* (מקרבן), and the verb used to describe priestly sacrificial worship in the Bible *makriv* (מקריב). See, for example, Lev. 3:1, 7. Thus the true role of Aaron was not about bringing sacrifices but about bringing people closer to Torah.

37. For example, Rabbi Yaakov b. Shimshon (France, 11th cent.), in *Mishnat Reuven*, Avot 1:12, writes: "'A lover of people'—this is a different matter and is not connected to being a disciple of Aaron." This view is also held by Rabbenu Behayei in his *Kitvei Rabbenu Behayei: Pirkei Avot,* and Rabbi Yosef b. Shushan in his commentary on Mishna Avot, *Peirushei Rabbenu Yosef b. Shushan al masekhet Avot*. It should also be noted that the words "lover of peace and pursuer of peace" are commonly found together, such as in Sanhedrin 6b: "But Aaron loved peace pursued peace, and would place peace between people." Similarly, in *Derekh eretz zuta* 11:11, 18, 20: "Loves peace, pursues peace, greets with peace, and replies with peace." Thus, it is possible that when Hillel said, "Be of the disciples of Aaron," he meant only "Be a lover of peace and a pursuer of peace" and not "a lover of people who draws them closer to Torah."

38. For example, Rabbi Yona of Gerondi (Spain, 13th cent.), in his commentary on Avot, *Peirushei Rabbenu Yona miGerondi al masekhet Avot,* 1:12, writes: "These people are disciples of Aaron, who used to act this way, loving people and drawing them closer to Torah. For when Aaron would sense that someone was sinning in private he would go to him and make a connection with him." Similarly, Abarbanel, *Nahalat Avot* 1:12, writes that all of Aaron's work of bringing peace between people "was in order to draw them closer to Torah . . . for the ultimate goal was to draw them closer to the Torah and to its study. And therefore, he constantly made the effort to greet each person with God's name (i.e., to say "*shalom*" to them)."

Several other commentaries, among them Rabbi Yosef b. Yehuda ibn Aknin (Morocco, Egypt; 12th–13th cent.), in his *Sefer mussar: Peirush Mishnat Avot l'Rabbi Yosef b. Yehuda,* Becher edition (Berlin: Tzvi Hirsch Itzkovski, 1910); Meiri, *Beit haBehira,* Avot; Rabbi Ovadia of Bartenura (Italy, Palestine; 15th cent.) in *Peirush Rabbenu Ovadia miBartenura* on Avot; and Maimonides in his commentary on Mishna, *Masekhet Avot im peirush Rabbenu Moshe b. Maimon,* Avot 1:12, also connect this section of the mishna with the legend of Aaron greeting the wicked with *shalom* and thereby preventing them from doing wrong.

39. *Mishnat Rabbi Eliezer: Midrash sheloshim ushtayim middot,* ed. H. G. Enelow (New York: Bloch Publishing, 1933), chap. 4, 74.

40. See H. L. Strack and Günter Stemberger, *Introduction to the Talmud and Midrash,* trans. Markus Bockmuehl (Minneapolis: Fortress Press, 1992), 259–265.

41. The root of the verb "sinned" is *sarah*. *Sarah* is an Aramaic translation of the Hebrew *avla* (unrighteousness or sin), which is found in Malachi 2:6. For other examples, see below, n. 100; *Targum Yonatan,* II Sam. 19:20, 24:17.

42. Unless otherwise indicated, all biblical citations are translated from *The Holy Scriptures: According to the Masoretic Text* (Philadelphia: Jewish Publication Society, 1917), with slight alterations made to modernize the language.

43. *Sifra,* 1:2 (45d) (MS Vatican 66).

44. The immediate context for the midrash's question is a discussion about the cousins of Aaron, who came to take away the bodies of Nadav and Avihu after they died in the

Tabernacle. The midrash states: "'And Moses called Mishael and Eltzafan, the sons of Uziel the uncle of Aaron' (Lev. 10:4). Is it not already known that Uziel is the uncle of Aaron, as it is said, 'And the sons of Kehat: Amram, and Yitzhar, and Hebron, and Uziel' (Ex. 6:18)? If so, why does it need to say here 'uncle of Aaron'? It likens the actions of Uziel to the actions of Aaron: Just as Aaron would pursue peace in Israel, so too, Uziel would pursue peace in Israel. And how do we know that Aaron would pursue peace (*rodef shalom*) in Israel?"

45. There were early attempts to identify also Moses as a pursuer of peace, such as this: "Moses, too, was a lover of peace, as it is said (Deut. 2:26): 'I sent messengers out of the wilderness of Kedmot [to Sihon king of Heshbon with words of peace]'" (*Sifrei*, Deut. 199, 237). See also below, n. 79, where both Aaron and Moses are described as being peacemakers.

46. It should be noted that some commentaries and scholars were not satisfied by these scriptural proofs that Aaron was a pursuer of peace. The Maharal of Prague writes in *Derekh hayim*, Avot 1:12, that it was Aaron's relationship to the Israelite people that led the rabbis to associate him so strongly with peace: "While certainly Aaron was a lover of peace and a pursuer of peace, nevertheless this is not mentioned explicitly anywhere in the Bible. There is only a hint in Scripture (Mal. 2:6): 'He walked with Me in peace and uprightness.' But Hillel was not relying on that passage when he said, 'Be of the disciples of Aaron: a lover of peace and a pursuer of peace,' as though everyone would know that verse. . . . The reason he said, 'Be of the disciples of Aaron,' is that Aaron was the high priest, and a high priest is uniquely able to bind Israel together so that they become a unified nation. . . . The matter [of Aaron as a *rodef shalom*] is at its core reflective of Aaron's position, as since he was the high priest he would make peace throughout the world. For there always needs to be peace between individuals, as well as peace between Israel and their Father in heaven, and this way everything will be peaceful. And this matter was done by Aaron in particular more than anyone else in the world."

Marc Gopin also did not accept these midrashic proofs as the primary motivation for identifying Aaron as the ideal pursuer of peace; see above, n. 2.

47. In its biblical context, the difference in wording may not have been significant.

48. This is how *Avot d'Rabbi Natan* B understands the midrash (see below, n. 73), that the word "all" (*kol*) is mentioned only regarding Aaron and not Moses, which hints to the fact that not everyone loved Moses.

The parallel midrash in *Kalla rabbati* 1:3 seems to understand the contrast between the two verses as being between "the children (understood here to mean "sons") of Israel" and the "whole *house* of Israel," meaning that when Moses died only the men wept, but when Aaron died the men and the women mourned him. For a summary of how medieval commentaries were divided over these two ways of understanding the contrast between Aaron and Moses, see Roth, "Tradition of Aaron," 33n68, 69.

49. For a discussion on other rabbinic sources that use this verse as a proof text that Aaron was a pursuer of peace, as well as other interpretations of whom the verse may be referring to (such as Pinhas, Aaron's grandson), see Roth, 19n17.

50. Ginat, *Blood Revenge*, 64 (case 16); 73–74 (case 24); 74–77 (case 25).

51. Ginat also mentions several cases in which the social, and occasionally political, status of the third side rose as a result of a successful *sulha* process. See, for example, case 23, 72–73.
52. On the interests of third-party mediators in international conflicts, see I. William Zartman and Saadia Touval, "International Mediation," in *Leashing the Dogs of War: Conflict Management in a Divided World*, ed. Chester A. Crocker, Fen Osler Hampson, and Pamela Aall (Washington, DC: United States Institute of Peace Press, 2007), 437–54.
53. Abraham ibn Ḥayim, *Korban Aharon* (Dessau, 1656), *Shemini* 37, 100b, n. 37.
54. *Hagahot haMaharid*, *Shemini* 3, 1:37.
55. This is not the only way to explain Aaron's behavior in contrast to the behavior of Moses. The seventeenth-century Polish commentator Rabbi Avraham Gumbiner wrote (*Zayit ra'anan*, *Shemini* 526) that Aaron "did not want to assert his own authority in front of Moses," pointing to the Talmud's comment (Arakhin 16b) that even "humility that is not for its own sake" is preferable to "rebuke for the sake of rebuke." In other words, Aaron knew rebuking the people was proper, and *would have* rebuked them, but he shrank from doing so out of humility, so as not to undermine the authority of Moses. We can conclude from this that Aaron's avoidance of rebuke reflected his moral qualities, but in and of itself it was not his highest moral quality. The midrash expresses a perspective on Aaron's gentleness with the people that is different from the one we saw in the commentaries on the mishna that had described him—unequivocally and positively—as a "pursuer of peace." Other commentaries reject Rabbi Gumbiner's explanation and favor that of ibn Ḥayim (see Roth, "Tradition of Aaron," 20n23).
56. See Kaminsky, *Fundamentals*, 223–61, where he argues that this is the very essence of the halakhic requirement of *tokhaḥa*, rebuke.
57. Found in *Avot d'Rabbi Natan* A, chap. 12.
58. Indeed, a later midrash, *Tanḥuma* (*Ḥukat* 10; MS Cambridge 1212), blames the very use of harsh words as contributing to a slow process of wearing away at the love a king has for his subject: "A parable: A king had a beloved subject who would be coarse with him, using harsh words against him. But the king did not get angry with him. Eventually, [the subject] stood up and was coarse with him in front of his legions. The king sentenced him to death."
59. For an example of an educational unit on this topic, see Pardes Rodef Shalom Schools Program, unit 6: Constructive Communication through Tochacha, 2016. https://elmad.pardes.org/pcjcr/.
60. For an in-depth discussion on the relationship between these two rabbinic terms for compromise, *bitzua* and *peshara*, the various rabbinic opinions about them found in *Tosefta* Sanhedrin, and a comparison to contemporary forms of Alternative Dispute Resolution, see Ḥayim Shapira, "The Debate over Compromise and the Goals of the Judicial Process," in *Diné Israel* 26–27 (2009–2010): 183–228. Earlier scholars who attempted to compare the rabbinic concept of *peshara* did not distinguish between it and *betzua*, and between these two terms and arbitration as opposed to mediation. See Ira Yitzchak Kasdan, "A Proposal for P'sharah: Jewish Mediation/Arbitration

Service," *Jewish Law Articles: Examining Halacha, Jewish Issues and Secular Law* (1990), https://www.jlaw.com/Articles/psharah3.html. He writes, "The terms *peshara* and *bitzua* are used interchangeably by the Talmud in the first chapter of *Massechet Sanhedrin* and . . . apparently refer to both arbitration and mediation processes." Similarly, Steinberg, "Conflict Prevention," 7, writes that the process of *peshara* is "translated variously and inconsistently as mediation and/or arbitration, reflecting the fact that these procedures were considered to be very similar."

61. It should be noted that this is a minority opinion within Jewish law and not accepted as normative. The law follows the opinion of Rabbi Yehoshua b. Korha, who stated that compromise actually leads to peace and is therefore commendable.
62. Rabbi Eliezer uses the Hebrew word *botze'a* in its rabbinic meaning—compromiser—rather than in its biblical meaning, which probably refers to greed or violent robbery.
63. *Tosefta* Sanhedrin 1:2 (MS Vienna 46). See also the parallels in BT Sanhedrin 6b and JT Sanhedrin 1:1.
64. There are commentators who do not address this problem, since ultimately Jewish law does not support Rabbi Eliezer's view that it is forbidden to compromise. There are also commentators who indeed identify the "pursuit of peace" with compromise, yet do not address the problem of Aaron as a peacemaker. See Rabbi Eliezer b. Rabbi Yoel Halevi (also known as the Raviyah; Germany, 12th cent.), *Sefer Raviyah, Avi ha'ezer* (Debretzky edition, Bnei Brak, Israel: 1999/2000), vol. 4, 1013; Commentary of *Talmid HaRamban*, Sanhedrin 6b (Lifschitz ed., 13).
65. These points appear at the end of Rabbi Eliezer b. Natan's rulings pertaining to tractate Sanhedrin, *Sefer Ra'avan, Even ha'ezer, hiddushim leSanhedrin* 4 (Jerusalem: Wagshal, 1984); Y. Z. Dinur, *Hiddushei haRitzad*, vol. 3 (Jerusalem: Mossad Harav Kook, 1990), 243–44.
66. Rashi, Sanhedrin 6b, s.v. "*aval Aharon*."
67. *Yad Rama*, Sanhedrin 6b, s.v. "*tanu rabbanan*."
68. Rabbi Yeshayahu di Trani, Sanhedrin 6b, in Rabbi Yaakov Halevi Lifschitz, *Sanhedri gedola lamasekhet Sanhedrin*, vol. 5, part 2 (Jerusalem: Harry Fischel Institute, 1972, 6–7).

    On disagreements among early-modern and modern authorities as to whether Jewish law follows the Riaz's opinion, see Lifschitz, 7n25–26.
69. Ittai Lifschitz describes the halakhic ramifications of this distinction. Ittai Lifschitz, "*Hapeshara bamishpat haIvri*" [in Hebrew] (PhD diss., Bar-Ilan University, 2004), 95, 89–100.
70. *Tosafot* Sanhedrin; see E. E. Urbach, *The Tosaphists: Their History, Writings, and Methods* [in Hebrew] (Jerusalem: Bialik Institute, 1986), 657–58.
71. Tosafot *Sanhedrin* 6b, s.v. "*aval Aharon*."
72. Rabbi Alexander Zusslin Hakohen, *Sefer ha'agguda*, Sanhedrin 6b.
73. *Avot d'Rabbi Natan* B, chap. 25. Moses is explicitly portrayed as a judge in tannaitic midrashic sources, such as in *Mekhilta d'Rabbi Shimon b. Yohai* (J. N. Epstein and Ezra Tzion Melamed edition [Jerusalem: Mekitz Nirdamim, 1955], 16:31, 115): "A woman sinned against her husband. She says, 'He sinned against me,' and he says, 'She sinned against me.' They came to Moses for judgment. He says to them: 'In the morning there will be a decision. At sunrise, if manna is found at the house of the

NOTES 289

husband, it is known that she sinned against him. If manna is found at the house of her father, it is known that he sinned against her.'" Moses determines, or rather presides over, the judicial ruling expressed by the presence of manna at the home of the justified party on the following morning; he does not attempt to make peace between the two quarreling sides, seeking only to clarify the truth of the situation. See also parallels in *Mekhilta d'Rabbi Yishmael* (Shaul Horovitz and Yisrael Avraham Rabin edition [Frankfurt am Main, 1931], *Vayasa* 5, 171); Yoma 85a.

74. Law of Courts, 79c, *Gishur*.
75. The most articulate argument made against the ADR movement was made by Owen Fiss, who wrote in his article, "Against Settlement" (1075): "I do not believe that settlement as a generic practice is preferable to judgment or should be institutionalized on a wholesale and indiscriminate basis. It should be treated instead as a highly problematic technique for streamlining dockets. Settlement is for me the civil analogue of plea bargaining: Consent is often coerced; the bargain may be struck by someone without authority; the absence of a trial and judgment renders subsequent judicial involvement troublesome; and although dockets are trimmed, justice may not be done. Like plea bargaining, settlement is a capitulation to the conditions of mass society and should be neither encouraged nor praised." Owen Fiss, "Against Settlement," *Yale Law Journal* 93 (1984): 1073–90.
76. See, for example, the debate between two Ohio district judges, the Honorable John C. Crastley and the Honorable Dan Aaron Polster, over passing a law that would forbid any judge who attempted to mediate a conflict from later serving as the trial judge of the case.

John C. Cratsley, "Judicial Ethics and Judicial Settlement Practices: Time for Two Strangers to Meet," *Ohio State Journal on Dispute Resolution* 21, no. 3 (2006): 569–96, https://kb.osu.edu/dspace/bitstream/handle/1811/77239/OSJDR_V21N3_0569.pdf; Dan Aaron Polster, "The Trial Judge as Mediator: A Rejoinder to Judge Cratsley," *Ohio State Journal on Dispute Resolution's Mayhew-Hite Report* 5, no. 1 (2006), https://www.mediate.com/articles/polsterD1.cfm.
77. Michal Alberstein, "Judicial Conflict Resolution (JCR): A New Jurisprudence for an Emerging Judicial Practice," *Cardozo Journal of Conflict Resolution* 16 (2015): 879–965.
78. Exodus Rabba 8:5 (MS Jerusalem 5977 24): "'And he went, and met him [in the mountain of God, and he kissed him]' (Ex. 4:27). When it says, 'Loving-kindness [JPS ed.: mercy] and truth meet; [righteousness and peace have kissed each other]' (Ps. 85:11), 'loving-kindness' refers to Aaron . . . while 'truth' refers to Moses. . . . 'Righteousness' refers to Moses, of whom it is said: 'He executed the righteousness of the Lord' (Deut. 33:21), and 'peace' refers to Aaron, of whom it is said: 'He walked with Me in peace and uprightness' (Mal. 2:6). 'Have kissed each other,' as it says: 'And he kissed him.'"

This same verse in the book of Psalms was interpreted also in the opposite way, namely that these values do not come together in love and harmony but rather are in direct conflict with one another. See Genesis Rabba 8:5.

79. There is, however, one late midrash (11th cent.) that portrays both Aaron and Moses as peacemakers between God and Israel as well as between people, perhaps even working side by side (*Seder Eliyahu rabba*, MS Vatican 31, chap. 18, 106): "Go and learn from Moses and Aaron who . . . made peace between [the people of] Israel and their Father in heaven, between [the people of] Israel and the rabbis, between fellow rabbis, between two people, [and] between husband and wife. And as a result of their ways, a good name was made for them, for their children, [and for] their grandchildren until the end of generations. [As it says]: 'These are that [same] Moses and Aaron' (Ex. 6:26)."
80. For background on these sources, see H. L. Strack and Günter Stemberger, *Introduction to the Talmud and Midrash*, 225–27, 229–30, 231.
81. Avot d'Rabbi Natan, Chap. 12, 24b. The text presented is based on MS New York 25, with variants according to Hans-Jürgen Becker and Christoph Berner, *Avot d'Rabbi Natan: Synoptische Edition beider Versionen* (*Avot d'Rabbi Natan:* A synoptic edition of both versions), Text and Studies in Ancient Judaism Series 116 (Tübingen: Mohr Siebeck, 2006).
82. Avot d'Rabbi Natan, Version B, chap. 24, 25b. The text presented is based on MS Parma 327, with variants according to Becker and Berner, *Avot d'Rabbi Natan*.
83. *Kalla Rabbati*. Michael Higger edition, 216–17. The text presented is based on MS Parma 327.
84. Daniel Sperber, *Masekhet derekh eretz zuta and Perek hashalom*, 3rd ed. (Jerusalem: Tzur-Ot, 1994), 201–2. The text presented is according to MS Oxford 2339.
85. Three of the four versions (all but *Avot d'Rabbi Natan* B; see Tables 2.1, 2.2) preface these legends with the verse from Malachi 2:6, cited in the tannaitic sources already noted. The rabbis seem to have identified within this verse the basic components of Aaron's method of pursuing peace as expressed in the legends. The verse says, "In peace (*shalom*) and uprightness he walked (*halakh*) with Me, and turned (*heshiv*) many (*rabim*) away from iniquity (*avon*)." In each of the three versions, the context is that Aaron would walk to one of the sides in conflict and pursue peace. Moreover, the verse seems to hint that Aaron not only turned the wicked from sinning, but also pursued peace between people who were fighting. The Hebrew word for fighting used in two of the versions (*Avot d'Rabbi Natan* A and *Kalla rabbati*) is *ravu* or *meriva*, which seems to be a play on the verse's word for "many"—*rabim*, as in "he turned *many* away from iniquity." Employing the word *ravim*, "fighting," which has the exact same spelling as *rabim*, "many," allows the verse to be read: "He turned *people [who were] fighting* from sin."
86. *Avot d'Rabbi Natan* A, chap. 12, 24b–25a. A similar story is cited in version B, with minor variants. There the person says to himself, "Woe is me! Tomorrow Aaron will come and inquire of my well-being. How will I *respond to him (meshivo)*?" See below, n. 88, for the possible significance of his using the words "respond to him."
87. In medieval Jewish law, some ruled it was forbidden to say *shalom* to a wicked person. See, for example, *Sefer ḥaredim* (Kunszentmiklós, Hungary: Yitzḥak Leib Schwartz, 1935), 4:37, 122–23.
88. The statement attributed to Rabbi Meir here connects two seemingly separate stitches of Malachi 2:6: "In peace and uprightness he walked with Me" on the one hand, and

"He turned many away from iniquity" on the other. There may also be a play on words in version B, where it says the sinner says to himself, "How will I respond to him," since the Hebrew word used for "respond to him" (*meshivo*) has the same Hebrew root as "turned" (*heshiv*) in the verse.

Aaron's greeting of peace relates to another stitch of the verse: "Iniquity was not found on his lips." That is to say, we would expect Aaron to rebuke a sinner and point out the "iniquity" the sinner is committing. But this was not Aaron's way, as we already saw in the tannaitic *midrash*, the *Sifra, Mekhilta d'miluim*, which states that Aaron, as opposed to Moses, would not rebuke the sinner directly.

89. See above, n. 38.
90. Michael Rothenberg, *Hayesodot ha'erchi'im shel hapeshara* (master's thesis, Hebrew University, 2001), 130–31, cites a similar but later midrash (*Tanḥuma*, Buber B, Ḥukat, 131), which tells how Aaron would greet an individual on their way to doing a sin at night, and through giving that person the benefit of the doubt he would succeed in preventing them from doing evil. Rothenberg understands that this was an example of conflict prevention, as Aaron prevented the potential sinner from doing wrong against another person and thereby forestalled a future dispute in court.

Gopin, *Eden and Armageddon*, 180–81, emphasizes this method of conflict resolution in a few places. In his discussion on "conflict prevention and the interpersonal relationship," he writes, "The talmudic rabbis mandated that one should greet everyone with a loving, or literally 'beautiful,' face. . . . Honor, as an intentional peacemaking act, is a rather under-utilized strategy of conflict prevention and conflict resolution at the current time. . . . Any Jewish methodology of conflict resolution would have to focus on honor and the necessary engagement with the face of the enemy." For more on the role of the third party in preventing conflict through showing respect to the other, see Gopin, *Bridges*, 130–31. Ury, *The Third Side*, 120–22, similarly lists "respect" as one of the methods a third-party peacemaker can employ when trying to prevent conflicts, though he doesn't mention simply greeting others as one of the examples of how to offer respect.
91. Mathew 5:47 (English Standard Version [ESV]).
92. *Sahih al-Bukhari*, vol. 1, book 2, Belief 11: "A man asked the Prophet, 'What sort of deeds or [what qualities of] Islam are good?' The Prophet replied, 'To feed [the poor] and greet those whom you know and those whom you don't know,'" https://www.sahih-bukhari.com/Pages/Bukhari_1_02.php.
93. *Kalla rabbati* 3:1, ed. Michael Higger (New York: Debe Rabanan, 1936).
94. See the opinion of Rabbi Shmuel de Uçeda cited above on pages 44–45.
95. See Shabbat 88b: "The Sages taught: Concerning those who are insulted and do not insult, who hear their shame and do not respond, who act out of love and are joyful in suffering, the verse says" (Judges 5:31): "But they that love Him are as the sun when it goes forth in its might."
96. http://elmad.pardes.org/wp-content/uploads/2015/11/The-Rodef-Shalom-who-Runs-to-Say-Shalom-First.pdf.
97. For an example of how Jewish and Islamic sources on greeting people with *shalom/salaam* were used in an event, see Elḥanan Miller, "'Those Wishing to See the Face of God Must See the Face of the Other.'"

98. See above pages 47–48.
99. In all four of the Minor Tractates that discuss Aaron's pursuing peace, the order of the examples is: greeting the wicked, making peace between individuals, and making peace between husband and wife (see Tables 2.1, 2.2). However, since the legends of Aaron pursuing peace between individuals is a primary focus in this chapter, I have chosen to explore the legends of him pursuing peace between husband and wife before discussing his efforts between two individuals.
100. The word for sin here is *sarah*, as in the *Sifra* that we saw above, n. 41.
101. There is an emphasis on Aaron "going"—literally, walking—both to the husband and to the wife, echoing the verse: "In peace and uprightness he *walked* with Me."
102. *Avot d'Rabbi Natan* B, chap. 24, 25b.
103. *Kalla rabbati* 3:1, 217.
104. Tricia S. Jones and Ross Brinkert, *Conflict Coaching: Advancing the Conflict Resolution Field by Developing an Individual Disputant Process* (Los Angeles: Sage Publications, 2007), 4–5.
105. Isak Svensson, "Guaranteeing Peace: The Credibility of Third-Party Mediators in Civil Wars," in *International Conflict Mediation: New Approaches and Findings*, ed. Jacob Bercovitch and Scott Sigmund Gartner (New York: Routledge, 2008), 115.
106. Svensson, 120. On page 218, we will see a case (as part of Table 5.1, case 29) that took place in Germany in the fifteenth century where the third-party peacemaker was a guarantor but then passed away, and the question arose as to whether or not the agreement was still valid.
107. The story about Rabbi Meir is in JT Sota 1:4 and Leviticus Rabba 9:9 (Table 3.1, case 6). The story was first cited by commentaries on Mishna Avot by Rabbi David haNagid (Egypt, Syria, Palestine; 1212–1300), the grandson of Maimonides, in his commentary on Mishna Avot, *Midrash David*. After citing the story about Rabbi Meir, he writes: "See the awesome love Rabbi Meir had in making peace so that there would be peace between husband and wife. And so would Aaron the high priest make peace between fellows, and go from home to home and make peace between husband and wife."

    A shortened version of the same story is found in the commentary of Rabbi Yosef b. Shushan on Mishna Avot *Peirushei Rabbenu Yosef b. Shushan al masekhet Avot*, but it is told about Aaron and not Rabbi Meir. Aaron is also the protagonist in the story as it appears in *Merkavat haMishna*, the commentary of Rabbi Yosef Alashkar, but there he adds: "And a story like this happened to Rabbi Meir." Similarly, in the commentary of Rabbi Yosef b. Hayim Yaavetz, the reworked story is juxtaposed to the story of Aaron pursuing peace between husband and wife from *Avot d'Rabbi Natan* B; likewise, in the commentary attributed to Rashi on Mishna Avot (Vilna ed.).
108. Vilna ed. This commentary is known as *Peirush hameyuhas l'Rashi* (attributed to Rashi) or Pseudo Rashi—presumably inaccurately. It is not to be confused with the actual commentary of Rashi.
109. Gopin, *Eden and Armageddon*, 80, 136–37, 182–86; Steinberg, "Jewish Sources," 17–18; Roness, *Conflict and Conflict Management*, 64–67, 140; Schimmel, *Wounds Not Healed*, 155. Other scholars who have mentioned this legend of Aaron in the context

of Jewish models of conflict resolution include Yitzchok Adlerstein, "Lawyers, Faith, and Peacemaking: Jewish Perspectives on Peace," *Pepperdine Dispute Resolution Law Journal* 7, no. 2 (2007): 177–87; Everett Gendler, ". . . Therefore Choose Life," in *The Challenge of Shalom: The Jewish Tradition of Peace and Justice*, ed. M. Polner and N. Goodman (Philadelphia: New Society Publishers, 1994), 14; Moshe Drori, "*Lidmutam shel hashofet Moshe Rabbenu vehamegasher Aaron hakohen*," *Alon hashoftim al shem hashofet Baruch z"l* 3 (January 2011): 14; Elisheva Hacohen and Aviad Hacohen, "*Velo yakhlu ledabro leshalom: Pishur, gishur, veyishuv sikhsukhim*," *Mishpat Ivri* 54 (2002), http://www.daat.ac.il/mishpat-ivri/skirot/54-2.htm; Hershey H. Friedman and Abraham Weisel, "Should Moral Individuals Ever Lie? Insights from Jewish Law," SSRN website, August 28, 2013, http://dx.doi.org/10.2139/ssrn.2317563; and Heidi M. Tauscher, "Spiritual Practices for Mediation Challenges: Pragmatic Mediation Applications from Five Major World Religious Traditions," American Bar Association website, Section of Dispute Resolution, May 25, 2003, http://www.abanet.org/dispute/spiritual_tool.pdf.

110. Most traditional commentaries and modern scholars do not cite this version of the legend. The only commentator (as far as I have found) who did cite it is Rabbi Matitya b. Moshe HaYitzri (Spain, 14th–15th cent.) The only contemporary scholar who refers to it is Roness, *Conflict and Conflict Management*, 65. I chose to cite this version because I feel it contains the most articulated version of Aaron's methods, which is the subject of our study.

Most commentaries and scholars cite the version found in *Avot d'Rabbi Natan* A, with minor changes. Among them are Rabbi Yaakov b. Shimshon, Rabbi Yosef b. Yehuda ibn Aknin, Meiri, Rabbi Ovadia of Bartenura, and Rabbi Yitzhak b. Shlomo of Toledo. Several modern scholars, such as Gopin, Tauscher, Schimmel, and Kaminsky, also cite this version. The reason for its popularity is most likely because it is the one found in the most common printed edition of the Babylonian Talmud (Vilna).

Gopin, *Eden and Armageddon*, 183n82, also cites one section from *Avot d'Rabbi Natan* B. He refers to the J. D. Eisenstein edition of *Otzar midrashim*, vol. 1 (New York, 1915), 81, which itself cites *Avot d'Rabbi Natan* B. Steinberg, "Jewish Sources," 17, and Kaminsky, *Fundamentals*, 54n73, also cite the version of *Derekh eretz zuta*.

111. I have used *appease* here as the translation of *lefayes*, even though I have generally used *reconcile* for words from this root throughout the book. In this case, the grammatical context requires "appease."
112. *Kalla rabbati* 3:1.
113. For example, in both versions of *Avot d'Rabbi Natan*, the conflict is portrayed to be rooted in concerns about humiliation (version A, "I am embarrassed before him") and honor (version B, "who is greater than I"). See Table 2.2.
114. *Avot d'Rabbi Natan* A, chap. 12, s.v. "*shnei bnei adam she'osim meriva zeh im zeh*."
115. See also Avruch, *Culture*, 52.
116. Version B. The version in *Derekh eretz zuta* is the sparsest, including no details of the actual encounter between the two parties.

117. Gopin, *Eden and Armageddon*, 183, points to a different version found in *Otzar hamidrashim*, 81 (not on 78, as he writes in n. 82). That version reads: "And he said, 'Woe is me, for I have sinned against my fellow who is greater than I.' Here is [Aaron] standing in the marketplace—[and Aaron says,] 'Go in your kindness and ask forgiveness of him.'" According to this version, Aaron is the one who tells each party to go to the marketplace and ask forgiveness from the other. This version is indeed based on *Avot d'Rabbi Natan* B, as it says earlier on that page, "And we read in *Avot d'Rabbi Natan*." It seems that "Here I am," rendered as הרי אני (MS Parma) and הריני (MS Vatican), was shortened to simply הרי, "here is," yielding the mistaken version in *Otzar haMidrashim*.
118. Antoun, "Institutionalized Deconfrontation," 163, writes that the kiss and hug between rivals symbolize the climax of the *sulha* reconciliation process. While it may be more prevalent in traditional cultural conflict resolution processes, it is not entirely absent from modern-Western ones. See, for example, Kenneth Cloke, "Revenge, Forgiveness, and the Magic of Mediation," *Conflict Resolution Quarterly* 11, no. 1 (1993). There, he calls upon mediators to create a ceremony of forgiveness that would include expressions of forgiveness, exchanging of promises, and a kiss and hug or handshake.
119. For example, the version in the commentaries of Rabbis Yaakov b. Shimshon and Yitzḥak b. Shlomo of Toledo in *Peirushei Rabbenu Yitzhak b. Shlomo miToledo al masekhet Avot* reads, "Until they reconciled with one another and kissed each other." The version in the commentary of Rabbi Yosef b. Avraham Ḥayun (Lisbon, 15th cent.), *Milei d'Avot* 1:12, reads, "Until they reconciled (*mitpaysim*) with each other and made peace between them." In several other medieval commentaries, such as *Peirush hameyuḥas l'Rashi* (Kasher and Blecharovitz edition), the legend simply concludes with the words, "until he reconciled them."
120. Gopin, *Eden and Armageddon*, 137; Roness, *Conflict and Conflict Management*, 66; Kaminsky, *Fundamentals*, 54; Schimmel, *Wounds Not Healed*, 155; Drori, "*Lidmutam*," 12; Tauscher, Spiritual Practices," 15; Steinberg, "Jewish Sources," 18.
121. Adlerstein, "Lawyers, Faith, and Peacemaking," 180–81.
122. Abu-Nimer, "Contrasts," 152.
123. Gopin, *Eden and Armageddon*, 137, and especially 185. Other scholars also note Aaron's method. See HaKohen, Mediation; Drori, *Lidmutam*, 12; Schimmel, *Wounds Not Healed*, 155; Tauscher, "Spiritual Practices," 14–15.
124. Gopin, *Eden and Armageddon*, 137.
125. Pely, *Muslim/Arab Mediation*, 46.
126. Jabbour, *Sulha*, 26–28.
127. Ibid., 31–32. See also Pely, *Muslim/Arab Mediation*, 80.
128. Jabbour, *Sulha*, 42: "The members of the accused family speak through the mediators. They cannot speak to the family of the deceased directly. We talk to them as if we are acting on behalf of the killer." Likewise, Ginat, *Blood Revenge*, 59, writes: "In the societies under discussion, when mediation is required in matters of blood disputes, the disputing parties are always physically separated. Thus, in blood disputes the mediator or mediators are always also 'go-betweens'; the role is one and the same, and indeed, this term precisely defines their function."

129. Ibid., 80.
130. For more about the tensions between local Jewish customs and the law as Rabbi ibn Ḥaviv saw it, see Yosef Hacker, *Megurashei Sefarad v'tze'etzaeihem baEmperia haOttomanit bame'a ha-16* (Jerusalem: Hebrew University Faculty of Humanities, 1967).
131. Rabbi Yaakov ibn Haviv, *Ein Yaakov* (Thessaloniki, 1516), on JT Yoma 8:9. Ibn Ḥaviv based his position on the words of the sage Shmuel in the Jerusalem Talmud (Yoma 8:9 [45c]): "One who sinned against his fellow must say to him, 'I have wronged you.' If he accepts [the apology], then good; if not, he must bring people and appease him in front of them."
132. See, for example, Rabbi Yisrael Meir Kagan, *Mishna Berura* 606:1:2, "Laws of the Eve of the Day of Atonement": "And it is correct to go by himself to him, and he should not first send a middle man who would convince [the other party] to accept the appeasements. And if it is difficult for him to go first by himself, or if he knows that the reconciliation is more likely through the means of middle man who would broker [peace] between them, he can do it through the middle man."
133. For more on this topic see, Kaminsky, *Fundamentals*, 312–16, "The Obligation of Personally Going to Ask for Forgiveness"; Roth, "Tradition of Aaron," 102–6.
134. Rabbi Ḥayim Palagi, *Leḥayim beYerushalayim*, JT Yoma 8:7.
135. There is not necessarily a direct contradiction here since the offending side did not ask or even know of Aaron's intervention. Moreover, Aaron seems to be intervening in a case where both sides are convinced that the other needs to come and appease them, and therefore without Aaron's intervention there would never be a reconciliation. Perhaps this is the intention of Rabbi Ovadia Yosef (*Shut Yeḥaveh da'at* 5:44), who simply wrote that Rabbi Palagi's words can be refuted. However, below, 229–230, in Chapter 5, I bring the words of Rabbi Joseph Molkho who seems to understand ibn Haviv's (add line under H) ruling as indeed including cases like that of the Aaron legend, in which neither side requested the intervention of the third-party, yet such interventions are not allowed since they lead to coercive and insincere forgiveness.
136. See Nicholas Tavuchis, *Mea Culpa: A Sociology of Apology and Reconciliation* (Palo Alto, CA: Stanford University Press, 1991), 49–50: "As the offender . . . I cannot have someone apologize on my behalf. . . . To request, encourage, allow or be subjected to such mediatory actions violates both the logic and the spirit of apology . . . such interventions are in short, self-defeating and antithetical to the apologetic agenda, which calls for direct exchange between particular wrongdoers and their victims. . . . It is most commonly found in what has been termed 'honor-sensitive' societies and in cultures where groups or collective membership interests and claims as well as institutionalized hierarchical arrangements take precedence over individuality and egalitarianism."
137. The other manuscripts read simply, "He is beating his chest and tearing his clothes," apart from MS New York 10484, which reads: "He is beating his chest and tearing his clothes and strangling his mind." See Table 2.2.
138. Gopin, *Eden and Armageddon*, 185.
139. King-Irani, "Rituals of Forgiveness," 132.
140. Pely, *Muslim/Arab Mediation*, 85–86.

141. Schimmel, *Wounds Not Healed*, 155.
142. Marc Gopin, "Judaism and Peacebuilding" (Coward and Smith), 126n18.
143. Friedman and Weisel, "Moral Individuals."
144. It is possible to see a biblical precedent for peacemaking by means of lying. In II Samuel 14:1–3, Joab attempts to intercede in the conflict between King David and his son Absalom and reconcile them through a lie.
145. Moses Maimonides, *Mishneh Torah*. See Laws of Robbery and Lost Articles 14:13.
146. The former chief rabbi of Israel, Rabbi Yisrael Meir Lau, in his *Shut Yaḥel Yisrael* (responsum 11), rules in accordance with the opinion that it is indeed a mitzva to change the truth for the sake of peace. In Chap. 5 (Table 5.1, case 31), we will see that a rabbi bending the truth in order to promote peace is acting in the "ways of the pursuers of peace (*rodfei shalom*), who change the truth for the sake of peace." He told each side in a conflict that the other side would win if the case was brought to court, and they should therefore drop their claims and reconcile.
147. Gerald Steinberg, "Jewish Sources," 18: "The precedence of social harmony over truth is reflected in the emphasis placed on the role of Aaron the high priest, who toiled to make amends between people and couples in order to maintain the peace. According to the midrash, Aaron would approach people he knew were in conflict in order to attempt to restore their relations. It is told how often he would fabricate a conversation of one side's regret in order to bring two disputing sides to resolve their conflict."
148. See Aalok, "ADR Dharma," 356, and notes there. Aalok, basing himself on Krishna's words to King Dhritarshtra in his attempt to make peace between the Kurus and the Pandavas in the Mahabharata war, writes as a recommendation to third-party mediators today, "If applicable, the mediator should point out that the other side is doing their dharma, so it is only fair for this party to do their duty as well. In order to get some further leverage for attaining peace . . . the mediator should inform each party that the other side is not scared but wants peace because it is the right thing to do." These suggestions, based on Krishna's telling each side favorable things about the other, is very similar to the method credited to Aaron in rabbinic literature.
149. *Sahih al-Bukhari* 3:49, 857, cited in Abu-Nimer, *Nonviolence*, 63.
150. Pely, *Muslim/Arab Mediation*, 26.
151. Ginat, *Blood Revenge*, 70.
152. James D. D. Smith, "Mediator Impartiality: Banishing the Chimera," *Journal of Peace Research* 31, no. 4 (1994): 445.
153. Andrew Kydd, "Which Side Are You On? Bias, Credibility, and Mediation," *American Journal of Political Science* 47, no. 4 (2003): 597–611. Kydd writes, "Thus if the mediator is unbiased and simply wants to minimize the chance of war, she will face an insuperable incentive to lie. Lying will make peace more likely, telling the truth will make war more likely. Thus the unbiased mediator faces a serious credibility problem."
154. Despite the talmudic ruling that clearly saw lying for the sake of peace as a positive act, there are nevertheless later rabbinic authorities who express various degrees of discomfort with this. Rabbi Yeshayahu Halevi Horowitz (Prague, Safed;

1558–1630), known as the Shelah haKadosh, writes in his book *Shnei Luḥot haBrit* (section entitled "Regarding Matters of the Pillar of Peace," 248): "And even though it is a mitzva to change [the truth] for the sake of peace, in any event, if a person is able to make something up that will allow the angered party to be reconciled, without having to change [the truth], then 'Keep far from a false matter' (Ex. 23:7)." Rabbi Yaakov Etlinger (Germany, 1798–1871), in his commentary *Arukh laNer* (Yevamot 65b), writes: "'It is permissible to change [the truth]' does not mean to tell a complete lie, but rather to mislead slightly." And Rabbi Yehuda b. Shmuel of Regensburg (Ashkenaz, 12th–13th cent.), *Sefer Hasidim* (ed. Mordekhai Margaliot [Jerusalem: Mossad Harav Kook, 1956/7]), 426, rules: "That which they said, 'It is permissible to change [the truth] for the sake of peace,' refers only to matters of the past."

155. See, for example, Leviticus Rabba 27:5.
156. Nazir 23b; Horayot 10b.
157. Rabbi Yehoshua Heschel of Rimanov, *Siftei tzaddikim*, Eccl. 3:15.
158. *Kalla rabbati* 3:1.
159. Gopin, *Eden and Armageddon*, 183–84.
160. In Chap. 3 (Table 3.1, case 6), we shall see the story of Rabbi Meir making peace between husband and wife; in Chap. 4 (Table 4.2, case 18), the example of Rabbi Azulai sacrificing his honor to make peace between family members, and in Chap. 5 (Table 5.2, case 34) the story of the lay mediator who ends up becoming the pursued party after he agrees to be the guarantor of the agreement.
161. *Hadith of Sunan Abu-Dawud*, English translation, 4877, book 42, *hadith* 123; https://sunnah.com/abudawud/43/123. This appears in the chapter regarding humility (48).
162. Pely, *Muslim/Arab Mediation*, 85.
163. Jabbour, *Sulha*, 48.
164. Ibid., 56–57.
165. Ibid., 56–57.
166. Rabbi Moshe Ḥayim Ephraim of Sudilkov, *Degel Maḥaneh Ephraim*, Leviticus, *Aḥarei Mot*, s.v. "*vekhapper hakohen*."
167. Rabbi Moshe Ḥayim Ephraim of Sudilkov.
168. Ibid.
169. Katja Favretto, "Should Peacemakers Take Sides? Major Power Mediation, Coercion, and Bias," *American Political Science Review* 103, no. 2 (2009): 248–63: "Without prejudging what type of offer the third party will make, two ideal types emerge in equilibrium: the third party can either make an offer both sides are certain to accept or it can make an offer that will only be accepted if the threat of military intervention is credible." A good example of this can be found in NATO's controversial decision in 1999 to take military action as an act of humanitarian intervention in the former Yugoslavia.
170. Quran, *sūrat* I 49:9 (Yusaf Ali trans.), http://corpus.quran.com/translation.jsp?chapter=49&verse=9.
171. Hamzeh, "Role of Hizbullah," 111–12.

172. Fredrik Barth, *Political Leadership among Swat Pathans* (London: Athlone Press, 1968), 99.
173. For various roles that a third-party peacemaker can take on, in particular that of being an "equalizer," see Ury, *The Third Side*, 154–61.
174. A similar model of saints as peacemakers can be found in Emrys Peters's *The Bedouin of Cyrenaica: Studies in Personal and Corporate Power* (Cambridge, UK: Cambridge University Press, 1990). There he describes the role of the Marabatin bi'l Baraka, or "clients of the goodness," as being "granted the use of land and water by their nobles in return for the spiritual services they give the Bedouin and they are able to administer in this way by virtue of the fact that they are accredited with divine goodness (*baraka*). They succour the sick, they write amulets for a number of purposes, they circumcise the young boys, and they are always present at peace gatherings. These clients of the goodness are found in small numbers, dispersed among the tribal sections" (40–41). In times of conflict, such as after a homicide, they intervene as intermediaries, going back and forth between the sides in attempt to set an agreed-upon amount for "blood money" (*diya*). Once this is set, they bring the sides together in a peace meeting, where their attendance gives it the "weight" of their *baraka*. The main purpose of the meeting is to restore normal relationships between the sides, symbolized by eating together out of the same bowl (64).
175. Ernest Gellner, *Saints of the Atlas* (Chicago: University of Chicago Press, 1969), 8.
176. Ibid., 81, describes how the *igguramen* facilitate the annual elections of the tribal chiefs.
177. Ibid., 220. Regarding the altar in the Tabernacle, and later in the Temple, serving as a place of refuge, see Exodus 21:14; I Kings 2:28. Regarding the Levite cities functioning as cities of refuge, see Makkot 10a.
178. Ibid., xviii, defines *baraka* as "sanctity, holiness, manifested also in prosperity and magical powers."
179. Ibid., 126.
180. Ibid., 8.
181. Ibid., 126.
182. Ibid., 129. Aaron did not engage in settlement agreements but only in reconciliation and in shifting people's perceptions of the other. Granted, this might be an oversimplification of the image of Aaron as a third-party mediator, especially in light of *Tosefta* Sanhedrin 1:2, cited above (n. 63), which seems to place him in the context of brokering some kind of noncoercive compromise (*peshara*) agreements.
183. Ibid., 85.
184. Ibid., 220. The case involved a murder that took place in the saint's dwelling, which is supposed to be a sanctuary. The protocol is for the murderer's side to pay the blood money to the *agurram* himself. The latter then hands it to the victim's side, after which there is reconciliation between the two feuding parties. As Gellner tells it, in this particular case the *agurram* realized the perpetrator would not pay, so the *agurram* gave the money to the victim secretly, as if it was on behalf of the perpetrator. Thus, during the ceremony, it appeared as though the blood money had been paid, and reconciliation was achieved.

Gellner claims that this story and others like it have not only left the reputations of the saints unblemished, but have actually enhanced them, and may even have been retold by the saints for the purpose of strengthening their communal reputation as third-party peacemakers. As Gellner writes, "These stories are not to the saints' discredit locally, for they illustrate both generosity and skill in mediation, and it is not impossible that some of them are put about or encouraged by the saints themselves."

185. Ginat, *Blood Revenge*, 82n19.
186. See above, ns. 1, 2, 6.
187. For a good example of the shift from Aaron's children being referred to as "pursuers of peace" to the rabbis being identified thus, see Meiri, *Beit haBeḥira*, Yoma 71b, with regard to the conversation between Shmaya, Avtalyon, and the high priest. Quoting the Talmud, Meiri explains: "[Shmaya and Avtalyon] said to [the high priest]: 'May simple Israelites (*bnei amamya*) who behave like Aaron go in peace'—that is, Shmaya and Avtalyon are *rodfei shalom* (pursuers of peace) and ethical people; and 'May [priests] who do not behave like Aaron not go in peace'—that is, [the priests] are argumentative and competitive over priestly honors, and they speak ill of Torah scholars."
188. With regard to the idea of Hillel molding the image of Aaron into being similar to himself, see Bamberger, "Aaron," 208: "[W]hen the Pharisees had finished painting the portrait of Aaron . . . the first high priest had become the ideal Pharisee. In fact, he had virtually become Hillel!"

Chapter 3

1. Catherine Hezser, "Classic Rabbinic Literature," in *The Oxford Handbook of Jewish Studies*, ed. Martin Goodman (Oxford: Oxford University Press, 2002). Classical rabbinic literature includes all ancient Jewish literary works that preserve the traditions of tannaitic (70–200 CE) and amoraic (3rd–5th cent. CE) rabbis in the Land of Israel and Babylonia: the Mishna, the *Tosefta*, and the Jerusalem and Babylonian Talmuds, as well as the various volumes of Midrash and the Minor Tractates.
2. Gittin 52a, based on MS Vatican 130. There is one minor textual variant: in MS Vatican 140 and the printed editions, it says only that Rabbi Meir "stopped them," but does not say "and settled them down."
3. See 68. The symmetry between the disputing parties is implied throughout the story: "There were two people"; "[they] quarreled with one another"; "[he] stopped them"; "he made peace between them." Moreover, "this man whom Rabbi Meir has driven from this house" implies that it is the home of both people. Further evidence of a familial relationship between the sides comes from the context of the story, which appears in the tractate Gittin in the midst of a discussion about guardianship of young orphans. In the story immediately preceding the one cited above, we are told how Rabbi Meir tried very hard to defend the rights of young orphans, forbidding their guardian from selling their possessions. We are thus led to wonder why

this story about Rabbi Meir making peace between two people appears between two stories about the laws governing guardians of minors. A possible answer is that, at least according to the redactor of the Talmud, the story relates to orphaned minors who were living together in the same house. For a differing opinion, see Moshe Lavee, "*Kabbalat ha'aḥer veha'aḥerut: Tahalikhei havlata vetishtush besifrut Ḥazal*" [Acceptance of others and otherness: Processes of emphasis and ambiguity in rabbinic narratives], *Mishlav* 37 (2001): 101.

4. See, for example, *Tosefta* Pe'a 4:9, *Tosefta* Bava Metzia 3:20.
5. Bava Batra 16a: "Reish Lakish said: Satan, the evil inclination, and the Angel of Death are all one."
6. Rashi, Eruvin 26a. There is some variation in Rashi's wording among the different manuscripts. For more on these textual variants, see Roth, "Tradition of Aaron," 124n19. For more on the connection between strife and Satan in rabbinic literature, see *Sifrei*, Num. 42 (Horowitz edition, 46): "Great is peace, for even if Israel is worshiping idolatry but peace is between them, it is as if God said, 'Satan cannot touch them.'"
7. Ury, *The Third Side*, 15.
8. Ecclesiastes Rabba 4:9:1. The comment appears in a discussion of the statement in Ecclesiastes 4:12: "A threefold cord is not readily broken."
9. See also Quran, *Surah Al-Isra'* 17, *Ayah* 53 (https://quran.com/17/53): "And tell My servants to say that which is best. Indeed, Satan induces [dissension] among them. Indeed, Satan is ever, to mankind, a clear enemy."
10. Houston, *Manual for the Peacemaker*, 66. For the various traditions of this legend, see Buck, "Deganawida," 92ff.
11. Rabbi Moshe Isserles, *Shut HaRema* 17.
12. Rabbi Hayim Yosef David Azulai, *Avodat hakodesh* (Vilna, 1906/7), 1:7:

"Seek peace, and pursue it" (Ps. 34:15)—this is the attribute of Aaron the priest, who loved peace and pursued peace, and it is the medicine of life (*sama deḥayeh*). And if they said to seek peace among others, all the more so one should seek peace among members of his own home and relatives. And know that in a place where there is strife (*maḥloket*), the Divine Presence (*Shekhina*) goes away, Heaven forbid, for she is the Mother of Peace, and a home where there is strife is the dwelling place of the Other Side (i.e., Satan), Heaven forbid.

Rabbi Yehoshua Meir Hakohen of Volozhin, in his commentary *Sha'arei hakodesh* on Rabbi Azulai there, cites the Rabbi Meir story as Rabbi Azulai's source. A similar statement can be found in *Ben Ish Ḥai*, year 2, *Vayera* (end of *aleph*) 12, who, after quoting the legend commented, "Whoever is angry and creates conflict, that person strengthens the hands of Satan; and the opposite (i.e., harmony) expels him (Satan)."
13. *Shut Divrei yatziv*, vol. 2 (Netanya, Israel: Mekhon Shefa Ḥayim, 1996), *Oraḥ ḥayim* 123:4.
14. Gopin, *Eden and Armageddon*, 183–86.
15. Deuteronomy Rabba states here: "And the man was a scoffer."
16. This is not the only version of the legend. A late version of the story, translated into Hebrew, appears in Deuteronomy Rabba, *Shofetim* 15. A version with particularly meaningful variant readings can be found in Leviticus Rabba 9:9, annotated by

Mordecai Margulies (New York: Jewish Theological Seminary of America, 1993, 191–92). For further discussion on the textual variants of this legend, see Roth, "Tradition of Aaron," 139–44.

17. See Numbers 5:11–31.
18. This may also have sexual implications, as marital relations are encouraged especially Friday night. See, for example, Maimonides, *Mishneh Torah*, Laws of Sabbath 30:14.
19. See Shabbat 23b: "Rabba said: It is obvious to me [that between] the Hanukka lamp and the house lamp, the house lamp takes precedence, on account of peace in the home, as it is said (Job 5:24): 'You shall know that your tent is in peace.' [Between] the house lamp and [wine for] sanctifying the [Sabbath or festival] day, the house lamp takes precedence, on account of peace in the home." See also Shabbat 25b. Maimonides explains the precedence of the house lamp over the Hanukka lamp in *Mishneh Torah*, Laws of Megilla and Hanukka 4:14. He apparently connects the ruling in Shabbat 23b with the story of Rabbi Meir, which makes the same analogy to the *sota* ritual (discussed in the text): "For the [Ineffable] Name of God is erased in order to make peace between a man and his wife; great is peace, for the entire Torah was given to make peace in the world."
20. See, for example, Mishna Shabbat 2:6; Genesis Rabba 17:8, 60:16.
21. *Sifra, Emor* 14:3 (104d): "'If a man maims his neighbor' (Lev. 24:19) . . . I know only [that this applies] when he gives him a wound. How do I know [that the law applies] if he screamed in his ear, pulled his hair, spit and the spit reached him, took his cloak off of him, [or] uncovered the hair of a woman? Scripture states: 'He has done, so shall be done to him.'" See also Mishna Bava Kamma 8:6; Nedarim 67b. On the connection between the source in Nedarim 67b and the story of Rabbi Meir in the Jerusalem Talmud, see Shulamit Valler, "*Milḥama veshalom bayit al pi sifrut Ḥazal*," in *Shalom umilḥama betarbut haYehudim*, ed. Avriel Bar-Levav (Jerusalem: Merkaz Zalman Shazar, 2006), 29.
22. Valler, 19, analyzes the husband's anger:

> The reason for the husband's anger is his displeasure at the inordinate amount of time, in his view, that his wife spent in the company of Rabbi Meir and his Sabbath evening lecture. This reason may have at its base any of several causes. The husband may have been jealous of his wife's spiritual enjoyment, something he did not share and of which perhaps he was incapable. He might have been angry at having been left alone (part of the time, in the dark) on a Friday night, waiting for her longer than usual. Or he may have been enraged because he suspected that she preferred the rabbi to him, a possibility supported by the husband's demand that she spit in the rabbi's face.

> Marc Gopin, *Eden and Armageddon*, 183, writes in a similar vein: "There were men at the time that hated the rabbis as intellectual elitists, and in this story, this resentment is probably compounded with the classic male jealousy when women dare to know more than men do, especially when they learn from another man." It is unclear to what extent the narrator considered the husband's oath to be reasonable or, alternatively, despicable. The version in Deuteronomy Rabba, however, as noted earlier, clearly disapproves of the husband, whom it calls a scoffer (*leitzan*).

23. See also the medieval legend of Aaron pursuing peace between husband and wife (Table 2.1, case 3).
24. MS Munich 95.
25. See Valler, "*Milḥama*," 16–17.
26. See ibid., 17n15, where she offers several ways to understand Rabbi Shimon's response.
27. Ibid., 27.
28. Ibid., 33.
29. Gopin, *Eden and Armageddon*, 185.
30. Ibid., 184.
31. Ibid., 186.
32. Pardes Rodef Shalom Schools Program, Unit 2, "Strategies of the Rodef Shalom", Teacher's Guide, 12, 2016. https://elmad.pardes.org/pcjcr/.
33. Regarding power imbalances in the *sulha* process, see Abu-Nimer, *Nonviolence*, 107, who writes about the asymmetric nature of conflicts in the context of the *sulha* process and how the process often favors the stronger side.
34. Ginat, *Blood Revenge*, 62–63 (case 14).
35. This story appears in multiple versions in classical rabbinic literature. The earliest version appears to be the one in JT Mo'ed Katan 3:7 (83c), as well as in JT Berakhot 2:1 (4b) with only very minor differences; see Yaakov Sussman, "*Masoret limud umasoret nusaḥ shel haTalmud haYerushalmi*," in *Meḥkarim besifrut hatalmudit* (Jerusalem: Israel Academy of Sciences and Humanities, 1983), 13–14. Another version of the story appears in Yevamot 96b, and differences will be pointed out in the notes below. An additional version of the story appears in the margins of MS Leiden of JT Shekalim 2:5 (47a), which then entered into the body of the text in the first printed editions. That version combines elements of the two texts from the Jerusalem Talmud and the one in Yevamot. For more information on the problems with the text in the Shekalim version, see Sussman, 12–76, and on this story specifically, 22n59.
36. Leaning on a student while walking is a general custom of honor a student shows for his teacher. For examples in the Jerusalem Talmud, see Ketubot 9:2 (33a), Kiddushin 1:7 (61a), Avoda Zara 3:8 (43b), Horayot 3:4 (48b), Beitza 1:7 (60c). For examples in the Babylonian Talmud, see Shabbat 140a, Avoda Zara 37a. For a dissenting opinion, see Rabbi Naftali Frankel, *Korban ha'eida*, on JT Mo'ed Katan 3:7, who claims that "Rabbi Yoḥanan was very heavy and therefore needed to rely on someone else in order to walk."
37. Literally, "did not ask about my well-being."
38. See Michael Sokoloff, *Dictionary of Jewish Palestinian Aramaic* (Baltimore: Johns Hopkins University Press, 1990), 35, s.v. "*adori*."
39. Some later rabbis even ruled, based on this story, that this is the appropriate way for students to relate to teachers. See Louis (Levi) Ginzberg, *Peirushim veḥiddushim baYerushalmi* (New York: JTS, 1940), 243–44; Ofra Meir, "'*Muvtaḥ ani bazeh shemoreh hora'a beYisrael' (Pesahim 3b): Lidmuto shel Rabbi Yoḥanan beyaḥaso letalmidav*," in *Alei Siaḥ* 15–16 (1982), n. 14.

Two classical rabbinic texts support the accuracy of this custom. The first is from the Babylonian Talmud (Berakhot 27b): "The rabbis taught: Rabbi Elazar Ḥisma says . . . one who greets his teacher or returns his teacher's greeting . . . causes the Divine Presence to distance itself from Israel."

The second ostensible proof is from a slightly later work that lists the differences in customs between Babylonian and Palestinian Jews, and the Babylonian custom of not greeting teachers is listed as difference number 38. See Mordekhai Margaliot, *Hahilukim shebein anshei haMizrah uvnei Eretz Yisrael* (Jerusalem: Reuven Mass, 1938), 151–52. See also *Hagahot Maimoniyot* (Rabbi Meir b. Yekutiel Hakohen of Rothenberg [Germany, 13th cent.]) on Maimonides, *Mishneh Torah*, Laws of Torah Study 5:5. See also *Hagahot haRema,* Yoreh De'ah 242:16, s.v. 'yesh ormim'. See also *Divrei hamudot* (Rabbi Yom Tov Lipman Heller [Bohemia, 17th cent.]) on *Piskei haRosh, Berakhot* 4:5, 23.

40. Meir, 15–16.
41. First, Rashi interprets Rabbi Elazar Hisma's statement (see above, n. 39) to mean not that one should refrain from greeting one's teacher but that one should do so properly and with a show of respect, rather than merely as one would greet a peer. Second, Ginzberg, *Peirushim vehiddushim,* 243, argues that Rabbi Elazar Hisma's statement is unlikely to mean what it appears to mean (i.e., that the Babylonian custom was not to greet one's rabbi), because he is a Palestinian rabbi, and it does not stand to reason that he would be reporting and supporting a specifically Babylonian custom.

With regard to the list of differences between Palestinian and Babylonian Jewish customs, there is reason to doubt its reliability. It is from an anonymous work of dubious origins, and its author might even have used our story from the Jerusalem Talmud as the source for this particular Babylonian custom. See Robert Brody, *The Geonim of Babylonia and the Shaping of Medieval Jewish Culture* (New Haven: Yale University Press, 1998), 112–13; Rabbi Yissachar Tamar, *Alei Tamar,* JT Mo'ed Katan 47.

42. See, for example, Nazir 20b; Bava Kamma 73b; Sanhedrin 98a; Berakhot 3a; Ta'anit 20b. Likewise, see *Piskei haRosh,* Berakhot, Chaps. 4, 5; *Be'ur haGra* and *Arukh hashulhan, Yoreh de'a* 242:39.
43. See Mo'ed Katan 24b, printed edition (in contrast to MS Columbia); *Masekhet Sefer Torah* (Vilna, 1883), 1:5, which is a late rabbinic text.
44. Yevamot 96b.
45. See, for example, Meiri, *Beit haBehira,* Yevamot 96b; Maimonides, *Mishneh Torah,* Laws of Torah Study 5:9; *Tur* and *Shulhan arukh, Yoreh de'a* 242.
46. JT Sanhedrin 1:1 (13a).
47. JT Megilla 1:12 (72c), JT Yevamot 12:6 (13a), JT Gittin 1:4 (40c). See Hanokh Albeck, *Mevo letalmidim* (Tel Aviv: Dvir, 1969), 226n151.
48. See Albeck, 224–27.
49. JT Yevamot 3:9 (5a). See also JT Yevamot 15:5 (15a), where Rabbi Yohanan similarly insists that Rabbi Elazar learned another law on the same subject. This incident appears as well in JT Sanhedrin 5:2 (22d). Ginzberg, *Peirushim vehiddushim,* 242–43, also notes that Rabbi Yohanan is likely wrong in his assessment of the sources of Rabbi Elazar's knowledge.
50. Mishna Yevamot 10:9. For more on this, see Roth, "Tradition of Aaron," 148n172.

51. See Jenny R. Labendz, *Socratic Torah: Non-Jews in Rabbinic Intellectual Culture* (New York: Oxford University Press, 2013), 35–80.
52. This section of the story appears to be a later addition to the original version in the Jerusalem Talmud. See JT Shekalim 2:1; *Midrash Shmuel* 19:4 (Buber ed.). It is also possible that this section is based on a similar story in JT Avoda Zara 3:8 (43b). Meir, "*Muvtah Ani*," argues that this section of the story is a final attempt to convince Rabbi Yohanan to see things differently, after the original explanation regarding Babylonian customs did not convince him.
53. Berakhot 17a.
54. Mishna Avot 5:11.
55. Yevamot 96b.
56. See Moshe Herr, "*Bein batei knessiot levein batei teatra'ot vekirkasa'ot*," in *Knesset Ezra*, ed. Shulamit Elitzur, Moshe Herr, A. Sha'anan, and G. Shaked (Jerusalem: Yad Ben-Zvi Press, 1994), 107, for examples of political sermons, and there in n. 13 for evidence of corruption on the part of the Patriarch during this period.
57. In the Jerusalem Talmud's version of this story (Sanhedrin 2:5 [20c]), the rabbi preaches in the synagogue of Tiberias, where both Reish Lakish and Rabbi Yehuda Nesiya live.
58. In the Jerusalem Talmud this line reads, "The king took it all," with no reference to the Patriarch.
59. The version in Genesis Rabba says "Rabbi," but the version in the Jerusalem Talmud says "Rabbi Yehuda Nesiya," and this is clearly who is intended.
60. In the Jerusalem Talmud, all that is said to Rabbi Yehuda Nesiya is, "He [Yosei of Maon] is a great man." This illustrates an entirely different method of third-party peacemaking, namely, giving a character witness—a technique used to facilitate a direct meeting between the two parties in conflict. See Herr, "*Bein batei knessiot*," 111–12.
61. Genesis Rabba 80:1 (MS Vatican 30), 950–53.
62. Herr, "*Bein batei knessiot*," 111–12.
63. Ibid., 113, explains this as a reference to the state of the Temple in Jerusalem. It is likely, however, that the intention here is to the "house" of the Patriarch.
64. In the Jerusalem Talmud's version of this story, it is Rabbi Yehuda Nesiya who turns to Reish Lakish and says, "It's not enough that he insulted me to my face once? But to my face twice?"
65. As opposed to the other stories discussed in this chapter, these two have not attracted much attention from either classical rabbinic commentaries or contemporary scholars.
66. See Geoffrey Herman, *A Prince without a Kingdom* (Tübingen: Mohr Siebeck, 2012).
67. MS Munich 6; in nearly every manuscript the name of the place is different. See Roth, "Tradition of Aaron," 155n212.
68. Yoma 78a (MS Munich 6).
69. See Gittin 11a; Albeck, *Mevo*, 450–51.
70. Between the lines in MS Florence the word *ikpid* is added, meaning Rav Yosef became angry. This is also in MS Paris.

71. Added between the lines of MS Florence.
72. Added between the lines of MS Florence.
73. MS Florence continues here: "Rav Yosef sent Rav Dimi bar Yosef to rebuke [Rav Avya for not coming]." It would appear that there were two different versions of this legend that were combined into one in MS Florence (as well as in MS Oxford 366).

    There are many different versions of this legend, as well as a parallel story in Kiddushin 25a in which the third party sent to rebuke and excommunicate them discovers that the absent rabbis were indeed angry with the lecturer. For further discussion on the textual variants of this legend see Roth, "Tradition of Aaron," 155–57.
74. MS Florence. I chose MS Florence rather than MS Oxford 366, which the Academy of the Hebrew Language determined to be the best manuscript for this section, since only MS Florence preserves the two versions of this story that remained after several hands had revised this manuscript.
75. In the margins of MS Florence as well as in the Soncino and Vilna printed editions of the Talmud, the word חלש, "weak" or "ill," is added.
76. The larger literary setting of this story is the interpretation of a Scriptural verse, Ps. 50:23, which leads to a play on words involving *derekh eretz*—good manners or respectful behavior. I have not included the hermeneutical introduction and conclusion of the story both in the interests of readability and because it does not affect the content of the story. This story has been analyzed thoroughly by literary scholars of rabbinic legend, most notably Yona Frankel, *Darkhei haAggadah vehaMidrash* (Tel Aviv: Yad laTalmud, 1996), 245–47; Avigdor Shinan, "*Rabbi Yanai, harokhel, veha'adam hameshupa: Iyyun betashtitam shel shnei sippurim beMidrash Vayikra Rabba*," *Bikoret uFarshanut* 30 (1994): 15–23; and Shmuel Faust, "*Talmidei ḥakhamim ve'amei haaretz: Vayikra Rabba 9*," *Da'at: Limudei Yahadut veruaḥ* (Machon Herzog), http://www.daat.ac.il/DAAT/sifrut/agadot/talmidey-2.htm.
77. Margulies, *Vayikra Rabba*, 177, in his note to line 1, translates, "dressed in expensive and beautiful clothes," noting the possible implication that the man was wealthy. See Shinan, 20n21.
78. For an in-depth discussion of the textual variants of this story, see Roth, "Tradition of Aaron," 134–39.
79. Margulies, *Vayikra Rabba*, 177, note to line 4.
80. The phenomenon of a rabbi insulting someone because they fail a test of scholarship is found in other rabbinic stories as well; see Shabbat 108a, Bava Batra 22a.
81. This line is not in MS London, but it does appear in nearly all other manuscripts of this story. See Roth, "Tradition of Aaron," 136n88.
82. This bracketed text does not appear in MS London or MS Munich, or in the printed edition, but it appears in MSS Vatican, Paris, Jerusalem 1, Oxford 3, Oxford 51, and Sasson.
83. An alternative translation of this question is: "Why did you grant me kindness at my table?" See Frankel, *Darkhei haAggada vehaMidrash*, 246.
84. This version is found also in MS Munich and the printed edition. However, in other manuscripts such as MSS Vatican and Paris the text reads, "who were entering into [a fight with] each other until I separated them." See Margulies, *Vayikra Rabba*, 177.

85. This final line appears in MSS London and Munich and in the printed edition, but does not appear in the other manuscripts.
86. MS London.
87. See below; some textual witnesses include hints about his method, to which we will return later in this chapter.
88. See Frankel, *Darkhei haAggada vehaMidrash*, 246.
89. This phenomenon is mainly found in the Babylonian Talmud. See Shabbat 108a, Bava Batra 22a, Bava Kamma 59a.
90. Shinan, "*Rabbi Yanai*," 20.
91. The phenomenon of poking fun at and mocking the other side after claiming victory in a battle of wits is common in rabbinic literature. See above, n.89. Albert Rapp, "Phylogenetic Theory of Wit and Humor," *Journal of Social Psychology* 30, no. 1 (1949): 84–93, describes from an anthropological perspective how people would test newcomers to a community through a duel of wits, and the victorious side would cruelly mock and poke fun at the defeated side.
92. Faust, "*Talmidei hakhamim ve'amei haaretz*," identifies the guest's question as a riddle.
93. Frankel, *Darkhei haAggada vehaMidrash*, 623n67, explains that the guest's grabbing Rabbi Yanai was a symbolic act of grabbing back his inheritance. Faust, however, sees the guest as acting violently and out of control.
94. Ibid., 246. Prof. Rob Eisen pointed out to me orally that the guest may be gently poking at Rabbi Yanai by alluding to the irony that Yanai is a Greek name, and he is claiming to be the sole inheritor of the Torah, while the guest is a descendent of Yaakov (Jacob, who is also called Israel).
95. Faust, "*Talmidei hakhamim ve'amei haaretz*," and Frankel, *Darkhei haAggada vehaMidrash*, 247, both understand the guest's response as having a dual meaning, referring to both his general behavior and his immediate interaction with Rabbi Yanai.
96. Leviticus Rabba 9:3.
97. Rabbi Samson Raphael Hirsch (Germany, 1808–1888), who founded a religious movement around Torah and *derekh eretz*, wrote about this midrash extensively. See, for example, his commentary on Gen. 3:24. The expression even has its own entry in Wikipedia: https://en.wikipedia.org/wiki/Proper_behavior_precedes_the_Torah.
98. Shinan, "*Rabbi Yanai*," 20, writes that the guest is an example of "an absolute pursuer of peace."
99. According to MSS Vatican and Paris (see above, n.84), instead of the guest saying he "makes peace between them," he describes himself as engaging in conflict management, separating between two parties whom he found fighting and trying to bring about a ceasefire.
100. Lederach, *Preparing for Peace*, 83. On this phenomenon in general within rabbinic literature, see Labendz, *Socratic Torah*.
101. On Elijah's own peacemaking, see Mishna Eduyot 8:7: "Elijah does not come to push away or draw near, but to make peace in the world." This mishna is an elaboration on the biblical verse in Malachi 3:23.

102. On this part of the story, see Samuel Secunda, "'Dashtana ki derekh nashim li': A Study of the Babylonian Rabbinic Laws of Menstruation in Relation to Corresponding Zoroastrian Texts" (PhD diss., Yeshiva University, 2007), 20–23.
103. MS Munich 95 and the Pesaro printed edition read: "two brothers" (אחי).
104. MS Jerusalem, Yad HaRav Herzog.
105. See Ta'anit 21b.
106. As discussed, for example, in Chap. 2, 42–43.
107. In the Pesaro printed edition, this root is also found in the very beginning of the story, where Rabbi Beroka "sees a certain man": *hoza le'hahu gavra*, who turns out to be the jailor. In other words, Rabbi Beroka was able to see these people only on a superficial level, but could not perceive that they were people deserving of future reward in the World to Come.
108. MS Vatican 134, and the Pesaro and Vilna printed editions.
109. Rashi and Sokoloff (*Dictionary*, 436, s.v. "*hoza'a*" [1st entry]) both understand his name thus.
110. See Sokoloff, 436, s.v. "*hoza'a*" (2nd entry), with reference to Pesahim 105b, MS Munich 6.
111. See Menachem Tzvi Kaddari, *Hebrew Biblical Dictionary* [in Hebrew] (Ramat Gan, Israel: Bar-Ilan University, 1996), 284, s.v. "*haza*," who suggests this reading.
112. Rabbenu Hananel, Ta'anit 22a, s.v. "*ve'amru leh*." Abraham Joshua Heschel, the famous Jewish philosopher, claimed this tale was "particularly cherished" by the Ba'al Shem Tov, the founder of the Hasidic movement. See Abraham Joshua Heschel, *A Passion for Truth* (New York: Farrar, Straus & Giroux, 1973), 53.
113. Rashi, Ta'anit 22a, s.v. "*ad d'avdei shelama*."
114. Bruce D. Bonta, "Conflict Resolution among Peaceful Societies: The Cultures of Peacefulness," *Journal of Peace Research* 33, no. 4 (1996): 407. See also Grace Kyoon-Achan, "Indigenous Elders as the Mbasoron Tar (Repairers of the World) and Inukshuks (Way-pointers) of Peace," in Tuso and Flaherty, *Creating the Third Force*, 191, where she includes humor as one of the desirable qualities of the peacemaking elders. See also Maureen Flaherty and Cathy Rocke, with Margaret Lavallee and Billie Schibler, "Case Study—Reconstructing Communities: Indigenous Grandmothers Searching for Peace," in Tuso and Flaherty, *Creating the Third Force*, 382, where they describe the ability of these peacemaking grandmothers to have a sense of humor and laugh at themselves.
115. Peter T. Coleman and Morton Deutsch, "Some Guidelines for Developing a Creative Approach to Conflict," in Coleman, Deutsch, and Marcus, *Handbook of Conflict Resolution*, 408.
116. Rashi, Ta'anit 22a, s.v. "*tarhinan*"; Mishna Pe'a 1:1.
117. Maharal, *Netivot olam, Netiv hashalom*, chap. 2, p. 85.
118. See Chap. 5, 210–211.
119. Rabbi Yosef ibn Al-Nakawa, *Menorat hamaor*, ed. H. G. Enelow (NY: Bloch Publishing, 1929), chap. 20 ("*Derekh Eretz*"), 411. Rabbi Al-Nakawa also cites the previous legend (case 11) at 393–94.
120. *Avot d'Rabbi Natan* B, chap. 24. See Chap. 2, 42–43.

121. Pardes Rodef Shalom Schools Program, unit 2: The Strategies of the Rodef Shalom, 18, 2016. https://elmad.pardes.org/pcjcr/.
122. https://www.youtube.com/watch?v=YTOn7oVTuAw.
123. http://israelipalestiniancomedy.com/videos/.
124. Al-Aqsa and The Temple Mount in Judaism and Islam, published January 2, 2020, https://www.youtube.com/watch?v=waGElQvxUAk.
125. Hayward, "Women, Religion, and Peacebuilding," 317. Though less common, there are examples of women of faith serving as direct intermediaries between parties in conflict or between local communities and armed actors. They are able to approach these actors in part because as religious women, they are less likely to be seen as a threat by armed actors.
126. Pely, *Muslim/Arab Mediation*, 129. See also Kadayifci-Orellana, Abu-Nimer, and Mohamed-Saleem, "Islamic Framework for Peacebuilding," 22, 28.
127. A third possible example of a female third-party peacemaker in classical rabbinic literature is Ima Shalom (lit., mother of peace), who was the wife of Rabbi Eliezer and the sister of Rabban Gamliel, the Patriarch at the time. She might have played the role of a third-party mediator in the famous legend of the conflict between her husband and her brother (Bava Metzia 59b), in which she unsuccessfully labored to avoid further escalation of their antagonism against each other. It is also possible that she was named Ima Shalom since it was intended for her to marry Rabbi Eliezer, who was perhaps already understood to be a rival of Rabban Gamliel, in attempt to create peace between the two through a marriage alliance. However, I found no traditional or contemporary scholars who connect her name with peacemaking, whether in this legend or in any other legend told about her. Indeed, I found only those who claim this was the name given her at birth. For these reasons, I chose not to include the legend as a case study for this book.
128. The text used for this is the version of the scholia preserved in Ta'anit 18a, MS Jerusalem, Yad HaRav Herzog. The Scholium (pl. scholia) is the early commentary of *Megillat Ta'anit*. The same version of the story can be found in Rosh Hashana 19a and, with some variants, in the MS Parma edition of the scholia on *Megillat Ta'anit*, 28 Adar. See Vered Noam, *Megillat Ta'anit: Versions, Interpretation, History* [in Hebrew] (Jerusalem: Yad Ben-Zvi Press, 2003), 128–29.
129. This quotation is from the original *Megillat Ta'anit*; the rest of the story is the Babylonian Talmud's version of the Scholium.
130. In the Scholium version of this story, it reads "practice idol worship" instead of "not study the Torah."
131. The Parma edition of the Scholium (12:8, 129; MS Parma, Biblioteca Palatina, 2298 [1544]) adds the following after the words "go and demonstrate at night": "saying, 'Alas, in Heaven's name . . .'" In other words, as opposed to the version of the story in the Babylonian Talmud, here in the Scholium she explicitly instructs the Jews what to say when they demonstrate. And these are the exact same words that they are described as saying in the Babylonian Talmud version.
132. This line is missing in the version that appears in Ta'anit 18a but is found in the parallel version in Rosh Hashana 19a (MSS Munich 140).
133. Noam, *Megillat Ta'anit*, 129, lines 28–29.

134. For a complete summary of scholarly opinions with regard to the dating of this legend, see Noam, 312–13.
135. See Book of the Maccabees I, 1:41–50.
136. In Babylonian Aramaic, the word is *matronita*; see Sokoloff, *Dictionary*, 661. In Palestinian Aramaic the word is *matrona*; see Sokoloff, 303.
137. There is no way, of course, of identifying who this woman is, especially given the fact that historians are in disagreement with regard to when and if this event took place. Nevertheless, it is worth mentioning the opinion of Heinrich Graetz, *History of the Jews*, vol. 2, ed. Bella Löwy (New York: Cosimo, 2009), 432. He holds this story takes place in the wake of the bloody Bar Kokhba revolt during the rule of Antonius Pius, who nullified the edicts of Hadrian in 139/140 CE, and the woman is the widow of Tinius Rufus, who was the governor of Judea in the first century:

A noble Roman lady of Cæsarea or Antioch, who had pity on the sufferings of the Jews, advised them to petition the Roman authorities that the persecutions might cease. This lady was perhaps the wife of Rufus, and is said to have had inclination toward Judaism. Following this advice, a few men, headed by Jehudah b. Shamua, repaired to the governor to beg for mercy. In the gloomy darkness of their desolation they lamented—"O heavens, are we not your brothers, the sons of the same father? Why do you inflict on us unendurable sufferings?" Such lamentations appear to have induced the governor to petition the Emperor to pursue a milder course of conduct toward the Jews.

138. Rashi, Rosh Hashana 19a, s.v. *"hafginu."*
139. Maharsha, *Hiddushei Aggadot*, Rosh Hashana 19a, s.v. *"lo ahikhem."*
140. Moses Rosensohn, *Shalom ahim*, part 1 (Vilna, 1870). This was part of a series of publications known as *Marbei shalom* (Vilna, 1870). It should be noted that Rosensohn was shunned by the Orthodox Jewish community in Russia under suspicion that he was secretly trying to convert Jews to Christianity. See http://www.jewishencyclopedia.com/articles/12858-rosensohn-moses.
141. Gene Sharp, *The Politics of Nonviolent Action*, vol. 3 (Boston: Porter Sargent, 1973), 706.
142. See above, n. 131.
143. M. J. Mathey et al., "The Role Played by Women of the Central African Republic in the Prevention and Resolution of Conflicts," in *Women and Peace in Africa: Case Studies on Traditional Conflict Resolution Practices* (Paris: UNESCO, 2003), 41–42.
144. Berakhot 10a. This translation is based on MSS Oxford, Opp. Add. Fol. 23 (366), considered by the Academy of the Hebrew Language as the primary manuscript of this tractate of the Talmud. Significant variants are cited in brackets. The translation of Ps. 104:35 has been adjusted to reflect the Talmud's intended meaning.
145. MS Munich 95, MS Paris 671:4, and printed editions.
146. MS Munich 95, MS Paris.
147. In all other manuscripts her name appears.
148. In all other manuscripts it is added, with minor variants, "Furthermore, cast your eyes on the end of the verse, 'and the wicked be no more.' Because sins will cease, they will be wicked no more."
149. MS Florence, MS Munich 95, and printed editions.

150. Yifat Moniknadem, "Beruria as an Analogical Contrast to Rabbi Meir" [in Hebrew], *Derekh Aggada* 2 (1999): 42. This is how the verse from the book of Psalms is understood in a few places in rabbinic literature. See, for example, Berakhot 9b, where Rabbi Yehuda the son of Rabbi Shimon b. Pazzi quotes this verse in the context of the wicked actually dying.
151. Moniknadem, "Beruria as an Analogical Contrast to Rabbi Meir," 42.
152. Moniknadem, at ibid., 42, writes: "Beruria's use of the verse conceals within it a criticism of Rabbi Meir, that despite all of his learning and knowledge of Torah he did not think of using it properly when it came to a situation that related to him."
153. It could, however, be argued that Beruria is simply doing here what rabbis always do to one another in discussion, which is to quote biblical prooftexts to persuade the other side.
154. Gopin, *Bridges*, 36.
155. Pely, *Muslim/Arab Mediation*, 133–34.
156. Josephine Ntahobari and Basilissa Ndayiziga, "The Role of Burundian Women in the Peaceful Settlement of Conflicts," in *Women and Peace in Africa*, 20.
157. Greer Fay Cashman, "Martin Luther King Jr. Day still relevant in current era," *Jerusalem Post*, January 20, 2020, https://www.jpost.com/israel-news/martin-luther-king-jr-day-still-relevant-in-current-era-614729.
158. http://womenwagepeace.org.il/en/.
159. For further examples of contemporary Jewish religious women serving as peacemakers, see Kurtzer-Ellenbogen, Lucy, "Jewish Women in Peacebuilding: Embracing Disagreement in the Pursuit of 'Shalom,'" in *Women, Religion, and Peace: Exploring Experience, Probing Complexity*, Susan Hayward and Katherine Marshall eds., Washington DC: USIP press, 2015, 113–25.
160. Although it does appear that according to the *Tosefta* Sanhedrin piece cited in Chapter 2, Aaron would engage in bringing conflicting parties to a compromise agreement.

Chapter 4

1. See Chap. 1, 25 and fn. 93.
2. For the role of rabbinic responsa literature in the study of history, see Haym Soloveitchik, *Shut kemakor histori* [Responsa as a historical source] (Jerusalem: Merkaz Zalman Shazar, 1991).
3. Regretfully, I was unable to find examples of women serving as third-party peacemakers in later rabbinic literature. This is not to imply, of course, that women did not contribute to communal peacemaking, or that there is no surviving evidence of such peacemaking stories.
4. *Mishneh Torah*, Laws of Personal Development 5:7.
5. *Mishneh Torah*, Laws of Robbery and Lost Articles 14:13.
6. Yitzhak Yaakov Fuchs, *Halikhot bein adam leḥavero* (Jerusalem: privately printed, 2004), 1:17, cites Maimonides' statement from *Mishneh Torah*, Laws of Personal Development, as the source for the following: "There is a special obligation incumbent upon Torah scholars to attempt to make peace between people."
7. Rabbi Levi ibn Ḥaviv, *Shut Maharalbaḥ* 110.

8. Rabbi Ḥayim Shabtai, *Shut Torat Ḥayim* 3:32.
9. *Sefer ḥaredim*, Introduction, chap. 7, viii. See Preface, n. 7.
10. See Daniel Roth. "The Call to Rabbis and Lay Leaders to be Pursuers of Peace", Elmad, October 29, 2915. http://elmad.pardes.org/2015/10/the-call-to-rabbis-and-lay-leaders-to-be-pursuers-of-peace/. See also Daniel Roth, "Mikhtav ishi lerav hakehilah ulekehilato", Arutz Sheva, 11.2.2021 https://www.inn.co.il/news/467600
11. Rabbi Syracusty himself signed his name, "Yosef, son of my master, the perfect scholar, Rabbi Avraham el-Syracusty" (Meir Benayahu, "*Teuda min hador harishon shel megurashei Sefarad biTzefat*," in *Sefer Tzefat*, vol. 1 [Jerusalem: Yad Ben-Zvi and Hebrew University, 1953], 114). Rabbi Yosef Garson, in his eulogy (below), refers to him as "Syracusy." However, he became known as "Saragossi" in later literature, such as in Rabbi Elazar b. Moshe Azikri's *Sefer ḥaredim*, as we will see; his tombstone in Ein Zetun near Safed says "Saragossi." I have chosen, however, to refer to him the way he referred to himself: "Syracusty." On the life of Rabbi Syracusty, see Graetz, *History of the Jews*, vol. 4, 399; Solomon Rozness, *Divrei Yisrael beturgema* (Tel Aviv: Dvir, 1930), 189–92; and Benayahu, "*Teuda*," 114; Meir Benayahu, "*Derushav shel Rabbi Yosef b. Meir Garson*," in *Michael*, vol. 7 (Tel Aviv: Tel Aviv University, 1982), 98–99.
12. The year in which the land lies fallow, occurring once every seven years.
13. See above, n. 11.
14. Shabbat 88b. See also Chap. 2, n. 95, and Chap. 4, n. 152.
15. Benayahu, "*Derushav*," 162–64.
16. See Chap. 2, 44–45.
17. The idea of giving charity to the poor as a means of making peace between them and God has its roots in classical rabbinic literature. Mishna Avot 2:7 states, "One who increases charity increases peace." Leviticus Rabba 34:16 says, "Rabbi Yehuda, son of Rabbi Shimon, expounded: 'The poor man sits and complains, saying, "How am I different from so-and-so? Yet he sleeps in his bed and I sleep here! He sleeps in his own house and I sleep here!" Now, come forward and give him charity. I shall consider it as if you had made peace between him and Me!' Hence it is written 'Let him take hold of My strength, that he may make peace with Me; let him make peace with Me' (Isaiah 27:5)." For further explanation and other examples of kabbalists in Safed making peace between the poor and God, see Benayahu, "*Derushav*," 9.
18. *Sefer ḥaredim*, Introduction, chap. 8, viii.
19. Benayahu, "*Teuda*," 114; "*Derushav*," 99.
20. *Sefer ḥaredim*, Introduction, chap. 7, vii. Identifying the prophet Elijah as the one who will bring peace in messianic times is based on earlier rabbinic literature; see Chap. 3, n. 101.
21. Rabbi Ḥayim Yosef David Azulai, *Shem hagedolim* (Livorno: G. Falorni, 1774), 42. See also Rabbi Menaḥem Mandiaonfli, *Etzba ketana* (Izmir: Roditi, 1876), 3a, who writes, "Because of [the pursuit of peace] Elijah the prophet will come," and as a proof of this he quotes Rabbi Azikri verbatim, concluding, "Because [Rabbi Syracusty] constantly made peace, he merited to see Elijah."
22. Rabbi Pinḥas Eliyahu Horowitz, "Love of Neighbors," article 13, in *Sefer habrit* (Brno, 1797, later republished as *Sefer habrit hashalem*), part 2: *Divrei emet*, chap. 27, 52b. Horowitz's words would later be brought as a proof by Moses Rosensohn in his book *Shalom aḥim*, which was exclusively focused on proving that peacemaking is not

an internal Jewish principle, but includes Jews and non-Jews entirely as equals. On Rosensohn, see Chap. 3, 130, and n. 140. See also Rabbi Yosef Avraham Heller, *Shalom yihiyeh* (New York: Empire Press, 1989), 6, who also cites the same words of Rabbi Azikri as well as additional traditional sources that advance the notion that peacemaking and loving one's neighbor include non-Jews. Rabbi Yosef Nissim ibn Adhan, *Sefer ma'aseh Bereshit*, part 4 (Jerusalem: Keter, 1986), 539, commandment 695, also restates Rabbi Horowitz's words in *Sefer habrit* nearly word for word. Although he does not reference him explicitly there, he does refer to him elsewhere throughout his book.

23. See, for example, Rabbi Yaakov Yosef of Polonne, one of the first dedicated disciples of the Ba'al Shem Tov, who wrote, "We are taught it is a great *mitzva* to achieve peace between two people who quarrel. I will tell of an even greater *mitzva*, namely, to make peace between your body and your spirit, so that materialism does not conquer the spirit." (Lewis I. Newman, *Hasidic Anthology: Tales and Teachings of the Hasidim* [New York: Bloch Publishing, 1934], 311. This is a translation of Rabbi Avrahahm Kahana, *Sefer haHasidut* [1922], 126).

Rabbi Tzadok Hakohen of Lublin, of nineteenth-century Poland, writes: "It is said in the name of Rabbi Simha Bunim of Pesishcha . . . It is said (Ps. 38:4) "There is no peace in my bones because of my sin"- that the primary [cause] of separation and war is within a person's body, between his bones, caused by sin and the evil inclination, and from this emerges war on the outside" (*Pri tzaddik* [Lublin: 1900–1934], *Hanukka*, 160).

Hasidic rabbis were not the first to advance concepts of inner peace between body and soul within Judaism. See, for example, Horowitz, *Shnei Luhot haBrit, Shoftim, Torah ohr*: "And he should make peace between his body and soul, meaning he should cleanse his material [body], for if not the soul will be separate from the body. And this is the meaning of 'Torah scholars increase peace in the world' (Berakhot 19a). And a person is called a small world (*Tanhuma, Pekudei* 3)." These statements support Gopin's critique of rational conflict resolution methods that too often ignore the inner workings of the individual peacemakers. He writes, "The fact that one notices in religious literature, from East to West, from Buddhism to Judaism, a careful attention to nurturing the inner life and working on the moral life from an internal perspective suggests an important critique of current conflict resolution practice. Conflict resolution needs to address the most protean origins of anger, suffering, love, and benevolence and the skills of fair play and communication. Otherwise, deficiencies of character are bound to undermine the methods that are being taught" (*Eden*, 179–80).

24. Virgil Peterson, "The Rabbi's Resolution and the Power of Stories," *Conflict Resolution Notes* 11, no. 2 (September 1993).

25. Peterson cites as his source Ira Progoff, *The Dynamics of Hope: Perspectives of Process in Anxiety and Creativity, Imagery and Dreams* (New York: Dialogue House Library, 1985), 237–44.

26. Avraham Yellin, *Derekh tzaddikim* (Lvov, 1912), 49.

27. After citing another example of the power of prayer, the author concludes, "All that a person wants he makes happen through his prayers."

28. Martin Buber, *Ohr haganuz: Sippurei Hasidim* (Jerusalem/Tel Aviv: Schocken Press, 2005), 333. Buber also cites there another legend, which he calls "Making Peace." This

story tells how Rabbi Yaakov Yitzḥak Rabinowicz of Pesishcha (known as the Holy Jew; 1766–1813) once made peace as a young child between sheep fighting next to a river, and was then recognized by his uncle as a future leader of his people. See 361. (The original story can be found at the end of *Imrei Yehoshua*, vol. 2 [Piotrkow, 1926], in a supplementary section to the book entitled *Ateret Avot*, 2.)

29. Pinto, "Peacemaking as Ceremony," 176–77. See also Hamdesa Tuso, "Ararra: Oromo Indigenous Processes of Peacemaking," in Tuso and Flaherty, *Creating the Third Force*, 90.
30. For an example of prayer assisting in bringing sides to an agreement, see Little, *Peacemakers in Action*, 72–73. For an example of shared prayer and its inherent challenges in strengthening interfaith relationships after a formal peace agreement, see Little, 172.
31. Gopin, *Bridges*, 71.
32. https://jerusalemprayingtogether.wordpress.com/.
33. David M. Halbfinger, "In Israel, a Time to Pray Amid a Health Crisis," *NYTimes*, May 25, 2020, https://www.nytimes.com/2020/03/25/world/middleeast/israel-virus-prayer.html.
34. Shaul Stampfer, *Hayeshiva haLita'it* (Jerusalem: Merkaz Zalman Shazar, 2005), 39–42. This book has been translated into English as *Lithuanian Yeshivas of the Nineteenth Century: Creating a Tradition of Learning* (Liverpool: Littman Library of Jewish Civilization/Liverpool University Press, 2014).
35. Hillel Noah Steinschneider, *Ir Vilna* [The city of Vilnius], vol. 1 (Vilna: Widow and Brothers Romm, 1900), 90.
36. Stampfer, *Hayeshiva haLita'it*, 72.
37. Ibid., 79.
38. Ibid., 87.
39. See Preface, n. 7.
40. Rabbi Yaakov Lifschitz, *Zikhron Yaakov*, vol. 2, 34–35.
41. Baruch Epstein, *Mekor Barukh*, vol. 4 (Vilna: Widow and Brothers Romm, 1928), 1692–93.
42. Ibid.
43. Ibid.
44. It is puzzling that the agreement does not address one of the central issues in the conflict between the two rabbis, namely, their different study methods. It is difficult to account for this apparent lacuna.
45. Baruch Epstein, *My Uncle the Netziv* [translation of *Mekor Barukh*, vol. 4] (Brooklyn: ArtScroll Mesorah, 1988), 28; *Mekor Barukh*, 1696–99.
46. Lifschitz, *Zikhron Yaakov*, vol. 2, 35.
47. http://929.org.il.
48. See Jeremy Sharon, "Debate and Division Come under Discussion by Presidents, Judges and Rabbis," *Jerusalem Post*, February 17, 2019; https:// www.929.org.il/ pack/ מגשרים-בין-גיבורי-המקרא; https:// www.youtube.com/ watch?v=4KfKFeLNjUM&t= 128s.
49. https://pardes.org.il/mm.
50. Meir Benayahu, *Rabbi Ḥayim Yosef David Azulai*, vol. 1 (Jerusalem: Mossad Harav Kook, 1959). Prof. Benayahu is the grandson of former Chief Rabbi of Israel Rabbi Yitzḥak Nissin, who in 1960 brought over the remains of Rabbi Azulai from Levorno,

Italy, to be buried in Jerusalem. For the most updated list of books and articles that discuss Rabbi Azulai, see Oded Cohen, "New and Old Cultural Spaces in the Hida's World" [in Hebrew] (PhD diss., Tel Aviv University, 2016), 9–11.

51. On the role and social status of what was called the *shadar* (שד״ר), those who were sent to raise money on behalf of the Jewish communities in the Land of Israel in those days, see Cohen, "New and Old," 24–35, 289–92.
52. Benayahu, *Azulai*, vol. 1, 48.
53. Rabbi Hayim Yosef David Azulai, *Sefer ma'agal tov hashalem*, ed. Aharon Freimann (Jerusalem: Mekitzei Nirdamim, 1933). Freimann's edition was later translated into English by Benjamin Cymerman. I have used Cymerman's translation as the basis for my own, and will indicate where my translation diverges from his. See *The Diaries of Rabbi Ha'im Yosef David Azulai*, part II, trans. and ed. Benjamin Cymerman (Jerusalem: Bnei Issakhar Institute, Ohr Hamaarav Publishing House, 1997).
54. For a map of all the cities Rabbi Azulai visited, see http://mayaeh.tau.ac.il/blog/travels/חידא-חיים-יוסף-דוד-אזולאי/.
55. For an in-depth discussion on the relationship between Rabbi Azulai and non-Jews, see Cohen, "New and Old," 330–48. See also Benayahu, *Azulai*, 88. Azulai, *Ma'agal tov*, 120 (24 and 26 Kislev)/Cymerman, *Diaries*, part 2, 187, describes sitting and discussing Kabbala (Jewish mysticism) with a Christian scholar. At 122 (3 Tevet)/*Diaries*, 192–93, Rabbi Azulai describes how a Christian scholar opened up the Paris library especially for him in order to show him all the Jewish books and ancient manuscripts.

    He also notes, at 121 (29 Kislev)/*Diaries*, 188–89, "I must make mention here of the divine favor that I have such a good name [among the people]; and they hold my importance one hundred times more than I know I deserve. And I have constantly told them 'that I am a simpleton'—and they think this is just out of humility. Even among the gentiles—'the sages of Edom'—I have become famous, and they ask the Jews about me; and this is something amazing!" There are many more such examples.
56. Cohen, "New and Old," 295–99, briefly discusses what we have labeled cases 18, 20, and 23, focusing on Rabbi Azulai's understanding of his own self-image, as part of a larger discussion on how Rabbi Azulai was uninhibited with regard to actively inserting himself into community matters, whether they had to do with Jewish law and customs, ethical issues, or, as in these cases, peacemaking.
57. *Ma'agal tov*, 79 (16 Tammuz).
58. The same Hebrew letter expresses the sounds of *p* and *f*.
59. He writes this word in Hebrew as though it is an acronym.
60. *Ma'agal tov*, 79 (16 Tammuz); *Diaries*, 79. See also 50n63.
61. *Ma'agal tov*, 71n16 (21 Av); *Diaries*, 59n23.
62. *Ma'agal tov*, 71 (21 Av); *Diaries*, 59–60. Henceforth, the title *Signore* will be written as "S."

    Federica Francesconi, "An Alternative Path toward Emancipation: Jewish Merchants and Their Cross-Cultural Networks in the Eighteenth-Century Italian Ghettos" (*Avotaynu Online*: "Jewish Genealogy & Genetics," May 4, 2016), writes:

    > A preliminary examination of the sources reveals the existence of a network of Italian Jewish merchant families, such as the Fermis, Morpurgos, and Cohens,

who forged an oligarchy that functioned to help the community after 1555, which lasted more than two centuries.... At the time, the leadership of the Fermi, Morpurgo, and Cohen families was characterized by a high involvement within the organization of the Jewish community, broad commercial networks in the Mediterranean and in the New World, and finally, a certain degree of commercial cooperation with the Christian mercantile class of the city.

See http://www.avotaynuonline.com/2016/05/alternative-path-toward-emancipation-jewish-merchants-cross-cultural-networks-eighteenth-century-italian-ghettos/.

63. *Ma'agal tov*, 71 (21 Av); *Diaries*, 59–60. Since this case is especially lengthy, I will refer to Rabbi Azulai's diary entries only in the notes instead of bringing the exact quotes in the body of the text.
64. *Ma'agal tov*, 71 (22 Av); *Diaries*, 60.
65. Pius VI was elected on February 15, 1775, after Pope Clement XIV, who Azulai writes (*Ma'agal tov*, 72 [23 Av]; *Diaries*, 61) was a close friend of his host S. Pinḥas, passed away the previous September.
66. *Ma'agal tov*, 72 (18 Elul); *Diaries*, 62.
67. *Ma'agal tov*, 72 (22 Elul); *Diaries*, 63.
68. The extended family centered on two sets of siblings. I would like to thank my friend and colleague, Dr. Jenny Lebendz, for helping me map out this complicated family tree.

The "other" Cohen family siblings	Pinhas Cohen and his siblings
David (married to Reina)	**Pinḥas** (married to Giudecca [Judith], sister of David and Isaac Cohen)
Isaac	
Giudecca [Judith] (married to Pinḥas)	**Sapira** (married to Samuel Cagli)
	Reina (married to David Cohen)
	Giudecca [Judith] (lives in Pesaro, as do her son Avraham Halevi, married to the daughter of Joseph Morpurgo [of the distinguished Morpurgo family], and daughter Sarah, married to a son of the Matzliaḥ family)

The two sides of the conflict were:

Side 1	Side 2
David Cohen	**Pinḥas** Cohen
Isaac Cohen	**Sapira** (Pinḥas's sister) and her husband Samuel Cagli
Reina Cohen (David's wife and Pinḥas's sister)	(Giudecca [Judith], Pinḥas's sister, and her children Sarah and Avraham, who lived in Pesaro, were not part of the conflict.)
	Giudecca [Judith] Cohen (Pinḥas's wife and David and Isaac's sister)

Thus, David and Isaac were fighting with their sister Giudecca, and Pinḥas and Sapira were fighting with their sister Reina. Rabbi Azulai became involved when he was staying in Pesaro at the home of Avraham Halevi, and he received a letter from Rabbi Israel of Ancona that when he came to Ancona, he would stay with Pinḥas. Pinḥas happened to be in Pesaro at that time, but he didn't stay with his nephew Avraham Halevi (where Rabbi Azulai was staying), because Pinḥas was in a fight with Avraham Halevi's mother, who was Pinḥas's sister Giudecca. Instead, Pinḥas stayed with Matzliaḥ, his son-in-law's father (that is, the father of his daughter Sara's husband). Rabbi Azulai's very first accomplishment appears to have been to make peace between Giudecca and Pinḥas; the rabbi brought the two siblings together, but Giudecca pushed Pinḥas to make peace first with her daughter-in-law (daughter of Morpurgo), which he apparently did.

69. *Ma'agal tov*, 72 (22 Elul); *Diaries*, 63 (translation mine).
70. *Ma'agal tov*, 71n16 (23 Elul); *Diaries*, 63.
71. *Ma'agal tov*, 73 (27 Elul); *Diaries*, 63.
72. See Chap. 1, 23–24.
73. Lisa Schrich, "Ritual, Religion, and Peacebuilding," in Omer, Appleby, and Little, *The Oxford Handbook of Religion, Conflict, and Peacebuilding*, 516–40, and see especially 529.
74. *Ma'agal tov*, 73 (28 Elul); *Diaries*, 64.
75. *Ma'agal tov*, 73 (28 Elul); *Diaries*, 64.
76. *Ma'agal tov*, 73 (28 Elul); *Diaries*, 64.
77. Gopin, *Eden and Armageddon*, 179–80.
78. *Ma'agal tov*, 73 (Heshvan); *Diaries*, 66. This line is my translation.
79. *Ma'agal tov*, 73–74 (Kislev); *Diaries*, 66.
80. *Ma'agal tov*, 73–74 (Kislev); *Diaries*, 66.
81. *Ma'agal tov*, 74 (Tevet); *Diaries*, 67–68.
82. *Ma'agal tov*, 74 (Tevet); *Diaries*, 67–68.
83. *Ma'agal tov*, 74 (Adar); *Diaries*, 68.
84. *Ma'agal tov*, 74 (1 Nissan); *Diaries*, 68.
85. *Ma'agal tov*, 74 (3 Nissan); *Diaries*, 69.
86. *Ma'agal tov*, 74 (9 Nissan); *Diaries*, 69.
87. *Ma'agal tov*, 74 (9 Nissan); *Diaries*, 69.
88. *Ma'agal tov*, 74–75 (9 Nissan); *Diaries*, 69: "And it was a miracle (*nes*)! And the date was the 13th day of Nissan." (The date 9 Nissan is a reference point.) It appears that Rabbi Azulai is doing a play on words of the word miracle, *nes*, with the Hebrew month of Nissan in which the miracle of the exodus from Egypt took place.
89. *Ma'agal tov*, 75 (29 Nissan); *Diaries*, 69. Cymerman holds that this note was written by the cardinal himself. However, in my opinion, it might have been written by the cardinal's notary.
90. *Ma'agal tov*, 75 (29 Nissan); *Diaries*, 69.
91. *Ma'agal tov*, 75 (2 Iyar); *Diaries*, 70.
92. *Ma'agal tov*, 75 (4 Iyar); *Diaries*, 71.

93. Rabbi Azulai renders Finzi in Hebrew as "Pinto, [also] called Fintzi," and del Vecchio as "mil-Vecchio."
94. Ma'agal tov, 76 (16 Iyar); Diaries, 73. I inserted the words "[he had made]" and [deathbed].
95. Ma'agal tov, 76 (17 Iyar); Diaries, 74.
96. Benayahu, Azulai, 50n61, refers to this as an intentional tactic to influence Gedalia to make peace.
97. Ma'agal tov, 76 (18 Iyar); Diaries, 74.
98. Ma'agal tov, 77 (19 Iyar); Diaries, 74.
99. Ma'agal tov, 77 (19 Iyar); Diaries, 74.
100. Moses Vita Cohen was a prominent banker who had a close business and personal relationship with Pope Clement XIV.
101. A reference to Bava Kamma 91a.
102. Ma'agal tov, 77 (24 Iyar); Diaries, 75.
103. Ma'agal tov, 77 (19 Sivan); Diaries, 76. I used the word "arguing" instead of "discussing," and "compromise" instead of "settle."
104. On June 14 (27 Sivan), Rabbi Azulai met with the representatives of the community to speak with them about the secretive matter, despite the fact that he was very ill that day. On June 27 and 30 (10 and 13 Tammuz), he describes the internal deliberation between the representatives of the community over whether or not to accept the compromise agreement he was involved in brokering.
105. Ma'agal tov, 79 (16 Tammuz); Diaries, 79.
106. Ma'agal tov, 79 (19 Tammuz); Diaries, 79.
107. The words "speak peace to S. [Jacob Naquite]" are my translation, and differ from Cymerman's translation, which is "speak with S. Shalom." It is entirely clear from the continuation of the story that the name of the *gabbai* was not Shalom, but Jacob Naquite, and that the word *shalom* in the original Hebrew meant to speak *peace* to him. It is possible that Rabbi Azulai intentionally chose not to mention his name in this first passage of the story, instead referring to him as S., as a way of protecting his identity. Rabbi Azulai would often hide incriminating details about people out of fear of slander. Cymerman, however, who accidentally understood that the name of the *gabbai* was Shalom, struggles to weave this detail into the continuation of the story.

In my correspondence with Dr. Oded Cohen (see above, n. 50), he claims that from within the context of the story my reading makes sense, and that the name of the *gabbai* was indeed Jacob Naquite. Moreover, there have been cases where Cymerman has mistranslated the words of Rabbi Azulai, and as I mentioned earlier, there are instances in which Rabbi Azulai will try to hide people's identities. Dr. Cohen accedes that it is too difficult to determine which theory regarding the identity of the *gabbai* is correct, since there is no evidence within the manuscripts that we have on this section to attest to either theory, and that from a syntactical perspective it should have said, "to speak with S. *about* Shalom," and not just "to speak with S. Shalom." Nevertheless, I believe there is no other way to understand this story other than to say that this entry is referring to Jacob Naquite and not to an additional *gabbai* named Shalom.

108. *Diaries*, 178 (Heshvan 29).
109. *Maʾagal tov*, 117 (2 Kislev); *Diaries*, 179.
110. See Chap. 2, 72–73, and notes there.
111. *Maʾagal tov*, 118 (6 Kislev); *Diaries*, 180. Translation based on Cymerman. I have modified Cymerman's translation slightly by replacing "a meeting in the house of S. Daniel" with "at the yeshiva of S. Daniel."
112. See Maimonides, *Mishneh Torah*, Laws of Repentance 2:5. Maimonides requires the penitent to ask forgiveness from the offended party in public. The specific custom of asking forgiveness in front of the entire community in the synagogue is mentioned in several other rabbinic sources. See below, case 25, where the rabbis of Safed call upon the disputant rabbis of Cairo to reconcile with one another in front of the community, in the synagogue, on the Sabbath. See also Rabbi Shlomo Luria (the Maharshal; Brisk., Lublin; 1510–1573), *Yam shel Shlomo*, Bava Kamma, chap. 8, law 49, who rules that the one asking forgiveness must do so "during the [next communal] gathering in the Synagogue, before the taking out of the Torah from its ark."

For more sources on the custom of asking forgiveness in front of the community in the synagogue, see Roth, "Tradition of Aaron," 113–14. There I mistakenly claimed that this may have been an Ashkenazic custom, but the case of the rabbis of Safed clearly proves that the custom is not limited to the Ashkenazic community alone.

113. Rabbi Azulai greatly valued making peace between husband and wife. An additional story that testifies to this can be found in *Maʾagal tov*, 121 (29 Kislev); *Diaries*, 188–89. There, a very wealthy man offered him a great sum of money (1,000 *scudi*) for the Jewish community of Hebron if he would assist in convincing his wife to accept a *get* (a Jewish bill of divorce) from him. The rabbi, however, refused, adding that if the man would like him to help make peace between the man and his wife, he would be more than happy to do so for free.
114. *Maʾagal tov*, 121 (27 Kislev); *Diaries*, 188, Kislev 28. Translation based on Cymerman. I used the word "leaning" in place of Cymerman's "sliding down," since that is not the meaning of the word מטין. Cymerman, in n. 62, writes, "i.e., things were getting worse." I disagree with this assertion, as "leaning" can mean that things are unstable and can still go in either direction, toward divorce or toward reconciliation.
115. *Maʾagal tov*, 121 (28 Kislev); *Diaries*, 188. Translation based on Cymerman. I inserted "Hear, O Israel" for the Cymerman's transliteration, "*Shema, Yisrael*," and "talisman" for the transliterated "*segulah.*"
116. Deut. 6:4.
117. See *Maʾagal tov*, 76 (12 Iyar); *Diaries*, 72: "I met there the sage R. Judah Fano; and he told me [*inter alia*] that the Rema *z"l* once wrote on a small piece of parchment '*Shema Israel*' using the milk of a nursing mother and her nursing daughter mixed with lemon juice: with fasting and *tevilah* [ritual immersion] this is a wonderful talisman; for whosoever swallows this parchment, against apostasy: and it is tried and tested."

118. *Ma'agal tov*, 122 (first day of the New Moon of Tevet); *Diaries*, 190. Translation based on Cymerman. I substituted the word "persuasively" for "words of chastisement" since the original Hebrew, *divrei kibushin*, can mean either, and in this context it seems more likely that Rabbi Azulai was trying to engage in a persuasive conversation more than yelling at her, especially since it becomes clear that Rabbi Azulai changes his approach as a result of his conversation with her.
119. Benayahu, *Azulai*, 50n58, wrote: "In Bayonne he [attempted] to resolve a dispute that had been between Abraham Nounez and his wife for some eight years, and he advocated for the benefit of his wife."
120. *Ma'agal tov*, 111–12 (12 Tishri); *Diaries*, 163. Translation based on Cymerman. I replaced "And he set conditions (for reconciliation) that his wife" with "He accepted on the condition that his wife," since I understand that the conditions included several items not mentioned here that were to be sealed by her swearing on the Torah scroll, not that the swearing on the Torah was the sole condition.
121. *Ma'agal tov*, 111–12 (20 Tishrei); *Diaries*, 163–64. Translation based on Cymerman. I inserted the words "I instructed him and persuaded him" for "I consented to him and appeased him," which in my opinion is not an accurate translation of *vehoreiti lo ufiastiv*.
122. *Ma'agal tov*, 112 (21 Tishrei); *Diaries*, 164.
123. *Ma'agal tov*, 112 (23 Tishrei); *Diaries*, 165.
124. *Ma'agal tov*, 113 (1 Heshvan); *Diaries*, 167.
125. *Ma'agal tov*, 113 (2 Heshvan); *Diaries*, 168.
126. For a thorough presentation of the core Jewish sources on forgiveness see Kaminsky, *Fundamentals*, 299–405.
127. Reuben, Simon, and Levi, children of the biblical Jacob, often serve as pseudonyms in rabbinic literature when the writers did not want to record the original names of the disputants.
128. Rabbi Shmuel b. Moshe de Medina, *Shut Maharshdam* 10:145.
129. See above, Chapter 2, 80.
130. Pardes Rodef Shalom Schools Program, unit 5: The Rodef Shalom and Bullying Prevention—The Power of Community, 2016. https://elmad.pardes.org/pcjcr/.
131. *Shut HaMabit* 156:4 (Jerusalem: Yad haRav Nissim, 1990).
132. Meir Benayahu and Alexander Shibber, "*Peniyat ḥakhmei Mitzraim el haRidbaz veḥakhmei Tzefat lehash'ḥit maḥloket shepartza bakehilatam*," in *Sefer Tzefat*, 130.
133. Ibid., 132.
134. *Shut HaMabit* 1:293.
135. Ibid.
136. Ibid.
137. Ibid.
138. Benahayu and Shibber, "*Peniyat ḥakhmei Mitzraim*," 132.
139. Ibid.
140. *Shut HaMabit* 1:293.
141. Rabbi Yosef Karo. *Shut Avkat rokhel* 302:17.
142. *Shut HaRidbaz* 6:239 (Warsaw: 1881/2).

143. See above, 185.
144. Part of Rabbi Melchior's words can be found in a short video on FaceBook that brings highlights from the 2019 Keness Gishurim (Mediation Conference), https://www.facebook.com/177266925767574/videos/511045716252772.
145. *Teshuvot Rabbenu Avraham ben haRambam*, responsa 4–8, ed. Avraham Hayim Friemann and Shlomo Dov Goitein (Jerusalem, 1938), 13–25. For an overview of this conflict and Rabbi Avraham's management of it see Naftali Yaakov Hakohen, *Otzar hagedolim alufei Yaakov* (Bnei Brak, Israel, 1967–70), vol. 2, 96–97. See also Miriam Frankel, *"Ha'ohavim vehanedivim": Ilit manhiga bekerev Yehudei Alexandria biYemei haBeinaim* (Jerusalem: Yad Ben-Zvi and Hebrew University, 2007), 173–74. I would like to thank my friend and colleague Dr. Pinchas Roth for bringing these articles to my attention.
146. For an overview of the history of the conflict between the local Arabic-speaking Egyptian Jewish community and the immigrant community from Christian lands, including France and Italy, see Mordekhai Akiva Friedman, "Maimonides Appoints Rabbi Anatoly Muqaddam of Alexandria" [in Hebrew], *Tarbiz* 83, no. 1 (2015): 135–61. Friedman points out that Maimonides began the practice of appointing French immigrants to key rabbinic positions in Egypt and Alexandria, and that even in his days there was some strong opposition to this. The opposition stemmed from the fact that these rabbis did not speak Arabic, from the fact that they had different customs and traditions, and even from economic issues. Friedman suggests that Maimonides would often prefer the French immigrant rabbis because they were not only greater Torah scholars but also would be more loyal to the Torah and to his own vision for the rabbinate than those with local political ties.
147. Maimonides, *Mishneh Torah*, Laws of Repentance 3:7. See also Friemann and Goitein, *Teshuvot Rabbenu Avraham ben haRambam*, 4:15n6.
148. Referring to the talmudic ruling in Mo'ed Katan 16a.
149. For a discussion on the mutual excommunications in this case, see Frankel, "Ha'ohavim vehanedivim," 174.
150. Sota 45a. See Chap. 5, 239, where this expression is used in a similar situation.
151. *Teshuvot Rabbenu Avraham* 4:18.
152. This is an allusion to the statement in Shabbat 88b, which was also used above to describe Rabbi Syracusty; see above, Chap. 4, n. 14. See also Chap. 2, n.95, and corresponding text.
153. T*eshuvot Rabbenu Avraham* 4:24–25.
154. See Friedman, "Maimonides Appoints Rabbi Anatoly Muqaddam," 138n145.
155. It should be noted that despite his lack of success, Rabbi Avraham was remembered as a valiant peacemaker because of his sincere efforts. See Hakohen, *Otzar hagedolim*, 97, in which Rabbi Avraham is described with regard to his peacemaking efforts in this conflict as acting out of the "highest ethical qualities." Hakohen's *Otzar hagedolim* is a comprehensive listing of rabbis that includes extensive, albeit unverifiable, information about them.
156. The legend found in Rabbi Natan's book will be quoted as it is found in Adolf Neubauer, *Mediaeval Jewish Chronicles*, vol. 2 (Oxford: Clarendon Press, 1895), 79–80. Rabbi Natan's book is referred to there as *Seder olam zuta*. Textual variants will

be brought based on the variants cited in Neubauer's edition. I will also cite variants as found in the earlier printed edition of Rabbi Natan's work in Rabbi Avraham Zekhut, *Sefer yuḥasin* (Zhovkva [Zolkiew], 1799), 58b, as well as the more recent Menahem Ben-Sasson, "Hamivneh, hamegama, vehatokhen shel ḥibbur Rav Natan haBavli," in *Tarbut veḥevra betoldot Yisrael biYemei haBeinaim*, ed. Robert Bonfil, Menahem Ben-Sasson, and Rabbi Y. Hacker (Jerusalem: Merkaz Zalman Shazar, 1989), 185:17–186:25. Ben-Sasson's Hebrew-language article is based on a partial manuscript of Rabbi Natan's work, which is in Judeo-Arabic (Arabic words, Hebrew letters). Ben-Sasson also offers a complete summary of the history of Rabbi Natan the Babylonian's chronicles, including the debate over how to resolve the contradictions between this work and others such as *Iggeret Rav Sherira Gaon* (B. M. Levin edition [Haifa, 1921]). See also Brody, *Geonim of Babylonia*, 26–30.

157. In the Neubauer version he is called Nissim, which seems to be a play on words, as he is known for his miracles, *nissim*. However, Neubauer cites an alternative version where he is called Nissi. In the Zekhut and Ben-Sasson versions his name is Nissi, and this is how he is commonly referred to by scholars. See, for example, Louis (Levi) Ginzberg, *Geonica*, vol. 1 (New York: JTS, 1909), 28n1, who writes, "Nissi, the son of the Exilarch and brother-in-law of the Gaon Sar Shalom."

158. *Reish kalla* was a distinguished position in the Babylonian academies, directly below the head of the academy, known as the Gaon, and the Av Beit Din, head of the religious court. The position was granted to a well-respected leader of the community, who would sit at the head of one of the rows in the academy. See Brody, *Geonim of Babylonia*, 49–50. Rabbi Natan also describes how some twenty years after the incident cited above, David b. Zakkai consulted with Rabbi Nissi about whom to appoint as the new head of the academy of Sura. He eventually decided on Rabbi Sa'adya Gaon, despite Rabbi Nissi's warnings that he may cause upheaval—which he indeed did. See Neubauer, *Mediaeval Jewish Chronicles*, 80, and Brody, 238.

159. Neubauer, 79, sites other versions that the number was fourteen, which is also the number mentioned in Ben-Sasson's and Zechut's versions.

160. Neubauer, 79–80.

161. In Hakohen, *Otzar hagedolim*, vol. 3, 225, Rav Nissi (or Rav Nati, as he insisted was his actual name) is described as being an "expert in the Holy Names, opening the palace locks through a Holy Name." Similarly, Ginzberg, *Geonica*, 28, points out that in late rabbinic *midrashim*, this same miraculous tactic of mentioning God's Ineffable Name is used by the biblical Mordekhai from the book of Esther.

Many early historians seem to have felt varying degrees of discomfort from the use of magic here. On the other hand, J. Mann, "Inyanim shonim leḥeker tekufat haGeonim," *Tarbitz* 5 (1933): 154–55, asserts that what actually convinced the sides to ultimately make peace and reconcile was not Nissim's (as he refers to him) miracle, but a common enemy of Rabbi ben Meir, who was head of the academy in Palestine at the time and was challenging the Babylonian hegemony over the Jewish calendar. It should be noted that Mann also challenges the historical accuracy of Rabbi Natan's story in general, claiming that it was corrupt and that the conflict he is describing was actually between David b. Zakkai and a Rabbi Mevaser, not between David b. Zakkai and Kohen Tzedek Gaon, and he dates the conflict as taking place in

the summer of 922. This is due to his preference for the seemingly parallel version of the event in *Iggeret Rav Sherira Gaon*, 119–20.
162. See, for example, *Avot d'Rabbi Natan* A, chap. 12, 56, which states, "Whoever makes use of the Ineffable Name of God loses their portion in the World to Come."
163. Mishna Sota 7:6.
164. JT Yoma 3:7.
165. Buck, "Deganawida," 92 (6).
166. Neubauer, *Mediaeval Jewish Chronicles*, 80. It should be noted, however, that there were heads of *yeshivot* who were blind, for example, Rav Yosef. See Chap. 2, 112–113, case 10.
167. Neubauer, 79–80.
168. This may likewise be true of female peacemakers in patriarchal societies. On the role of religious women as mediators, see Chapter 3, n. 125.
169. In an interview to the religious Zionist newspaper, Arutz Sheva in Hebrew, I cited some of the examples of rabbis serving as peacemakers discussed in this chapter as part of my argument for why rabbis today need to serve as peacemakers and sharpen their skills in resolving conflicts. See, Shimon Cohen, "Ha'im lerabanim yesh kelim leyashev sikhukhim?" ("Do rabbis have the tools to resolve conflicts?," Hebrew), *Arutz Sheva*, 9, December, 2020, https://www.inn.co.il/news/459988. The interview took place the same day Mosaica held a large conference for community rabbis regarding their role as mediators. See also Barukh Chizki, "HaRav Yackov Ariel: 'rak bekihilah megubeshet rav yakhol liphoal'" ("Rabbi Yackov Ariel: 'Only within a united community can a rabbi operate,'" Hebrew), *Arutz Sheva*, 8, December, 2020, https://www.inn.co.il/news/459983. And Ahrenberg, Yonatan and Matanya Yadid, "Legasher bimkom lehakhriah" ("To mediate instead of to determine", Hebrew), *Bisheva*, 3.12.2020 https://www.inn.co.il/news/459442. This last article, written by two religious Zionist rabbis, draws heavily on the sources of this chapter to encourage rabbis to serve as mediators and peacemakers within their communities.
170. Ironically, the Islamic leaders I have worked with are often more inclined to refer to me as "Doctor" (because of my PhD) than as "Rabbi." I have understood this as connected to the fact that within a Palestinian-Islamic context, an academic doctor (in particular, of religious studies) is often considered to be more distinguished and knowledgeable as a religious leader than a sheikh; and, perhaps by association, than a rabbi.

Chapter 5

1. Hacohen and Hacohen, "*Velo yakhlu*," state this explicitly: "The *mitzva* of pursing after peace and conflict resolution is the obligation of all people and not only the court." Their words were later quoted by Israeli municipal judge Ron Shapiro in his rulings.

2. *Midrash hagadol, Va'era* 6:23, 103. The original source of this midrashic comment that *Midrash hagadol* is quoting from is unknown.
3. See also Chap. 2, n. 45, for an early midrash that identifies Moses as a "lover of peace." In Chap. 2, n. 79, we saw the later *Seder Eliyahu rabba* identifying Moses as a pursuer of peace like Aaron.
4. See Hacohen and Hacohen, "*Velo yakhlu*," n. 7, for references to the source of this tradition.
5. JT Pe'a 1:1 (15d): "'And bringing peace between people'—as it is written, 'depart from evil, and do good; seek peace, and pursue it.'" See similarly in Kiddushin 4a and Yevamot 109a–b.
6. Rabbi Yisrael Lifschitz, *Tiferet Yisrael*, Pe'a 1:1, distinguishes between "acts of loving kindness" and "bringing peace": "'Bringing peace' means even if [one or] both sides don't want [to make peace]; even in such a case one should make every effort to persuade them to mediate the peace between them. And for this reason the author of the mishna did not say to make peace, but rather to bring peace, meaning to bring counsel from afar to those (in conflict) through one's soft words; to bring peace between them."
7. See Chap. 3, 123.
8. One of the fundamental principles governing the development of Jewish law during the medieval and early-modern eras is that at the core of *halakha* are 613 biblical commandments (see Makkot 23b), which are derived from the text of the Five Books of Moses, called the Written Law. They in turn are elaborated on and supplemented by the Oral Law, which is found in the talmudic corpus of rabbinic writings. Medieval and modern Jewish law codes and responsa literature further fine-tuned their details and applications. Numerous medieval and early-modern rabbis created books listing their versions of the 613 commandments, but these volumes rarely make mention of the pursuit of peace as one of them, despite the great interest in peacemaking apparent in many early rabbinic sources.
9. The earliest medieval source that makes reference to a commandment to be a peacemaker is the 8th–9th century Babylonian book *Halakhot gedolot*. The author counts "love of peace and true justice" as one of the 613 biblical commandments (listed as positive commandment 37). However, he includes no further discussion of what the commandment entails or what its Torah source is. Other rabbis who were determined to include the pursuit of peace as one of the commandments connected it to a verse in the Torah. Rabbi Elazar b. Moshe Azikri, for example, counted *bakesh shalom* (seek peace) as a positive commandment among the 613 biblical commandments by connecting it to a verse in Deuteronomy (20:10): "When you draw near to a city to wage war against it, you shall call upon it (first) to make peace." Part of the commandment to seek peace includes seeking peace between individuals, such as between husband and wife, as he writes, "And the Holy One, blessed be He, commanded to have his Name blotted out . . . in order to place peace between a husband and wife" (*Sefer ḥaredim* 4:46, p. 26). For more on this see Kaminsky, *Fundamentals*, 52–53, and notes ad loc.

10. Rabbi Yitzhak of Corbeil, *Sefer amudei gola*, also called *Sefer mitzvot hakatzar* (Cremona, Italy, 1955), *siman* 8. For more sources that quote this position, see Kaminsky, 52n66.
11. It is, however, unclear if he means bringing peace between two people through a third side, which is the focus of our study, or bringing peace between the conflicting sides without third-party intervention. From his words, "and judging *him* favorably," it seems that the commandment is focused on bringing peace between the conflicting individual and his foe without a third party. In the continuation of the piece, Rabbi Yitzhak cites several stories and laws from earlier rabbinic texts, and all of them deal exclusively with interpersonal reconciliation and forgiveness. Moreover, he makes no mention of third-party peacemaking. Perhaps this is because the pursuit of peace is mentioned here as a subcategory of loving your neighbor as yourself. For further discussion with regard to why Rabbi Yitzhak of Corbeil seems to be defining this commandment exclusively as pertaining to interpersonal and not third-party peacemaking, see Roth, "Tradition of Aaron," 93n65.
12. See E. E. Urbach, *The Tosaphists*, 571–74. See also Haym Soloveitchik, "Three Themes of *Sefer Hasidim*," *AJS Review* 1 (1976): 325–27, which describes the notion of "acting for the common good" among Hasidut Ashkenaz.
13. See Urbach, 571–74.
14. Rabbi Eliezer of Worms, introduction to *Sefer haroke'ah* (Warsaw, 1880).
15. *Sefer haroke'ah*, "The Root of Good Character Traits," 6.
16. Yisrael Ta-Shma, *Talmudic Commentary in Europe and North Africa, part 2: 1200–1400* [in Hebrew] (Jerusalem: Magnes, 2000), 19–21.
17. Rabbenu Yona Gerondi, *Sha'arei teshuva* (Vilna, 1922), 3:12, 42. See also his commentary on Mishna Avot 1:12.
18. See Yom-Tov Assis, *The Golden Age of Aragonese Jewry* (London: Littman Library, 1997), 110–11. *Berurim* also had the authority to force their will upon the community: "The *berurim* and all other leaders, whatever their titles, enjoyed the authority vested in them by the ruler and the community. Specific charters were issued to different communities enabling their elected leaders to rule and take measures against members who failed to abide by their decisions" (113). My thanks to Dr. Yehudah Galinsky for bringing this important reference to my attention.
19. Ta'anit 22a. This is the Aramaic phrase used in the Talmud, which I have translated as "we are jesters," but Rabbi Yona translated it here as "we are joyful people," therefore emphasizing the importance of happiness as a requirement for communal peacemakers.
20. Rabbenu Yona Gerondi, *Iggeret hateshuva*, day 2, rule 4.
21. For an example of how Rabbenu Yona's words serve as a precedent for third-party peacemaking in contemporary Jewish law, see Y. Y. Fuchs, *Halikhot*, 36 (1:18). Fuchs refers to Rabbenu Yona as the source for the following law: "It is worthy to appoint in every place men and women who should be at the ready to make peace between a person and his fellow, a husband and wife, and parents and children. And they should be happy people who know how to appease and reconcile. And anyone who makes peace between people joyfully and goodheartedly is promised a share in the World to Come." Note that Fuchs here omits the necessity

mentioned by Rabbenu Yona that these individuals have the authority to enforce their peacemaking.
22. Rabbi Yitzhak bar Sheshet, *Shut HaRivash* (Vilna, 1879), responsum 228.
23. Rabbi Hayim Palagi, *Tzeva'ah mehahayim* (Jerusalem, 1995), 55–56, letter 36.
24. For a photo and short article (in Hebrew) of rabbis holding the Rabbi Palagi text on parchment, see "For the First Time: Religious Zionist Rabbis Attend Mediation and Conflict Resolution Conference," *Arutz Sheva*, 4 December, 2019, https://www.inn.co.il/news/420136.
25. This assertion is based primarily on searching the electronic database of the Responsa Project of Bar-Ilan University.
26. My intention is not to claim the legends of Aaron have any sort of direct influence on these individuals' specific methods. Rather, those who refer to members of their own communities specifically as "pursuers of peace" recognized a connection between the work of these individuals and an extant Jewish tradition of peacemaking.
27. See Chap. 2, 42–43.
28. *Shut Ri Migash* 101.
29. Ibid.
30. With regard to this legal issue, see Rabbi Yitzhak b. Yaakov Alfasi, *Shut HaRif* 235, and notes ad loc.
31. The sources appear in *Shut Mahari Bruna* (Jerusalem: 1960) 78. See Yisrael Yuval, *Hakhamim bedoram* [The sages in their generation] (Jerusalem: Magnes, 1989), 384n157; Avraham Fuchs, "Historical Material in the Responsa of Rabbi Yisrael Bruna" [in Hebrew] (PhD diss., Yeshiva University, 1974), 38n48. I would like to thank my friend Dr. Pinchas Roth for drawing my attention to these important sources.
32. Yuval, *Hakhamim*, 364–98; A. Fuchs, "Historical Material," 16–43.
33. *Shut Mahari Bruna* 78. The letter is signed by Rabbi Peretz. See Yuval, 384n159.
34. *Shut Mahari Bruna* 78.
35. It is not entirely clear what the parties disagreed about regarding the document. One possible point of contention might have been the reference to Rabbi Eliezer being "in Prague." Did it mean when he was physically within the city, or did it mean while he was a resident of the city, even while he traveled? See Yuval, *Hakhamim*, 387n165. Another issue might have been the division of roles. Various rabbinic responsibilities could overlap or be ambiguous, and the document could not have possibly discussed every conceivable role a rabbi might play. A. Fuchs, "Historical Material," 38–39, writes, "It is possible that Rabbi Eliyah was the rabbi not only of the city of Prague but of all of Bohemia, since in one of the responsa he is referred to as the 'leader of the state.' Due to how busy he was, he would sometimes leave Prague. Rabbi Eliezer of Passau took advantage of that fact until a dispute broke out between them. . . . It is possible that when Rabbi Eliyah of Prague was absent from the city, it was permissible for [Rabbi Eliezer] to fulfill other roles as well."
36. *Shut Mahari Bruna* 283.
37. Rabbi Yaakov Weil, *Shut Mahari Weil* (Jerusalem: 1959), responsum 151. See Yuval, *Hakhamim*, 367: "The important members of the community related to the conflict as if it did not affect them at all."

38. Yuval, 378.
39. Rabbi Yisrael Isserlein, *Sefer terumat hadeshen, Pesakim veketavim* 73 (Jerusalem: Shmuel Avitan, 1958), 16–17.
40. *Shut Mahari Bruna* 282. Another example of Rabbi Eliezer personally insulting Rabbi Eliyah is found in Rabbi Peretz's letter to Rabbi Eliezer (*Shut Mahari Bruna* 278), which describes how Rabbi Eliezer neglected to call up Rabbi Eliyah to the Torah after a groom, which was the custom for rabbis of the congregation.
41. Known as the Maharik, 1420–1480. See *Shut Maharik* 185.
42. *Shut Maharik* 6, which describes a dilemma over communal monies presumed to have been in Ḥayim Ḥalfan's house after he passed away.
43. The *ketuba* is the marriage contract required by Jewish law. It contains the amount of money owed to the woman upon divorce or death of the husband. While there is a base value to the *ketuba*, often grooms added an additional amount as well.
44. For further discussion of this conflict and the rabbi's peacemaking method, see Roth, "Tradition of Aaron," 40–43.
45. Rabbi Meir Katznellenbogen of Padua, *Shut Maharam Padua* 29.
46. Mishna Avot 5:17. For references to this concept in the context of conflict resolution studies, see Kaminsky, *Fundamentals*, 17n43, and text ad loc.
47. Rabbi Shaul Yeshua b. Yitzhak Abutbul, *Shut Avnei shayish* (Jerusalem, 1930), 2:28.
    Although the two men are mentioned with the honorific כה"ר, which generally indicates a rabbi, here the title is used out of respect for their status as lay leaders. There is ample evidence that these individuals were laypeople as noted below.
48. Rabbi David Ovadia, *Kehilat Tzefru: Divrei yemei haYehudim bakehilat hakadosh Tzefru beMa'arav haPenimi (Marocco)*, vol. 1 (Jerusalem: Moreshet Yahadut Marocco, 1975), 77, letter 441.
49. For more information on Moroccan Jewish community leaders in this period, see Shlomo Deshen, *The Mellah Society: Jewish Community Life in Sherifian Morocco* (Chicago: University of Chicago Press, 1989), 46–61. Deshen defines these leaders as men of social and economic status who were able to pay taxes. They would issue ordinances, though the number of leaders required to establish an ordinance was not set.
50. Ovadia, *Tzefru*, vol. 1, 77, letter 441; vol. 2, 35, document 399; 191, document 591; 44, document 409.
51. Ovadia, vol. 1, 12, letters 8, 9.
52. *Avnei shayish* 1:17. Additional examples of this phenomenon can be found in several places in *Avnei shayish*: Responsum 1:17: "*Rodfei shalom* intervened and mediated . . . and it was established, and it has been signed and witnessed by those signed here, and it is established: Meir Sabbaḥ, Shlomo b. Yehoshua ibn Ḥuta" (both of whom are rabbis according to Ovadia); responsum 2:113: "*Rodfei shalom* stepped in. . . . Signed: the great Rabbi Shaul Yeshua Abutbul"; ibid.: "*Rodfei shalom* stepped in . . . and once they compromised, each went home in peace. And for proof, it is signed here and established: Yisrael Yaakov Uziel and Joseph b. Zikhri" (both of whom are rabbis according to Ovadia).
53. *Shut Avnei shayish* 1:82.
54. Mo'ed Katan 25b.

55. *Shut Avnei shayish* 1:82.
56. This is consistent with Deshen's description of litigants turning to other judges and courts even after there was a ruling. See Deshen, *Mellah Society*, 76–77.
57. See in particular the opinion of Rabbi Yeshayahu di Trani's comment, which says that pursuing peace is allowed "even after the case has been closed" (Chap. 2, n. 68, and note there), as well as the opinion of Rabbi Alexander Zusslin Hakohen *Sefer ha'agguda*, Sanhedrin 6b, (Chapter 2, 58n.72.).
58. *Shut Avnei shayish* 1:63.
59. Ibid., 1:63.
60. Ibid., 1:17.
61. Ibid., 1:14.
62. Ibid., 2:113.
63. Ibid., 1:2.
64. Ibid., 1:28.
65. *Shut Yismah levav, Orah hayim* 23.
66. *Shut Avnei shayish* 2:113.
67. Ibid., 1:17.
68. Ibid., 1:63.
69. Ibid., 2:113.
70. Ibid., 1:14.
71. Ibid., 1:2.
72. Ibid., 2:28.
73. Rabbi Raphael b. Mordekhai Bardugo, *Shut Mishpatim yesharim* (Krakow: 1890/91), 1:250.
74. *Shut Avnei shayish* 1:20.
75. The term *rodfei shalom* can be found in vol. 1, 228, 329, 404; vol. 2, 38, 55, 60. The term *metavchei shalom* can be found in vol. 1, 11, 38; vol. 2, 2, 250; and vol. 3, 338. Both of these terms are often prefaced in the letters and documents with a description of the conflicting sides having a *harvot amarim*, which may be translated as "a sword [fight] of words." It is also interesting to note that in a couple of places there are instances where non-Jewish third-party mediators were called in to make peace and bring the sides (i.e., families) to a compromise agreement; see vol. 3, 45, n. 24*: "They brought in non-Jews to make peace between them"; vol. 2, 42: "And they brought non-Jews in, and they tried to mediate between them but did not succeed." These non-Jewish third parties were brought in ostensibly because they were considered to have high social status and the power to force one side or another to agree to make peace.
76. Ovadia, *Tzefru*, vol. 3, 100.
77. I am translating *lefasher beineihem* as "mediate between them" throughout this chapter, although the verb is more strictly translated as "effect a compromise." The Hebrew phrase is used to refer variously to compromise or to mediation; sometimes, however, the meaning is left vague.
78. *Shut Avnei shayish* 1:92.
79. *Shut Mishpatim yesharim* 2:212.

80. Rabbi Ḥayim Mordekhai Labaton, *Shut Nokhaḥ hashulḥan, Ḥoshen mishpat* 13.
81. Rabbi Ovadia Yosef, *Shut Yabia omer* (1995), 2:9.
82. Ibid.
83. Chapter 3, 71–73, fn. 132.
84. *Shulhan Gevoah, Orach Chaim Vol. 2*, 606:1:2, 55a.
85. Regarding Rabbi Malkho's assumption that rabbinic law requires forgiveness to be sincere, see Kaminsky, pp. 354–5.
86. See Avraham Ya'ari, *Letters of the Land of Israel* [in Hebrew] (Ramat Gan, Israel: Masada, 1971), 206–7.
87. I am grateful to my student and colleague, Dr. Ofer Ashual, for referring me to this story, and for his sharp insights and reflections on it.
88. Ben Ish Ḥai, *Shut Torah lishmah* 257.
89. See Chap. 2, n. 184, in which I cite a case from Gellner, *Saints*, 220, in which the Saints secretly paid the compensation money for one of the sides in the conflict in order to uphold the peace agreement. Hamzeh, "Role of Hizbullah," 113, cites cases where Hezbollah peacemakers pay what is owed to the other side when the obligated party cannot afford it themselves. Based on this, Kadayifci-Orellana, Abu-Nimer, and Mohamed-Saleem, in "Understanding an Islamic Framework," 29–30, write, "In some cases, if the family of the offender cannot afford the whole amount of compensation, third parties contribute money to settle the payment."
90. Rabbi Yosef al-Ḥakham compares this case to that of a guarantor for a woman's *ketuba* payment in the case of a divorce. In such a case, Maimonides does not require the guarantor to pay, since he performed a *mitzva* in serving as the guarantor in the first place; but the Ra'avad requires the guarantor to pay. According to Rabbi Yosef al-Ḥakham, in the case of a peacemaker serving as a guarantor, even the Ra'avad would not require the guarantor to pay.
91. *Shut Torah lishmah*, 257.
92. Sometimes the compromisers (*pashranim*) are also known as "well-respected individuals" (*nikhbadim*). See, for example, *Shut Maharshdam, Yoreh de'a* 1:147, cited below 237–238.
93. See, for example, Rabbi Shlomo b. Avraham Hakohen, *Shut Maharshakh* 2:228: "In any event, since the *pashranim* made a compromise and the claimant *agreed to the compromise that was made*, the litigant had no grounds on which to complain about Reuben anymore." See also Shabtai, *Shut Torat Ḥayim* 1:25: "*He compromised* with Shimon according to [what was agreed upon with] the *pashranim*."
94. *Shut Ḥayim bayad*, 69.
95. *Shut Torah lishmah* 339. See also *Shut Avnei shayish* 1:92, where he refers to the peacemakers as both *metavkhei shalom* (mediators of peace) and *pashranim* (compromisers).
96. See, for example, the sixteenth-century *Shut HaRema* 78: "I was asked: Reuben and Simon chose for themselves two *pashranim* and [the disputants] made a formal, legally binding agreement to uphold whatever compromise they would establish for them (*she'yifashru*)."

These compromisers were sometimes called "compromiser [rabbinic] judges" (*dayanim pashranim*). See, for example, *Shut Torat Ḥayim* 1:71: "In addition to this, when the judges who were the *pashranim* (compromisers) came, who were chosen by the two parties to arbitrate between them (*lefasher beineihem*) regarding their differences . . ."; *Shut Maharit* (Rabbi Yosef Trani; Safed, Turkey; 16th–17th cent.), 2:98: "They agreed that the judges who were *pashranim* would arbitrate between them (*she'yifashru beineihem*), and this is the decree that the judges decreed." I have translated the term *lefasher beineihem* in this case as "arbitrate between them," as this is clearly what the context necessitates.

97. *Shut HaRivash*, 127.
98. For another example where the *pashranim* attempted to intervene in the conflict numerous times, see Rabbi Avraham b. Yitzhak Entebbe, *Shut Mor veohalot* (Livorno, 1843), 4:5: "Compromisers stepped in three times."
99. *Shut HaRivash*, 127.
100. Ibid.
101. See Rabbi Yoel Sirkis, *Shut Habaḥ* 21: "A fight began between them, and *pashranim* stepped in and compromised for them, and they both agreed."
102. *Shut Maharshdam, Yoreh de'a* 1:147.
103. Ibid.
104. While it seems that the intercommunal conflict was resolved by these *pashranim*, the rest of the query goes on to tell of a conflict that took place between one of the communities and a particular individual who wanted to leave one community and join the other. He claimed all prohibitions had been lifted, and the community claimed that this particular one was still valid even after the nullification and burning of all of the other bans made by each community against the other.
105. See Shabbat 116b, where it states, "The Name of God can be destroyed in order to make peace; all the more so those texts (of heresy) that cause conflict."
106. See, for example, "Weapons Become the Flame of Peace in Mali," https://www.flickr.com/photos/unitednationsdevelopmentprogramme/8904895089; "Symbolic Weapons—Burning Ceremony in Congo Brazzaville," http://www.afrol.com/articles/18515.
107. See *Tosefta* Sanhedrin 1:2; Chap. 2, n. 63.
108. Rabbi Aharon b. Yosef Sasson, *Shut Torat emet* 155 (Venice, 1626).
109. *Shut Avkat rokhel* 206.
110. Ibid.
111. Sota 45a. For an elaboration of this phrase, see Chap. 4, 192.
112. *Shut Avkat rokhel* 206: "But since inside of him [the *kohen*] deceived [the *ḥakham*], holding him as his enemy and hating the *ḥakham* in the way that the wicked inherently hate Torah scholars, he did not ask to be released from the excommunication. And the *ḥakham* did not release him. . . . And since then, [the *kohen*] has not spoken with the *ḥakham* for good or for bad. Even when the *ḥakham* would say hello he would not respond.

Another example of an unsuccessful asymmetric reconciliation encounter between a *ḥakham* and a lay leader in which the ceremony of forgiveness took place

but the sides evidently did not truly reconcile can be found in *Shut Ḥayim bayad* 57, in a letter addressed to Rabbi Ḥayim Palagi of nineteenth-century Izmir.
113. See Chap. 4, 192; *Teshuvot Rabbenu Avraham* 4:18.
114. These roles and the lines of separation between them were complex and sometimes fraught with conflict. See Brody, *Geonim of Babylonia*, 35–82. Concerning this conflict in particular, see 237–39 and notes there.
115. On the relationship between Jewish bankers and the Geonim, especially Sa'adya Gaon, see Brody, 65–66. See also Norman A. Stillman, *Jews of Arab Lands: A History and Source Book* (Philadelphia: Jewish Publication Society, 1979), 35–39. At 35, Stillman writes, "The ultimate reconciliation between Sa'adya and ben Zakkai was brought about through the good offices of the wealthy Bishr b. Aaron in 937." Stillman notes that these wealthy bankers often sided and shared more common interests with the rabbis against the Exilarch, a claim that does not seem to be relevant to our case.
116. This is a talmudic reference to Sanhedrin 110a.
117. *Seder olam zuta* (in Neubauer, *Mediaeval Jewish Chronicles*, 82).
118. On the talmudic practice of dialoguing on the basis of the interlocutor's identity and cultural background and its parallel in the Socratic dialogues of Plato, see Labendz, *Socratic Torah*.
119. Sanhedrin 110a. For an in-depth discussion on the prohibition against holding on to a dispute, see Kaminsky, *Fundamentals*, 62–65.
120. Sanhedrin 110a. This tension between rabbis and descendants of the house of David is reminiscent of the conflict seen earlier between Hodaya b. Yishai and Rabbi Yosef b. Gershom in Cairo (case 26).
121. Neubauer, *Mediaeval Jewish Chronicles*, 82.
122. Est. 10:3. In that context, "peace" more likely refers to welfare, but its usage may nevertheless be significant.
123. See Chap. 1, 25–26.
124. Kobi Nachshoni, "Israeli-Palestinian Peace Initiative Helped Resolve Temple Mount Standoff," *Ynetnews*, July 27, 2017, https://www.ynetnews.com/articles/0,7340,L-4995939,00.html.
125. Mordechai Mironi, "*Al migbalot hapishur ve'al besorot hagishur*," *Din uDevarim* (2011): 487–536, http://weblaw.haifa.ac.il/he/Journals/din_udvarim/gilionF2/487-536.pdf.
126. Prof. Mordechai Mironi argues there are still important differences between *gishur* and *pishur*, and it seems most likely that *pishur* is more similar to Aaron and other non-Western traditional cultural models of mediation. See previous note.

Conclusion

1. Regarding the first category, the conflict case, I will return to discuss this critical question at the end of this chapter as part of my discussion in the section entitled "The Scope of Third-Party Peacemaking in Judaism."

2. Case 15 describes Rabbi Syracusty's general practice of peacemaking, and is therefore inconclusive with regard to whether he acted alone or with others.
3. Case 11 is a legend about a lay peacemaker but not directly about him serving as a third party, and case 31 is not a description of actual third-party lay peacemakers but rather of a rabbi alluding to them. I am therefore not including these cases here.
4. See Chap. 2, 55–59, 94–99.
5. This pertains to the community of Posen, which was discussed in case 29, Chap. 4, 218.
6. It should be noted that the lay peacemaker in this case did not serve as a guarantor of the reconciliation but rather of the compromise agreement.
7. I am not including the three articles I have published on this topic to date: "The Peacemaker in Jewish Rabbinic and Arab Islamic Traditions," *Journal of Religion, Conflict, and Peace* 4, no. 2 (Spring 2011); "The Pursuit of Peace in Medieval Judaism," in *Religion and Peace: Historical Aspects*, ed. Yvonne Friedman (London: Taylor & Francis/Routledge, 2017), 146–58; and "From the Diary of a Rabbinic Peacemaker: Case Study of a Traditional Jewish Process of Reconciliation and Conflict Resolution," *Journal of Living Together* 6, no. 1 (2019).
8. For a discussion on the difference between religious "cultural peacebuilding" and "structural peacebuilding" in general and within the context of the Jewish/Israeli–Muslim/ Palestinian conflict in particular, see Wang, "Strategic Engagement and Religious Peace-Building," 71–82.
9. See Chap. 1, 10.
10. Gittin 55a–b.
11. *Mekhilta d'Rabbi Yishmael, d'bahodesh* 11, 244. This passage can also be found in *Sifra, Aharei Mot* 8, chap. 3, 92d. There the list is slightly different: "The person who makes peace between a man and his wife, between family and family, between city and city, [between] state and state, between nation and nation."
12. Rashi, Ex. 20:22: "Then in the case of one who makes peace between a man and his wife, between family and family, between a man and his fellow, how much more so that punishment will not come upon him (*Mekhilta d'Rabbi Yishmael*)." (Translation from *Chumash with Targum Onkelos, Haphtaroth and Rashi's Commentary: Shemot*, trans. and ann. A. M. Silbermann in collaboration with M. Rosenbaum [Jerusalem: Feldheim Publishers, 1934].) Rashi comments here on the prohibition against using tools on the stones for the altar. The stones of the altar must remain complete (in Hebrew, *sheleimot*) and never be struck because they make peace (in Hebrew, *shalom*, from the same root as *sheleimot*) between the people and their Father in heaven. He goes on to compare peace between man and God to peace between people. (There are no textual variants to this passage in Rashi, and therefore we cannot ascribe the omission in Rashi of the words "nation and nation and government and government" to a later copier.)
13. Rabbi Hayim Hirschensohn, *Nimukei Rashi*, vol. 2 (Y. Wieder, 1929), 101a.
14. *Nimukei Rashi*, Ex. 20:21.
15. Rabbi Yosef Nissim Adhan, *Sefer ma'aseh Bereshit* 1:97, commandment 41.

Bibliography

Academic Sources

Abu-Nimer, Mohammed. "Conflict Resolution in an Islamic Context: Some Conceptual Questions." *Peace and Change* 21, no. 1 (January 1996): 22–40.
Abu-Nimer, Mohammed. "Contrasts in Conflict Management in Cleveland and Palestine." In *Traditional Cures for Modern Conflicts*, edited by I. William Zartman, 141–52. Boulder, CO: Lynne Rienner Publishers, 2000.
Abu-Nimer, Mohammed. "An Islamic Model of Conflict Resolution: Principles and Challenges." In *Crescent and Dove: Peace and Conflict Resolution in Islam*, edited by Qamar-ul Huda, 73–88. Washington, DC: United States Institute of Peace Press, 2010.
•Abu-Nimer, Mohammed. *Nonviolence and Peace Building in Islam: Theory and Practice*. Gainesville: University of Florida Press, 2003.
Ackermann, Alice. "The Idea and Practice of Conflict Prevention." *Journal of Peace Research* 40, no. 3 (2003): 339–447.
Adlerstein, Yitzchok. "Lawyers, Faith, and Peacemaking: Jewish Perspectives on Peace." *Pepperdine Dispute Resolution Law Journal* 7, no. 2 (2007): 177–87.
Albeck, Hanokh. *Mevo letalmidim*. Tel Aviv: Dvir, 1969.
Alberstein, Michal. "Judicial Conflict Resolution (JCR): A New Jurisprudence for an Emerging Judicial Practice." *Cardozo Journal of Conflict Resolution* 16 (2015): 879–965.
Anderson, Royce. "A Definition of Peace." *Peace and Conflict: Journal of Peace Psychology* 10, no. 2 (2004): 101–16.
Antoun, Richard T. "Institutionalized Deconfrontation: A Case Study of Conflict Resolution among Tribal Peasants in Jordan." In *Conflict Resolution in the Arab World: Selected Essays*, edited by Paul Salem, 140–75. Beirut: American University of Beirut, 1997.
Appleby, R. Scott. *The Ambivalence of the Sacred: Religion, Violence, and Reconciliation*. Lanham, MD: Rowman & Littlefield, 2000.
Assis, Yom-Tov. *The Golden Age of Aragonese Jewry*. London: Littman Library, 1997.
Auerbach, Yehudith. "Conflict Resolution, Forgiveness and Reconciliation in Material and Identity Conflicts." *Humboldt Journal of Social Relations* 29, no. 2 (2005): 41–80.
•Augsburger, David W. *Conflict Mediation across Cultures*. London: Westminster John Knox Press, 1992.
• Avruch, Kevin. *Culture and Conflict Resolution*. Washington, DC: United States Institute of Peace Press, 1998.
Bamberger, Henry. "Aaron: Changing Perceptions." *Judaism* (Spring 1993): 201–13.
Barth, Fredrik. *Political Leadership among Swat Pathans*. London: Athlone Press, 1968.

Becker, Hans-Jürgen, and Christoph Berner. *Avot d'Rabbi Natan: Synoptische Edition beider Versionen* [*Avot d'Rabbi Natan*: A synoptic edition of both versions]. Text and Studies in Ancient Judaism Series, no. 116. Tübingen: Mohr Siebeck, 2006.

Benayahu, Meir. "Derushav shel Rabbi Yosef b. Meir Garson." In *Michael*. Vol. 7. Tel Aviv: Tel Aviv University, 1982, 42–205.

Benayahu, Meir. *Rabbi Hayim Yosef David Azulai*. Vol. 1. Jerusalem: Ben-Zvi Institute, and Mossad Harav Kook, 1959.

Benayahu, Meir. *Teuda min hador harishon shel megurashei Sefarad biTzefat.* ("Certificate from the first generation of deportees Spain in Safed", Hebrew). In *Book Asaf*. Mosad Harav Kook, 1953, 109–125.

Benayahu, Meir, and Alexander Scheiber. "Peniyat hakhmei Mitzraim el haRidbaz vehakhmei Tzefat lehash'hit mahloket shepartza bakehilatam." In *Sefer Tzefat*, 125–134. Vol. 1. Jerusalem: Ben-Zvi Institute and Hebrew University, 1962.

Ben-Sasson, Menahem. "Hamivneh, hamegama, vehatokhen shel hibbur Rav Natan haBavli." In *Tarbut vehevra betoldot Yisrael biYemei haBeinaim*, edited by Robert Bonfil, Menahem Ben-Sasson, and Rabbi Y. Hacker, 137–196. Jerusalem: Merkaz Zalman Shazar, 1989.

Bonta, Bruce D. "Conflict Resolution among Peaceful Societies: The Cultures of Peacefulness." *Journal of Peace Research* 33, no. 4 (1996): 403–20.

Brody, Robert. *The Geonim of Babylonia and the Shaping of Medieval Jewish Culture*. New Haven: Yale University Press, 1998.

Buber, Martin. *Ohr haganuz: Sippurei Hasidim*. Jerusalem/Tel Aviv: Schocken Press, 2005.

Buck, Christopher. "Deganawida: The Peacemaker." In *American Writers*, supplement 26, edited by Jay Parini, 81–100. n.p.: Charles Scribner's Sons, 2016.

Burger, Ariel. *Hasidic Nonviolence: R. Noson of Bratzlav's Hermeneutics of Conflict Transformation*. Boston: Boston University Press, 2008.

Burton, John. *Conflict and Communication: The Use of Controlled Communication in International Relations*. London: Macmillan, 1969.

Cloke, Kenneth. "Revenge, Forgiveness, and the Magic of Mediation." *Conflict Resolution Quarterly* 11, no. 1 (1993): 67–78.

Cohen, Oded. "New and Old Cultural Spaces in the Hida's World." [In Hebrew.] PhD diss., Tel Aviv University, 2016.

Cohen, Stuart A. *The Three Crowns: Structures of Communal Politics in Early Rabbinic Jewry*. Cambridge, UK: Cambridge University Press, 2007.

Coleman, Peter T., and Morton Deutsch. "Some Guidelines for Developing a Creative Approach to Conflict." In *Handbook of Conflict Resolution: Theory and Practice*, 3rd ed., edited by Peter T. Coleman, Morton Deutsch, and Eric C. Marcus, 478–490. San Francisco: Jossey-Bass, 2014.

Coleman, Peter T., Morton Deutsch, and Eric C. Marcus, eds. *The Handbook of Conflict Resolution: Theory and Practice*, 3rd ed. San Francisco: Jossey-Bass, 2014.

Cratsley, John C. "Judicial Ethics and Judicial Settlement Practices: Time for Two Strangers to Meet." *Ohio State Journal on Dispute Resolution* 21, no. 3 (2006): 569–96.

Cymerman, Benjamin, trans. and ed. *The Diaries of Rabbi Ha'im Yosef David Azulai*. Part II. Jerusalem: Bnei Issakhar Institute, Ohr Hamaarav Publishing House, 1997.

Deshen, Shlomo. *The Mellah Society: Jewish Community Life in Sherifian Morocco*. Chicago: University of Chicago Press, 1989.

Deshen, Shlomo. *Tzibbur veyehidim: Sidrei hevra bakehilot Yehudei Maroco bame'ot ha-18–19*. Tel Aviv: Ministry of Defense, 1983.

Dinur, Y. Z. *Hiddushei haRitzad*. Vol. 3. Jerusalem: Mossad Harav Kook, 1990.

Drori, Moshe. "*Lidmutam shel hashofet Moshe Rabbenu vehamegasher Aaron hakohen*." *Alon hashoftim al shem haShofet Baruch z"l* 3 (January 2011): 1–14.
*Eilberg, Amy. *From Enemy to Friend: Jewish Wisdom and the Pursuit of Peace*. Ossining, NY: Orbis Book, 2014.
*Eisen, Robert. *The Peace and Violence of Judaism: From the Bible to Modern Zionism*. New York: Oxford University Press, 2011.
Epstein, Rabbi Baruch. *Mekor Barukh*. Vol. 4. Vilna: Widow and Brothers Romm, 1928.
Epstein, Rabbi Baruch. *My Uncle the Netziv*. [Translation of *Mekor Barukh*, vol. 4.] Brooklyn: ArtScroll Mesorah, 1988.
Evans-Pritchard, E. E. *The Nuer*. Oxford: Oxford University Press, 1940.
Faust, Shmuel. "*Talmidei hakhamim ve'amei haaretz: Vayikra Rabba 9*." *Da'at: Limudei Yahadut veruah*. August 12, 2006. Machon Herzog. http://www.daat.ac.il/DAAT/sifrut/agadot/talmidey-2.htm.
Favretto, Katja. "Should Peacemakers Take Sides? Major Power Mediation, Coercion, and Bias." *American Political Science Review* 103, no. 2 (2009): 248–63.
Firestone, Reuven. *Holy War in Judaism: The Fall and Rise of a Controversial Idea*. Oxford: Oxford University Press, 2012.
Fisher, Ronald J. *Interactive Conflict Resolution*. Syracuse, NY: Syracuse University Press, 1997.
Fisher, Ronald J. "Methods of Third-Party Intervention." *Berghof Handbook for Conflict Transformation*. Berlin: Berghof Research Center for Constructive Conflict Management, 2001. http://edoc.vifapol.de/opus/volltexte/2011/2579/pdf/fisher_hb.pdf.
Fisher, Ronald J. "Social-Psychological Processes in Interactive Conflict Analysis and Reconciliation." In *Reconciliation, Justice, and Coexistence: Theory and Practice*, edited by Mohammed Abu-Nimer, 25–45. Lanham, MD: Lexington Books, 2001.
Fiss, Owen. "Against Settlement." *Yale Law Journal* 93 (1984): 1073–90.
Flaherty, Maureen, and Cathy Rocke, with Margaret Lavallee and Billie Schibler. "Case Study—Reconstructing Communities: Indigenous Grandmothers Searching for Peace." In *Creating the Third Force: Indigenous Processes of Peacemaking*, edited by Hamdesa Tuso and Maureen P. Flaherty, 371–90. Lanham, MD: Lexington Books, 2016.
Francesconi, Federica. "An Alternative Path toward Emancipation: Jewish Merchants and Their Cross-Cultural Networks in the Eighteenth-Century Italian Ghettos." *Avotaynu Online: Jewish Genealogy & Genetics*. May 4, 2016. http://www.avotaynuonline.com/2016/05/alternative-path-toward-emancipation-jewish-merchants-cross-cultural-networks-eighteenth-century-italian-ghettos.
Frankel, Miriam. "*Ha'ohavim vehanedivim*": *Ilit manhiga bekerev Yehudei Alexandria biYemei haBeinaim*. Jerusalem: Yad Ben-Zvi and Hebrew University, 2007.
Frankel, Yona. *Darkhei haAggada vehaMidrash*. Tel Aviv: Yad laTalmud, 1996.
Friedman, Hershey H., and Abraham Weisel. "Should Moral Individuals Ever Lie? Insights from Jewish Law." SSRN website, August 28, 2013. http://dx.doi.org/10.2139/ssrn.2317563.
Friedman, Mordekhai Akiva. "Maimonides Appoints Rabbi Anatoly Muqaddam of Alexandria." [In Hebrew.] *Tarbiz* 83, no. 1 (2015): 135–61.
Fuchs, Avraham. "Historical Material in the Responsa of Rabbi Yisrael Bruna." [In Hebrew.] PhD diss., Yeshiva University, 1974.
Fuchs, Yitzhak Yaakov. *Halikhot bein adam lehavero*. Jerusalem: privately printed, 2004.
Gellner, Ernest. *Saints of the Atlas*. Chicago: University of Chicago Press, 1969.
Gendler, Everett. ". . . Therefore Choose Life." In *The Challenge of Shalom: The Jewish Tradition of Peace and Justice*, edited by M. Polner and N. Goodman. Philadelphia: New Society Publishers, 1994.

Ginat, Joseph. *Blood Revenge: Family Honor, Mediation, and Outcasting*. Portland, OR: Sussex Academic, 1997.

Ginzberg, Louis (Levi). *Geonica*. Vol. 1. New York: JTS, 1909.

Ginzberg, Louis (Levi). *Peirushim vehiddushim baYerushalmi*. New York: JTS, 1940.

Goh, Bee Chen. *Law without Lawyers, Justice without Courts: On Traditional Chinese Mediation*. Aldershot, England: Ashgate, 2002.

Gohar, Ali, and Lisa Schrich. "Ritual and Symbol in Justice and Peacebuilding: Lessons from Pukhton Tribes on the Jirga." In *Creating the Third Force: Indigenous Processes of Peacemaking*, edited by Hamdesa Tuso and Maureen P. Flaherty, 455–470. Lanham, MD: Lexington Books, 2016.

√ Gopin, Marc. *Between Eden and Armageddon: The Future of World Religions, Violence, and Peacemaking*. Oxford: Oxford University Press, 2000.

◀ Gopin, Marc. *Bridges across an Impossible Divide: The Inner Lives of Arab and Jewish Peacemakers*. New York: Oxford University Press, 2012.

√ Gopin, Marc. *Holy War, Holy Peace: How Religion Can Bring Peace to the Middle East*. Oxford: Oxford University Press, 2002.

Gopin, Marc. "Judaism and Peacebuilding." In *Religion and Peacebuilding*, edited by Harold Coward and Gordon S. Smith, 111–27. Albany: SUNY Press, 2004.

Gopin, Marc. "Judaism and Peacebuilding in the Context of the Middle East Conflict." In *Faith-Based Diplomacy: Trumping Realpolitik*, edited by Douglas Johnston, 91–102. NY: Oxford University Press, 2003.

Graetz, Heinrich. *History of the Jews*. Vols. 2, 4. [Originally published in 1894.] Edited by Bella Löwy. Philadelphia: 1893 (vol. 2), 1894 (vol. 4).

Hacker, Yosef. *Megurashei Sefarad v'tze'etzaeihem baEmperia haOttomanit bame'a ha-16*. Jerusalem: Hebrew University Faculty of Humanities, 1967.

Hacohen, Elisheva, and Aviad Hacohen. "*Velo yakhlu ledabro leshalom: Pishur, gishur, veyishuv sikhsukhim.*" *Mishpat Ivri* 54 (2002). http://www.daat.ac.il/mishpat-ivri/skirot/54-2.htm.

Hakohen, Naftali Yaakov. *Otzar hagedolim alufei Yaakov*. Bnei Brak, Israel, 1967–70.

Hamzeh, Nizar. "The Role of Hizbullah in Conflict Management within Lebanon's Shi'a Community." In *Conflict Resolution in the Arab World: Selected Essays*, edited by Paul Salem, 93–121. Beirut: American University of Beirut, 1997.

Hayward, Susan, and Katherine Marshall, eds. *Women, Religion, and Peacebuilding: Illuminating the Unseen*. Washington, DC: United States Institute of Peace Press, 2015.

Herman, Geoffrey. *A Prince without a Kingdom*. Tübingen: Mohr Siebeck, 2012.

Herr, Moshe. "*Bein batei knessiot levein batei teatra'ot vekirkasa'ot.*" In *Knesset Ezra*, edited by Shulamit Elitzur, Moshe Herr, A. Sha'anan, and G. Shaked, 105–19. Jerusalem: Yad Ben-Zvi Press, 1994.

Hertog, Katrien. *The Complex Reality of Religious Peacebuilding: Conceptual Contributions and Critical Analysis*. Lanham, MD: Lexington Books, 2010.

Heschel, Abraham Joshua. *A Passion for Truth*. New York: Farrar, Straus & Giroux, 1973.

Hezser, Catherine. "Classical Rabbinic Literature." In *The Oxford Handbook of Jewish Studies*, edited by Martin Goodman, 115–140. Oxford: Oxford University Press, 2002.

Houston, Jean. *Manual for the Peacemaker: An Iroquois Legend to Heal Self and Society*. Wheaton, IL: Quest Books, 1995.

Irani, George E. "'The Best of Judgments': Rituals of Settlement (Sulh) and Reconciliation (Musalaha) in the Middle East." In *Creating the Third Force: Indigenous Processes of Peacemaking*, edited by Hamdesa Tuso and Maureen P. Flaherty, 55–76. Lanham, MD: Lexington Books, 2016.

Irani, George E. "Islamic Mediation Techniques for Middle East Conflicts." *Middle East Review of International Affairs (MERIA)* 3, no. 2 (June 1999).
Irani, George E., and Nathan C. Funk. "Rituals of Reconciliation: Arab-Islamic Perspectives." *Arab Studies Quarterly (ASQ)* 20, no. 4 (Fall 1998): 53–72.
Isaacs, Alick. *A Prophetic Peace: Judaism, Religion, and Politics*. Bloomington: Indiana University Press, 2011.
Jabbour, Elias. *Sulha: Palestinian Traditional Peacemaking Process*. Montreat, NC: House of Hope, 1996.
Jones, Tricia S., and Ross Brinkert. *Conflict Coaching: Advancing the Conflict Resolution Field by Developing an Individual Disputant Process*. Los Angeles: Sage Publications, 2007.
Kadayifci-Orellana, S. Ayse. "Ethno-Religious Conflicts: Exploring the Role of Religion in Conflict Resolution." In *The SAGE Handbook of Conflict Resolution*, edited by J. Bercovitch, V. Kremenyuk, and I. W. Zartman, 264–80. London: SAGE, 2009.
Kadayifci-Orellana, S. Ayse, Mohammed Abu-Nimer, and Amjad Mohamed-Saleem. *Understanding an Islamic Framework for Peacebuilding*. Birmingham: Islamic Relief Worldwide, 2012.
Kaddari, Menachem Tzvi. *Hebrew Biblical Dictionary*. [In Hebrew.] Ramat Gan, Israel: Bar-Ilan University, 1996.
Kaminsky, Howard G. *Fundamentals of Jewish Conflict Resolution: Traditional Jewish Perspectives on Resolving Interpersonal Conflicts*. Boston: Academic Studies Press, 2017.
Kaminsky, Howard G. "Traditional Jewish Perspectives on Peace and Interpersonal Conflict Resolution." EdD diss., Teachers College, Columbia University, 2005.
Kasdan, Ira Yitzchak. "A Proposal for P'sharah: Jewish Mediation/Arbitration Service." *Jewish Law Articles: Examining Halacha, Jewish Issues and Secular Law* (1990). https://www.jlaw.com/Articles/psharah3.html.
Kelman, Herbert C. "Informal Mediation by the Scholar/Practitioner." In *The Handbook of Interethnic Coexistence*, edited by Alan B. Slifka, 310–31. New York: Continuum, 1998.
Kelman, Herbert C. "Reconciliation from a Social-Psychological Perspective." In *The Social Psychology of Intergroup Reconciliation*, edited by A. Nadler, T. E. Malloy, and J. D. Fisher, 15–32. New York: Oxford University Press, 2008.
Kemp, Graham, and Douglas P. Fry, eds. *Keeping the Peace: Conflict Resolution and Peaceful Societies around the World*. New York: Routledge, 2004.
King-Irani, Laurie. "Rituals of Forgiveness and Processes of Empowerment in Lebanon." In *Traditional Cures for Modern Conflicts*, edited by I. William Zartman, 129–40. Boulder: Lynne Rienner Publishers, 2000.
Kotite, Phyllis. "Education for Conflict Prevention and Peacebuilding: Meeting the Global Challenges of the 21st Century." Paris: UNESCO, 2012. http://unesdoc.unesco.org/images/0021/002171/217106e.pdf.
Kurtzer-Ellenbogen, Lucy, "Jewish Women in Peacebuilding: Embracing Disagreement in the Pursuit of 'Shalom'." In *Women, Religion, and Peace: Exploring Experience, Probing Complexity*, edited by Susan Hayward and Katherine Marshall, 113–25. Washington, DC: United States Institute of Peace Press, 2015.
Kydd, Andrew. "Which Side Are You On? Bias, Credibility, and Mediation." *American Journal of Political Science* 47, no. 4 (2003): 597–611.
Kyoon-Achan, Grace. "Indigenous Elders as the Mbasoron Tar (Repairers of the World) and Inukshuks (Way-pointers) of Peace." In *Creating the Third Force: Indigenous Processes of Peacemaking*, edited by Hamdesa Tuso and Maureen P. Flaherty, 55–76. Lanham, MD: Lexington Books, 2016.

Labendz, Jenny R. *Socratic Torah: Non-Jews in Rabbinic Intellectual Culture*. New York: Oxford University Press, 2013.

Landau, Yehezkel. *Healing the Holy Land: Interreligious Peacebuilding in Israel/Palestine*. Washington, DC: United States Institute of Peace Press, 2003.

Lavee, Moshe. "*Kabbalat ha'aher veha'aherut: Tahalikhei havlata vetishtush besifrut Hazal*" [Acceptance of others and otherness: Processes of emphasis and ambiguity in rabbinic narratives]. *Mishlav* 37 (2001): 75–114.

Lawrence, Cassandra, Dr. Sara Singha, Najla Mangoush, and Rev. Douglas Leonard. "Demystifying Religion in Mediation: Identifying Gaps in Training, Knowledge, and Practice." *Al Amana International*, 2017. https://www.peacemakersnetwork.org/our-work/network-publications/.

Lederach, John Paul. *Preparing for Peace: Conflict Transformation across Cultures*. Syracuse, NY: Syracuse University Press, 1996.

Lederach, John Paul. *Reconcile: Conflict Transformation for Ordinary Christians*. Harrisonburg, VA: Herald Press, 2014.

Lifschitz, Ittai. "*Hapeshara bamishpat haIvri*." PhD diss., Bar Ilan University, 2004.

Lifschitz, Rabbi Yaakov Halevi. *Sanhedri gedola lamasekhet Sanhedrin*. Vol. 5, part 2. Jerusalem: Harry Fischel Institute, 1972.

Lifschitz, Rabbi Yaakov. *Zikhron Yaakov*. Vol. 2. Kovno, 1924.

Little, David, ed. *Peacemakers in Action: Profiles of Religion in Conflict Resolution*. New York: Cambridge University Press, 2007.

Mann, J. "*Inyanim shonim leheker tekufat haGeonim*." *Tarbitz* 5 (1933): 273–304.

Margaliot, Mordekhai (Mordecai Margulies). *Hahilukim shebein anshei haMizrah uvnei Eretz Yisrael*. Jerusalem: Reuven Mass, 1938.

Mathey, M. J., et al. "The Role Played by Women of the Central African Republic in the Prevention and Resolution of Conflicts." In *Women and Peace in Africa: Case Studies on Traditional Conflict Resolution Practices*, 35–46. Paris: UNESCO, 2003.

Meir, Ofra. "'*Muvtah ani bazeh shemoreh hora'a beYisrael*' (*Pesahim* 3b): *Lidmuto shel Rabbi Yohanan beyahaso letalmidav*." In *Alei Siah* 15–16 (1982): 224–36.

Melchior, Rabbi Michael. "Establishing a Religious Peace." In *Coexistence & Reconciliation in Israel: Voices for Interreligious Dialogue*, edited by Ronald Kronish, 117–28. Mahwah, NJ: Paulist Press, 2015.

Mironi, Mordechai. "*Al migbalot hapishur ve'al besorot hagishur*." *Din uDevarim* (2011): 487–536. http://weblaw.haifa.ac.il/he/Journals/din_udvarim/gilionF2/487-536.pdf.

Moniknadem, Yifat. "Beruria as an Analogical Contrast to Rabbi Meir." [In Hebrew.] *Derekh Aggada* 2 (1999): 37–63.

Montville, Joseph. "The Healing Function in Political Conflict Resolution." In *Conflict Resolution in Theory and Practice*, edited by D. J. D. Sandole and H. van der Merwe, 112–27. Manchester: Manchester University Press, 1993.

Musalaha: A Curriculum of Reconciliation. Jerusalem: Musalaha Ministry of Reconciliation, 2011.

Nagat, Yitbarakh. "The *Schmagluch* Establishment's Conflict Resolution Methods in the Ethiopian Jewish Community: Self-Perceptions of Interveners Regarding the Decision Management Process." [In Hebrew.] Master's thesis, Bar-Ilan University, 2006.

Newman, Louis I. *Hasidic Anthology: Tales and Teachings of the Hasidim*. New York: Bloch Publishing, 1934.

Noam, Vered. *Megillat Ta'anit: Versions, Interpretation, History*. [In Hebrew.] Jerusalem: Yad Ben- Zvi Press, 2003.

Ntahobari, Josephine, and Basilissa Ndayiziga. "The Role of Burundian Women in the Peaceful Settlement of Conflicts." In *Women and Peace in Africa: Case Studies on Traditional Conflict Resolution Practices*. Paris: UNESCO, 2003.

Omer, Atalia. "Religious Peacebuilding: The Exotic, the Good, and the Theatrical." In *The Oxford Handbook of Religion, Conflict, and Peacebuilding*, edited by Atalia Omer, R. Scott Appleby, and David Little, 3–32. Oxford: Oxford University Press, 2015.

Ovadia, Rabbi David. *Kehilat Tzefru: Divrei yemei haYehudim bakehilat hakadosh Tzefru beMa'arav haPenimi (Marocco)*. 5 vols. Jerusalem: Moreshet Yahadut Marocco, 1975.

Peck, Connie, and Eleanor Wertheim, eds. "Strengthening the Practice of Peacemaking and Preventive Diplomacy in the United Nations: The UNITAR Approach." https://unitar.org/pmcp/sites/unitar.org.pmcp/files/sppd.pdf.

Pely, Doron. *Muslim/Arab Mediation and Conflict Resolution: Understanding Sulha*. New York: Routledge, 2016.

Pely, Doron, and Golan Luzon. "The Muslim/Arab Sulha and the Restorative Justice Model: Same Purpose, Different Approach." *Cardozo Journal of Conflict Resolution* 19 (2018): 289–307.

Peters, Emrys. *The Bedouin of Cyrenaica: Studies in Personal and Corporate Power*. Cambridge, UK: Cambridge University Press, 1990.

Peterson, Virgil. "The Rabbi's Resolution and the Power of Stories." *Conflict Resolution Notes* 11, no. 2 (September 1993): 29–30.

Pinto, Jeanmarie. "Peacemaking as Ceremony: The Mediation Model of the Navajo Nation." In *Creating the Third Force: Indigenous Processes of Peacemaking*, edited by Hamdesa Tuso and Maureen P. Flaherty, 163–86. Lanham, MD: Lexington Books, 2016.

Polster, Dan Aaron. "The Trial Judge as Mediator: A Rejoinder to Judge Cratsley." *Ohio State Journal on Dispute Resolution's Mayhew-Hite Report* 5, no. 1 (2006). https://www.mediate.com/articles/polsterD1.cfm.

Pratto, Felicia, and Demis E. Glasford. "How Needs Can Motivate Intergroup Reconciliation in the Face of Intergroup Conflict." In *The Social Psychology of Intergroup Reconciliation*, edited by A. Nadler, T. E. Malloy, and J. D. Fisher, 117–44. New York: Oxford University Press, 2008.

Progoff, Ira. *The Dynamics of Hope: Perspectives of Process in Anxiety and Creativity, Imagery and Dreams*. New York: Dialogue House Library, 1985.

Rapp, Albert. "Phylogenetic Theory of Wit and Humor." *Journal of Social Psychology* 30, no. 1 (1949): 84–93.

Riek, Blake M. et al. "A Social-Psychological Approach to Postconflict Reconciliation." In *The Social Psychology of Intergroup Reconciliation*, edited by A. Nadler, T. E. Malloy, and J. D. Fisher, 255–73. New York: Oxford University Press, 2008.

Roness, Michal, ed. *Conflict and Conflict Management in Jewish Sources*. Ramat Gan, Israel: Conflict Management and Negotiation Graduate Program, Bar-Ilan University, 2008. http://pconfl.biu.ac.il/files/pconfl/shared/conflict_handbook.pdf.

Roth, Daniel. "From the Diary of a Rabbinic Peacemaker: Case Study of a Traditional Jewish Process of Reconciliation and Conflict Resolution." *Journal of Living Together* 6, no. 1 (2019): 43–52.

Roth, Daniel. "The Peacemaker in Jewish Rabbinic and Arab Islamic Traditions." *Journal of Religion, Conflict, and Peace* 4, no. 2 (Spring 2011).

Roth, Daniel. "The Pursuit of Peace in Medieval Judaism." In *Religion and Peace: Historical Aspects*, edited by Yvonne Friedman, 146–58. London: Taylor & Francis/Routledge, 2017.

Roth, Daniel. "The Tradition of Aaron, Pursuer of Peace between People, as a Rabbinic Model of Reconciliation." [In Hebrew.] PhD diss., Bar-Ilan University, 2012.

Rothenberg, Michael. "*Hayesodot ha'erchi'im shel hapeshara*." Master's thesis, Hebrew University, 2001.

Rozness, Solomon. *Divrei Yisrael beturgema*. Tel Aviv: Dvir, 1930.

Salem, Paul. "A Critique of Western Conflict Resolution from a Non-Western Perspective." *Negotiation Journal* 9, no. 4 (1993): 361–69.

Sande, Ken. *The Peacemaker: A Biblical Guide to Resolving Personal Conflict*. 3rd ed. Ada, MI: Baker Books, 2003.

Schäfer, Peter. "Rabbis and Priests, or: How to Do Away with the Glorious Past of the Sons of Aaron." In *Antiquity in Antiquity: Jewish and Christian Pasts in the Greco-Roman World*, edited by Gregg Gardner and Kevin L. Osterloh, 155–172. Tübingen: Mohr Siebeck, 2008.

Schimmel, Solomon. *Wounds Not Healed by Time: The Power of Repentance and Forgiveness*. Oxford: Oxford University Press, 2002.

Schrich, Lisa. "Ritual, Religion, and Peacebuilding." In *The Oxford Handbook of Religion, Conflict and Peacebuilding*, edited by Atalia Omer, R. Scott Appleby, and David Little, 516–40. Oxford: Oxford University Press, 2015.

Schumer, Nathan Still. "The Memory of the Temple in Palestinian Rabbinic Literature." PhD diss., Columbia University, 2017.

Secunda, Samuel. "'*Dashtana ki derekh nashim li*': A Study of the Babylonian Rabbinic Laws of Menstruation in Relation to Corresponding Zoroastrian Texts." PhD diss., Yeshiva University, 2007.

Shapira, Hayim. "The Debate over Compromise and the Goals of the Judicial Process." *Diné Israel* 26–27 (2009–2010): 183–228.

Sharp, Gene. *The Politics of Nonviolent Action*. Vol. 3. Boston: Porter Sargent, 1973.

Shinan, Avigdor. "*Rabbi Yanai, harokhel, veha'adam hameshupa: Iyyun betashtitam shel shnei sippurim beMidrash Vayikra Rabba*." *Bikoret uFarshanut* 30 (1994): 15–23.

Sikand, Aalok. "ADR Dharma: Seeking a Hindu Perspective on Dispute Resolution from the Holy Scriptures of the Mahabharata and the Bhagavad Gita." *Pepperdine Dispute Resolution Law Journal* 7, no. 2 (2007): 322–72. http://digitalcommons.pepperdine.edu/cgi/viewcontent.cgi?article=1095&context=drlj.

Silbermann, A. M., trans. and ed., in collaboration with M. Rosenbaum. *Chumash with Targum Onkelos, Haphtaroth and Rashi's Commentary: Shemot*. Jerusalem: Feldheim Publishers, 1934.

Smith, James D. D. "Mediator Impartiality: Banishing the Chimera." *Journal of Peace Research* 31, no. 4 (1994): 445–50.

Sokoloff, Michael. *Dictionary of Jewish Palestinian Aramaic*. Baltimore: Johns Hopkins University Press, 1990.

Soloveitchik, Haym. *Shut kemakor histori* [Responsa as a historical source]. Jerusalem: Merkaz Zalman Shazar, 1991.

Soloveitchik, Haym. "Three Themes of *Sefer Hasidim*." *AJS Review* 1 (1976): 311–57.

Sperber, Daniel. *Masekhet derekh eretz zuta and Perek hashalom*. 3rd ed. Jerusalem: Tzur-Ot, 1994.

Stampfer, Shaul. *Hayeshiva haLita'it*. Jerusalem: Merkaz Zalman Shazar, 2005.

Stampfer, Shaul. *Lithuanian Yeshivas of the Nineteenth Century: Creating a Tradition of Learning*. [Translation of *Hayeshiva haLita'it*.] Liverpool: Littman Library of Jewish Civilization/Liverpool University Press, 2014.
Steinberg, Gerald M. "Conflict Prevention and Mediation in the Jewish Tradition." *Jewish Political Studies Review* 12, nos. 3–4 (Fall 2000): 3–21. Special edition of Jewish Approaches to Conflict Resolution. Jerusalem Center for Public Affairs. http://jcpa.org/wp-content/uploads/2000/10/conflict-prevention.pdf.
Steinberg, Gerald M. "Jewish Sources on Conflict Management: Realism and Human Nature." In *Conflict and Conflict Management in Jewish Sources*, edited by Michal Roness, 10–23. Ramat Gan, Israel: Conflict Management and Negotiation Graduate Program, Bar-Ilan University, 2008. http://pconfl.biu.ac.il/files/pconfl/shared/conflict_handbook.pdf.
Steinberg, Gerald M. "The Limits of Peacebuilding Theory." In *The Routledge Handbook of Peacebuilding*, edited by Roger MacGinty, 36–53. Oxford: Routledge, 2013.
Steinschneider, Hillel Noah. *Ir Vilna* [The city of Vilnius]. Vol. 1. Vilna: Widow and Brothers Romm, 1900.
Stephen, Walter G. "The Road to Reconciliation." In *The Social Psychology of Intergroup Reconciliation*, edited by A. Nadler, T. E. Malloy, and J. D. Fisher, 369–94. New York: Oxford University Press, 2008.
Stillman, Norman A. *Jews of Arab Lands: A History and Source Book*. Philadelphia: Jewish Publication Society, 1979.
Strack, H. L., and Günter Stemberger. *Introduction to the Talmud and Midrash*. Translated by Markus Bockmuehl. Minneapolis: Fortress Press, 1992.
Sussman, Yaakov. "*Masoret limud umasoret nusah shel haTalmud haYerushalmi*." In *Mehkarim besifrut hatalmudit*, 12–76. Jerusalem: Israel Academy of Sciences and Humanities, 1983.
Svensson, Isak. "Guaranteeing Peace: The Credibility of Third-Party Mediators in Civil Wars." In *International Conflict Mediation: New Approaches and Findings*, edited by Jacob Bercovitch and Scott Sigmund Gartner. New York: Routledge, 2009.
Ta-Shma, Yisrael. *Talmudic Commentary in Europe and North Africa, part 2: 1200–1400*. [In Hebrew.] Jerusalem: Magnes, 2000.
Tauscher, Heidi M. "Spiritual Practices for Mediation Challenges: Pragmatic Mediation Applications from Five Major World Religious Traditions." *American Bar Association website, Section of Dispute Resolution*, May 25, 2003. http://www.abanet.org/dispute/spiritual_tool.pdf.
Tavuchis, Nicholas. *Mea Culpa: A Sociology of Apology and Reconciliation*. Palo Alto, CA: Stanford University Press, 1991.
Tuso, Hamdesa. "Ararra: Oromo Indigenous Processes of Peacemaking." In *Creating the Third Force: Indigenous Processes of Peacemaking*, edited by Hamdesa Tuso and Maureen P. Flaherty, 77–103. Lanham, MD: Lexington Books, 2016.
Tuso, Hamdesa, and Maureen P. Flaherty, eds. *Creating the Third Force: Indigenous Processes of Peacemaking*. Lanham, MD: Lexington, 2016.
Urbach, E. E. *The Tosaphists: Their History, Writings, and Methods*. [In Hebrew.] Jerusalem: Bialik Institute, 1986.
Ury, William. *The Third Side: Why We Fight and How We Can Stop*. New York: Penguin Books, 2000.
Valler, Shulamit. "*Milhama veshalom bayit al pi sifrut Hazal*." In *Shalom umilhama betarbut haYehudim*, edited by Avriel Bar-Levav. Jerusalem: Merkaz Zalman Shazar, 2006.

Wang, Yvonne. "Strategic Engagement and Religious Peace-Building: A Case Study of Religious Peace Work in Jerusalem." *Approaching Religion* 4, no. 2 (2014): 71–82. https://doi.org/10.30664/ar.67551.
Wanis-St. John, Anthony. "Ancient Peacemakers: Examples of Humanity." In *Peacemaking: From Practice to Theory*. Vol. 2. Edited by Susan Allen Nan, Zachariah Cherian Mampilly, and Andrea Bartoli, 578–89. Santa Barbara, CA: Praeger, 2011.
Witty, Cathie J. *Mediation and Society: Conflict Management in Lebanon*. New York: Academic Press, 1980.
Ya'ari, Avraham. *Letters of the Land of Israel*. [In Hebrew.] Ramat Gan, Israel: Masada, 1971.
Yetkin, Y. "Peace and Conflict Resolution in the Medina Charter." *Peace Review: A Journal of Social Justice* 18 (2006): 109–17.
Yuval, Yisrael. *Hakhamim bedoram* [The sages in their generation]. Jerusalem: Magnes, 1989.
Zartman, I. William, and Saadia Touval. "International Mediation." In *Leashing the Dogs of War: Conflict Management in a Divided World*, edited by Chester A. Crocker, Fen Osler Hampson, and Pamela Aall, 437–54. Washington, DC: United States Institute of Peace Press, 2007.

Unless otherwise indicated, all biblical citations are translated from *The Holy Scriptures: According to the Masoretic Text* (Philadelphia: Jewish Publication Society, 1917).

Rabbinic Literature

Classical Rabbinic Literature (200–1000 CE)
Unless otherwise indicated, all classical rabbinic literature sources are translations based on the manuscripts found in Ma'agarim, the Historical Dictionary Project of the Academy of the Hebrew Language (https://daf.hebrew-academy.org.il/new-site). Manuscript numbers will appear only in the notes. The bibliography will reflect the accepted academic editions, and likewise the notes will refer to the pagination of those editions. Textual variants are indicated in the notes.
Masekhet Sefer Torah. Vilna, 1883.
Avot d'Rabbi Natan. Solomon Schechter edition. New York: The Jewish Theological Seminary, 1997.
Genesis Rabba. J. Theodor-Chanoch Albeck edition. Jerusalem: Wahrmann Books, 1965.
Kalla Rabbati. Michael Higger edition. New York: Debe Rabanan, 1936.
Leviticus Rabba. Annotated by Mordecai Margulies. New York: Jewish Theological Seminary of America, 1993.
Mekhilta d'Rabbi Shimon b. Yohai. J. N. Epstein and Ezra Tzion Melamed edition. Jerusalem: Mekitz Nirdamim, 1955.
Mekhilta d'Rabbi Yishmael. Shaul Horovitz and Yisrael Avraham Rabin edition. Frankfurt am Main, 1930/1.
Midrash hagadol. Jerusalem: Mossad Harav Kook, 1947.
Midrash Tanhuma. Solomon Buber edition. Vilna, 1884/5.
Mishnat Rabbi Eliezer: Midrash sheloshim ushtayim middot. Also referred to as *Midrash agur*. Rabbi Menahem b. Yehuda di Luzzano [the Ramdal]. H. G. Enelow edition.

New York: Bloch Publishing, 1933.
Otzar midrashim. Vol. 1. J. D. Eisenstein edition. New York, 1915.
Seder Eliyahu rabba veSeder Eliyahu zuta [*Tanna d'Vei Eliyahu*]. Meir Ish Shalom [Friedmann] edition. Vienna: Ahiasaf, 1902.
Sifra [*Sifra d'Vei Rav: Hasefer hu Torat kohanim*]. Isaac Hirsch Weiss edition. Text translated from MS Vatian 66. Vienna: Yaakov Hakohen Schlossberg, 1862.
Sifrei al sefer Devarim. [*Sifrei* on the book of Deuteronomy.] Louis Finkelstein edition. Berlin: Ha'agguda hatarbutit haYehudit beGermania, 1940.

Medieval and Modern Rabbinic Literature (1000 CE to the Present)

Akeidat Yitzhak. Rabbi Yitzhak b. Moshe Arama. Pressberg: Victor Kittseer, 1849.
Alei Tamar. Rabbi Yissachar Tamar. Givataim, Israel: Atir, 1979.
Arba'a turim (*Tur*). Rabbi Yaakov b. Asher. Jerusalem: Machon Yerushalayim, 1993/4.
Arukh hashulhan. Rabbi Yehiel Mikhel Halevi Epstein. Warsaw, 1884/93.
Arukh laner. Etlinger, Rabbi Yaakov. Bnei Brak, Israel, 2003/4.
Avodat hakodesh. Rabbi Hayim Yosef David Azulai [the Hida]. Vilna, 1906/7.
Beit haBehira. Meir, Rabbi Menahem [the Meiri]. Jerusalem: Machon haTalmud haYisraeli haShalem, 1968.
Ben Ish Hai. Year 2. Rabbi Yosef Hayim. Jerusalem, 1932.
Be'ur haGra. Rabbi Eliyau b. Shlomo Zalman [the Vilna Gaon]. Jerusalem: Machon Shulchan haMelachim, 2004.
Commentary of Talmid HaRamban. In Lifschitz, Rabbi Yaakov Halevi. *Sanhedri gedola lamasekhet Sanhedrin*. Vol. 5, part 2. Jerusalem: Harry Fischel Institute, 1972.
Commentary on Tractate Sanhedrin. Rabbi Yeshayahu di Trani [the Riaz]. In Lifschitz, Rabbi Yaakov Halevi. *Sanhedri gedola lamasekhet Sanhedrin*. Vol. 5, part 2. Jerusalem: Harry Fischel Institute, 1972.
Degel mahaneh Ephraim. Rabbi Moshe Hayim Ephraim of Sudilkov. Berditchev, 1808/9.
Derekh hayim: peirush lemasekhet Avot. Rabbi Yehuda b. Betzalel Loew [the Maharal]. Hayim Halevi Pardes edition. Tel Aviv, 1975.
Derekh tzaddikim. Rabbi Avraham Yellin. Lvov, 1912.
Divrei hamudot al piskei haRosh [Rabbenu Asher ben Yehiel]. Babylonian Talmud. Rabbi Yom Tov Lipman Heller. Wagshal edition. Jerusalem, 1996/7.
Ein Yaakov. Rabbi Yaakov ibn Haviv. Thessaloniki, 1516–22.
Etzba ketana. Rabbi Menahem Mandiaonfli. Izmir: Roditi, 1876.
Hagahot haMaharid betokh Sifra hu Torat hayim. Rabbi Yaakov David Biderman. Warsaw, 1865.
Hagahot Maimoniyot [Commentary on Moses Maimonides' *Mishneh Torah*]. Rabbi Meir b. Yekutiel Hakohen of Rothenberg. Jerusalem, 1982.
Hagahot haRema. Rabbi Moshe Isserles [the Rema]. Jerusalem: Morasha leHanchil, 1992–2005.
Halakhot gedolot. Jerusalem: Machon Yerushalayim, 1992.
Hiddushei Aggadot. Rabbi Shmuel Eidels [the Maharsha]. Jerusalem, 1964.
Hiddushei haRama al masekhet Sanhedrin. Rabbi Meir Halevi Abulafia. Thessaloniki, 1797/8.
Iggeret hateshuva. Rabbi Yona b. Avraham Gerondi [Rabbenu Yona]. Farkas, Slovakia, 1911.
Iggeret Rav Sherira Gaon. B. M. Levin edition. Haifa, 1921.

Kitvei Rabbenu Behayei: Pirkei Avot. Rabbenu Behayei b. Asher. Rabbi Hayim Dov Chavel edition. Jerusalem: Mossad Harav Kook, 1970.
Korban Aharon. Rabbi Avraham ibn Hayim. Dessau, 1656.
Korban ha'eida. Rabbi Naftali Frankel. Jerusalem, 1931.
Lehayim beYerushalayim. Rabbi Hayim Palagi, Jerusalem, 2000.
Masekhet Avot im Nahalat Avot leDon Yitzhak Abarbanel. Rabbi Don Yitzhak Abarbanel. Zilberman edition. Jerusalem: Yad haRav Nissim, 2005.
Masekhet Avot im peirush Rabbenu Moshe b. Maimon. Rabbi Moses Maimonides. Translated by Yitzhak Shailat. Jerusalem: Ma'aliot, 1994.
Menorat hamaor. Rabbi Yosef ibn Al-Nakawa. H. G. Enelow edition. New York: Bloch Publishing, 1929.
Merkavat haMishna. Rabbi Yosef Alashkar. Lod, Israel: Orot Yahadut haMagreb, 1993.
Midrash agur. See Mishnat Rabbi Eliezer, below.
Midrash David al Pirkei Avot. Rabbi David haNagid [David ben Avraham Maimuni]. Jerusalem: Siah Yisrael, 1987.
Midrash Shmuel. [Commentary on Mishna Avot.] Rabbi Shmuel b. Yitzhak de Uçeda. Venice, 1585.
Milei d'Avot. Rabbi Yosef b. Avraham Hayun. In *Peirushei Rishonim lemasekhet Avot*. Moshe Shlomo Kasher and Yaakov Yehoshua Blecharovitz edition. Jerusalem: Machon Torah Sheleima, 1972/3.
Mishna berura. Rabbi Yisrael Meir Kagan [the Hafetz Hayim]. Jerusalem, 1976/7.
Mishnat Reuven al masekhet Avot im peirush Rav Yaakov b. Rav Shimshon. Mordekhai Katznellenbogen edition. Jerusalem: Mossad Harav Kook, 2005.
Mishneh Torah. Rabbi Moses Maimonides [the Rambam]. Translated by Eliyahu Touger. Brooklyn: Moznaim, 2013.
Nahalat Avot. See Masekhet Avot im Nahalat Avot leDon Yitzhak Abarbanel, above.
Netivot olam. Rabbi Yehuda b. Betzalel Loew [the Maharal]. Warsaw, 1872/3.
Nimukei Rashi, vol. 2. Rabbi Hayim Hirschensohn. Hoboken, 1930.
Peirush hameyuhas l'Rashi. Also referred to as Pseudo Rashi. Moshe Shlomo Kasher and Yaakov Yehoshua Blecharovitz edition. Jerusalem, 1974.
Peirush Rabbenu Ovadia miBartenura. Rabbi Ovadia of Bartenura. In *Mishnayot zekher Hanokh*. Jerusalem: Wagshal, 1999.
Peirushei Rabbenu Yitzhak b. Shlomo miToledo al masekhet Avot. Rabbi Yitzhak b. Shlomo of Toledo. Moshe Shlomo Kasher and Yaakov Yehoshua Blecharovitz edition. Jerusalem, 1965.
Peirushei Rabbenu Yona miGerondi al masekhet Avot. Rabbi Yona b. Avraham Gerondi [Rabbenu Yona]. Jerusalem: Machon Torah Sheleima, 1980.
Peirushei Rabbenu Yosef b. Shushan al masekhet Avot. Moshe Shlomo Kasher and Yaakov Yehoshua Blecharovitz edition. Jerusalem, 1967/8.
Pirkei Avot im peirush haYaavetz. Rabbi Yosef b. Hayim Yaavetz. Jerusalem: Mekhon Ma'oz ha-Torah, 1990.
Piskei haRosh. Rabbenu Asher ben Yehiel. Vilna, 1979/80–1986/7.
Pri tzaddik. Rabbi Tzadok Hakohen. Lublin, 1900–1934.
Ruah Hayim al masekhet Avot. Rabbi Hayim of Volozhin. Vilna, 1859.
Seder olam zuta. Natan b. Yitzhak [Rabbi Natan b. Yitzhak HaBavli]. In Neubauer, Adolf. *Mediaeval Jewish Chronicles*. Vol. 2. Oxford: Clarendon Press, 1895.
Sefer amudei gola [*Sefer mitzvot hakatzar (Semak)*]. Rabbi Yitzhak of Corbeil. Cremona, Italy, 1956/7.
Sefer ha'agguda. Rabbi Alexander Zusslin Hakohen. Krakow, 1570/1.

Sefer habrit. Part 2: *Divrei emet.* Rabbi Pinhas Eliyahu Horowitz. Brno, 1797.
Sefer ha'ikkarim hashalem. [Book of principles.] Rabbi Yosef Albo. Vol. 4. Jerusalem: Horev, 1995.
Sefer haredim. Rabbi Elazar Azikri. Kunszentmiklós, Hungary: Yitzhak Leib Schwartz, 1935.
Sefer haroke'ah. Rabbi Eliezer of Worms. Warsaw, 1880.
Sefer Hasidim. Rabbi Yehuda b. Shmuel of Regensburg. Mordekhai Margaliot edition. Jerusalem: Mossad Harav Kook, 1956/7.
Sefer ma'agal tov hashalem. Rabbi Hayim Yosef David Azulai [the Hida]. Edited by Aharon Freimann. Jerusalem: Mekitzei Nirdamim, 1933.
Sefer ma'aseh Bereshit. Rabbi Yosef Nissim Adhan. Jerusalem: Keter, 1986.
Sefer mussar: Peirush Mishnat Avot l'Rabbi Yosef b. Yehuda. Rabbi Yosef b. Yehuda ibn Aknin. Becher edition. Berlin: Tzvi Hirsch Itzkovski, 1910.
Sefer Ra'avan. Even ha'ezer, hiddushim leSanhedrin. Vol. 4. Rabbi Eliezer b. Natan. Jerusalem: Wagshal, 1984.
Sefer Raviyah. Avi ha'ezer, vol. 4. Rabbi Eliezer b. Yoel Halevi [the Raviyah]. Debretzky edition. Bnei Brak, Israel: 1999/2000.
Sefer terumat hadeshen. Rabbi Yisrael Isserlein. Reprint of Aaron Walden Warsaw edition. Jerusalem: Shmuel Avitan, 1958.
Sefer yuhasin. Rabbi Avraham Zekhut. Zhovkva (Zolkiew), 1799.
Sha'arei teshuva. Rabbi Yona b. Avraham Gerondi [Rabbenu Yona]. Vilna, 1922.
Shalom ahim. Moses Rosensohn. Vilna, 1870.
Shalom yihiyeh. Rabbi Yosef Avraham Heller. New York: Empire Press, 1989.
Shem hagedolim. Rabbi Hayim Yosef David Azulai [the Hida]. Livorno: G. Falorni, 1774.
Shnei luhot habrit. Rabbi Yeshayahu Halevi Horowitz [the Shelah haKadosh]. Jerusalem: Oz veHadar, 1993.
Shulhan arukh. Rabbi Yosef Karo. Jerusalem: Machon Yerushalayim, 1992/3.
Shulhan Gevoah, Orach Chaim Vol. 2. Rabbi Joseph Molkho. Thessaloniki, 1755.
Shut Avkat rokhel. Rabbi Yosef Karo. Leipzig, 1858/9.
Shut Avnei shayish. Rabbi Shaul Yeshua b. Yitzhak Abutbul. Jerusalem, 1930.
Shut Divrei yatziv. Vol. 2. Rabbi Yekusiel Yehuda Halberstam. Netanya, Israel: Machon Shefa Chaim, 1996.
Shut Habah. Rabbi Yoel Sirkis. New York, 1965/6.
Shut HaMabit. Rabbi Moshe b. Yosef di Trani. Jerusalem: Yad haRav Nissim, 1990.
Shut HaRema. Rabbi Moshe Isserles [the Rema]. Edited by Asher Ziv. Jerusalem, 1970/1.
Shut HaRidbaz. Rabbi David b. Zimra. Warsaw: 1881/2.
Shut HaRif. Rabbi Yitzhak b. Yaakov Alfasi. Jerusalem, 1968/9.
Shut HaRivash. Rabbi Yitzhak bar Sheshet. Vilna, 1879.
Shut Hayim bayad. Rabbi Hayim Palagi. Izmir, 1872/3.
Shut Maharalbah. Rabbi Levi ibn Haviv. Brooklyn, 1961/2.
Shut Maharam Padua. Rabbi Meir of Padua Katznellenbogen. Krakow, 1881/2.
Shut Mahari Bruna. Rabbi Yisrael of Bruna. Jerusalem, 1959/60.
Shut Mahari Weil. Rabbi Yaakov Weil. Jerusalem, 1958/9.
Shut Maharik. Rabbi Yosef Colon b. Shlomo Trabotto. Jerusalem, 1972/3.
Shut Maharit. Vols. 1, 2. Rabbi Yosef di Trani. Tel Aviv, 1958/9.
Shut Maharshakh. Vol. 2. Rabbi Shlomo b. Avraham Hakohen. Jerusalem, 1969/70.
Shut Maharshdam. Vols. 1, 2. Rabbi Shmuel b. Moshe de Medina. New York, 1958/9.
Shut Mishpatim yesharim. Rabbi Raphael b. Mordekhai Bardugo. Krakow: 1890/91.
Shut Mor veohalot. Rabbi Avraham b. Yitzhak Entebbe. Livorno, 1843.

Shut Nokhah hashulhan. Rabbi Hayim Mordekhai Labaton. Buenos Aires, 1999/2000.
Shut Ri Migash. Rabbi Yosef ibn Migash. Jerusalem, 1958/9.
Shut Torah lishmah. Rabbi Yosef Hayim [the Ben Ish Hai]. Jerusalem, 1975/6.
Shut Torat emet. Rabbi Aharon b. Yosef Sasson. Venice, 1626.
Shut Torat Hayim. Rabbi Hayim Shabtai. Jerusalem, 2003/4.
Shut Yabia omer. Rabbi Ovadia Yosef. Jerusalem, 1995.
Shut Yahel Yisrael. Rabbi Yisrael Meir Lau. Jerusalem, 2003.
Shut Yehaveh da'at. Rabbi Ovadia Yosef. Jerusalem, 1976–80.
Shut Yismah levav. Rabbi Yeshua Shimon Hayim Ovadia of Sefrou. Jerusalem, 1993/4.
Siftei tzaddikim. Rabbi Yehoshua Heschel of Rimanov. Bnei Brak, Israel: 1999/ 2000.
Teshuvot Rabbenu Avraham ben haRambam. Freimann and Goitein edition. Jerusalem, 1938.
Tiferet Yisrael: Yakhin uvo'az. Rabbi Yisrael Lifschitz. In *Mishnayot zekher Hanokh*. Jerusalem: Wagshal, 1999.
Tzeva'at mehahayim. Rabbi Hayim Palagi, Jerusalem, 1995.
Yad Rama. See Hiddushei haRama al masekhet Sanhedrin, above.
Yam shel Shlomo. Rabbi Shlomo Luria [the Maharshal]. Jerusalem, 1995/ 6.
Zayit ra'anan. Rabbi Avraham Gumbiner. Venice, 1743.

Islamic Sources

Hadith of Sahih al-Bukhari. Vol. 1, book 2; vol. 3, book 49. https://sunnah.com/bukhari/53h.
Hadith of Sunan Abu-Dawud. https://sunnah.com/abudawud/43/123.
Ibn Ishaq. *Sirat Rasonl Allah*. https://archive.org/stream/Sirat-lifeOfMuhammadByibnIshaq/SiratIbnIahaqInEnglish#page/n13/mode/2up.

News Paper Articles

Ahren, Raphael. "Using an Old- New Formula in the Search for Peace: New Pardes Program Combines Judaic, Conflict Studies." *Haaretz*, September, 17, 2010. https://www.haaretz.com/1.5114327.
Ahrenberg, Yonatan, and Matanya Yadid. "Legasher bimkom lehakhriah" ("To mediate instead of to determine", Hebrew). Bisheva, December 3, 2020. https://www.inn.co.il/news/459442.
Arutz Sheva, 8, December, 2020. https://www.inn.co.il/news/459983.
Barukh, Chizki. "HaRav Yackov Ariel: 'rak bekihilah megubeshet rav yakhol liphoal' " ("Rabbi Yackov Ariel: 'Only within a united community can a rabbi operate,' " Hebrew).
Cohen, Shimon. "Ha'im lerabanim yesh kelim leyashev sikhukhim?" ("Do rabbis have the tools to resolve conflicts?" Hebrew). *Arutz Sheva*, 9, December, 2020. https://www.inn.co.il/news/459988.
Gelfond Feldinger, Lauren. "Jewish Peacemaking Program in Jerusalem Creates a Niche." *Haaretz*, July 13, 2012. https://www.haaretz.com/conflict-resolution-with-ajewish-twist-1.5299093.
Ghert-Zand, Renee. "9 Adar Encourages Conflict, Constructively." *Times of Israel*, February 9, 2014. https://www.timesofisrael.com/9-adar-encourages-conflict-but-ina-constructive-way/.

Halbfinger, David M., "In Israel, a Time to Pray Amid a Health Crisis," *NYTimes,* May 25, 2020, https://www.nytimes.com/2020/03/25/world/middleeast/israel-virus-prayer.html.

Hoffman, Gil. "Sheikh, Rabbi Hope Baseless Love, Joint Fast Will Stop COVID- 19." *Jerusalem Post,* July 27, 2020. https://www.jpost.com/israel-news/sheikh-rabbi-hope-baselesslove-joint-fast-will-stop-covid-19-636492.

Kronish, Ron. "The Pursuit of Religious Peace in the Israeli-Palestinian Conflict." *Times* of Israel, May 24, 2020. https://blogs.timesofisrael.com/the-pursuit-of-religious-peacein-the-israeli-palestinian-conflict/.

Miller, Elhanan. "'Those Wishing to See the Face of God Must See the Face of the Other.'" *plus 61j Media,* June 6, 2019. https://plus61j.net.au/panel5/wishing-see-facegodmust-see-face/.

Nachshoni, Kobi. "Israeli-Palestinian Peace Initiative Helped Resolve Temple Mount Standoff." *Ynetnews,* July 27, 2017. https://www.ynetnews.com/articles/0,7340,L-4995939,00.html.

Roth, Daniel. "Mikhtav ishi lerav hakehilah ulekehilato", Arutz Sheva, 11.2.2021, https://www.inn.co.il/news/467600

Roth, Daniel. "The Call to Rabbis and Lay Leaders to be Pursuers of Peace", Elmad, October 29, 2915. https://elmad.pardes.org/2015/10/the-call-to-rabbis-and-lay-leaders-to-be-pursuers-of-peace/

Sharon, Jeremy. "150 Organizations Worldwide Prepare to Mark Adar 9 as Jewish Day of Constructive Conflict." *Jerusalem Post,* February, 26, 2015. https://www.jpost.com/Diaspora/150-organizations-worldwide-prepare-to-mark-Adar-9-as-Jewish-Day-of-Constructive-Conflict-392343.

Sharon, Jeremy. "Debate and Division Come under Discussion by Presidents, Judges and Sharon, Jeremy. "150 Organizations Worldwide Prepare to Mark Adar 9 as Jewish Day of Constructive Conflict." *Jerusalem Post,* February, 26, 2015. https://www.jpost.com/Diaspora/150-organizations-worldwide-prepare-to-mark-Adar-9-as-Jewish-Day-of-Constructive-Conflict-392343.

Sharon, Jeremy. "Debate and Division Come under Discussion by Presidents, Judges andRabbis." Jerusalem Post, February 17, 2019.

Sharon, Jeremy. "Pardes Institute Encourages Jews to Engage in 'Constructive Conflict' for New Adar Holiday." *Jerusalem Post,* February 8, 2014. https://www.jpost.com/Jewish-World/Jewish-News/New-holiday-encourages-Jews-to-engage-in-constructive-conflict-340786.

Slivko, Sidney, "Pursuing Peace in the Classroom: Israeli Center Promotes Conflict Resolution as a Core Jewish Value," *New York Jewish Week,* February 5, 2014, https://jewishweek.timesofisrael.com/pursuing-peace-in-the-classroom/.

Index

Tables are indicated by *t* following the page number.

Aaron, 16, 88*t*, 89*t*
   as calming influence, 73–74
   disciples of, 39–42, 208, 285n38
   drawing people to the Torah, 50–51, 285n38
   emissary of offender, role as, 71–73
   greeting wicked with *shalom*, 62–64, 290n88, 291n90
   humility and self-sacrifice of, 77–81
   as ideal Jewish peacemaker, 13–14, 41, 99, 281n2
   initiative taken by, 70
   as lover of peace, 42–47
   as lover of people, 50–51
   lying in peacemaking, 75–77, 296n147
   marital peacemaking by, 64–67
   meeting separately with each side, 71
   Moses compared to, 51–55, 287n55, 290n79
   overview, 37–38, 67–70
   as pursuer of peace, 42–47, 286n46
   Rabbi Meir compared to, 100
   Rabbi Syracusty compared to, 147–148
   Reish Lakish compared to, 110
   saint peacemaker compared to, 84–87
   Yaakov bar Iddi compared to, 107
Abarbanel, Don Yitzhak, 47–48, 285n38
Abaye, 112–113, 137*t*
Abraham, 15
Abulafia, Meir Halevi, 57
Abu-Nimer, Mohammed, 11, 18–19, 23–24, 28–29, 70, 272n44, 276n93, 278n115, 328n89
Abutbul, Shaul Yeshua, 222–223, 228
accounts, 4–7. *See also peacemakers by name*
Adlerstein, Yitzchok, 70
ADR (alternative dispute resolution), 59, 289n75
adultery, *sota* ritual for, 97–98
Agriboz, anonymous visiting rabbi in, 180–184, 205*t*
agurram, 84–87, 298n184
Alashkar, Moshe, 220–221
Alashkar, Shlomo, 185–189
Albo, Yosef, 284n27
Alfasi, Yitzhak b. Yaakov (the Rif), 75
alternative dispute resolution (ADR), 59, 289n75
ambivalence of the sacred, 10
Ami (Rabbi), 106–107
Ancona, Italy
   mefashrim peacemaking in, 236
   Rabbi Azulai peacemaking in, 163–169, 178–179, 203*t*
Anderson, Royce, 48
anger absorbers, 78–79, 99
anonymous visiting rabbi in Agriboz, 180–184, 205*t*
Anschel Segal, 217–218
appeasement, by Rabbi Meir, 95–100
Appleby, Scott, 10
Arab-Islamic peacemaking. *See also sulha process*
   cross-cultural comparisons, 27–31
   emissaries in, 73
   humility in, 78
   lying in, 75
   models of conflict resolution, 11
   use of force in, 80–81
Assi (Rabbi), 106–107
Assis, Yom-Tov, 324n18
Augsburger, David, 22, 279n124
aveilut (mourning), 13

Avot d'Rabbi Natan, 58, 88*t*, 89*t*, 144
   Aaron as calming influence in, 73–74
   lovers and pursuers of peace in, 42–43
   marital peacemaking in, 64–65
   pursuers of peace in, 69, 282n13
   shalom greeting in, 62
Avraham b. Moshe b. Maimon, 190–195, 205*t*, 240, 3210n155
Avruch, Kevin, 22, 23
Azikri, Elazar b. Moshe, 145–146, 148, 323n9
Azulai, Hayim Yosef David (the Hida), 94–95, 149, 203*t*, 300n12
   Ancona, peacemaking in, 163–169
   Bayonne, peacemaking in, 175–177
   Bordeaux, peacemaking in, 172–173
   Ferrara, peacemaking in, 171–172
   Lugo, peacemaking in, 169–171
   marital peacemaking, 174–177, 318n113
   Paris, peacemaking in, 174–175, 318-19nn117–121
   peacemaking methods, 177–178
   practical implications, 178–179
   relationship with non-Jews, 313n55

Babylonian Talmud. *See also specific legends*
   Aaron as peacemaker in, 56
   changing of truth in, 75
   lay peacemakers, 208
   matronit legend, 128–129
   Rabbi Meir peacemaking, 92–95
   Rabbi Yaakov bar Iddi peacemaking, 104–107
Baghdad, peacemaking in
   by Bishr b. Aharon, 240–245
   by *metavkhei shalom*, 233–235
   by Rabbi Nissi, 195–199, 205*t*
Bamberger, Henry, 281n2, 299n188
Bardugo, Refael, 229
Bar Shalom, Adina, 135
Barth, Fredrik, 80–81
battle of wits, 115–120, 306n91, 306n94
Bayonne, peacemaking efforts of Rabbi Azulai in, 175–177, 203*t*
Bedouin saint peacemaker, Aaron compared to, 84–87

Bee Chen, Goh, 23
bending of the truth, 296n154, 296nn146–147
   in Aaronic peacemaking, 75–77
   by Reish Lakish, 107–111
   by Yaakov bar Iddi, 103–107
Ben Ish Hai, 234–235
Berber saints, 84–87
Berlin, Naftali Tzvi Yehuda (the Netziv), 155–158
Beroka (Rabbi), 121–126
Beruria (wife of Rabbi Meir), 132–134, 139*t*, 310nn152–153
berurim, 210–211, 324n18
Between Eden and Armageddon: The Future of World Religions, Violence, and Peacemaking (Gopin), 12–14, 270n22, 291n90, 294n117, 301n22
biblical conflict narratives, 159, 160–161
Biderman of Wyszogród, Yaakov David, 54
Bishr b. Aharon, 240–245
bitzua (compromise), 55–60, 287n60
blessing (*berakha*) of peace, 85
blood money, 86, 277nn109–110
Bonta, Bruce, 123
Bordeaux, peacemaking of Rabbi Azulai in, 172–173, 179, 203*t*
borerim (arbitrators), 236–237
bringing peace, 208, 209, 323n6
Buber, Martin, 152, 313n28
bullying prevention, 184
burning causes of conflict, 237–238
Burundi, female peacemakers in, 134

Cairo, rabbinic peacemakers in
   Avraham b. Moshe b. Maimon, 190–195, 205*t*
   Moses Benjamin and Moses Dammuhi, 184–189, 205*t*
calming influence of peacemakers
   Aaron, 73–74
   Rabbi Meir, 92–95
ceasefires, 26, 76, 277n108
Central African societies, role of elderly women in, 131
Chacour, Abuna, 20
charity to poor, 147–148, 311n17

Chinese mediators, 23
Christianity, 20, 63
cities of refuge, 16
classical rabbinic literature, third-party peacemakers in, 91, 137t. *See also* Aaron; Meir (Rabbi)
    Abaye, 112–113
    Beruria (wife of Rabbi Meir), 132–134
    distinguished simpleton, 115–120
    jesters, 121–126
    practical implications, 114–115, 126–127, 134–135
    Rafram, 111–112
    Reish Lakish, 107–111, 114–115
    Roman noblewoman, 128–132
    Yaakov bar Iddi, 103–107, 114–115
Cohen, David, 164–169, 315n68
Cohen, Giudecca, 163, 315n68
Cohen, Isaac, 164–169, 315n68
Cohen, Oded, 317n107
Cohen, Pinḥas, 163–169, 315n68
Cohen, Stuart A., 40
Coleman, Peter T., 123
collectivism, 255
communal rabbi, role of, 144–145
compensation money, 328n89
compromise agreements
    in Bishr b. Aharon peacemaking, 244–245
    in Rabbi Azulai peacemaking, 167–168, 170, 172, 177–178
    in rabbinic peacemaking in Volozhin, 154–162
    in *rodfei shalom* peacemaking, 224
    role of third-party peacemakers, 200, 256, 261
conflict coaching, 65
conflict management, Biblical examples of, 15–16
Conflict Mediation across Cultures (Augsburger), 22
conflict prevention, 13
    by Aaron, 62, 291n90
    lovers of peace, 42–43, 45
"Conflict Prevention and Mediation in the Jewish Tradition" (Steinberg), 14
conflict resolution. *See also peacemakers by name*
    cross-cultural comparisons, 27–31
    humor in, 123, 126–127
    Interactive Problem-Solving Workshops, 32–35, 35t
    Islamic models of, 11
    Jewish models of, 12–17
    modern-Western compared to traditional models, 27–31
    in other religious traditions, 18–21
    principles in legend of *matronit*, 130
    traditional cultural models, 23–27
conflict transformation, 13, 14, 21, 94, 120
constructive communication, 54, 55
constructive conflict, 13, 15, 17
Creating the Third Force: Indigenous Processes of Peacemaking (Tuso and Flaherty), 22
creative reframing, 75
cultural models of third-party peacemaking. *See* traditional cultural models of third-party peacemaking
cultural peacebuilding, 261–262
cultural religious peacebuilding, 49
Culture and Conflict Resolution (Avruch), 22

David b. Zakkai, 195–199, 240–245
Deganawida, 19–20, 93–94, 197
de Medina, Shmuel b. Moshe, 181, 182–183, 237–238
de Molinio, Yitzḥak, 184–189
derekh eretz (ethical behavior), 116, 118, 119–120
Derekh eretz zuta, 68, 70, 88t, 89t
Derekh tzaddikim, 151
Deuteronomy 34:8, 52, 58, 66
Deutsch, Morton, 123
di Curiel, Yisrael b. Meir, 185–187
Diner, Yosef Tzvi Halevi, 56
direct peacemaking, 72–73
disciples of Aaron, 39–42, 208, 285n38
disputes between rabbis, *rodfei shalom* peacemaking in, 216–219, 249t
di Trani, Moshe b. Yosef (the Mabit), 185–189
doctor, parable of, 80, 83
Dovid Tevele b. Moshe, 154–158

Eidels, Shmuel (the Maharsha), 130
Eilberg, Amy, 284n31
Eisen, Robert, 10, 306n94
Elazar b. Pedat, 103–107
Elazar Ḥisma, 302n39, 303n41
elderly women, role in peacemaking, 131
elicitive approach, 21, 120, 133
Eliezer b. Natan (the "Ra'avan"), 56, 59
Eliezer b. Rabbi Yosei the Galilean, 55–56
Eliezer of Passau, 216–219, 325n35, 326n40
Eliezer of Worms, 210
Elijah, 121–126
elite religious peacebuilding, 49
Eliyah of Prague, 216–219, 325n35, 326n40
emissary of offender, role of Aaron as, 71–73
Epstein, Baruch, 157, 158–159
ethical behavior (*derekh eretz*), 116, 118, 119–120
Etlinger, Yaakov, 296n154
Evans-Pritchard, E. E., 23
exceptionally distinguished simpleton, 115–120, 139*t*
Exodus (book of)
 23:5, 13
 4:27, 60
Ezekiel 16:44, 109–110

Favretto, Katja, 297n169
female peacemakers, 126–127, 139*t*, 308n127, 322n168
 Beruria (wife of Rabbi Meir), 132–134, 310nn152–153
 matronit, 128–132, 309n137
 practical implications, 134–135
Ferrara, peacemaking of Rabbi Azulai in, 171–172, 203*t*
Fisher, Ronald J., 280n140
Fiss, Owen, 289n75
Flaherty, Maureen P., 22
force, use of, 80
forgiveness
 in IPSW model, 33
 Prophet Muhammad as model of, 19
 public ceremonies, 318n112, 330n112
 in Rabbi Azulai peacemaking, 173
 sulha process, 26

forgiveness-reconciliation models, 16
France, peacemaking of Rabbi Azulai in
 in Bordeaux, 172–173, 179, 203*t*
 in Paris, 174–175, 203*t*, 318–19nn117–121
Francesconi, Federica, 315n62
Friedman, Hershey H., 75
Friedman, Mordekhai Akiva, 320n146
Friemer, Yosef, 154–158
Froman, Hadassa, 135
Fuchs, Avraham, 325n35
Fuchs, Yitzhak Yaakov, 325n21
Fundamentals of Jewish Conflict Resolution: Traditional Jewish Perspectives on Resolving Interpersonal Conflicts (Kaminsky), 17
Funk, Nathan, 29–30

Garson, Yosef, 147–148
Gellner, Ernest, 84–85, 86, 298n184
Genesis Rabba, 108–109
Germany, peacemaking between rabbis in, 217–218
Gerondi, Yona, 124, 210–211, 285n38, 325n21
Ginat, Joseph, 53, 71–72, 75–76, 86, 275n80, 276n100, 277n109, 278n118, 294n128
gishur, 59, 248
goal of conflict resolution process, 29, 30
Gopin, Marc, 10, 11, 12–14, 41, 71, 74, 75, 77–78, 99, 101–102, 133, 270n22, 281n2, 283n25, 291n90, 301n22, 312n23
Graetz, Heinrich, 309n137
greetings
 with *shalom*, 62–64, 290n88, 291n90
 for teachers, 104, 302n39, 303n41
guarantor, peacemakers as, 66, 218, 234, 328n90

Hacohen, Aviad, 322n1
Hacohen, Elisheva, 322n1
hadith of Sunan Abu-Dawud, 78
Hakham, Yosef al-, 328n90
Hakohen, Shlomo b. Avraham, 328n93
Halakhot gedolot, 323n9
Halberstam, Yekusiel Yehuda, 95
Halfan, Ḥayim, 219–220
Hamzeh, Nizar, 80–81

haNagid, David, 292n107
hand-shaking ceremony, 26, 277n114
happiness of peacemakers, 210–211, 324n19
jesters, legend of, 121–126
hashuvim (distinguished individuals), 239–245, 250t
Hasidic peacemaker, 150–154
Hasidut Ashkenaz, 209–210
Hayim of Volozhin, 154–155, 282n14
Hayward, Susan, 268n4, 322n168
healing through peacemaking, 13
Herr, Moshe, 109
Hertog, Katrien, 11, 269n5, 269n6, 269n7, 273n59, 273n60
Heschel, Abraham Joshua, 307n112
Heshel, Yehoshua, 76–77
Hezbollah peacemakers, 80, 276n93, 328n89
Hillel, 39, 87, 124, 299n188
Hinduism, 19, 75, 272n50
Hirschensohn, Rabbi Hayim, 265–266
historical accounts, 4–7. *See also peacemakers by name*
Hodaya b. Yishai, 190–195
Horowitz, Pinhas Eliyahu, 149, 311n22
Horowitz, Yeshayahu Halevi, 296n154
Houston, Jean, 94
humility
of Aaron, 63, 66–67, 77–81
of jesters, 124
in peacemaking, 83
of Rabbi Meir, 94, 95–100
humor, role in peacemaking, 121–127
husbands and wives, peacemaking between. *See* marital peacemaking

ibn Adhan, Yosef Nissim, 266–267
ibn Al-Nakawa, Yosef, 124
ibn Haviv, Levi, 144
ibn Haviv, Yaakov, 72–73, 295n131
ibn Hayim, Abraham, 54
ibn Himar, Iyad, 78
ibn Migash, Yosef, 214–216
ibn Tibbon, Yaakov, 184–189
ideal Jewish peacemaker, 13–14, 41, 99, 281n2
Iftar of Mediation, 49
Iggeret hateshuva (Rabbenu Yona), 210–211
igurramen, 84–87, 298n184

Ima Shalom, 308n127
indigenous processes of peacemaking. *See* traditional cultural models of third-party peacemaking
Infugao people, Philippines, 23
inheritance disputes, *rodfei shalom* peacemaking in, 219–220, 249t
initiative in peacemaking
in *sulha* process, 276n102
taken by Aaron, 43, 65, 70
of third-party peacemakers, 255
inner peace, 46, 150, 166, 283n24, 312n23
Interactive Conflict Resolution, 32–35, 35t
Interactive Problem-Solving Workshops (IPSW), 32–35, 35t, 74
intercommunal peacemaking, role of *pashranim* in, 237–238
interreligious relations, 130
Irani, George, 29–30
Iroquois legend, 19–20, 93–94, 197
Islam. *See also* Arab-Islamic peacemaking
conflict resolution models, 11, 27–31
Jewish-Muslim relations, 81–82, 126–127
Prophet Muhammad, 18–19, 63, 78, 272n49, 291n92
Saints of the Atlas Mountains, 84–87
Israel, Hayim Avraham, 165–168
Israeli Palestinian Comedy, 126
Israeli-Palestinian conflict, 127, 134–135, 247, 261–262
Italy, peacemaking in, 219–221. *See also* Azulai, Hayim Yosef David (the Hida)

Jabbour, Elias, 71, 78–79, 276n102, 278n118, 278n119, 294n128
Jacob, 15
jaha (respected delegation), 25, 26, 71, 74, 78–79, 275n87
Jerusalem Talmud, 295n131. *See also specific legends*
character witness in, 304n60
lay peacemaking in, 208
Rabbi Meir peacemaking, 95–96
Rabbi Yaakov bar Iddi peacemaking, 103–107
Reish Lakish peacemaking in, 107–111, 304n64

jesters, legend of, 121–126, 139t
Jesus, 20, 63
Jewish imperative for peacemaking
   by lay peacemakers, 208–213
   by rabbis, 143–146
Jewish models of conflict
   resolution, 12–17
Jewish-Muslim relations, 81–82, 126–127
"Jewish Sources on Conflict
   Management: Realism and Human
   Nature" (Steinberg), 14–17
jirgamar (gray-bearded elders), 23–24
judges, relationship with mediators, 59–60
judicial compromise, 55–60
judicial conflict resolution (JCR), 60

Kadayifci-Orellana, S. Ayse, 23–24,
   276n93, 328n89
Kagan, Yisrael Meir, 295n132
Kalla rabbati, 62–63, 88t, 89t
   humility of Aaron in, 77
   marital peacemaking in, 65
   peacemaking between two individuals
   in, 67–69, 70, 71
Kaminsky, Howard, 17, xii
Karo, Yosef, 185–187, 239
Katznellenbogen, Meir, 220–221
ketuba (marriage contract), 219, 223–224,
   229, 326n43, 328n90
Klein, Menashe, 98
kohanim (priestly class), 37, 40
Kohen Tzedek Gaon, 195–199
Krishna, 19, 75, 272n50, 296n148
Kydd, Andrew, 296n153

Lafayette, Bernard, 46
lay peacemakers, 139t, 207, 249t. *See also*
   rodef/rodfei shalom (pursuer(s) of peace)
   Bishr b. Aharon, 240–245
   disputes between rabbis, peacemaking
   in, 216–219
   in early-modern Morocco, 222–228
   exceptionally distinguished simpleton,
   115–120
   ḥashuvim, 239–245
   inheritance disputes, peacemaking in,
   219–220
   jesters, 121–126
   Jewish imperative for, 208–213
   marital peacemaking by, 214–216
   mefashrim, 235–238
   metavkhei shalom, 228–235
   nikhbadim, 239–245
   pashranim, 235–238
   practical implications, 126–127, 246–248
   in seventeenth-century Safed, 230–233
   way of pursuers of peace, discussion of,
   220–221
Lederach, John Paul, 20, 21, 120, 273n60
legends of third-party peacemakers, 4, 6–7.
   See also peacemakers by name
Lelov, Dovid of, 150–154, 202t
leopard-skin chief, 23
Levin, Yehoshua Heschel, 155
Leviticus 19:18, 209
Leviticus Rabba 9:3, 116
Lifschitz, Yaakov, 157, 158, 159–160
Lifschitz, Yisrael, 323n6
listening to victims, 74
Lithuania, rabbinic peacemakers in, 154–162
Loew, Yehuda, 43
Lord Krishna, 19, 75, 272n50, 296n148
lover of people, Aaron as, 50–51, 285n37
lovers of peace, 42–47, 63, 282n14, 283n21
Lugo, peacemaking efforts of Rabbi Azulai
   in, 169–171, 203t
lying in peacemaking, 16, 296n144,
   296n154
   by Aaron, 75–77, 296nn146–147
   practical implications, 82–83
   by Reish Lakish, 107–111
   by Yaakov bar Iddi, 103–107

Mahameed, Ibtisam, 133, 134–135
Maharal of Prague, 43, 124, 286n46
Mahloket Matters: How to Disagree More
   Constructively, the Beit Midrash Way
   project, 161
Maimonides, 75, 143–144, 318n112,
   320n146
makhloket (disagreement for the sake of
   Heaven), 15, 17
Malachi 2:5–6, 52–53, 62, 73, 290n85,
   290n88
Mann, J., 321n161
Marabatin bi'l Baraka, 298n174

marital peacemaking
　by Aaron, 64–67, 282n8
　by *mefashrim*, 236
　by *metavkhei shalom*, 229
　by Rabbi Azulai, 174–177, 318n113, 318–19nn117–121
　by Rabbi Meir, 95–100, 301n22
　by *rodfei shalom*, 214–216, 222–227, 249t
Marshall, Katherine, 268n4
matronit, legend of, 128–132, 134–135, 139t, 309n137
McLean, Eliyahu, 152–153
mediation. *See* third-party peacemaking
mediators, 59–60, 248
　metavkhei shalom, 228–235, 248, 250t
medieval and early-modern lay peacemakers, 207, 249t. *See also rodef/rodfei shalom* (pursuer(s) of peace)
　Bishr b. Aharon, 240–245
　disputes between rabbis, peacemaking in, 216–219
　in early-modern Morocco, 222–228
　hashuvim, 239–245
　inheritance disputes, peacemaking in, 219–220
　Jewish imperative for, 208–213
　marital peacemaking by, 214–216
　mefashrim, 235–238
　metavkhei shalom, 228–235
　nikhbadim, 239–245
　pashranim, 235–238
　practical implications, 246–248
　in seventeenth-century Safed, 230–233
　way of pursuers of peace, discussion of, 220–221
medieval and early-modern rabbinic peacemakers, 141–143, 202t, 203t, 205t. *See also* Azulai, Hayim Yosef David (the Hida)
　anonymous visiting rabbi in Agriboz, 180–184
　Avraham b. Moshe b. Maimon, 190–195
　Dovid of Lelov, 150–154
　Jewish imperative for rabbinic peacemaking, 143–146
　misnaged peacemakers of Volozhin, 154–162

Moses Benjamin and Moses Dammuhi, 184–189
　Nissi al-Nahrawani, 195–199
　Yosef Syracusty, 146–150
meetings between sides
　burning causes of conflict, 237–238
　forgiveness in, 318n112, 330n112
　in private spaces, 34
　in public spaces, 69
　in Rabbi Azulai peacemaking, 173
　in *sulha* process, 26–27, 277n112, 277n114
　meeting with sides separately, 71, 255–256, 276nn103–104
mefashrim (compromisers), 235–238
Megillat Ta'anit, 128
Meir (Rabbi), 14, 137t, 292n107
　Beruria (wife of), 132–134, 310nn152–153
　as calming influence, 92–95
　humility and appeasement in peacemaking of, 95–100
　marital peacemaking by, 301n22
　practical implications, 100–102
Meir, Golda, 126
Meir, Ofra, 104
Mekhilta d'Rabbi Shimon b. Yohai, 288n73
Melchior, Michael, 189
Menahem Mandiaonfli, 311n21
Menahem Meiri, 283n21
metavkhei shalom (mediators of peace), 228–235, 248, 250t
Minor Tractates, examples of peacemaking by Aaron in, 61
　as calming influence, 73–74
　emissary of offender, role as, 71–73
　greeting wicked with *shalom*, 62–64
　humility and self-sacrifice in, 77–81
　initiative taken by Aaron, 70
　lying in peacemaking, 75–77
　marital peacemaking, 64–67
　meeting separately with each side, 71
Minstrel, Shlomo Shlumiel, 230–233
Mironi, Mordechai, 330n126
Mishna, portrayal of Aaron in
　disciples of Aaron, 39–42
　drawing people to the Torah, 50–51
　as lover and pursuer of peace, 42–47

Mishna Avot 1:12, 66
Mishna Pe'a 1:1, 208
Mishnat Rabbi Eliezer, 51
Mishneh Torah, 143–144
misnaged peacemakers of Volozhin, 154–162, 202t
mitzvah regarding peacemaking, 144, 209, 323n8, 323n9
modern-Western models, 27–31
Mohamed-Saleem, Amjad, 328n89
Molkho, Joseph, 229–230
monkalun (advisors), 23
Morocco, *rodfei shalom* peacemaking in, 222–228
Mosaica, 280n143
　Aaron model used by, 81–82
　Iftar of Mediation, 49–50
　Rabbis as Mediators project, 213
　Religious Peace Initiative, 49, 83, 247, 262
　Temple Mount/Al-Aqsa Mosque video project, 126–127
Moses, 58, 286n48, 287n55, 287n58, 290n79
　comparison to Aaron in *Sifra*, 51–55
　comparison to Aaron in *Tosefta* Sanhedrin, 55–60
　as judge, 288n73
　as pursuer of peace, 286n45
Moses Benjamin, 184–189, 205t
Moses Dammuhi, 184–189, 205t
Moshe Elbaz, 222
Moshe Hayim Ephraim of Sudilkov, 79–80, 99
Moshe Isserles, 94
mourning, 13
Muhammad (Prophet), 18–19, 63, 78, 272n49, 291n92
musalaha. See *sulha* process
muslihs (facilitator of the *sulha*), 25
Muslims. See also Arab-Islamic peacemaking
　Jewish-Muslim relations, 81–82, 126–127
　Prophet Muhammad, 18–19, 63, 78, 272n49, 291n92
　Saints of the Atlas Mountains, 84–87

Nachshon, 208
Nagat, Yitbarakh, 24
Nahalat Avot, 47
Name of God, invoking, 196–197

Naquite, Jacob, 172–173, 317n107
Natan b. Yitzhak the Babylonian, 195, 240–242
Navajo model, 30–31
negative peace, 48
nikhbadim (well-respected individuals), 239–245, 250t
Nissi al-Nahrawani, 195–199, 205t, 321n161, 321nn157–158
non-Jewish third-party mediators, 327n75
non-Jews, pursuing peace among, 51, 149, 263–266, 311n22
non-rabbinic peacemakers. See lay peacemakers
nonviolence, 130, 134
Nounez, Abraham, 175–177
Nuer people in South Sudan, 23
Numbers (book of)
　20:29, 52, 58, 66, 73
　6:22–27, 85

Otzar hamidrashim, 294n117
Ovadia, David, 227–228
Ovadia, Yeshua Shimon Hayim, 223–224

Pacha, Nalkot, 81
Palagi, Hayim, 73, 211–212, 213, 235–236
paradigmatic peacemakers, 18–21. See also Aaron
Pardes Rodef Shalom Retreat, 101
Pardes Rodef Shalom Schools Program
　Aaron legend in, 82–83
　anonymous visiting rabbi in Agriboz legend used in, 184
　jester legend in, 126
　Rabbi Meir legend in, 100–101
　Rabbi Yaakov bar Iddi legend in, 114–115
Paris, peacemaking of Rabbi Azulai in, 174–175, 203t, 318–19nn117–121
particularism, 10
pashranim (compromisers), 235–238, 250t, 328n93, 328n96, 329n101, 329n104
Pe'a, 208
Pely, Doron, 31, 74, 75, 78, 133
Peretz b. Eliyahu of Corbeil, 58
Perpignan, S. Elia, 174–175

personal self-sacrifice
  of Aaron, 66–67, 77–81
  in IPSW model, 36t
  of Rabbi Azulai, 172–173
  in *sulha* process, 36t
  of third-party peacemakers, 258
peshara (compromise), 14, 287n60
Peters, Emrys, 298n174
Peterson, Virgil, 150–151
Petit, Moses and Solomon, 172–173
Pinto, Jeanmarie, 30
Pinto, S. Barukh Solomon, 169
pishur (compromise), 248, 330n126
piyus (reconciliation), 69
poor, peacemaking efforts with, 147–148, 311n17
popularity of peacemaker, 53
Posen, Germany, 218
positive peace, 48
postmodernism, influence of, 27–28
post-trauma, 13
power discrepancies, 68–69, 102, 113–114
  in Abaye legend, 112–113
  in *metavkhei shalom* peacemaking, 230–235
  practical implications for, 114–115
  in Rafram legend, 111–112
  in Reish Lakish legend, 107–111
  in Yaakov bar Iddi legend, 103–107
pragmatic mediation, 30
Prague, *rodfei shalom* in, 216–219
prayer, power of shared, 151–154, 313n30
Praying Together in Jerusalem, 153
priestly class during Second Temple period, controversy over, 37, 40
proactivity in peacemaking, 45
  of Aaron, 62, 65, 70
  of non-rabbinic peacemakers, 124, 125
  of pursuers of peace, 42–43
  of Rabbi Syracusty, 148
  in *sulha* process, 276n102
  of third-party peacemakers, 255
Problem-Solving Workshops, 32–35, 35t
Psalms (book of)
  104:35, 132–133
  34:15, 42, 208, 209, 282n12, 282n14, 312n23
  85:11, 60

psychology, influence on contemporary Western culture, 27
public ceremonies
  burning causes of conflict, 237–238
  forgiveness in, 318n112, 330n112
  in Rabbi Azulai peacemaking, 173
  in *sulha* process, 26–27, 277n112, 277n114
Pukhtoon in Afghanistan and Pakistan, 23–24
Purim, peacemaking around, 243–244
pursuers of peace, 282nn13–214, 283n21. *See also rodef/rodfei shalom* (pursuer(s) of peace)
  Aaron as, 42–47, 70, 76–77
  meaning of *shalom*, 47–50
  rabbinic obligation as, 143–146
  shared prayer used by, 152–153

Quran, 80, 300n9

Rabbenu Ḥananel b. Ḥushiel, 122–123
Rabbenu Yona, 124, 210–211, 285n38, 325n21
rabbinic peacemakers, 137t, 141–143, 202t, 203t, 205t. *See also* Azulai, Ḥayim Yosef David (the Ḥida); Meir (Rabbi)
  Abaye, 112–113
  anonymous visiting rabbi in Agriboz, 180–184
  Avraham b. Moshe b. Maimon, 190–195
  Dovid of Lelov, 150–154
  Jewish imperative for, 143–146
  misnaged peacemakers of Volozhin, 154–162
  Moses Benjamin and Moses Dammuhi, 184–189
  Nissi al-Nahrawani, 195–199
  practical implications, 114–115
  Rafram, 111–112
  Reish Lakish, 107–111, 114–115
  Yaakov bar Iddi, 103–107, 114–115
  Yosef Syracusty, 146–150
Rabbis as Mediators project, 213
Rafram, 111–112, 137t
rationalism, 29
rationalist realism, 14

Ravina (Rabbi), 111–112
reconciliation
  in Aaronic peacemaking, 69
  cross-cultural comparisons of conflict resolution, 30
  forgiveness-reconciliation models, 16
  in IPSW model, 33, 36*t*
  role of third-party peacemakers, 256–258
  in *sulha* process, 26–27, 36*t*, 277n112, 277n114, 278n115, 278n119, 294n118
  teshuva process, 13
  without third parties, 72–73
Regensburg, Germany, 217–218
Reish Lakish, 107–111, 114–115, 137*t*
religious peacebuilding, 268n4
  general discussion, 9–11
  Jewish models of conflict resolution, 12–17
  in other religious traditions, 18–21
Religious Peace Initiative, Mosaica, 49, 83, 247, 262
reputation of peacemaker, 66, 183, 195
responsa literature, 141–142, 214
restorative justice, 31
Ri Migash, 214–216
ritual space, in Rabbi Azulai peacemaking, 165–166
rodef/rodfei shalom (pursuer(s) of peace), 214, 248, 249*t*
  community volunteers as, 211–212
  compromise by, 59
  disputes between rabbis, peacemaking in, 216–219
  in early-modern Morocco, 222–228
  greeting others with *shalom*, 64
  inheritance disputes, peacemaking in, 219–220
  marital peacemaking by, 214–216
  rodef tzedek versus, 55
  role models, 41–42, 76–77
  shared prayer used by, 152–153
  training as, 264–265
  way of pursuers of peace, discussion of, 220–221
rodef tzedek (pursuers of justice), 55
role models of peacemakers, 260–261
  Aaron as, 39–41

  in other religious traditions, 18–21
  practical implications, 41–42
  Rabbi Syracusty, 149
Roman noblewoman, legend of, 128–132, 134–135, 139*t*, 309n137
Roness, Michal, 282n9
roots of conflicts, cross-cultural comparison of, 28–29
Rosensohn, Moses, 130

Sa'adya Gaon, 240–245, 330n115
Sadat, Anwar, 126
Safed, lay peacemakers in, 230–233
Sahih al-Bukhari, 291n92
Saints of the Atlas Mountains, 84–87, 298n184
Salem, Paul, 27–28
Sande, Ken, 20
Saragossi, Yosef, 146–150
Sasson, Aharon b. Yosef, 239
Sayyid, Sayyid Ibrahim Amin al, 80–81
Schäfer, Peter, 50
Schimmel, Solomon, 75
Schirch, Lisa, 165–166
schmagluch, 24
Schumer, Nathan Still, 281n2
science, influence of, 28
scope of Jewish peacemaking, 10, 263–266
secret meetings, in Rabbi Azulai peacemaking, 171–172
Seder olam zuta (Natan), 195, 240–242
seeking peace, 13
Sefer haredim, 148
Sefer haroke'ah, 210
self-revelation, cross-cultural differences in, 28
self-sacrifice. *See* personal self-sacrifice
Selya, Micah, 213
Senigallia, S. Gedalia, 169–171
Serero, Menahem, 225
settlement mediation, 30
Sha'arei Teshuva (Rabbenu Yona), 210
Shabbat 23b, 301n19
Shabtai, Hayim, 144–145, 146
shalom
  greeting wicked with, 62–64
  meaning of, 47–50, 284n27, 284n31
shalom bayit (peace within the home), 15, 16

shared prayer, 151–154, 313n30
Sharp, Gene, 130
Sheshet, Yitzhak bar, 211, 236
Shimon (Rabbi), 97–99
Shimon b. Elazar, 282n13
Shlomo b. Maimon, 222
Shlomo Yitzhaki (Rashi), 56–57, 59, 92–93, 123, 129, 265–266, 332n12
Shut Avkat rokhel, 330n112
Shut Avnei shayish, 326n47, 326n52
shuttle diplomacy, 71
Sifra, portrayal of Aaron in, 51–55
Sikand, Aalok, 19, 296n148
Simha Bunim Bonhart of Pesishcha, 312n23
simpleton, legend of, 115–120, 139*t*
Sirkis, Yoel, 329n101
social harmony, precedence over truth, 75–76, 296n147
social justice, 134, 147–148
social status of peacemakers, 143, 254–255. *See also* Azulai, Hayim Yosef David (the Hida)
  anonymous visiting rabbi in Agriboz, 180–184
  Avraham b. Moshe b. Maimon, 190–195
  Dovid of Lelov, 150–154
  misnaged peacemakers of Volozhin, 154–162
  Moses Benjamin and Moses Dammuhi, 184–189
  Nissi al-Nahrawani, 195–199
  in *sulha* process, 276n97
  Yosef Syracusty, 146–150
Soloveitchik, Yosef Dov, 155–158
sota ritual, 97–98
Spain, *rodfei shalom* in, 214–216
Spector, Yitzhak Elhanan, 154–162
spousal conflict. *See* marital peacemaking
Steinberg, Gerald, 14–17, 75, 296n147
Stillman, Norman A., 330n115
stories, defined, 5
storytelling, in peacemaking, 150–151
structural peacebuilding, 261–262
success of interventions, 258–259
sulha process, 274nn75–76, 275n81
  Aaronic peacemaking compared to, 71, 84

anger absorbers, 99
blood money in, 277nn109–110
comparing to modern-Western models, 31
creative reframing in, 75
five components of, 278n118
general discussion, 24–27
humility in, 78
indirect involvement of women in, 133
initiative in peacemaking, 276n102
IPSW model compared to, 32–35, 35*t*
jaha in, 25, 26, 71, 74, 78–79, 275n87
listening to victims, 74
meetings with both sides, 276nn103–104, 294n128
patience of mediators in, 276n100
Rabbi Azulai peacemaking compared to, 171–172
reconciliation ceremony, 26–27, 277n112, 277n114, 278n115, 278n119, 294n118
social status of peacemakers, 276n97
types of cases overseen by, 275n80
supernatural powers, in peacemaking, 196–198, 321n161
Svensson, Isak, 66
Syracusty, Yosef b. Avraham El-, 63, 146–150, 202*t*

Ta'anit 22a, 121–126
Talmud. *See* Babylonian Talmud; Jerusalem Talmud; Minor Tractates, examples of peacemaking by Aaron in; *specific legends*
Tanhuma, 287n58
Tannaitic literature, portrayal of Aaron in. *See also* Mishna, portrayal of Aaron in
  in *Sifra*, 51–55
  in *Tosefta* Sanhedrin, 55–60
taojie, 23
Tavuchis, Nicholas, 295n136
Temple Mount/Al-Aqsa Mosque video project, 127
teshuva (repentance) process, 13
third-party peacemaking. *See also* lay peacemakers; *peacemakers by name*; rabbinic peacemakers; *sulha* process
  common characteristics of peacemakers, 253–259

360 INDEX

third-party peacemaking (*cont.*)
  compromise agreements, 256
  cross-cultural comparisons, 28, 30
  defined, 1–2
  further areas of research, 259–263
  identity and number of peacemakers, 253–254
  initiative to intervene, 255
  in IPSW model, 32–33, 35*t*
  Jewish models of, 12–17
  meeting with each side, 255–256
  modern-Western versus traditional cultural models, 27–31
  non-Jew, 327n75
  in other religious traditions, 18–21
  reconciliation, 256–258
  scope of Jewish peacemaking, 263–266
  social status and connection to sides in conflict, 254–255
  success and failure of interventions, 258–259
  traditional cultural models of, 23–27
  transforming perspectives, 256–258
tokhaha (rebuke), 55, 200–201
Torah, role of Aaron in drawing people to, 50–51, 285n38
Torah scholars, peacemaking obligation of, 143–146, 267n7
Tosafot, 58, 59
Tosefta Sanhedrin, 55–60
Trabotto, Yosef Colon b. Shlomo, 219–220
traditional cultural models of third-party peacemaking. *See also* Sulha process
  comparing to modern-Western models, 27–31
  examples of, 23–27
  general discussion, 21–22
  Interactive Problem-Solving Workshops, 32–35, 35*t*
transformation, conflict, 13, 14, 21, 94, 120
transformative mediation, 30
transforming perspectives, 256–258
truth, changing, 16, 296n144, 296n154
  by Aaron, 75–77, 296nn146–147
  practical implications, 82–83
  by Reish Lakish, 107–111
  by Yaakov bar Iddi, 103–107
truth, clarifying
  by Abaye, 112–113
  by Rafram, 111–112
Tuso, Hamdesa, 22, 279n124
Tzadok Hakohen of Lublin, 312n23
Tzeva'ah mehahayim (Palagi), 211–212

Uçeda, Shmuel de, 40, 44, 282n14
Ukraine, rabbinic peacemaking in, 150–154
unburdening process, 74
unilateral gestures of aid, 13
universalism, 10
Ury, William, 93

Valler, Shulamit, 98–99, 301n22
Vecchio, S. Joseph del, 169–171
Vita Cohen, S. Moses, 171–172
Volozhin, *misnaged* peacemakers of, 154–162, 202*t*

Wang, Yvonne, 262
Wanis-St. John, Anthony, 19
wasit (mediator), 25
way of pursuers of peace, 220–221
Weil, Yaakov, 218
Weisel, Abraham, 75
white flag ceremony, 278n119
win-win model, 16, 18–19
Wolf, Shlomo Zalman Ze'ev, 154–162
women peacemakers. *See* female peacemakers
Women Wage Peace, 134–135
Written Law, peacemaking in, 209, 323n8, 323n9

Yaakov bar Iddi, 103–107, 114–115, 137*t*
Yaakov b. Shimshon, 285n37, 294n119
Yaakov Yitzhak Rabinowicz of Pesishcha, 313n28
Yaakov Yosef of Polonne, 312n23
Yaavetz, Yosef b. Hayim, 40–41
Yanai (Rabbi), 115–120, 306n91, 306nn93–395
Yehuda (Rabbi), 97–99
Yehuda b. Shammu, 128–129, 296n154
Yehuda Nesiya, 108–111, 304n60, 304n64
Yellin, Avraham, 151
Yeshayahu di Trani (Riaz), 57–58, 60

Yishmael (Rabbi), 119
Yisrael Isserlein, 218
Yisrael of Bruna (Mahari Bruna), 217–218, 219
Yitzhak b. Shlomo, 44, 294n119
Yitzhak of Corbeil, 209, 324n11
Yohanan bar Nappaha, 103–107
Yohanan b. Zakkai, 265
Yona Gerondi, 124, 210–211, 285n38, 325n21

Yosef b. Avraham Hayun, 294n119
Yosef b. Gershom, 190–195
Yosef b. Shushan, 282n8
Yosef Hayim, 234–235
Yosei (Rabbi), 42–43, 125, 214
Yosei of Maon, 108–111
Yuval, Yisrael, 326n37

Zimra, David b. (the Ridbaz), 148, 187
Zusslin Hakohen, Alexander, 58